Biology
and
Knowledge

Biology and Knowledge

An Essay on the
Relations between
Organic Regulations
and Cognitive
Processes

Jean Piaget

THE UNIVERSITY OF CHICAGO PRESS
CHICAGO AND LONDON

THE UNIVERSITY OF CHICAGO PRESS, CHICAGO 60637
EDINBURGH UNIVERSITY PRESS, EDINBURGH

© 1971 by The University of Chicago and The University of Edinburgh
All rights reserved
Published in 1971
Printed in the United States of America

International Standard Book Number: 0–226–66775–8
Library of Congress Catalog Card Number: 70–157421

Originally published in Paris as *Biologie et connaissance: Essai sur les relations entre les régulations organiques et les processus cognitifs*, © Editions Gallimard, 1967. Translated into English by Beatrix Walsh

Contents

Preface

The aim of this work is to discuss the problems of intelligence and of knowledge in general (in particular, logico-mathematical knowledge) in the light of contemporary biology. It is therefore a gathering of interpretations rather than of experimentation. But this theoretical essay is the work of an author who has been engaged for forty-five years in psychological experimentation in development and who therefore intends to adhere as closely as possible to the facts. It may, nevertheless, be permissible to recall that this author was trained as a biologist, that for a decade he published only in zoology, that he continued in this vein in 1929 and 1966 (*Revue Suisse de Zoologie*), and that he did a little work in botany (in 1966 in *Candollea*), all the while acquainting himself as fully as possible with the main currents of contemporary biology.

The plan of the present book is as follows: First, the problems are posed and defined (chapter 1), and, to this end, it is shown why the study of the psychological development of cognitive functions never ceases to raise biological questions allied to those of embryogenesis and, by consequence, to those of the relations between the organism and the environment, especially in matters of regulation.

In chapter 2, the methods to be used for

rationally comparing cognitive mechanisms to organic processes are defined, pains being taken to avoid the kind of reductionism that suppresses problems by means of too facile a comparison of the superior functions of knowledge to elementary behaviors.

Chapter 3, still of an introductory nature, attempts to disencumber the epistemology of biologists so as to show how the problems that biologists present to one another and the interpretations that they offer are constantly parallel to questions and explanatory theories that can be found, though expressed very differently, in the realms of the psychology of intelligence and the analysis of knowledge.

With chapter 4 we tackle the central problems, seeking to relate the structures and functions of the organism itself with those of various forms of knowledge (knowledge of the subject, not of the biologist).

Chapter 5 reviews the intermediaries between this material organization of the living being and the superior forms of cognitive organization. The various levels of behavior are examined, and an attempt is made to isolate the epistemological questions raised by the analysis of these levels.

Chapter 6 seeks to determine to what extent these questions are, at the present time, susceptible to biological solution, and the conclusions, in chapter 7, provide a partial synthesis of the book.

1 Posing the Problem

Among leading ethologists today there is a realization that the problems of knowledge, including the higher forms of human knowledge such as mathematics, can no longer remain outside the scope of biology. Biology must, for its own sake, provide some interpretation of knowledge in its purely organic aspects, these aspects, both phylogenetic and ontogenetic, being very much the field of the biologist. For instance, Konrad Lorenz, in a recent article, following up several others on the same topic, stated that "the learning apparatus of the human species ought to be as much the subject of biological and phylogenetic study as other apparatus." He goes on to say that "even if one takes no interest in the theory of knowledge as an epistemologist, one is compelled to do so as a biologist."[1] Darwin himself, during the period when he was writing his famous *Notebooks* on evolution (1837–39), was also making notes on psychology. These notes contain ideas which he later elaborated about man, the emotions, etc. Among them is to be found this fundamentally important statement: "Whoever achieves understanding of the baboon will do more for metaphysics than Locke did, which is to say he will do more for philosophy in general, including the problem of knowledge."

1. "Die Entstehung der Mannigfaltigkeit," *Die Naturwissenschaften,* 1965.

Section 1. Preliminary Considerations[2]

By and large, most biologists agree that knowledge consists basically of information drawn from our environment (acquired experience) in the form of reality and of figurative or motor responses to sensorial stimuli (pattern $S \rightarrow R$), and having no internal or autonomous structure. This, of course, leaves out of account the question of instinct and all the hereditary aspects of the mechanisms of perception or intelligence levels insofar as they are linked with the development of the brain. Moreover, since the genetic system, center of the living structure, is usually thought of as dependent solely on endogenetic factors, with no relation to the influence of environment except insofar as there may be selection after the event, there could be no relation between the living structure in its genetic or even its ontogenetic sources on one hand and, on the other, the building up of the type of knowledge which is a reflection of environment. Such knowledge might, at the very most, play some part in the process of selection, but it could only be a very minor part.

The psychology of development has, by contrast, given an entirely different picture of the way in which knowledge and the intelligence are formed—a picture that makes us consider problems much closer to those major biological questions now under discussion among embryologists and specialists in heredity and variation, the reason being that all knowledge presupposes a physical structure.

We must here define our terms. For the time being we shall pick out only a few main types of cognitive function, such as may concern almost the entire animal kingdom. First come those allied to a chain of actions whose programming is inherited: a matter of reflex or instinctive actions. Second, we shall talk of "perception" in the case of a proximate structure of given sensorial evidence; as such, perception can already be seen to intervene in instinctive behavior and to be a no less essential part of kindred behavior. Third, we shall classify together in a primary group all those types of acquired behavior that are made in succession by the individual and called, respectively, apprenticeship, experiment, etc. In this last main group, which extends from the Protozoa right up to the human mind, distinctions are usually made between "conditioned" behavior, the formation of

2. The scope of this work, already touched upon in the Preface, will be set out at the end of chapter 2 after the clarification of the questions of method.

habits of varying complexity, various types of memory, and various levels of intelligence. But, on one hand, the facts reveal (particularly in the course of the first year's development in a human being) the existence of remarkably stable agencies between the forming of basic habits and the dawning of sensorimotor intelligence. Thus, it is never by virtue of anything but an artificial demarcation or arbitrary judgment that the first workings of a human intelligence can be pinpointed. And thus also, every time we use the term intelligence, which has no meaning on its own, we shall need to define what level of development we are talking about among all those levels of acquired behavior. (This we shall do, for the moment, without raising the obvious problem of antecedent conditions of a hereditary nature.) On the other hand, various kinds of behavior—so different from one another that their only common feature is the conservation of the past or, to put it more explicitly, the utilization of something acquired previously—are generally designated "memory." In most cases, memory is thus fused with habit or with that special aspect of habit which involves the recognition of signs. As for evocative memory, which develops in man from about the age of two years, it probably only represents the figurative aspect (recollection images) of the conservation of intelligence schemata. We shall presently return to the subject of these schemata.

That being so, in order to understand how the biological problem of knowledge is posed, it is vital to begin by ridding oneself of the oversimplified ideas one has of such knowledge, in the case of perception and acquired behavior, when one thinks of it as a mere registering of the data furnished by environment. First of all, of course, from the types of acquired cognitive behavior and especially from the higher forms of intelligence, two aspects should be defined— essentially different from each other in the part taken in their elaboration by the actions of the subject or organism, on one hand, and by the objects themselves or their environment, on the other. These aspects of knowledge are the logico-mathematical and the exogenetic (empirical apprenticeship and experimental behavior). Logico-mathematical structures, which imply, ipso facto, a preponderant share of activity and organization that are internal (if not entirely endogenetic—a problem to be discussed in chapter 6) can be seen (although constantly fused with exterior data from which they can only be distinguished on the higher levels of thought) at all stages of acquired behavior and even of perception—perhaps even of certain instincts. For instance, Gestalt perceptives consist of geometrization; the practical intelligence of chimpanzees dominates the detour problems, which imply the intervention of a "group of displacements"; the sensorimotor schemata follow their own logical pattern; and so on. Although logico-mathematical knowledge takes on a differentiated form only in the higher ranges of human intelligence, we shall, nonetheless, be compelled subsequently to consider it one of the three main categories of knowledge, coming between innate structures and knowledge based on physical or external experience, and we may simply affirm that it is not based on mere exogenetic recordings. As for knowledge of this third type (which ranges from empirical apprenticeship to experimental behavior) we must emphasize right away that, on every level, it is *richer* in itself than whatever it absorbs from its environment. Furthermore, it adds something to its environment, namely, structure elements that were not furnished in that form by events or objects outside the organism. In short, there is a new assessment of knowledge. Whereas in the past it was thought to be comparable to phenotypes, that is to say, radically distinct from genotypes, today it is seen to be much more assimilable to phenotypic variations, insofar as they are the product of interreaction between genes and environment and also insofar as they are relative to reaction norms.

1. Cognitive Assimilation

The essential starting point here is the fact that no form of knowledge, not even perceptual knowledge, constitutes a simple copy of reality, because it always includes a process of assimilation to previous structures.

We use the term assimilation in the wide sense of integration into previous structures. This word is already used in biology with widely differing meanings: chlorophyllous assimilation is a transformation of visible light into energy which is integrated into the functioning of the organism; "genetic assimilation" (Waddington) is the incorporation into the genetic system of characteristics which were initially allied to some interreaction with the environment. The meaning common to all these usages is, in fact, integration with previous structures, which may remain unaffected or else be modified to a greater or lesser degree by this very integration, but without any break of continuity with the former state—that is, without being destroyed and simply by adapting themselves to the new situation.

Assimilation, thus defined in very general functional terms, plays a necessary part in all knowledge. When a naturalist classifies the creatures he has collected, his perceptions are assimilated into an already existing system of concepts (or logical categories), which constitute a previous structure in relation to his present activity. When a man or an animal perceives an object, he identifies it as belonging to certain categories, either conceptual or practical. Otherwise, on the purely perceptual plane, he perceives it by the intermediary of functional or spatial schemata (as a shape standing out against a background, as occupying position in space, etc.). Thus he assimilates it into structures that are more or less complex and on varying levels, all of them previous to his perception of the moment. When a baby pulls his blanket toward himself in order to reach some object that is on it but out of his reach, he is assimilating this situation into perceptual schemata (the connecting thought is "on it") and active schemata (the behavior of the cover on which the object is lying). In short, any type of knowledge inevitably contains a fundamental factor of assimilation which alone gives significance to what is perceived or conceived.

In the past, psychologists as well as many physiologists used the term "association" rather than "assimilation." Pavlov's dog associates the sound of a bell with getting food and subsequently begins to salivate when hearing the bell, just as though the food were there. But association is only one stage, singled out artificially from the whole process of assimilation. The proof of this is that the conditioned reflex is not stable on its own and needs periodic "confirmation": if you continue only to sound the bell without ever following it up with food, the dog will cease to salivate at the signal. This signal, therefore, has no significance outside a total schema, embracing the initial need for food and its eventual satisfaction. "Association" is nothing but a piece of arbitrary selection, a single process picked from the center of a much wider process (most people today realize how much more complex the conditioned reflex is than was at first thought: in neurological terms to the extent that it depends on reticular formation and not only on the cortex; and in functional terms by causing the intervention of feedbacks, etc.).

The importance of the concept of assimilation is twofold. On one hand, as we have just seen, it implies meaning, an essential notion because all knowledge has a bearing on meaning (indices or perceptual signals of great importance even at the instinctive level and then right on up to the symbolic function in anthropoids and man, not to mention bees and dolphins). On the other hand, this concept expresses the fundamental fact that any piece of knowledge is connected with an action and that to know an object or a happening is to make use of it by assimilation into an action schema.

2. Action Schemata

Knowing does not really imply making a copy of reality but, rather, reacting to it and transforming it (either apparently or effectively) in such a way as to include it functionally in the transformation systems with which these acts are linked.

In studying phenomena, the physicist does not confine himself to setting down a description of what they appear to be, but controls what happens to them, in such a way as to isolate the various facts and to cause variations in them so that they are assimilated into the logico-mathematical transformation system. It may be said that he is thus making a new description of them, and a more profound one this time, and that, for his purposes, mathematics acts simply as a kind of language. But mathematics is much more than that, since it alone can enable him to reconstruct reality and to deduce what phenomena are, instead of merely recording them. The point is that, to do this, mathematics uses operations and transformations ("groups," "operators") which are still actions although they are carried out mentally, and these actions are, moreover, so important that not even the slightest physical phenomenon can be written up without logico-mathematical tables which reinforce the statement and render it comprehensible.

As for mathematics itself, it must not be thought that there is no more to it than the mere mensuration of immediate reality, although it is very well adapted to perform that function. What it actually does goes far beyond immediate reality (dealing in the various forms of infinity, space, function, and so on). Mathematics consists not only of all actual transformations but of all possible transformations. To speak of transformations is to speak of actions or operations, the latter being derived from the former, and to speak of the possible is to speak not simply of a linguistic description of some ready-made immediate reality but of the assimilation of immediate reality into certain real or virtual actions.

Logic, for its part, is not to be reduced, as some people would have it, to a system of notations inherent in speech or in any sort of language. It also consists of a system of operations (classifying, making series, making connections, making use of combinative or "transformation groups," etc.), and the source of these operations is to be found beyond language, in the general coordinations of action.

The active nature of knowledge is manifest from the start in its most elementary forms. Sensorimotor intelligence consists of the direct coordination of actions without any representation or thought. Perception is meaningless without some accompanying action: to perceive a house, as Weizsäcker said, is not to see an object whose image enters your eye but rather to spot an object that you yourself are about to enter.

Thus, if all knowledge at all levels is linked to action, the part played by assimilation becomes clear. Actions are not, in fact, haphazard occurrences, but repeat themselves whenever similar situations arise. To put it more precisely, they reproduce themselves exactly if there is the same interest in a similar situation, but they are differentiated or else form a new combination if the need or the situation alters. We shall apply the term "action schemata" to whatever, in an action, can thus be transposed, generalized, or differentiated from one situation to another: in other words, whatever there is in common between various repetitions or superpositions of the same action. For example, we shall apply the term "reunion schemata" to behavior such as that of a baby piling up bricks or an older child assembling objects in an attempt to classify them; and we shall find this schema repeated time and time again, right up to logical operations such as the linking of two classes of things ("fathers" plus "mothers"="parents"). In the same way, "order schemata" will be recognized in widely differing kinds of behavior, such as making use of certain means "before" achieving a goal, arranging bricks in order of size, constructing a mathematical series, and so forth. Other action schemata are much less general, and their completion does not involve such abstract interiorized operations: for example, the schemata involved in swinging a suspended object, in pulling something on wheels, in sighting an object, and so forth.

To say that all knowledge presupposes some assimilation and that it consists in conferring meanings amounts, in the final analysis, to the affirmation that to know an object implies incorporating it into action schemata, and this is true from elementary sensorimotor behavior right up to the higher logico-mathematical operations.

3. The Stimulus/Response Pattern

These action schemata and, a fortiori, the operative schemata deriving from them, comprise an organization, and this fact immediately brings us into the realm of biology. In the first place, it is axiomatic that the most elementary schemata into which perceptions may be assimilated are reflex or instinctive ones, that is, hereditary as to a large part of their programming. A mobile is perceived in motion because it sets off an optokinetic reflex. The redbreast of the male robin is perceived by the female as a sexual indication and, by another male, as an object of aggression, etc. No doubt it will be said at this juncture that perception is one thing, independent of motion, and that motor response is another, set in action by perception but not assimilating it.

However, the point is that the pattern $S \rightarrow R$, which constitutes the set figure of association, is inadequate in this simplified form because an object can constitute a perceptive stimulus S only insofar as the organism perceiving it is sensitized (a thing which may remain permanent in a given specimen but without affecting other specimens, or else may be momentary under the influence of hormones, etc.). Now this sensitivity to the stimulus S means precisely that the latter is assimilated in a schema, the manifestation of which constitutes the response R. What we should say, therefore, is what a colleague said in one of our seminars: "In the beginning was the Response!" or, at least, we should write $S \leftrightarrows R$, or $S \rightarrow (A) \rightarrow R$ (where A stands for assimilation into a schema).

But most schemata, instead of corresponding to a complete inherited apparatus, are built up a bit at a time, and even give rise themselves to differentiations, by adaption to a modified situation or by multiple and varying combinations (for example, reciprocal assimilation with or without new accommodations[3]). Might it not

---

3. We shall apply the term "accommodation" (by analogy with "accommodates" in biology) to any modification produced on assimilation schemata by the influence of environment to which they are attached. But just as there is no assimilation without accommodation (whether previous or current), so in the same way there is no accommodation without assimilation; this is as much as to say that environment does not merely cause a series of prints or copies to be made which register themselves on the subject, but it also sets in motion active adjustments; which is why every time we speak of accommo-

be said, in such cases where historical or ontogenetic analysis is often possible, that progressively elaborated schemata constitute exclusively products of acquired experience and are thus entirely attributable to exterior environment? To say as much would be to leave out of account their internal action. Of course, the contents of each action schema depend partly on environment and partly on the objects and events to which it is attached. But that in no way means that its form or function can be independent of internal factors. In the first place, even down at the level of Coelenterata and Echinoderms, action depends on the nervous system, and, however elementary it may be, this is inherited, a fact which presupposes some collaboration from the genome. Second, and still on the behavioral level, no schema ever has a clear-cut beginning: it always derives, by means of successive differentiations, from a series of earlier schemata having their origin far back in reflex or spontaneous initial movements. Third, and most important of all, a schema always includes actions performed by the subject (or organism) which are not derived in themselves from the properties of the object or environment.

For example, piling things up is related to an additive schema which is dependent on the powers of the organism and not solely on the properties of the objects; before being piled up, the objects did not constitute a collection, and the act of piling them up is none of their doing, even if they did allow themselves to be piled up. To lay things out in a straight line means introducing some kind of order into things, not getting order out of them, for they were not in line previously. And even supposing the subject could perceive objects which had already been piled or lined up, it would still be necessary for the eye to take in these elements as a whole or to follow them one by one, or several at a time, in order that the pile or row be perceived as a whole. If the shape of the whole is quite small, one glance will surely be enough to recognize it as a pile or line; but can a newborn child take things in, in the same way, before he is able to assimilate the datum into reunion or order schemata?

To sum up, in biological terms it would be out of the question to consider the organization of action schemata independently of

---

dation the phrase "accommodation of assimilation schemata" is to be understood. For example, in an infant five or six months old, the seizing of things by both hands is an assimilation schema, but the stretching out or bringing nearer of the hands according to whether the object is near or far is an accommodation of that schema.

endogenetic factors, if for no other reason than that, as was fundamentally the case with all previous ones, these schemata constitute dynamic or functional forms indissolubly linked to the static or anatomical forms represented by the structure of the organs. In parenthesis it must be added that we are here speaking of structure insofar as it results from morphogenesis. Most instincts are allied to specialized organs, it is true, but it is nonetheless true that perception and acquired behavior, including the higher types of operative intelligence, do, in a more supple way, manifest certain functional possibilities or "reaction norms" of the anatomical and physiological structure of the species. In a word, the general coordinations of action upon which the building up of most basic types of knowledge is conditional, presuppose not only nervous coordinations but coordinations of a much more deep-seated kind, those which are, in fact, interactions dominating the entire morphogenesis.

4. Equilibration and Autoregulation

However, although the considerations we have just dealt with will need to be referred to again, in more detailed fashion, when we come to the question of the biological sources of logico-mathematical knowledge (section 20), there is another aspect of the general coordination of actions, which controls their evolution even up to the operations of the mind, and which is just as closely involved with the central problems of contemporary biology: the question of equilibration or autoregulation.

Leaving out of consideration, for the moment, the problem of instinct, which is considerable, let us note that perception and acquired behavior alike, whether elementary or higher, do, in fact, contain autoregulatory processes. Thus, the immediate problem is to establish what the connections are between them and the large number inherent in the organism itself.

Such processes are to be noticed at all levels of learning. On the perceptual level, one of the most remarkable is that which regulates constancy of size, shape, etc. In the case of size constancy, the zoologist von Holst has admitted the existence of a hereditary system of feedbacks. This system is of a complex nature but such that the apparent diminution of a perceived object, with increased distance is corrected by reafferences which are released by the very perception of the increasing distance. Likewise, I myself have made the point elsewhere that there exist perceptual regulators such that "apparent size" $\times$ "distance" = "actual size," but this was on the plane of acquired, not innate, behavior, and the point was made for two reasons: (1) In the young child, size at a distance is reduced, just as are distances themselves, while apparent size, if it projects, is much more accurately evaluated—at a distance of four meters, for example—by a six-year-old than by an adult (unless the latter is a draughtsman). This would seem to prove that regulation is inferior at its inception to what it later becomes. It may even be null at the initial stage (it is only from six months onward that perception of size becomes constant). (2) Even more important, the concept of a size constancy leads, in adults, to no exact evaluation at all, as might have been expected in an innate mechanism, but, on the contrary, to a fairly strong superconstancy or supercompensation—for example, when a rod 8 or 9 centimeters long is seen at a distance of 3 or 4 meters to be the equal of a rod 10 centimeters long at a distance of 0.5 or 1.0 meters; there is, thus, a sort of wariness, arrived at by perception, not by reasoning, which protects the human being against error and which is relevant to the theory of games or decisions (with Bayes's criterion or even the "minimax" criterion). This once again argues an acquired structure rather than a hereditary one.[4] W. P. D. Tanner and his team at Michigan were able to elaborate, on this same model of the strategy in information games, their theory of perceptual thresholds.

In the second place, it is obvious that all learning by trial and error (or groping) presupposes feedback structures of such a kind that the lesson learned by each trial has a chain reaction on those that follow, each referring back to the point of departure and having a progressive anticipation of success or failure (as when a man learning to ride a bicycle takes evasive action against a probable fall, before it happens, by holding himself steady while the wobbling diminishes).

In the third place, operations of thought and especially those of elementary logico-mathematical thought, taken as a whole (that is to say, adding and multiplying of classes, relating of numbers or spatial measurement, connections, isomorphisms, etc.), can be considered as a vast autoregulatory system which gives autonomy

4. We are not stating, in any case, that this superconstant is general, but that it arises from regulator mechanisms. Moreover, many other examples of this are to be found, for instance, the overcompensations in certain experiments carried out by H. Werner on the orientation, vertical and otherwise, of right hands in space.

and coherence to the process of thought (see section 14). Now, when I tried to analyze the factors in the formation of these processes in a child, I was forced to the conclusion that their prime cause was a factor of gradual equilibration in the sense of auto-regulation. If equilibrium in action is defined as an active compensation set up by the subject against exterior disturbances, whether experienced or anticipated, this equilibration will explain, among other things, the more general character of logico-mathematical operations—that is, their reversibility (to every direction operation there corresponds an inverse one which cancels it out: $P \cdot P^{-1} = 0$).

It goes without saying that these regulatory mechanisms, in knowledge at all levels, raise the problem of their relationship with organic regulations. At every stage of development of the living structure it is clear that, in fact, the essential question is that of the regulation mechanisms. At the physiological level of the synergy of functions, the problem underlying all these questions is that of homeostasis: the equilibrium of each open system and the hormonal or nervous regulations which assure coordination in the whole living entity. At the stage of ontogenetic development (see section 2) the central problem is that of the dynamic equilibrium of "channeled" formations—"homeorhesis," which Waddington has rightly differentiated from homeostasis. As for the genetic system itself, the genome is today no longer conceived as a mosaic of detached, atomic elements, but rather as an organized system, containing regulatory genes alongside structural genes and having an internal metabolism which preserves its structure as an entity by dint of perpetually renewing itself.

The central problem with which this book will have to deal is, therefore, that of the relationships between cognitive and organic regulations at all levels.

Let us, then, bring this short summary of preliminary data to a close.

In an original article of great interest called "The Generalized Principle of Photophysiology and the History of Life" (*Scientia* 57 [1963] :5), F. Chodat and H. Greppin write: "living beings are macromolecular and quantuma 'machines,' endowed with memory, and custodians of a very complicated logical structure such as is necessary to ensure the being's autonomy in the face of environmental aggression (the destruction of information by entropy . . .)." In fact, what our problem amounts to is the relationship between the "memory" or "logic" belonging to behavior or to mental activity, and the kind of "memory" or "logic" that Chodat and Greppin rightly place in organic life, not in their capacity as psychic properties—such as the theory of vitalism so unjustifiably leans on to cover up the gaps in its scientific explanation—but by reason of their being an expression of autoregulatory mechanisms.

As I have already pointed out, I do not consider "memory" and "logic" to be two distinct departments: the essential data are the perceptual sensorimotor or operational schemata; the conservation of these action schemata is what constitutes memory, and their organization is what constitutes logic, but conservation cannot take place without organization nor organization without conservation. But the essential point about the statements I have just made is that such cognitive schemata imply no absolute beginning but are built up by a progression of equilibrations and autoregulations.

If they have no absolute beginning, as, for instance, by the intervention of a cause exterior to the system and emanating from the environment, it is because such formative interventions are assimilated into already existing schemata which they simply serve to differentiate: thus, cognitive schemata are derived step by step, each from the preceding one, and in the last analysis they always depend upon coordination of the nervous system and the organic system, in such a way that knowledge is necessarily interdependent on the living organism as a whole.

If they do develop, on the other hand, by means of regulations such as add to information and resist entropic increases, it is because they constitute a special part—although what exactly that part is remains to be determined—of vast regulator systems by means of which the organism as a whole preserves its autonomy and, at the same time, resists entropic decay.

Section 2. The Epigenetic System and the Development of Cognitive Functions

Before we try to formulate our main hypothesis it still remains for us to go more explicitly into the generalized statements which have led up to it, and to examine more closely the basic introductory material afforded by the rather striking parallel between the problems raised by organic embryogenesis and the kind of mental

embryology which constitutes the development of individual intelligence, of perceptions, and so forth. It is from these that we draw
most of our facts about the nature of knowledge.

1. Preformation and Epigenesis

The problem that has always arisen before one could tackle ontogenesis has been preformation or epigenesis. With the usual veering of
fashion in the history of ideas, the tendency of many writers today
is to return to the more or less strict preformation standpoint. Their
grounds for this are that the chain or helical structure of the DNA
or desoxyribonucleic acid molecule is susceptible of a combinatorial
arrangement of its elements where "combinatorial" covers, by definition, the set of all possibilities. But if it is difficult, from the
phylogenetic point of view, to conceive of man as preformed in
bacterium or virus, it is every bit as hard to make out how, from
the ontogenetic point of view, the main stages of "determination" or
induction, and, most important, of the final functional "reintegration" of differentiated organs, could already be present in the initial
stages of segmentation. Furthermore, Waddington has stated
categorically that the idea of an entirely predetermined system in
the DNA, however fashionable it may be at the moment, is just
unacceptable in embryology. At the symposium on this subject at
Geneva in 1964, in the course of discussion about the regulations of
development, he made a very profound comparison between
epigenetic construction and a progression of geometric theorems in
which each is rendered indispensable by the sum of those preceding
it, though none is directly derived from the axioms underlying the
original one.

The comparison of epigenesis with a progressive mathematical
construction comes home to us all the more forcibly because the
growth of elementary logico-mathematical operations during the
ontogenesis of intelligence in a child raises the same problem of preformation or epigenetic construction as that which forms the basis of
discussion about causal embryology.

We shall, indeed, find ourselves compelled to trace the origin of
logico-mathematical operations back to an abstraction made from
the general coordination of actions. On the one hand, such operations cannot possibly be based on the objects themselves, since
abstraction from objects can give rise only to non-necessitous statements (in the sense of deductive necessity) or, to put it more pre-

cisely, to judgments which are merely probable, whereas it is characteristic of logico-mathematical operations that they have an internal necessity attributable to their complete reversibility (and therefore not physical): for example, if $i = \sqrt{-1}$, then $i \times i = -1$. On the other hand, reunion, order, and interchangeable schemata are to be found in the general coordination of action, and these constitute the practical equivalent and even the motor equivalent of future interiorized operations.

If these elementary logico-mathematical operations are based on the coordination of actions, by means of reflective[5] abstraction drawn from sensorimotor schemata, do we have to conclude that the whole of mathematics is laid down in advance to our nervous system? Not only is this unthinkable, but the facts prove that logic itself, even in its most "natural" forms, is by no means innate in human beings in the sense that it exists at any age. Even the transitivity of equals or of cumulative differences ($A = C$ if $A = B$ and $B = C$, or $A < C$ if $A < B$ and $B < C$) is by no means obvious to a child of four to six years when he has to make a comparison between lengths and weights on first perceiving A and B simultaneously, next B and C, but not A and C (A subsequently being hidden and so presenting the problem).

The task of finding out about this transitivity raises all the main problems of epigenesis. Is this transitivity inherent in the genotype of the human species? If so, why does it not automatically come into play at about seven or eight years (and about nine or ten for weights)? Because, it will be said, new conditions are indispensable if the inherent virtual is later to become actual: for example, the intervention of regulatory genes or the collaboration of a number of genes not so far synergic (by reference to genetic or genic coadaptation, to use the currently accepted term). However, as these differentiated regulations are not made at any definite age in the particular case but may be accelerated or retarded according to conditions of exercise or acquired experience, they certainly exercise factors which are indirectly connected with environment.

Can it then be said that transitivity is utterly unconnected with the actions of the genome and solely dependent on phenotypic actions of the organism in relation to environment? In that case, how can it become "necessary" and generalizable? Because those actions which exert an influence on environment are influenced in their

5. For reflective abstraction see section 20, subsection 4.

turn by the more generalized forms of internal coordinations of action? If that were so, would then generalized coordinations depend, in their turn, on the most common and deep-seated coordinations of the nervous system, which brings us back to the genome?

The evidence thus proves that the problem of preformation or epigenesis has nothing about it that appertains specially to organic embryogenesis, and it crops up in its most acute form every time we discuss the ontogenesis of cognitive functions. It may be objected that the problem is settled in advance, since the various aspects of intellectual behavior are phenotypic reactions and a phenotype is the result of interaction between the genotype and the environment. That is indisputable, but one still needs to explain in detail how, in the field of knowledge as in that of organic epigenesis, this collaboration between the genome and the environment actually works —especially those details which concern autoregulations or progressive equilibrations which admit of the exclusion of both preformism and the notion of a reaction caused entirely by environment.

2. *The Sequential Character of Stages*

In this attempt at elucidation, the first step forward should be an examination of the sequential character of development. We call sequential a series of stages, each one of which is a necessary part of the whole and a necessary result of all the stages that precede it (except for the first one), as well as naturally leading on to the next stage (except for the last one). This seems to be the case with the embryogenesis of Metazoa, since the main stages constantly repeat themselves in the same order. However, no experiments have yet been done to control the impossibility of doing away with one stage, though these will doubtless be performed some day if someone succeeds in isolating processes which entail considerable speeding up or slowing down of the succession of stages. A further argument in favor of the sequential character and generality of the stages is the fact that, in mosaic-type embryos, namely at the initial level studied, those which have shown incomplete regeneration when separated from a blastomere reach a stage of partial control if the seed is split at the virgin egg stage (Ascidies de Dalcq).

Now this same problem about the sequential character of stages appears again in psychology in connection with the development of the cognitive functions. It is important to note that in this sphere the stages became increasingly clear and sequential in relation to controls that are better differentiated and of wider application.

Psychologists have relied too much on the notion of stage. Some speak as though it were nothing but a series of actions, not always, though "generally," in a constant order, and supposedly sharing a dominant characteristic, nothing more—which opens the door to arbitrary thinking. This is what Freud means by stages, for example, as far as the affective is concerned.

When it comes to intelligence, however, we use the term stage where the following conditions are fulfilled: first, where the series of actions is constant, independently of such speeding up or slowing down as may modify the middle range of chronological age[6] in terms of acquired experience and social environment (like individual aptitude); second, where each stage is determined not merely by a dominant property but by a whole structure which characterizes all further actions that belong to this stage; third, where these structures offer a process of integration such that each one is prepared by the preceding one and integrated into the one that follows. For example, without going into great detail about particular stages, three main periods can be seen in the case of operative intelligence:

A. A sensorimotor period (from birth up to one and one-half to two years) during which sensorimotor schemata ranging up to acts of practical intelligence by means of immediate comprehension (using a stick or a piece of string, etc.) are established as well as practical substructures of future notions (permanent object schema, spatial deplacement "group," sensorimotor causality, etc.).

B. A period that begins when the semiotic function (language, game symbols, picture making) manifests itself and goes through the preparatory phase of preoperative representation (nonconservation, etc.). This ends not later than the eighth or ninth year with the setting up of operations which are called "concrete" because they still have a bearing on objects (classifying things, putting them in series, noting connections, understanding numbers).

C. A period beginning at about the age of eleven or twelve which is characterized by propositional operations (implications, etc.) with their combinatorial quality and their possible transformations made by relation to a quaternary group—a combination of

6. In psychology the distinction is always made between chronological and mental age.

two elementary reversibility forms (inversion or negation and reciprocity).

A stage system of this kind (stages which can actually be even further differentiated into substages) makes up a sequential process: it is not possible to arrive at "concrete" operations without undergoing some sensorimotor preparation (which explains why, for example, blind people, having badly coordinated action schemata, may be retarded). It is also impossible to progress to propositional operations without support from previous concrete operations, etc. Thus, one is confronted with an epigenetic system whose stages may be characterized by fairly precise structures: coordination of sensorimotor schemata reaching certain invariables and an approximate reversibility (though in successive actions); "groupings" of concrete operations, that is, those elementary structures which are common to classifications and serializations, etc.; and combinatorial with a quaternary group at the third degree.[7]

By contrast, in the field of primary perceptions (or field effects) no comparable system of stages is to be found, and, as to behavior of medium complexity (perceptive activity in exploration, etc., and mental images), an intermediary situation is found halfway between an absence of stages and stages limited by their progressive integrations. Thus, everything seems to happen as though the more complex—in their organization and autoregulation systems—cognitive systems are, the more their formation is dependent on a sequential process comparable to a biological epigenesis.

3. Chreods

If a detailed study is to be made, that is, if the evolution of broad concepts or of particular operative structures is to be studied separately, then each one may give rise to its own respective stages in the midst of which is to be found the same sequential process. But the interesting thing about this point is that it presents us with differentiated channels, each one of which is nevertheless relatively even and follows its own course while still giving proof of varied interactions with the rest.

7. This sequential character of the stages of intelligence certainly seems to prove the necessity of an endogenic factor in nervous maturation, but by no means excludes either the intervention of the environment (experience) or, more particularly, the interaction of environment and maturation at the center of a process of equilibration or progressive autoregulation.

Waddington has suggested the name "chreods" (necessary routes) to describe developments particular to an organ or a part of an embryo, and he applies the term epigenetic system (or, epigenetic "scene") to the sum of the chreods, taken as being—to a greater or a lesser degree—channeled. But the main interest of this idea is not just in the names he gives things (or in the symbolic patterns thereby presented to us, of channels, some wide, some narrow, that the processes must follow). It is, rather, in a new concept of equilibrium as something which is, as it were, kinematic and which, in determining such processes, is nevertheless quite distinct from homeostasis: there is a kind of "homeorhesis" when the formatory process, deviating from its course under outside influence, is brought back on course by the interplay of coercive compensations. In Waddington's opinion, such a mechanism is dependent upon a network of interactions rather than upon the action of individual genes; each group of genes is not even homeorhetic, and its return to a moral course or chreod presupposes, in this way, a complex interplay of regulations. It is true that some influence systematically exerted by the environment may eventually lead to lasting deviations in the chreod and to the consolidation of a new homeorhesis, but this is not the moment to raise such a problem (see section 12, subsection 3). On the contrary, we would do better to emphasize the fact that the chreod and its homeorhesis do have a space-time aspect, not merely a space one. Differentiation in chreods is regulated both in time and space. The various channelings as well as the autocorrections which assure their homeorhetical equilibrium are under the control of a "time tally," which might well be described as a speed control for the processes of assimilation and organization. It is, then, only at the completion of development or at the completion of each structural achievement that homeorhesis gives place to homeostasis or functional equilibrium. In the latter case, the question naturally arises of determining the relationship between the two.

It is impossible to take note of such a picture without immediately thinking of the far-reaching analogies it has with the development of schemata or ideas in the intelligence, and with that of operational structures.

To put the matter in a familiar way, let us begin by noting that these analogies are very far from being universally accepted; very rarely have I been able, in America, to expound any aspect of my stage theory without being asked, "How can you speed up this development?" And that excellent psychologist, J. Bruner, has gone so far as to state that you can teach anything to any child at any age if only you set about it the right way. My answer to this is in the form of two questions: first, would it ever be possible to make the theory of relativity or even the simple handling of propositional or hypothetico-deductive operations comprehensible to a four-year-old? And, second, why does a human baby not discover the continued presence of something that he sees you hide beneath a screen until he reaches the age of nine months and upward, whereas kittens (in a study made by H. Gruber when he discovered the same preliminary stages in them as in us) do so at three months, even though they make no further progress in coordinating successive positions?

The truth, it seems to me, is that every notional or operational construction implies some optimum length of time, the expression of the most favorable transformation or assimilation speeds. This is because such a construction contains a certain number of necessary stages whose itinerary is the equivalent of a "chreod." In the sphere of the mind, where social influences are added to factors of physical experience (material environment), deviations easily occur, and short circuits too. Thus, the natural way for the mind to attain the concept of whole numbers consists of syntheses of inclusion of classes and the sequence of transitive asymmetrical relationships, in spite of the fact that the latter two systems develop along partly independent lines. Now the natural structure of the number concept can be modified in various ways. First of all, as is done by many parents, it can be taught the child verbally—10 to 20, etc. But this only modifies the child's comprehension very slightly; we are constantly coming across subjects of four to five years old who will deny the equality of two piles of objects, even though they have counted what is in each pile as being perhaps 7 or 10, because the way the objects were arranged in space or subdivided into small groups was changed each time. In such cases, outside influences, such as counting out loud, only produce a slight deviation leading back to the "chreod" at the four- to five-year-old level, for lack of any means of assimilation at higher levels. In other cases, a genuine acceleration can be set up, but only at one point (for example, in experiments where transfers are made one at a time in succession, thus facilitating, by repetition of the same actions, the synthesis of inclusions and the serial order).[8] This local synthesis is not necessarily followed by comprehension, nor will it guarantee retention of the number in transfer experiments between groups of objects arranged differently on different planes.

Briefly, intellectual growth contains its own rhythm and its "chreods" just as physical growth does. This is not, of course, to say that the best teaching methods, by which we mean the most "active" ones, cannot, to a certain extent, speed up the critical ages dealt with so far, but this speeding up cannot be indefinitely continued.

4. Maturation and Environment

The epigenesis of the cognitive functions, like any other, does, in fact, presuppose an increasingly close collaboration between the factors of environment and the genome, the former increasing in importance the larger the subject grows.

The factors relative to the genome are certainly not to be left out of account, in spite of what some scholars, empirically oriented, have said about all knowledge being drawn from outside experience. At this stage of our knowledge, these factors certainly cannot be tested in detail, but the best indication that they do intervene is the fact that the maturation of the nervous system is continuous right up to the age of fifteen or sixteen years. This, of course, in no way implies that ready-made knowledge is written into the nervous system from the outset in the way that "innate ideas" are, and, even if this idea proves acceptable in the case of certain instincts (to which we shall return in chapter 5), there does not seem to be any similar phenomenon where human knowledge is concerned. On the contrary, heredity and maturation open up new possibilities in the human child, possibilities quite unknown to lower types of animal but which still have to be actualized by collaboration with the environment. These possibilities, for all they are opened up in stages, are nonetheless essentially functional (having no preformed structures) in that they represent a progressive power of coordination; but this very power is what makes possible the general coordinations

8. In this case, it was the putting of beads, simultaneously, one in each hand, into transparent bottles. See Inhelder and Piaget, *La formation des raisonnements récurrentiels,* Etudes d'épistémologie génétique, 17 (Presses Universitaires de France, 1963), chap. 2.

of action on which logico-mathematical operations are based, which is why the continuous maturation of the nervous system that goes on until fifteen or sixteen years is a factor by no means to be ignored.

Such maturation does not, moreover, depend solely on the genome. But it does depend on that among other things (with the intervention of exercise factors, etc.), and, in general terms, it is admitted today that every phenotypic growth (including, therefore, cognitive functions in general) is the product of close interreactions between the genome and the environment.

The analysis of this collaboration remains, it is true, very complex and has scarcely been touched on so far. At this point we might begin by referring to an idea for which we are indebted, once more, to Waddington. This time it dates back to the work he did in 1932 on the phenomena of induction in the embryos of hens and ducks, to the idea of "competence," or the physiological state of a tissue, which permits it to react in a specific way to given stimuli. Competence is naturally subject to time conditions such as we talked about earlier, and a tissue may be competent at one particular phase without having been so previously or even remaining so afterward.

Surely no one can fail to see the analogy between this notion in relation to the embryonic mechanism and the facts brought out by experiments in the field of learning in logico-mathematical operations. The work of such people as Inhelder, Sinclair, and Bovet opened this up. When mechanisms favorable to the acquisition of knowledge are thus presented (for example, retaining the idea that there is the same amount of liquid when changing it from one vessel to another of a different shape), the results are utterly different according to the stage of the child's development, and the particular presentation which causes one subject to learn more quickly about a constant quantity will leave another utterly unmoved. The explanation of this again lies in the fact that sensitivity to stimuli (not only perceptual stimuli but in some cases those which set up a reasoning process) is a function of such assimilation schemata as are available to the subject. In this case, then, "competence" is a particular instance of what we call cognitive "assimilation," but assimilation schemata are built up by the interplay among the subject's powers of coordination and by the data of experience and environment.

To put it briefly, the epigenetic process which is the basis of intellectual operations is rather closely comparable to embryological epigenesis and the organic formation of phenotypes. Of course, the part played by environment is much larger, since the essential function of knowledge is to make contact with environment. To the effects of physical environment we must add those of social environment (for the individual genome is always the reflection of multiple crossbreedings and of a fairly broad range of "population"). But the essential question does not concern the quantitative sum of the respective influences exerted by endogenitive and external factors; rather, it has to do with qualitative analogies, and from that point of view it seems obvious that internal coordinations of the necessary and constant type, which make possible the integration of exterior cognitive aliment, give rise to the same biological problem of collaboration between the genome and the environment as do all the other forms of organization which occur in the course of development.

5. *Homeorhesis and Homeostasis*

The various chreods that are characteristic of epigenetic growth, together with their space-time regulations in the shape of homeorhesis, eventually reach an adult state that is more or less in equilibrium and is of a homeostatic nature. We must now, therefore, compare these two kinds of equilibrium—the one, as it were, temporal or historical, and the other no less dynamic in its processes, though synchronic—and we must also point out the analogy between this situation and the question of equilibrium in the epigenesis of cognitive functions.

In a nutshell, the problem is one of the relations between equilibrium as a process and equilibrium as a final state. On this essential point we must not exclude the possible existence of a certain qualitative difference between embryological epigenesis, at least in its initial stages and not in its overall growth, and ontogenesis of the cognitive functions, at least as studied from birth onward, that is, throughout those phases which are already functional.

Embryologists do, in fact, draw a distinction between three main periods in ontogenesis. The first is one of initial segmentation with possibilities of regulation in the sense of the total regeneration of any part experimentally cut away. Second comes a period of determination or differentiation of the organs, with the possibility of varied inductions but without complete regeneration. Third is the phase of functional activity or, to quote Weiss, "reintegration"—an excellent way of expressing it—which suggests how the functional whole thus set up is a projection of the morphogenetic whole that was an essential part of the initial adaptations. Of course, the kind of ontogenesis of the cognitive functions that we are discussing principally concerns the infant state (or, in other species, the larva condition)—growth that took place before the initial stages of the third phase described above, while the embryological problem of the relation between homeorhesis and homeostasis must be considered in connection with the whole series of stages.

Looked at from this angle, homeostasis is late in developing, unless we are going to relate it theoretically to the early regulations of the first phase, which at this juncture would be no more than a fancy. On the contrary, the facts as they appear at the moment suggest that an epigenetic evolution takes place, in the course of which chreods are gradually differentiated, each one attaining a certain degree of independence. On the other hand, a complex of interactions is set up at the third stage, functional integration, but the point is that these are functional, having ceased to be structural, and are dominated by the nervous system. This being so, little relation can be seen between these interactions and the chreods, for though the latter serve finally to bring about the structural elaboration of each of the organs which can function only when this has been effected, they certainly did not prepare the way for the functioning itself, which depends on new integration factors. In a word, homeorhesis makes homeostasis possible by ensuring the structural composition of the organs, but homeostasis is brought about by the setting in motion of these organs under the influence of new interactions. These interactions are no longer diachronic but synchronic and are released by the nervous system.

If the foregoing description is not altogether accurate and if closer links are to be found between homeorhesis and homeostasis, we shall simply conclude that the analogy between organic ontogenesis and ontogenesis of the cognitive functions is even stronger than has been supposed here. Meantime, a difference (now to be expounded) still remains, which, it must be emphasized, depends fundamentally on the fact that the formation of the intelligence, etc., only takes place in the course of phases which have already become functional.

In the cognitive field, chreods can indeed be singled out which are more or less independent, each with its own homeorhesis, and forms of final equilibrium (in the sense that they continue to exist in a stable condition while still being capable of eventual integration into wider fields of equilibrium) which might be the cognitive equivalent of homeostasis. (This comparison has frequently been made in connection with Gestalts, etc., and we shall be making it again in connection with operative structures.) However, in the main, equilibrium is the product of equilibration; in other words, there is a continuity or, at the very least, a close relationship between the formatory process and the equilibrium resulting from it.

As far as the relative independence of "chreods" is concerned, one can cite the example of the relatively disconnected evolution of notions such as weight or visually evaluative quantities (length, etc.). Whereas serialization, transivity, and conservation are to be found in the latter field at seven or eight years, we have to wait until the child reaches nine or ten for him to structure the idea of weight by the same process. The countless "time lags" of this nature are an indication of the relative independence of such chreods, whereas interactions brought about by simple generalization might well seem quite easy, logically speaking.

On the contrary, where continuity between progressive equilibration and the final forms of equilibrium is concerned, it is so constant in the realm of cognitive functioning that we need make only one comment about it. Equilibration constitutes a very general process (although it advances, as we have just seen, sector by sector over itineraries that have no immediate connections). This process amounts, in the main, to putting up active compensations against outside perturbations: such compensations varying, of course, according to the levels and schemata of the subject but always bringing about a reaction to the perturbations that are experienced or anticipated. Operational equilibrium, on the other hand, is essentially characterized by reversibility (inversion or reciprocity) or, more particularly, by a stable form of compensation systems. Obviously, then, there is a continuity between the equilibrium attained and the process of equilibration itself. This central problem, however, leads us directly to the exploration of the hypothesis which has guided me in writing this book and which, therefore, will now be examined.

Section 3. Guiding Hypothesis about the Relation between Cognitive Functions and the Living Organization

This hypothesis of mine is not only very simple but banal in the extreme. It may nonetheless serve to throw light on certain points, for it seems to me that people have not gone nearly far enough in the consequences that can be drawn from it.

1. The Hypothesis

Life is essentially autoregulation. The explanation of evolutionary mechanisms, for so long shackled to the inescapable alternatives offered by Lamarckism and classical neo-Darwinism, seems set in the direction of a third solution, which is cybernetic and is, in effect, biased toward the theory of autoregulation. But if organic regulations thus appear more and more to be the central properties of life, there remains the task of describing those organs that bring about regulations. Now, the living being, for all it contains such mechanisms, does not possess differentiated organs for regulation, unless we consider as such an organ the nervous system, which in another respect is the instrument of cognitive functions (and, to a certain extent, the endocrine system, though in constant interaction with the nervous system). Then again, organic regulation must include, as a fundamental element of ever-increasing importance, exchanges with the environment. These exchanges are subject to their own progressive adjustments. But even here there is still no organ specially designed for the regulation of these exchanges, unless, once again, it be the nervous system, acting as a source of information about the environment and also as a source of active transformations operating on the environment.

Cognitive processes seem, then, to be at one and the same time the outcome of organic autoregulation, reflecting its essential mechanisms, and the most highly differentiated organs of this regulation at the core of interactions with the environment, so much so that, in the case of man, these processes are being extended to the universe itself.

Let us take the terms of this interpretative hypothesis one by one so as to weigh up its various and complementary meanings.

To take it in its general sense first, it should be noted right away that there is nothing contradictory in considering these cognitive functions as being, at one and the same time, a result or reflection of organic autoregulation and a differentiated organ which has a determining effect on them in the field of exchanges with the environment. This, in fact, is exactly what happens with the nervous system; even in the embryonic state this system first appears as a product of differentiation at the determination and induction stage (neurula, neurobiotaxis, etc.)—which in no way prevents its serving, at the functional reintegration stage, as an essential organ in these new regulations.

This said, the primary meaning of the hypothesis is that knowledge is not a copy of the environment but a system of real interactions reflecting the autoregulatory organization of life just as much as the things themselves do. The entire first section has shown why, but it may be restated in more biological terms, since section 2 is written with reference to embryological development.

If one adopts this position, it is remarkable that the nervous system has its origin in, and develops from, the ectoderm: neural blood disc and trough in the course of nerve formation. On one hand, the nervous system will subsequently participate in all the internal regulations of the organism (even in mechanisms so seemingly independent as the coagulation of the blood), without on that account being a product of the endoderm or even of the mesoderm. On the other hand, its ectodermic origin would seem to predetermine its having a special sensitivity to outer stimuli, but that by no means implies that it merely picks up inputs or related information, for it reacts to them by active movements and responses that produce a modification in the environment. And in the last analysis the nervous system is certainly not limited, as was believed for a long time, to making interventions merely in the form of responses or reactions ($S{\rightarrow}R$, which we have already commented on in section 1, subsection 3) for it gives proof of spontaneous initiating activities, such as those substantiated by electric shock tests or the ones studied by Adrian in connection with the behavior of worms (see also, under this head, the work of Bullock, etc.).

This picture, admittedly only a rough sketch, corresponds to the main, though equally sketchy, outlines of the cognitive process. Indeed, knowledge does not start in the subject (through somatic knowledge or introspection) or in the object (for perception itself contains a considerable measure of organization), but rather in interactions between subject and object and in other interactions originally set off by the spontaneous activity of the organ as much as by external stimuli. Starting from these primitive interactions in which the parts played by internal and external factors are indistinguishable (as well as subjectively fused), knowledge is then built up in two complementary directions, while still based on actions and action schemata outside which it has no hold either on the exterior world or on internal analysis.

The first of these directions, which develops much earlier in the animal kingdom because it is the most essential for adaptation to environment, is the conquest of objects or knowledge of environmental data, which will eventually enable the subject to comprehend the exterior world objectively. But conquest of the object is in no case (whether perception, elementary learning, or intelligent representation) a simple copy of reality, since there necessarily intervene certain factors of organization and regulation dependent on the fact that all knowledge is linked to action and that the evolution of actions presupposes coordination.

The second direction, which is almost certainly confined to human intelligence, involves becoming conscious of the internal conditions of these coordinations, a development which leads, by means of "reflection," to the making of logico-mathematical constructions. These, in the human child, are even to be observed in elementary form before there is any systematized physical knowledge.

From the point of view of the regulatory functions of the nervous system, is there a connection between this second line of development and the general autoregulations of organic life? None whatever, it would seem. And yet if we think of cybernetic models, which are, so far, the only ones throwing any light on the nature of autoregulatory mechanisms, we notice at once that they all bring some sort of logic into play (or at least some sort of binary arithmetic, which amounts to the same thing). Moreover, the essential function of logical operations, if they are to function effectively and in a living way, is to set up systems of control and autocorrection. Since logic, in psychological terms, is abstracted by reflection, not about objects, but about general coordinations of action, it would not be very daring to form the opinion that there is in existence a common fund of regulatory mechanisms which belong to the nervous regulatory systems in all their forms, and of which the general coordinations of action are only one manifestation among others. And since the nervous system is not a State within a State but the differentiated product of organic and morphogenetic coordinations, there is no a priori reason to set an initial limit to regressive analysis.

To sum up: to suppose, as our ruling hypothesis does, that cognitive functions are reflections of the essential mechanisms of organic autoregulation is a perfectly valid proposition. No more than that, but it is at least a beginning. What remains to be done is the easier part, namely, to show that they are also differentiated regulatory organs.

2. Internal Regulatory Organs

Before proceeding, let us recall that, outside the nervous system and the cognitive functions, there exist no differentiated organs acting as functional regulators, for the reason that organic regulators with the type of structure that terminates in cycles are self-conserving by means of a compensatory mechanism. For example, there is such a thing as homeostasis or a static internal environment, and this is made manifest by a certain permanence of the blood elements (globules and plasma with all that goes to make them up), particularly by the constant level of *pH*. But there is no such thing as an organ of homeostasis which acts as a kind of equilibrium, simply expressing the interaction of all the factors involved.

As Professor Max Aron has said so profoundly in his provocative book *Les problèmes de la vie*: "In the field of speculative biology, homeostasis presents some disturbing problems. It is both cause and effect, causing the normal functioning of tissues and organs, which draw the material necessary for their activity from the internal environment and also deposit their rejects in it, and at the same time dependent itself upon a number of organs: the kidneys, the liver, and the endocrine glands" (p. 130).

But to say that homeostasis is both cause and effect means simply that it is a feedback system, in other words, a form of autoregulation; and if any fault can be found in the interesting work from which we have just quoted, it is that it tends to leave out of account those cybernetic modes of thought which do, however, lend intelligibility to such situations, in principle at least.

However, to speak of feedback implies a system that functions independently and that has no need of a regulator to control its workings from the outset. It may be replied that such regulators do exist in the shape of nervous and endocrine systems. But they are a later development. A. A. Markosjan, who has made a very close study of the coagulation of the blood (including work on over twenty biochemical factors), demonstrates that we are dealing with a phylogenetic system, long established, perhaps even as far back as in the Coelenterata and certainly in the invertebrates, and containing its own regulator, only at a later stage coming under the control of endocrine glands and, eventually, of the nervous system.

The great interest of these hormonal and nervous controls is, therefore, that they reveal a tendency to specialization in that they set up differentiated organs of regulation. But at this juncture a careful distinction must be made between two sorts of regulation: structural and functional.

Structural regulation is that which occurs when the modifications brought about are either anatomical or histological, whereas functional regulation has an influence only on the exercise of physiological reaction of the organs. As an illustration of structural regulation we can cite the embryological experiment in which a blastomere is split up only to come together again as a whole embryo. On the other hand, the speeding up of coagulation in the case of threatened asphyxia at birth is brought about by functional regulation.

Now the fundamental truth on which we base our argument is that the nervous system alone constitutes a specialized organ of functional regulation as well as being the instrument of cognitive functions, whereas the endocrine system consists of an organ (likewise the only one) of both structural and functional regulations (leaving out of account such structural nervous residues as chemical mediators).

It is well known, indeed, that, even in the embryo, genital hormones differentiate the sexual organs, a thing which in itself amounts to a structural regulation. But one can go farther and, as scholars such as E. Wolff and L. Gallien have done, reach the conclusion that there is no natural difference between formative "inductions" of organs during the secondary period of embryogenesis and morphogenetic actions of an endocrine nature. On the other hand, the endocrine system shows an early tendency to differentiation at the induction or "determination" stage, which would seem to prove a continuity of function, from embryonic life onward, between the inductive processes and hormonal activity. It is only at the second stage, in concert with the nervous system, that the endocrine system becomes capable of functional regulation. The setting in motion of the genital system by the hormones so long after they have established the structural differentiations of sex, is a good example of the way in which structural regulation becomes functional.

We are increasingly aware of the close coordination between the endocrine and nervous systems. This fact should be remembered if we are to understand the growing specialization in the direction of the differentiation of an organ from functional regulations. On one hand, hormones react, in certain cases, upon the effectors, and by reciprocation there exists a nervous control of secretions (nervous centers upon which the hypophysis, etc. depends). On the other hand, and this is a point of particular interest, a kind of "neuro-secretion" is manifest throughout the nerve axones. This phenomenon was discovered as long ago as 1929 by the Scharrers, working on annelids, but it made no impact at first. Since then, however, an increasing number of instances of it have been found in the higher forms of life. It shows the connection between the chemical transmissions of hormones and the electrochemical transmissions of nerves (a fact which adds to our knowledge of chemical mediators such as adrenaline, etc.).

To sum up, throughout the main lines of development a progressive change can be observed from morphogenetic to structural auto-regulations and finally to functional regulations. The endocrine system is a specialized regulator organ, having an effect on both these categories at the same time, and only the nervous system appears to be a differentiated organ, whose special function is to bring functional regulators into play, both internally and where exchanges with environment are concerned.

3. Cognitive Functions and Regulation of Exchanges

If we come now to cognitive functions, we are simply at an extension of this process of specializing differentiation, but with no break of contact with the morphogenetic and structural origins of the living organization.

The points to remember, as a starting-off ground, are that there is no sphere in which the organism is subjected passively to environmental influences and that, on the contrary, the organism plays an essentially active part in relation to them. From the physico-chemical angle, the living being is no mere replica of the bodies surrounding it, for it presents an organization which preserves them by assimilation, and this organization includes some autoregulation. In genetic terms, the genome is in no sense the product of environmental influences but is an organized system, supplying "responses" to environmental tensions (Dobzhansky and Waddington) and containing its own "norms of reaction." In terms of embryology, however, epigenetic development implies a series of exchanges with some internal control imposing choices on the materials used. In physiological terms, the system of regulations gives proof of a continuous activity which, once again, does not merely submit to exchanges with the environment but, rather channels and controls them. In neurological terms the nervous system is not subjected to some constraining influence from the stimuli but shows spontaneous action, reacting only to stimuli which sensitize it—that is, it assimilates them actively into schemata established before it made its response.

As far as the last stage (that is, behavior) is concerned, exactly the same thing happens. Every animal, from protozoan up to man, presents behavior patterns; the vegetable kingdom shows equal evidence of reaction processes, but at a slower pace. Fear of anthropomorphism has often led to attempts to interpret behavior as a matter of passive experiences, beginning with the recording made by perception and followed by a series of associations, all imposed from the outside and merely being copied. But are we to believe that an organism which is active at every stage of growth should, on reaching the apex of its development, reverse the process and become a mere slavish imitator of its surroundings?

As distinguished an embryologist and geneticist as Waddington considers, on the contrary, that one of the essential feedbacks involved in selection is the fact that, while still under the influence of the genome, animals "choose" and "modify" their environment before submitting to its influences, which then help to form the genotype (see *The Strategy of the Genes* [1957], p. 107, fig. 13). That is just what behavior is: a mixture of choice from, and effect upon, the environment, exerting optimal control over exchanges. Learning is no exception to this definition, for, as the living creature acquires new conditioning or new habits, it assimilates signals and organizes action schemata that it then imposes on the environment at the same time as it is itself undergoing environmental influence.

Thus, there is active assimilation at the behavior level (see section

1, subsections 1–3), and the cognitive functions, just like any other function, have to observe the common laws of assimilation and accommodation. Action schemata are just as much "forms" of living organization as are other schemata, only they are functional forms with a dynamic structure and not material ones (in the sense of having any concrete form).[9]

It thus goes without saying that if the nervous system is a specialized organ of the functional regulations, then this structuring of environment by behavior must, in its turn, involve some specialized organ. The nervous system exerts its influence upon the whole field of functional regulations in their twin aspects of internal regulation (coordination of the various physiological mechanisms) and regulation of exchanges with the environment. Now, such exchanges may themselves be physical (digestion, breathing, excretion, etc.) or functional (behavior, that is, the entire system of action schemata). For there to be functional exchanges there must be organs of an even more differentiated kind, such as the sense organs and motor agencies, as well as nervous coordinations (and, in the last resort, cerebral and even cortical organs), all of which make learning possible.

However, such superficial considerations as these by no means exhaust all that there is to be said about cognitive functions, for the good reason that the nervous system does, in fact, enable these active exchanges to build up as modifications of the organism's environment and vice versa. This still leaves us with the problem of why cognitive functions, as such, are set up: for example, in the form of conscious intelligence (in which case it must be remembered that intelligence evolves imperceptibly from acquired conduct [section 1, introduction] and that there are no grounds for limiting consciousness to man only) or in the form of logico-mathematical operations.

The causal and cybernetic reason for this is that the functional exchanges characteristic of behavior presuppose, as does any other form of living organization, their own regulations, and that an autoregulation in this case is even more indispensable than usual because a fluid, unbounded area is involved, much less subject to restricting conditions than are material systems such as breathing. Modification of the environment according to possibilities of an

9. On the other hand, the structural regulations noted in section 3, subsection 3, apply to material structures.

endlessly open kind can lead anywhere, and if the only brake were selection as the old mutationists understood it (that is to say, elimination by a once-for-all sorting-out process, of the death-or-survival kind, and not reorganization consequent upon some modification of the genome's proportions), then the human race would have died out long ago. Every living organization, at every level of evolution, contains autoregulations, and the same thing applies, a fortiori, I would say, in the field of behavior.

It would follow that cognitive functions, seen in this light, are specialized organs of autoregulation controlling the exchanges underlying all behavior. But having said as much, if we are to continue the argument in biological terms, we shall have to explain how such cognitive autoregulations might be formed. Now in biological terms there is no need to base our argument on neoformations when the elements are already at hand and all we have to do is differentiate between them and regroup them. What needs to be explained is where cognitive functions get the instruments of autoregulation which they are to exert. Specialized organs they may be, but they certainly neither create nor conjure up everything for themselves: they have to work in concert with the rest of the organism.

We can answer this simply enough: cognitive autoregulation makes use of the general systems of organic regulation such as are found at every genetic, morphogenetic, physiological, and nervous level, and forthwith adapts them to their new situation (new, that is, by relation to the preceding levels, but still present in every animal series). This situation constitutes the exchanges with environment that form the basis of behavior.

That is why there are to be found in all kinds of knowledge, even human knowledge of the highest and most purely scientific kind, the principal functional constants that are characteristic of autoregulation at every level.

Thus, in their most generalized form, the operational structures of the intelligence are transformation systems of a kind which maintains the system as an invariant totality. This same definition could be applied to the living organism itself, since its two basic properties are that it serves as the field for multiple interactions (=transformations), though at the same time leaving unchanged both the overall form (=conservation) and even a certain number of invariant relationships.

The way in which the whole is conserved throughout a series of transformations presupposes some regulation of these, which in turn implies the interplay of conservation and regulatory corrections. This regulator mechanism thus corresponds, as we have said, to reversibility of operations in the shape of inversions or reciprocities, which make it possible to follow the course of the transformations without being caught up in the irreversible advance of increasing entropy (in two senses, that of thermodynamics, in the case of biological questions, and information systems, in the case of knowledge).

This kind of reversible mobility reveals itself in the organic field, where it is never anything but approximate, as well as in the cognitive field, where it may become operational, after a series of sensorimotor approximations and preoperational representations, by means of the complementary interplay of retroactions or retrocontrols (negative feedbacks of all kinds) and anticipations.

The whole of logic, whether we are talking about so-called natural logic or the systematized axioms of professional logicians, is, in essence, a system of autocorrections, whose function it is to distinguish between true and false and produce some means of abiding with the truth. It must be this normative function, within its well-defined limits, that principally distinguishes conscious cognitive mechanisms from the mechanical workings of physiological autoregulations. And yet, as soon as there is any organic autoregulation, failures of a temporary or pathological kind, just because of their approximate and incomplete character, can be set against the usual successes—an approximate equivalent of "errors" and coherent functioning. To put it another way, there is, even in this field, a certain connection between the biological and the cognitive, and this takes the form of an unidentified analogy between the "normal" and the "normalizer." Here it must be pointed out that such a notion of the "normal" is specifically biological, for a connection that is neither cybernetic nor biological but physical would not recognize things as normal or abnormal but merely as regular or fortuitously variant.

4. The Equilibration Factor

There are, as I think we established at Geneva in 1964 during our symposium on developmental regulations, three main factors in organic growth: programming by the genome, environmental influence, and equilibration or autoregulation factors. The two last are, properly speaking, neither hereditary (since they impose themselves *motu proprio* in terms of situations) nor acquired from outside (since internal regulation is involved). At the conference just mentioned, one leading embryologist seemed to adopt my point of view, though saying he needed time to think about it, whereas a famous physiologist openly expressed disagreement, pointing out that regulations or equilibrations are the direct expression of the causal interactions involved, each of whose elements are either predetermined from the genome onward or acquired under environmental influence.

The physiologist was probably right as far as his own field was concerned, because it is a fact that homeostatic regulations do not contain the necessary regulator organ. (It is nonetheless true that even if the hemoglobin or *pH* level, etc., are genetically stable, the actual laws of equilibration or displacements of equilibration are physical laws, not inherent but merely dominant, and the same thing may apply in the case of the open system of biological laws, properly speaking.) But the embryologist and even the psychologist (myself) were perhaps right, too, the former because he was thinking of epigenetic growth, which is not merely an agglomeration of innate and acquired elements but an organization trying to reach a certain level of equilibrium, and I myself because I was thinking of cognitive functions, which are meant to serve as autoregulation or equilibration organs in the field of behavior exchanges.[10]

Here, then, is the conclusion of this summary of our guiding hypotheses. The living organization is an equilibrated system (even if one avoids the term and substitutes Bertalanffy's "stable states in an open system"). But this organic equilibrium only represents a relative sort of stability in those very fields where it is best protected. The genome is isolated to the maximum degree from its environment, although it cannot be so completely; its equilibrium is nevertheless upset by mutations, etc., despite these ideal conditions. The epigenetic system is more open, but it finds its equilibrium by means of a number of processes, among them homeorhesis. Physiological systems are even more "open," and yet they react by homeostasis

10. Moreover, if one does not bring in the equilibration factor, one very soon reduces one's argument to a sort of integral reductionism, wherein knowledge is simply an innate preformation or else a copy, pure and simple, of external objects. Now, we know it is not innate, and, if a copy is being made, the model must be known, which means that there is a knowledge copy, and this can only be known by means of the copy itself.

of the interior environment—an environment all the more remarkably stable as the various animal groups are evolved and differentiated. The role of the nervous system is to be open to external stimuli and to react to them by means of its effectors; its increasing mobility does not prevent there being remarkably mobile equilibrium in the overall reactions. Finally, behavior is at the mercy of every possible disequilibriating factor, since it is always dependent on an environment which has no fixed limits and is constantly fluctuating. Thus, the autoregulatory function of the cognitive mechanisms produces the most highly stabilized equilibrium forms found in any living creature, namely, the structures of the intelligence, whose logico-mathematical operations have been of inescapable importance ever since human civilization reached the stage of being consciously aware of them.

2   Methods of Approach and Control

In making hypotheses about any doctrine one tends to experience a kind of euphoria, so that it is vital to take a balanced view if one's doctrine itself is to be well balanced. The wider these hypotheses range, the more intense the care which must be taken in deciding upon one's methods of approach and control. At this point, therefore, it will be valuable to devote a chapter to the examination of possible methods.

Section 4: What Methods Not to Follow

If a fruitful comparison is to be made between the organization characteristic of cognitive functions and the structures of the living organization, either at the different levels of the individual organism or at the different levels of evolution in organized entities, there are two methods to be avoided. It is not really a question of methods here but of tendencies which come naturally to the human mind but threaten to falsify everything if they are not guarded against by systematic methodological precautions. We are referring, first, to that tendency or method which leads people to project into structures or phenomena of inferior order the characteristics of structures or phenomena of a higher order (intelligence, intentional consciousness, etc.).

38

Second, there is the method or tendency which consists of suppressing the original characteristics of the higher orders and reducing them outright, and hence, to a greater or lesser extent verbally, to the processes of the lower orders (reducing intelligent comprehension to the level of conditioned associations, etc.). In both cases the comparison between cognitive functions and elementary forms of organization becomes inoperable simply because, by reducing either the superior or the inferior to the other level at the outset, one is suppressing one of the two terms of comparison.

1. Cuénot's "Combinatorial Intelligence"

It should not be thought that this method, by which concepts significant only in relation to the higher orders are used to interpret mechanisms of a lower order, is to be accounted for simply through the ignorance of philosophers and psychologists as far as biology is concerned. It is an unfortunate fact that biologists who know no psychology do sometimes employ ideas which are really only applicable to the behavior of the higher orders when they are trying to patch up gaps in their theories about the lower orders.

An example of this kind will make a good stepping-off ground for us, and will prevent the attempt at a systematic comparison that is being made in this book from being distorted at the outset by our succumbing to the very tendencies just referred to.

The well-known biologist Cuénot, whose work in general is of undeniable value, has written a little book called *Invention et finalité en biologie* (Flammarion, 1941), which is a model of clarity and even of intellectual honesty insofar as he advances no hypothesis without revealing the scruples or difficulties he may have about it. This book is based on pure, systematic anti-Lamarckism, with no allowance made, consciously at least, for the influence of environment on hereditary mechanisms. It constitutes an excellent examination of one kind of mechanism, explaining every form of adaptation by fortuitous mutations and late selection. However, Cuénot, who knew nothing of cybernetics or, for that matter, of the new genetic theories on populations (he published his book in 1941, after all), sees only one possible set of alternatives: mechanism (with the sole meaning of chance and selection by elimination) or finality. He then takes the latter line of thought, although he does his best to keep it prudently under control. Thus it comes about that, when examining von Uexküll's theory that the cell is not a machine but an operator of a machine (something that is self-evident from the cybernetic angle), Cuénot cautiously reaches the conclusion, which will probably be dismissed as "mythical," that "the germinal cell has a kind of combinatorial intelligence, an immanent power equivalent to that intentionality which is the very basis of the human tool."

What can such a formula mean, then, when we have to undertake a methodological analysis of it? To begin with, we find three hypotheses which are still valid today, provided we modify their conceptualization: first, the genome is not an aggregate of discontinuous elements with variations of a purely fortuitous nature, but it holds possibilities of some combinations which are not due to chance; second, these combinations are susceptible of being guided, with regulations, thus furnishing what Bigelow and others have described as "mechanical equivalents of finality"; third, these combinations and regulations may produce the equivalent in tools or instruments.

In Cuénot's work these hypotheses are further attached to two concepts—"intelligence" and "intentionality"—which may have meaning provided they are analyzed closely in relation to behavior at the higher level, but which have none at all if applied to the problems of the genome.

In fact, the word "intelligence" is nothing but a collective term, used to designate a considerable number of processes and mechanisms whose significance becomes clear only if they are analyzed singly and in the order in which they develop. On the other hand, to interpret them by recourse to the very concept which is under analysis, namely, intelligence itself, is merely to classify intelligence and go round in a circle, as in the famous formula whereby sleep is ascribed to dormitive properties. Intelligence would be better defined, for example, as a coordination of conceptual operations or sensorimotor schemata, or something on that order, whereas nothing like that can be applied to the genome. To attribute intelligence to the genome is no more than stating that it is capable of new combinations in response to the problems raised by any particular situation, but the real problem is to describe and explain these combinations and not to invoke a sort of general utility concept such as "intelligence," which adds nothing to what has already been said.

As for "intentionality," matters become even worse. Such a concept might have meaning in the case of conscious thought, but it has none at all outside mental activity. Was Cuénot trying to attribute consciousness to the genome? If that was the case, it still would not take us any farther, since the vital question in analyzing an intentional act of the intelligence is to understand where it gets its knowledge and information. Thus, to attribute intelligent intentions to the genome is to lend it some previous knowledge which must then be explained. More than that: if the genome constructs "tools" by means of intentional intelligence, that means it knows what it is doing, in which case it is obvious that it knows all about its environment, since it is the environment that poses all its problems. So really, in this hypothesis, there is understood an inevitable action of the environment on the genome, but this action is supposed to take place by means of psychic powers: physico-chemical reactions are entirely ruled out!

By and large, the use of psychological terms, in this particular case, presents us with the double drawback that it explains nothing and ends up in contradiction of one of the central theses of the book: the nonintervention of environment in the mechanism of heredity. Explaining the processes of combination by "intelligence" or by regulations actuated by "intentionality" amounts, in fact, to exactly the same thing as explaining life as a vital force. Attributing such powers to the genome leads into the same error as occurs in all vitalist interpretations—the presupposition of some prior knowledge of the environment in the organism, to which the organism has to respond.

The first rule in the method that should be adopted when cognitive functions are being compared to the various forms of biological organization will thus be not to start off by attributing the former to the latter! Now this is not as easy as one might think, since any finalist explanation which fails to provide in detail the causal interpretation of the controlled process under analysis really amounts to bringing into play the question of mental processes. And this attribution of the mental to the biological is rendered all the more systematic and dangerous when it is done under cover like this, unconsciously, or when the author realizes what he is affirming and has two answers ready: that mental life is preformed in the organism and that its preformation is an "unconscious" one, a fact which permits us to endow this organic unconscious with intentional finality and other characteristics of mental life.

On this point Cuénot's text is particularly revealing and merits more careful discussion from the point of view of method. In effect, what Cuénot is asking himself is whether, with his "combinatorial intelligence," it would be possible to "attribute to one cell alone this overriding capacity, capable of superseding and even of improving upon the work of the superior brain and skillful hands of a human being. How can one believe in the psychoid of a single germinal cell?" To this, Cuénot's reply is simply that if one accepts "the inventive function of the brain, that slate upon which ideas are written and from which orders are transmitted, then why should one refuse to believe that other cells have such a function? In any case, the germinal cell has locked within it all the power of the entire nervous system and the entire structure" (pp. 222–23).

Such an amazing piece of reasoning proves to the psychologist that a biologist of repute may very well know all about the problems of evolution and organic embryogenesis without suspecting for one moment that the intelligence, too, undergoes a kind of phylogenetic evolution and epigenetic development. Failing to realize this or to examine the psychogenetic data closely enough, the biologist then goes on to speculate on psychological matters, especially on cognitive functions. His thinking is exactly like that of the "spermatists" and "ovists," who thought they could see a little ready-made man in the center of the spermatozoid or egg. But Cuénot is not content with the historic speculations about seed fusion; he goes even further by tracing his homunculus back to the invertebrate level, as is shown by his explanations of "co-aptations" etc.,[1] which means endowing the seed of all animals with human intelligence.

This preformist attitude does not merely situate intelligence in the initial stages of life, a thing which in itself is as debatable from the psychological as from the biological point of view, but it extends to the very heart of intelligence. In effect, Cuénot's image of the slate shows clearly that "ideas" precede commands, which is certainly true of a grown man but utterly untrue of the lower levels in which action precedes reflection. Expressed in biological terms, Cuénot's definition amounts to saying that "the organism is a box in which are placed the structural characteristics that are the prime movers of the functions." The first thing everyone will want to know

1. It is known that Cuénot applies the term "co-aptation" (and not co-adaptation) to the adjustment of two separable pieces of an organ (like a button and a buttonhole in a snap fastener), built up separately during embryogenesis before they began to function.

is where these characteristics come from; this is the real problem. Lamarck's reply used to be that they were the products of the functions, and this we still partly accept as true on the phenotypic plane. Cuénot, however, by invoking the "intelligence," even though he calls it a slate (on which, as a rule, nothing is written to begin with), forgets that the central problem is to find out where his "ideas" come from, and that the functions are certainly the dominant factor here. Supposing someone describes for us the combinatorial mechanisms, from the genome of a protozoan up to that of man, and from the germ to adult intelligence, that are capable of responding to external tensions, but without losing sight of the structural differences between each level of intelligence. There will no longer be any need to attribute intelligence to the lower levels. Of course, there will still remain the problem of establishing what functions there may be in common between all these structures, and people who agree with Cuénot will reply that there exist certain functional constants which may be designated "intelligence" among other things. But at least then they will know what they are talking about instead of simply projecting a mental element into an organic question.

2. *Psychomorphism*

We have laid a good deal of emphasis on this question of psychomorphism as raised by a professional biologist, because Cuénot gives much franker expression than is usual to an idea which is, in fact, commonly held and is certainly characteristic of those who espouse vitalism or noncybernetic finalism. Cuénot's reason is the same as theirs: the vitalist is not satisfied with the normal mechanist explanations, especially those unlikely powers that are supposed to be the outcome of chance; and can one be surprised at that? However, he is unwilling to wait for progress to be made along other lines, and so he tries to find models among the higher levels of intelligence and in human behavior. Then, since he is persuaded that he knows about mental life through the direct experience of, and introspection about, his own body, he comes up with notions such as finality or totality—which he sees as a form having substance, on the model of the "ego"—or even creative force, on the model of "spiritual energy." It does not occur to him to make any epistemological criticism of these illusory notions, since they appear axiomatic to him.

These types of attitude or implicit method have, however, two grave shortcomings. The first, which need not surprise us, since everyone fancies himself a psychologist, is their total ignorance of the work done in experimental psychology, which ought to be enough to cure any biologist of his introspective illusions. Just one small indication of this is the remarkable fact that in the field of scientific psychology there are hardly any vitalists by comparison with the number of biologists. The second shortcoming is much more surprising, namely, the absence of any genetic, or at least any ontogenetic, examination of the problem, when biologists begin to talk about mental life. It is as though they thought the higher levels of mental life were predetermined and inherent from the moment of conception in all forms of organic life. All scholars unfamiliar with the work done in comparative and growth psychology evince this kind of antihistoric preformism. It is to be explained not only by the unconscious ignorance of which we have just spoken but also, as we noted earlier, by their naïve use of the notion of the subconscious according to which the higher characteristics of mental life are actually supposed to be present in all living things, although, as it were, blanketed and blindfold.

Beyond all doubt, the father of all this vitalism, both explicit and doctrinal, was Aristotle, for whom the soul had a shape like the body, both in essence and in motive power. In his analysis of the biological fact he draws up three categories: the vegetative soul, the feeling and active soul, and the spiritual soul. Indeed, there is a passage in the book *Des animaux à l'homme*, by P. Chauchard (Presses Universitaires de France, 1961), in which, after very kindly referring to what I have written about the relations between physiological causality and the "implications" of the conscious mind, the author suggests that my work acknowledges both the specificity of the higher type of mind and its organic conditioning. From this he concludes that I am returning to Aristotle in the actual sense of regarding the soul as having the same shape as the body (p. 179). It will thus be permissible for us to dwell on this point a little in order to prevent the present work's being read in this light.

In Aristotle, as in all other vitalist writing, there is one far-reaching tenet, namely, the connection between the living organization— that is, forms, whether structural or dynamic—and mental functions, particularly cognitive ones. It is this connection that we must, in fact, try to underline, and I readily admit that on this score the father of biology was the first to recognize it, so that it is an idea with a long history. But when we come to interpreting this connection, however close it may be, the contemporary view seems to have completely inverted that taken by Aristotle. When you come down to it, the soul for Aristotle is the motor of the body, whereas for the psychologist cognitive functions arise out of organic and motor life. On the other hand, for Aristotle the lower form of life is dependent on the higher, whereas for the modern psychologist cognitive functions spring from the organic and motor life of the living creature. Then again, for Aristotle the lower is, as it were, dependent on the higher; while the evolutionist sees the higher as deriving from the lower in the process of time, so that, for him, if there is any direction in it at all, such direction comes from regulatory systems and not at all from any kind of finalist predetermination. So there we have a double and fundamental inversion in interpretation, which means that, in order to retain the formula, it would be necessary to turn it upside down and say, "The shape of the body is the soul," or, to be more precise, "Organic forms contain cognitive forms as inescapable resultants."

There is little point in adding to this the statement that "forms" can mean a multitude of things. When you have the organicist L. von Bertalanffy, along with numerous contemporary thinkers who accentuate the idea of totality, striving to translate the idea of organization into terms of logico-mathematical structures, then the idea of "form" leads to just that kind of methodology to which we shall be referring shortly (see subsections 4–5). On the other hand, there is Driesch, the prey of his own discovery of structural regulation in the blastula of sea-urchins, drawing the immediate conclusion that it is not to be explained in any mechanistic terms and trying to fill in the scientific gaps, which he thus finds irremediable, by calling on Aristotle's entelechy. This takes him back to the traditional position in which the lower is subordinated to those forms said to be higher, so that he is actually turning his back on the possibility of any kind of knowledge.

3. Reduction of the Higher to the Lower

This idea, which keeps cropping up, of reducing the lower to the higher, may render all rational interpretations impossible, but its inverse seems to us equally unacceptable inasmuch as it is bound sooner or later to suppress the essential terms of the problem. Here again we are up against a perpetually recurring tendency, which even had a romantic phase in the nineteenth century with materialist metaphysics[2] and Le Dantec's retarded subject. It manifests itself nowadays in more subtle form when people try to reduce psychology to physiology pure and simple.

As for cognitive functions, the only ones which need concern us here, reductionist thinkers are seeking to play down the higher kind of intelligence as being a set of associations and elementary conditionings. Above all, they see its origins exclusively in language insofar as language is a second system of signalization (in the theory of conditioned reflexes) or a form of general syntax and semantics. It goes without saying that if these conclusions are admitted, our problem is solved out of hand, in the sense that the higher cognitive functions simply become part of the action of the physical and social environment on the organism. This amounts to saying that they are purely phenotypic variations in the old meaning of the term and in their quality of being a copy of some outer reality.

Three points must be made in relation to this. The first is that if, as has already been seen (section 1, subsection 1), the notion of association is a concept artificially confined within the assimilation process, then intelligence must be first and foremost a matter of the construction of mental assimilation schemata. Now this construction is both infinite (viz. the endless combinations of logico-mathematical schemata) and bound up in an internal organization, which reflects not only the properties of objects but also the properties of action coordinations. Thus, all the associationist accounts bypass what is, from the biological point of view, the central problem, namely, to discover what the organic conditions were previous to these coordinations and constructions; and it is this problem which we must now examine instead of suppressing it at the outset by artificially restricting the subject.

The second point to be made is that language, although it is of course an essential instrument in cognitive constructions at the higher level, offers in itself no complete explanation and cannot help us sidestep the problems which arise. First, it should be noted that language is merely one particular instance of the semiotic or symbolic function, and that this function as a whole (imitation with

2. This is contemptuously called by Soviet writers "dogmatic" or "vulgar materialism," since it has absolutely no connection with dialectical materialism, which is, indeed, a kind of evolutionist constructivism and not at all reductionist in principle.

a time lag, system of gestural symbols, symbolic play, mental image, written or drawn pictures, etc.), and not language alone, is what causes sensorimotor behavior to evolve to the level of representation or thought. From the biological point of view it is therefore important to begin with a study of the semiotic function in all its manifestations. This in itself presents a fine problem of comparative ethology before ever developing into a question of human psychology. In the latter field, imitation would seem to constitute an essential mechanism in the formation of this semiotic function insofar as sensorimotor imitation is already a sort of representation, though a representation by acts, and imitation, first altered and then interiorized, indubitably constitutes the starting point of the mental image.

On the other hand, once language is established as being a particular, although very important, type of semiotic function, it in no way exhausts the operations of the intellect, because their origin remains sensorimotor. Mathematics are, in fact, not simply a system of notations at the service of physical knowledge, but an instrument of structuralization, because it is of the nature of operations to produce transformations. The fact that the latter may be expressible in "symbols" does not in any sense reduce their active and constructive nature: thus, the psycho-biological problem of the construction of mathematical entities cannot possibly be solved by linguistic considerations.

The third point that has to be considered in connection with distorted logical reduction has to do with consciousness, a phenomenon that can only be analyzed in man (and then only from the moment when he learns to speak) but is nonetheless a natural phenomenon and may even be quite widespread, at least in the animal kingdom. Now, the reductionists incline to the view that consciousness is not a phenomenon but merely an "epiphenomenon." The behaviorists go even farther and make this field taboo, saying that no one who wants to be considered a scientist can talk about consciousness. The reason they give is that introspection is so deceptive, which, of course, is perfectly true; but they are leaving out of account objective methods of approach. If one wants to study, at one and the same time, the particular behavior of a subject (say, a child's capacity for generalization or his capacity for formulating, on demand, the resemblances and differences between different objects) and the language he uses to describe or justify his actions, it is perfectly possible to analyze the stages by which he becomes conscious of them by relating them to his positive behavior. This is how Claparède demonstrated that, when the child is making a series of generalizations, he has much more difficulty in bringing out the resemblances between two objects than their differences: the consciousness, in a case like this and often in others, is arrested by anything that blocks or disrupts normal procedure, whereas there is nothing to capture the consciousness (insofar as making generalizations is concerned) so long as the normal procedure goes on without outside interference. Further to this, research is going on now in neurology on the subject of "vigilance"; and electroencephalographic recordings are some way toward being able to distinguish objectively between conscious reactions and various automated actions.

Thus it will be seen that the way in which the positivists ban, as it were, the study of consciousness is an essential part of their position. It is a position which scientists, in their commonsensical way, sometimes confuse with the "positive" or "scientific." This means that a limit is set to the extension of research, experiment is actually surrounded by barriers, with the sole result that methodological prophecies are constantly being shown up as false by subsequent discoveries. Consider, for instance, the extraordinary statements made by Auguste Comte on the subject of atomism, the calculation of probabilities, the microscope, astral physics, and so on, fields in which his vetoes have been either totally ignored or contradicted. This has done nothing to undermine his prestige in the eyes of those who never read him and therefore find it all the easier to remain faithful to the positivist idea, which has been transmitted by means of slogan.[3]

Leaving positivism aside, we can see that consciousness, far from being of no consequence in the biology of cognitive functions, makes use of specific notions that are quite outside physical or physiological causality. A physical process is, in fact, assimilable to notions like space, mass, force, effort, energy, and causality, as compensatory between actions and reactions—all of them notions that are meaningless where consciousness is concerned unless the deceptive analogies of introspection are relied upon. On the other hand,

3. We might note here, as evidence of what I am saying, that Soviet psychologists, who have nothing positivist about them since the science of their nation is dialectic, are in fact making a study of consciousness.

consciousness sets up a system of interpretations whose basic notions are designation and "implication" as between meanings: for example, 2 is not the "cause" of 4, but its meaning "implies" that $2 + 2 = 4$, which is not at all the same thing. These implications may be naïve or simple, but they may also be elaborated by a scientific type of reasoning such as produces the "pure" sciences of logic and mathematics. That is why we say consciousness cannot be left out of account, since it is the very basis of the formal systems on which our comprehension of matter depends. Neurology, for instance, is unlikely ever to come up with an explanation of why 2 and 2 make 4, but its advances in the sphere of theoretic elaboration will be made by the use of structures and logico-mathematical models once it comes to interpreting the organic processes which make the act of thinking explicable.

It should be added that the situation just described is by no means a vicious circle. Physiological causality and conscious implication may be mutually irreducible, but they nonetheless have certain points of contact and even a measure of parallelism. The well-known principle of psycho-physiological parallelism is really nothing more than a principle of isomorphism midway between causality and implication. The best example of this isomorphism is to be found in cybernetic "thinking machines" or servomechanisms and the like; the latter do, in fact, afford a highly perfected model of what may well be the mechanical or causal equivalent of a system of implications (because they have a logical basis), but they remain quite outside the sphere of conscious significance, since the only thing which translates their causal series into significant implications is the consciousness of their inventors or readers.

The interpretation of consciousness offered here has, therefore, nothing contradictory about it when set against biological explanations of the cognitive functions. On the contrary, it is in harmony with them insofar as causality is not identical with, but complementary to, implication.

Section 5. Methods Used

Our present study is an essay in epistemological elaboration and not a piece of experimental research. Research on the relations between the act of knowing and life may take the form of work on heredity in intelligence or perceptive mechanisms, of investigations into epigenetic or even biochemical conditions of memory and learning (with the necessary intervention RNA, etc.), but such is not at all my line of country.

For at least forty-five years I did experimental work on the psychogenesis of the human child's intelligence. In addition to this, I did two small pieces of research, one about adaptation to environment in the aquatic mollusc (*Limnaea*) and the other on a case of morphogenetic anticipation in one vegetative type (*Sedum*). I did this to keep alive the biological interests which were first roused when I embarked on a career as a zoologist. But the present work is quite simply the fruit of epistemological analysis made by a man who admittedly knows something about experimentation, but in other fields. It will be true, nonetheless, that such analyses, if they are not to remain purely speculative, must necessarily conform to the demands of certain methods.

We have just completed the examination of those that we think should be avoided. Now is the time, therefore, to make clear what methods we actually intend to follow. It being understood that, if we are to make a fruitful comparison between biological organization and the cognitive functions, it is wrong to begin by projecting the latter into the former, or to suppress the latter by reducing them to the status of the former, what we must do now is to make clear under what conditions such a comparison might be fruitful with respect to any approaches taken, or verifiable with respect to any controls we could set up.

1. Comparison of Problems

One initial method of approach, although it can hardly be said to have any built-in control, is to bring out the close relationship between cognitive and biological problems. We have already seen this in the case of the epigenesis of intelligence and ontogenetic development of an organic nature, but this is merely a particular instance, and the method to be followed in comparing the main problems is a much more general one. The method underlying this general form is to list the problems common to biological studies and psychological research into cognitive functions or scientific epistemology. Now, in any attempt to set up such a list it immediately becomes apparent that these common problems are either of an entirely local or of the most general kind—the kind, in fact, which is bound to recur at every important juncture in the study of biology.

The local problems are self-evident, and we shall not be concerned with them here. For example, the analysis of an act of perception or of a sensorimotor schema raises the question of their nervous mechanisms, the study of intelligence takes us back to that of the cerebral cortex, and the problem of instinct leads to the neurological and genetic questions which are presenting such insoluble difficulties at the present time.

As for the general problems which are our main concern in this work, it is impossible to formulate them without at once being struck by the close connection between vital mechanisms and cognitive ones. All knowledge, in fact, of whatever nature it may be, raises the problem of the relations between subject and object, and this problem can lead to many solutions according to whether one attributes such knowledge to the subject alone, to an action by the object, or to the interactions of both. Now, since the subject is one aspect of the organism, and the object a sector, as it were, of the environment, the problem of knowledge, seen from this point of view, corresponds to the problem of the relations between the organism and its environment—undeniably the most general question in the whole of biology. Equally undeniable is the way in which this question keeps cropping up, and every time it arises there arise with it a series of possible solutions, each as different from the other as are the epistemological or psychogenetic ones.

It may be objected here that this is mere playing on words, and that if the subject is closely allied to the organism and the object to its environment, the relation characteristic of an act of cognition —such as that "the subject S perceives a shape" or "understands the theory of Pythagoras" or "is reducing the molecule of water to a compound of hydrogen and oxygen"—has no connection at all with a vegetative organism withering away for lack of light, yet capable of transmitting its characteristics independently of its environment or capable of transforming light into energy. Obviously if one begins by detaching acts of cognition from their psychological and physiological conditions, with the purpose of studying them, along with introspection, as pure states of consciousness affecting a purely "mental" subject, then one will see no connection between the two groups of phenomena. But if one remembers that perceptive forms have corresponding nervous forms, that the theorem of Pythagoras presupposes operations corresponding at source to sensorimotor schemata (displacement, union, and so on), that physical cognition is a composite of experimental data and various logico-mathematical operations, and so on, then one will discover, in every act of cognition, a construction of shapes along with problems of organization and transformation. The question of determining the relations between what arises from the environment and what is attributable to the action of the subject thus becomes the identical equivalent, so far as shapes, schemata, or operations are concerned, of a problem of relations between environment and organism.

So much being understood, the problem of the relations between the organism and its environment—which is surely the major question in the whole field of biology, with every solution to every question in every realm of life whatever depending on it—may be divided into three great subproblems.

1. The relations between the organism and its environment in the field of general or phyletic formative structures (genome, hereditary adaptation, and the mechanisms of evolution). Whether it be a matter of the Lamarckian solutions, the schema of aleatory mutations and of selection by the environment, or contemporary cybernetic solutions, it is obvious that in each is constantly to be found the question of the living being's dependence on, or relative independence from, its environment.

2. The relations between the organism and its environment in the sphere of ontogenetic growth (preformation or epigenesis), and of phenotypical variation.

3. The relations between the internal organization and things brought to it from the outside (for example, chemical or energy nourishment drawn from the environment) in the mechanism of the regulations at every level (genetic, epigenetic, physiological, and so on).

One is struck by the discovery of this same triad when facing the basic problems connected with the act of knowing.

1. The relations between the subject and the object in knowledge involving some part of the innate. That sort of cognition is frequently found in animals. (There is no need to make any pronouncement on the degree of innateness or on the absence of consciousness, and we restrict ourselves here to the field of per-

ceptive stimuli and triggered behavior, that is, "knowing what to do," which is a form of "knowing." It is this sort of thing that we designate "instinctive.") Such innate cognitive structures may well exist in man also, for instance, where spatial perception is concerned or, more precisely, in the spatial characteristics of perception. (Nothing can be served, however, by making any final judgment about such structures at this juncture since we are concerned only with the problems themselves.) It is even possible that there may be in man, not exactly those "innate ideas" that Descartes speaks of, but a priori categories, in the Kantian sense, of conditions that exist previously to experience. Furthermore, those biologists who believe in such a priori schemata, as does, for instance, Konrad Lorenz, who is both a great theorist about instinct and a convinced Kantian, all go so far as to say that such schemata are assimilable into genetic innateness: "The discovery, so important and so fundamentally new, which Kant made is that thought and human perception do, in fact, possess functional structures anterior to all individual human experience." Now, "we believe it possible to show the close relationship, a relationship that is functional and probably genetic too, between those *a priori* in animals and those in man."[4] Whether or not such hypotheses are accepted, they raise the problem of the relations between subject and object in knowledge of a supposedly hereditary kind and, as we have just seen in quotations from these texts, in the same terms as those in which the problem of heredity and environment are expressed.

2. The relations between subject and object in individual learning and the knowledge drawn from experience.

3. The relations between subject and object in the regulation and equilibration of knowledge and, especially, in the setting up of logico-mathematical operational structures, the hypothesis being that the operations involved in the latter constitute one particular form of regulation (and a very important one since it will be a matter of levels of achievement and generalization of cognitive regulator mechanisms; this we shall seek to demonstrate in section 14).

There is, then, a parallel to be drawn between the general problems and, as will also be seen in chapter 3, sections 8–9, this parallel-

---

4. Konrad Lorenz, "Kants Lehre vom Apriorischen im Lichte der gegenwärtigen Biologie," *Blätter für deutsche Philosophie* 15 (1941): 94–125. Both quotations appear on page 100.

ism becomes increasingly close if we look at it from the angle of the various solutions, with their various possibilities, that have been put forward in the past.

2. Functional Connections

The convergence of the problems as well as the guiding hypothesis formulated in section 3 with respect to cognitive functions immediately raise a central question, which must be the object of a second method of approach: the comparative study of cognitive functions and vital functions in general. Perhaps it would have been better to start by making such an examination, but one must first be made aware of the problems before one can identify the functions.

Indeed, if a confrontation of the cognitive functions with the organic functions is to be brought about, the preliminary business is to reach an understanding of what the term function means. Now, this concept is used in two distinct senses: there is the mathematical function $y = f(x)$, and the biological function, such as that of breathing or assimilation generally. The mathematical type of function is an operation which carries out a set of transformations; or, if you prefer, it is an operation which has been projected into the modifications of the variables; in other words, it is itself the law of transformation. (In point of fact, function and operation are almost synonymous in use, but people speak of operation when they are putting the emphasis on actions of the subject and of function when they are thinking of the links between the variables.) Biological function seems, at first glance, to be of a quite different order of reality, since it conjures up ideas of functioning and, above all, of functional utility which are foreign to the mathematical function as a whole. Thus, it implies the existence of a system, that is to say, a self-supporting structure or cycle, and it embraces activities which help it to be self-supporting. Biological function, then, has this in common with mathematical function: they each contain the idea not only of variations but also of determining activities. It is highly likely that if analysis of all biological functions were really pushed home, they could all be expressed in terms of mathematical functions, but there must be added to this the notion of an overall autoregulatory system, the functioning of which is expressed by the biological function, and the individual characteristic of which must be respected by the mathematical functions that are ultimately used to determine both that overall functioning and the biological function.

So much being taken for granted, the first striking observation to be made is that cognitive functions are more nearly related to biological functions in this precise sense of autoregulation than they are to the mathematical function in general. (Naturally, this by no means excludes the possibility of their being translated into mathematical functions, such as are adequate to their autoregulatory character, nor does it prevent their being the origin of mathematical functions in general.)

It is nonetheless true, autoregulation apart, that since we have laid stress on that aspect in setting forth the terms of our master hypothesis (section 3), the query may arise whether there may be other functions in common between cognition and life. Biological functions serve to maintain or preserve life, and cognitive functions to enable us to know about it and understand it. What do these sets of functions have in common, apart from the commonplace and altogether inadequate statement that perceptions, intelligence, and, above all, instinct all play a part in the conservation of life? That is why a comparative study of functions is the second and inevitable method of both approach and control.

For Aristotle, who was always trying, in his epistemology, to follow the commonsense line, knowing meant taking possession of the "forms" of reality that surround us in the world. Thomas Aquinas follows up Aristotle's idea by his insistence on this kind of realism, maintaining that, in the act of knowing, the subject "becomes" the object; this comes about only in the mind, not materially, of course, but the *intentio* is simply the process by which the "essence" is attained so that, in "becoming" the object, the subject is really returning to its essential form, its nature, which is external to ours.

There has been a complete reversal of this opinion since the time of Kant. Some have considered knowing to be, as it were, an incorporation or integration of the object in forms that are part of the subject (in other words, a priori forms). So much so that if Aristotle's terminology is to be preserved along with the Thomist theory of the subject's becoming the object, it could also be said that the object becomes the subject or at least loses its identity at a certain point in the act of knowing.

Suppose we confine ourselves to those "problems" we were talking of in section 5, subsection 1. We can see at once the possible transfer of a historical discussion of this kind to the sphere of exchanges between organism and environment. Take the action of light on a green plant: should we say that light becomes chlorophyll or that the chloroplast becomes light?[5] Phrased in this way, the question is meaningless, and it is obvious that, at that level of growth, interactions are produced of such a kind that there can be no sense in establishing any static line of demarcation between the organism and the contributions of the environment.

We shall therefore say that the primary function of knowing is that it is an "assimilation," by which we mean an interaction between subject and object. The nature of this interaction is such that it involves at one and the same time an accommodation of the most extensive kind to the characteristics of the object and an equally extensive incorporation into antecedent structures, however those structures may be built up. In the course of this assimilation the subject becomes the object, if you like, since it is clear that it accommodates its schemata to it, but, in order to do so, it never abandons or changes its nature: it "includes" it, "takes hold" of it, or "comprehends" it, to use the various terms which by their etymology denote both a taking possession of and a collaboration.

But assimilation is only a functional notion, not a structural one, that is to say, there are a great many different assimilation structures—a fact which allows us to include cognitive structures among them. The assimilation of chlorophyll is not comparable to the case of mineral salts being absorbed into the roots of a plant, or to that of respiration in sea or land creatures, or to that of the many kinds of digestion. Thus, it is obvious that cognitive assimilation must represent all sorts of other forms; it is a functional, not a material, incorporation of objects, in the sense that it integrates them into action or perception schemata and so does not submit them to chemical transformations, except, that is, to physiological reactions such as belong to elementary perception.

But if we go beyond assimilation, a certain number of other functions or functional properties are common both to the various forms of knowledge and to organic life, in particular all those which

5. The philosopher will be quick to point out that the comparison does not hold, because it is matter that is under discussion in this case, whereas knowing has to do with "essence"; but what is an "essence" if not a logico-mathematical structure leading to the understanding of a material object?

used to be covered by the inclusive and imprecisely analyzed notion of finality until recent days, when cyberneticians have succeeded in supplying teleonomic (not teleological) models or mechanical equivalents of finality. Among these are the properties of functional utility, of adaptation, of controlled variation, and, above all, of anticipation. Anticipation is, in fact, along with retroactions, one of the most generally found characteristics of the cognitive function. Anticipation intervenes as soon as perception dawns, and in conditioning and habit schemata, too. Instinct is a vast system of surprising kinds of anticipation, which seem to be unconscious, while the inferences of thought promote anticipations of a conscious kind, instruments that are constantly in use. Now, can it be said that most biological functions are also anticipatory? Embryogenetic growth is only a systematic anticipation of subsequent states and functions. Thus we are obliged to make a close analysis of the points of contact and of divergence between organic and cognitive anticipation.

We should note, further, while on the subject of these functional analogies, the suggestive way in which the language of the biologists and that in vogue among psychologists or epistemologists in the various fields of learning is today converging at many points. The language of "information" is, in fact, now in common use among biologists as it is also among those who study language and intelligence. In connection with this, people are always talking about the information of the genome or about transmissions of information aimed at securing the action of the genome on ontogenetic growth. Schmalhausen talks of information coming from the environment through the channel of selection, and so on. Now this sort of language is no more anthropomorphic or psychomorphic than that of "programming," introduced, as it constantly is, into the analyses of the genetic program which is enforced in the course of embryogenesis. Such language applies to programmed machines and the "information" they manipulate, a fact which will lead us (subsection 4 below) to talk about the use of cybernetic models as an approach method when comparing life and learning.

3. Structural Isomorphisms

First, however, we must point out the importance of a method of structural comparison that is complementary to the functional comparisons we have just been talking about. The methods are not identical because the same function may well be fulfilled by widely differing structures or organs, and a structure may remain the same while changing its function. In fact, since structures are much more numerous and variable than functions, it is impossible to interpret one in terms of the other, and so one is compelled to follow a different method with each.

This distinction is rendered all the more necessary by the fact that the functions they have in common can still hardly be rendered in terms precise enough to permit internal verification, and yet structural isomorphisms can be expressed in algebraic or logistic terms, which both impose precision and facilitate controls.

Furthermore, the notion of isomorphism, or, as Bertalanffy calls it, "formal homology," makes possible the introduction of degrees of connection, a thing that is almost meaningless when functional comparisons are in question. Under this head we shall talk about "partial isomorphisms" at the risk of disturbing the logicians, for whom an isomorphism is either total (bi-univocal connection between the elements of a structure A and those of the structure A' and between the unifying links in A and those in A', including their sense of direction) or else nonexistent. The drawback to the notion of partial isomorphism is, in fact, that it would be perfectly possible to establish links of this kind between any body and any thing: a flea is a partial isomorph of the moon, since both objects have a relatively closed surface and both move, and so forth. But partial isomorphisms do acquire some fruitful significance if the two following considerations are fulfilled: (a) when it is possible to point out transformation processes such as may give a lead from one of the structures under comparison to the other; (b) when it is possible to show a connection between these transformations and some actual and observable process of a historic or genetic nature (epigenetic, etc.).

Now these two conditions may indeed be fulfilled in the case of a comparison between organic and cognitive structures in the form of filiations by means of differentiation or neoconstructions, or in the form of collateral relationships arising from a common origin.

For example, order links ($A \rightarrow B \rightarrow C \rightarrow \ldots$) are to be found at every organic level. Genes are drawn up spatially in the DNA spirals. They intervene in a certain temporal order during epigenetic growth (thus we know that they are not the same genes that intervene at the various levels of larva, caterpillar, chrysalis, and the final insect form). There is an order of succession clear for all to

see, whether linear or cyclic, as the details of physiological functioning are worked out. When it comes to nerve structure, links are
found in order throughout the activation phases or during the carrying out of a reflex action or, a fortiori, of a complex instinct. As
for behavior acquired by means of learning and sensorimotor coordinations, the sequence link can clearly be seen to intervene, for
example, in the succession of means by which a desired object is
attained. So it is clear that, at the level of intellectual operations,
when a child undertakes to place a series of objects in a certain
order, the sequence he follows will not be due to the objects themselves, because it is he who is deciding on the order. Even if he
thinks the order he chooses is related to the objects, that will be
because his perception of them is ordered in a certain way by
means of his eye movements or his sense of touch, so that in a
general way he is displaying ordered behavior. Thus, sequence order
is part of the preliminary data in countless organic series, and our
problem as psychogeneticists is to show how this data comes to
be abstracted from the series by means of successive reconstructions, each reconstruction depending on the preceding data.

It seems, therefore, to be both legitimate and fruitful for us to
follow the method of singling out partial isomorphisms between
comparable structures at different levels. To take the particular case
of sequence links, a great many ordered or semiordered structures
can be found whose common elements are identifiable. Now, since
structures may be expressed much more precisely than functions,
in terms of logico-mathematics, it is thus possible to evaluate the
degrees of isomorphism with much less risk of error than if we were
to compare functional connections by means of language only. It
follows from this that the method based on structural isomorphisms
has much more built-in control than the methods we talked of previously; so we shall be led to rely on it whenever possible.

It is to be noted, in connection with this, that Woodger's attempt
to supply a logistic axiomatization of structures and biological
processes will naturally help us in our task. What Woodger wanted
to do was certainly not to arrive at a comparison of cognitive and
organic mechanisms. Still less was it to express the former in terms
of the latter, since, on the contrary, he tries to shed light on the
latter by using the most highly refined forms of structure relevant
to the former. But it goes without saying that, insofar as his attempt
is successful, by that very fact, whether he wants to or not, he has

isolated instances of partial isomorphism, if no more, between axiomatized organic structures and the cognitive structures which lead to this formalization.

4. Abstract Models

We now come to a fourth approach and control method: the use of abstract and cybernetic models.

The work done by Woodger has not really brought about any progress in biological explanation for the simple reason that he is a logician and brings forward no new explanatory strategies. What he is trying to do is to increase the rigor of biological reasoning, which may, of course, help indirectly but which essentially has to do with forms of knowledge in the subject in biology, not with the object of such knowledge, which is the organism, and still less with the organism as a subject or future subject of knowledge.

On the other hand, logico-mathematical models can be used in seeking an explanation of organic or biological mechanisms themselves, and it goes without saying that, insofar as such attempts are successful, an attempt can always be made to apply such strategies to such and such an aspect of growth in the cognitive functions, which would lead, should this succeed, to the highlighting of some analogies of a very instructive kind.

Mathematical attempts of this type may be aimed outright at achieving both a high degree of generalization and, at the same time, the quantitative precision achieved by equations in physics. This has been the method of procedure of certain American mathematicians such as Rachevsky and Rappaport, and of some Italians such as Fantappié, but the formulae they have each produced are so generalized as to be of little real significance so far as one can see.

A more modest method of approach, which may yet be more reliable, is to try to make a generalized statement but not a quantification. In other words, one can restrict oneself to qualitative and logical instruments, not in order to axiomatize the theories, as Woodger does, but in order to formalize the structures or processes so as to understand them better. This is the way J. B. Grize goes about it, in our Center for Genetic Epistemology, and it is hoped thus to obtain information about structural isomorphisms, if only partial ones, in the sense spoken of in section 5, subsection 3.

Mathematical methods, on the other hand, are being increasingly used, no longer to express the most general vital processes—a rather premature attempt since so little was known about them—but simply to resolve certain clearly defined problems concerning details of positive research. Thus, the part played by mathematics has been a fundamental one in genetics, for in this field it is important to determine, by means of theory and calculation, under what conditions it is possible to reach the experimental results that have been obtained. For example, through the use of mathematical deduction we have come to understand that the genome does not function as a collection of disconnected elements all reacting in a purely random way, but that regulatory or transformatory genes, as well as structural ones, have to be taken into account, and that, over and above those mutations which are partly due to chance, there still remain organized regroupings which have to be included in the study.

However, even leaving out of account the fact that such theoretical progress goes a long way toward reconciling genetic mechanisms with functional ones generally and hence in part with the functioning of cognitive mechanisms, the great contribution of mathematization, as far as regulatory processes are concerned, has been the construction of models—some cybernetic, some theoretical, and some concrete.

Cybernetics are, in fact, mainly a theory of guiding and communication: they offer an explanation of how one mechanism can direct others, or itself, by means of transmissions and the retroactive or anticipatory effects of information given.

Cybernetic models, more and more frequently used in every field of biology from genetics to ethology, are of very special interest to us because they give a direct expression to the structures which are involved in all cognitive mechanisms. What knowledge really consists of is not just the acquisition and accumulation of information, since that alone would remain inert and sightless, as it were. But knowledge organizes and regulates this information by means of autocontrol systems directed toward adaptation, in other words, toward the solving of its problems. Every cybernetic concept thus acquires immediate significance in the cognitive field, and the use of these concepts in biology is bound to contribute toward an increase in the number of structural isomorphisms that were discussed in section 5, subsection 3.

5. *The Epistemology of Behavior Levels*

The study of isomorphisms, both functional (section 5, subsection 2) and structural (subsection 3), and of their models (subsection 4) naturally leads to comparisons which not only bear on the extremes (such as the genome and logico-mathematical operations of human thought) but which inevitably follow step by step through each level of organization. Comparative analyses of this kind automatically finish up as systematic comparisons between different levels of what may be considered to be cognitive functions on every rung of the animal kingdom, if no more. In this way we can speak of "learning" or "memory" at the level of Protozoa, already regarding those processes as a beginning of cognitive reaction. This applies to all the problems concerning instinct and, in a general way, all the questions touched on by ethology in the field of behavior, whether "innate," to use the old term employed in English by some young ethologists, or "acquired."

But this internal comparison between the various levels of cognitive mechanism picks up what was said (section 5, subsection 1) about the comparison of problems. Indeed, it is very clear that as soon as we start talking of perception, of learning, of memory, or of any behavior that is wholly or partially innate, in the field of animal psychology or ethology, the questions which then arise may be expressed either in terms of the endogenetic organization of the living creature and the effect of environment, or else in terms of the internal organization of the subject and the properties of the object: the only difference is one of language, and the problems are identical.

The fifth method of approach and control that we must use in our research thus consists of what might be called a comparative epistemology of the levels of knowledge. If we take epistemology to mean, not the causal or psycho-physiological study of the factors enabling a piece of knowledge to function (for example, the nervous conditions and the material terms which go to express the variations of an act of perception), but the analysis of conditions of truth (adequation or adaptation) of the things known, the relaying of information between subject and object, it will be seen that the epistemological problem is to be confronted at every level. Just as a study can be made of the epistemological questions of space, time, causality, and the conservation of the object in the mind of the human young, from 1–3 months to 12–18 months, so also a great many analogous questions, some of them much wider, can and should be asked about the entire range of animal evolution.

It is impossible, for example, to pretend that any epistemology of the notion or schema of time or its relation to speed displacements or speed frequencies (rhythm), can be complete without taking account of the time reactions of a great many animal species. An instance of this is the relations between time reactions and rhythm in bees.[6]

In the same way, it is impossible to formulate a complete epistemology of space without taking into account examples of the remarkable orientation behaviors or reactions to the movement of the stars shown by various classes of animal. Such reactions lead to a hierarchy of "displacement groups," which are much more complex than those that the human infant can master at the sensorimotor stage.

When I was a student at the university, one of our lecturers, who was a Pure Logician and had once done some elementary biology, but none at all since 1910, put the following point to us by way of a concession to the claim that there must of necessity be a biological dimension to logical problems: "Obviously, if one could only penetrate the consciousness of an ant without losing one's human thought processes, every problem of knowledge would be solved." Now one does not really need to penetrate the consciousness of a subject to be able to assess the knowledge that its behavior reveals. One has to carry one's analysis as far as the study of this subject's development to be able to understand the relations in knowledge between subject and objects, in other words, between the action of the organism and the action of the environment.

It is thus clear that the study of behavior is the field in which comparative epistemology is likely to make the most decisive advances. Nor is there anything new about this conclusion. In an earlier chapter we saw how Konrad Lorenz, one of the pioneers of the "objectivist" approach in contemporary ethology, tried to show connections between his own brand of Kantianism and the question of how far behavior depends on innate qualities. The problem, raised by him in very stimulating fashion, is to know what conditions may exist before any act of knowing takes place. And the question about

6. In this connection, the remarkable work done by Bünning on rhythm in plants and animals should be borne in mind.

what exists before adaptation is the problem common to biology and the study of the cognitive functions.

6. Biological Epistemology

Yet another method of approach is by means of the epistemology of biological knowledge. Here we find ourselves on quite different ground, surely, from that of the methods discussed so far, because here it is a question of the sort of knowledge belonging to biology and not of the sort of knowledge we may have about the organism as a subject. Nevertheless, the epistemology of biological knowledge is highly instructive about the nature of the object to be known and therefore about the organism itself, which is why this sixth method, although indirect, cannot possibly be left out of account.

It is, in fact, possible to affirm—and, to our way of thinking, this is where all modern criticism is tending—that the object of an act of knowing is never completely independent of the activities of the subject. This is to be understood in the sense that, while objectivity is the ideal aimed at by every science, particularly by experimental science, such objectivity must nonetheless be subordinated to three conditions:

1. In the first place, objectivity is a process and not a state. This amounts to saying that there is no such thing as an immediate intuition touching the object in any valid manner but that objectivity presupposes a chain reaction of successive approximations which may never be completed. Some people, among them even dialectical materialists, insisting on the primacy of the object, have concluded from this that the object is only to be reached in the sense that a mathematical "limit" may be reached, which is to say never, or, if at all, only through the channel of a lower mechanism.

It seems obvious, therefore, that when a present-day biologist speaks of the genome, of DNA, of selection, of phenotypes, or even of a species or an individual, these notions are relative to a certain degree of approximation. Before comparing them to the notions of psychogenesis or of the analysis of cognitive functions, it may be useful to analyze their construction in both cases, for the examination of successive approximations is, in some ways, every bit as instructive as is that of actual states.

2. In the second place, approximations leading to the object are not of a merely additive nature (the cumulative effect of information piling up or linking on without further reaction). Rather, they

contain an additional process which is essential to decentering. By decentering is meant the liberation of subjective adherences or of pre-notions which are assumed to be accurate simply because they are simpler for the subject. Where biological notions are concerned, such subjective adherences will be assimilations, either conscious or intentional, of organic data to schemata based on introspection (see section 4, subsections 1–3). Among the pre-notions may be found atomist patterns, which always prove very coercive at the outset of an investigation before ideas of organized totality are formed.

3. In all branches of advanced experimental science, of which physics is the prototype, the attainment of objectivity is achieved not by taking the object in its naked state, as it were, but by explaining it and, even at that early stage, describing it by means of a logico-mathematical framework (classifications, interrelations, measurements, functions, and so on), because outside this framework no cognitive assimilation is possible. This framework is relative to the activity of the subject—a subject whose center has been displaced, of course, and which is therefore epistemic, not subjective in the sense of individual, but nonetheless a subject. Thus, it is impossible to talk about objectivity or object without referring back to the previous condition of the cognitive organization. Again, the comparison between the biologist's kind of knowledge and the knowledge of someone theorizing about psychogenetic growth or epistemology is one that must be made at this point in our argument.

To quote only one example, there is nothing more enlightening than a close analysis of the countless situations in which the mind of the biologist is torn between the schemata of predetermination and those of construction or epigenesis. This is a long way from being the case only in the field of embryology (section 2). It occurs in every situation in which some new characteristic presents itself. Now in a great many situations there is no really crucial experience to help one decide whether the regrouping under observation is setting up a new construction or whether it is an actualization of possibilities that were inherent in the given structure. Indeed, nothing is harder than making a rational appraisal of what the virtual state of a structure may have been, because, logically speaking, it has no significance at all outside the framework of conservation. Moreover, certain elements are preserved even in transformation, while others are modified: thus, a factor of decision intervenes almost inevitably, not merely a factor of information in choosing which hypotheses guide the new characteristic toward modification or conservation. To put it another way, the only controls possible are dependent less on facts which can be measured or isolated than on a total confrontation between the entire interpretive system adopted and the entire set of facts at the scientist's disposal while the research is in progress.

Such epistemological analyses, however, have this further advantage, from the point of view of the fruitfulness of our discussion: they actually converge with all the arguments about psychogenetics and epistemology, in which latter field there is permanent conflict of every kind between the a priori and the constructivist theories.

7. Application of Explicative Theories in Biology

One last method of approach remains for us to use, and this involves the application of the explicative theories of biology to such psychogenetic facts as are relevant to the cognitive functions.

To do this may seem rather bold, since we are not yet in possession of the biological data which would make comparison possible in specific fields, such as the part which may be played by hereditary factors in the elaboration of cognitive structures. For example, it is still well-nigh impossible, just as it was in mid–nineteenth century, to decide what may be hereditary in the structure of perceptions and spatial intuitions: the three dimensions, perhaps? Localizations themselves? Intuition about the continuous in its simpler, perceptual forms (including the contradictions implicit in them: *A* not differentiated from *B,* nor *B* from *C,* but *A* distinct from *C*)? And so on.

However, we cannot avoid making the confrontation, if only because we need to learn how to pinpoint the problems and set clearer limits to those zones in which we still know nothing and research is still to be done. But quite apart from the heuristic advantages to be gained, the confrontation has to be made because most biologists have left the existence of cognitive functions almost entirely out of account when trying to elaborate a general theory of adaptation. For them thus to be reminded of it, by having the field of vital adaptations widened to include cognitive adaptation, may well give them a fresh perspective. It does, indeed, strike one that vitalists and finalists have been alone in giving any systematic thought to the problem, for the simple reason that, for them, intelligence could not possibly be reduced to a mechanism. But apart from Lamarck, at one or two points, most theorists on evolution forget to pose the question of whether the adequacy of knowledge to objects could be brought back into their explicatory schemata.[7] We cannot refer to a single mutationist who has ever asked himself seriously what use his instruments for scientific comprehension would be if the convolutions of his cerebral cortex were brought about by mere chance mutations with selection—though after the event—of the aptest for survival alone (and not the aptest in intellectual competition).

A sort of revolution both in our biological and our epistemological views has been brought about by Waddington's declaration at the beginning of his work on the "strategy" of genes to the effect that no physical science can be complete so long as the term "Mind" (or mental life) is excluded from its vocabulary. Yet Waddington is by no means a vitalist or a finalist. It is just that, being a biologist whose work is inspired by cybernetics, he understands that no theory of organization and adaptation dares leave cognitive adaptations out of account.

So much being said, and without trying to anticipate what follows, the central problem for us now to discuss, by the application of method 7, is the adaptation of logico-mathematical structures to the physical world in the light of biological explanations of evolution and adaptation in general. It may be said, perhaps, that a problem such as this is utterly without meaning, and that one might as well expect biology to explain a thing like the discovery of America. Now that would be to confuse the issue seriously: biology does not have to explain the existence of America as an object, because that is a matter for geology, but the problem of the trends which compelled Christopher Columbus to set off on his exploration can certainly be of as much interest to the biologist as to the psychologist. On the other hand, in mathematics and logic the very object of knowledge becomes the problem, and, although one may be certain that $7 + 5 = 12$, there is complete disagreement about the nature of numbers, and it is highly likely that numbers do not exist apart from the behavior of the subjects. Therefore, it is easy enough to think of them, as logical empiricists do, as the expression of a

---

7. They have, of course, been concerned with the development of intelligence, cerebralization, etc., but only rarely (except for Lorenz and Rensch) with epistemological problems such as the adequacy of mathematical structures to reality.

language, a point of view which could reduce the biological problem to that of the organic conditions of all kinds of language. But even so, the question why logico-mathematical operations have a necessary character still has to be explained; and if this necessity were reduced, as people sometimes want to make us believe, to a tautology like $A = A$, there would still remain the question of the psychobiological nature of this identity. Is it a product of experience (but everything in nature keeps changing), of heredity (but by means of what mechanism?), of convention (but the inverse convention would be absurd), of equilibration (but by means of what regulations?), etc.? And if logico-mathematical structures are taken as being something much more than a language, having to do with the general coordinations of action, then the question of the biological roots of logical and mathematical operations becomes even more complex and much more central too. It is of enormous interest to look at the great doctrines of biological variation and adaptation from this point of view.

Now that the methods to be followed have been put before the reader, he will have seen what shape the following chapters will take. In chapter 3 an examination will be made of the problems common to biology and the study of what knowing is (method 1). This will lead to an analysis of the solutions proposed and thus to the use of method 6. We shall then note, first, the parallelism between the principal theories of biology and those of psychogenetics and epistemology, a parallelism all the more striking for having been generally ignored by both parties. After that we shall be able to apply all the more confidently those difficult methods 2 and 3, by which functions are compared and structural isomorphism is set up. For this we may or may not need to apply method 4 in using models common both to forms of living organization and to forms of knowledge: this will occupy us in chapter 4. Chapter 5 will be devoted to the epistemology of the lower types of cognitive function, and its principal aim will be to point out the existence of a sort of logic in the instinct and the necessary dependence on a hereditary framework in the building up of acquired knowledge. Having completed these analyses we shall then be able, in chapter 6, to embark upon an attempt to present a biological interpretation of the three main kinds of knowledge. The sort of innate knowing, or knowing what to do, characteristic of instinct naturally raises some important questions about hereditary adaptive variation. These questions are still being much discussed, having been raised again by all the talk of "population genetics." Acquired knowledge, especially the kind which depends on physical experience, is, of course, also a kind of phenotypic accommodation; however, just as, from the biological point of view, the phenotype's adjustment to its environment is never without some interaction on genotypic structures, so also experimental knowledge is never possible without logico-mathematical structuration. There then remains the central problem of the nature of these logical or mathematical operations. Such operations can be reduced neither to innate structures of the instinct type nor to mere imprints made or provoked by the environment and objects: the entire aim of this book will be to discover a third type of biological statute, without which our argument falls to the ground; for the amazing way in which logico-mathematical frameworks adapt themselves to physical experience is one particular case—and a very important one for our point of view—of the adaptation of an internal functioning of the mind or organism to the characteristics of the object or of the environment in general.

3 The Epistemology of Biological Knowledge

This chapter is to be interpreted in terms of methods 1 and 6. It is, in fact, very important to begin by method 1, namely, by trying to discover the ultimate parallelism between the problems raised by the biologist, the psychologist interested in intelligence, and the epistemologist. These problems, however, are not encountered in a stark form; they cannot be detached from the theories or overall concepts that cause them to be raised in the first place. Furthermore, it is impossible to compare these theories or general attitudes about life and knowledge in their separate spheres without also analyzing the notions and explanations that are used in doing so—in other words, without formulating an epistemology of the kinds of knowledge which belong to the biologist qua biologist and not to the organism qua subject. This shows, then, that the use of method 1 is in fact linked to the use of method 6, and that is why we take the two of them first, even though it may seem a digression to discuss biological knowledge at the beginning of our critical analysis.

Having shown this examination to be necessary, we must then point out that there are two aspects of it—aspects which prove so closely knit as to be inseparable, in the long run, but which it is useful to examine separately for the sake of clarity in setting forth the argument. Biological knowledge does,

70

indeed, contain two dimensions, and that is our first fundamental analogy with the study of cognitive functions—two dimensions, that is, that are much more distinct from each other than are the questions of dynamics and statics in mechanics or physics. There is a diachronic dimension, corresponding to the notions of evolution or of individual growth, and a synchronic dimension, corresponding to the problems of physiology. To be sure, the analogue of an evolutionary process is to be found elsewhere, as in thermodynamics, quite distinct from those "states" which analysis may artificially demarcate. There remains, however, the fundamental difference that increasing entropy as a function of time does not constitute a "development," even in closed systems (which, moreover, are the only ones in which the notion of entropy can be seen to have an unequivocal meaning). The diachronic dimension of vital phenomena is, on the other hand, essentially something that can be characterized by the notion of development, and as soon as the interpretation of this notion is undertaken, great problems arise in close analogy with cognitive questions. On the other hand, the synchronic dimension corresponds to problems centered on the notion of organization, which is likewise foreign, in its strict form, to physics and common to biology and to cognitive mechanisms.

Section 6. Diachronic Notions

The two main fields in which diachronic problems arise are variation, or evolution, and ontogenesis. Now, both of these undergo intervention by "development" but in two distinct senses which must first be set out in relation to each other.

1. Organic and Genealogical Development

If we restrict ourselves to the most general characteristics of the notion of development—the temporal transformation of structures in the double sense of differentiation of substructures and their integration into totalities—then it is clear that the evolution of organized creatures constitutes a kind of development, just as does the gradual formation of an adult organism from the sperm state. Nevertheless, we are immediately struck by the differences between these two types of development.

In the case of phylogenesis we are confronted with what may be called a "genealogical" or collective development by means of the formation of successive branches growing out of the common tree, or twigs growing from the branches. In this case there are, of course, transformations arranged in a time sequence, and they follow certain clear paths when studied in the context of the main lines of development: that is, in the dual directions of differentiation and integration. However, these two notions are concerned solely with individuals from the various phyla; thus, a bird has a more highly differentiated organism than a hydra and is better integrated if only because, should it accidentally be cut in two, it will not make two birds, whereas the separate pieces of a hydra will continue quite easily to live as separate entities. There is a further differentiation of phyla qua phyla, as follows: from a common ancestry, such as worms, there may descend different kinds of phyla, such as mollusks and vertebrates. But in such cases the phyletic differentiation is not accompanied by integration; for example, the different species of a genus do not constitute an organized whole (the "genus") in the same way that the different organs of one individual have an overall harmony characteristic of the individual organism.

If we thus suppose there to be a relative dissociation between integration and differentiation in the field of genealogical development, we shall, admittedly, at first appear to be ignoring the idea held by so many biologists today, that the species—a fundamental unit in evolution—constitutes an organized whole (though its level of integration is recognized to be lower than that of the individual). But the problem we are posing does not lie here; it is concerned exclusively with establishing whether differentiation and integration are directly or inversely proportional in genealogical development (including, according to their type, a hierarchy of logical classes, in the logical sense of the term: species, genus, families, orders, and so on) and in organic or ontogenetic development. Now, in development of this second kind one may allow (considering the principal stages of initial segmentation, then the determining factors, and finally their functional reintegration, as Weiss interprets it) that, by and large, integration is proportional to differentiation and sooner or later is bound to prove a necessary complement of it. In genealogical development, on the other hand, it is just possible, though difficult, to maintain that the more subspecies and varieties a species engenders, the better it is integrated. To say as much is to presuppose some proportionality between the richness of its genetic potentialities and its integration. This proportionality becomes inverted as one gradually passes from the species to the "genus," to the "family," to the "order," and so on, in the sense that the more species one of these units contains, or the more differentiated forms, the less it is integrated.[1]

Contrary to this first type of development, the second type intervenes in ontogenesis and may be classified as organic or individual (not collective) in the sense that whatever characteristics of development may be under discussion they can only be taken as applying to the individual organism on its own. There is an exception to this with respect to the formation of spermatozoids and ovules. These follow the direction of genealogical development.

Having said this, before undertaking an analysis of the notions involved in the interpretation of these two kinds of development, we should point out that both are to be met with again in the field of cognitive systems.

In the first place, where organic or individual development (type 2) is concerned, this is obviously characteristic of the formation of an individual intelligence, of a human being's intelligence, for instance; sufficient insistence was laid in section 2 on the analogies between organic epigenesis and the development of cognitive functions for it to be unnecessary to go over that again here.

As for the genealogical or collective development (type 1) of the same functions, whole series of examples can be given, without introducing phyletic or hereditary filiation, merely by generalizing the notion of genealogy to any kind of filiation whatsoever (social, national, and all those cases in which trees of filiation can be drawn up in terms of transformations in time). Thus, endless

1. This brings to mind the inverse proportion of "comprehension" and "extension" in elementary logical classifications. And if it should be objected that the species alone constitutes a natural totality, because genus, families, and so on are more artificial, there are two replies we can make. The first is that Zipf and Willis, with their laws of probability, have demonstrated the natural character of the kind of taxonomy which is as much a part of objective dichotomies as it is of the classifying operations carried out by a naturalist. The second is that, despite the criteria of cross-breeding, etc., the distinctive characteristics for species are very far from being as clear as has sometimes been claimed. For one thing, hybrids between different species are sometimes found to be fertile, and, for another, one has only to make a close study of the taxonomy of a group of slightly variable character to see the difficulty that arises in trying to distinguish between subspecies and species, or between what is subgenus or a section of a subgenus. Stebbins is one of several biologists who have pointed out this relativity.

varieties of cognitive reactions in the animal series (reactions belonging to the instincts, to learning, to forms of intelligence, and so on) are indubitably dependent on genealogical development, since they are not found together in the same individual. It is the same with the varieties of intelligence or thinking processes of individual members of the human species. It is the same again with the many theories which may arise during the same period, calling themselves "schools," with opposing points of view in the same branch of learning. Or again, these doctrines may develop one after the other in the course of a particular historical period, and some may be born of earlier ones which seem contradictory.

However, the interest in any comparison which might be drawn between the two types of development, biological and cognitive, is that if you take the kind of science whose findings can be proved beyond fear of contradiction, which is the case with logico-mathematical structures, these two types fuse and become one whole. In fact, such structures are built up progressively, both from the historical and the psychological point of view, and may be either invented or discovered[2] by particular individuals. This in itself is a kind of genealogical development. All the same, they do become logically integrated into an organized whole, which then constitutes a piece of organic development.[3] But it is obvious that this fusion

2. As to the question of invention and discovery in mathematics, see section 20, subsection 4.

3. It must be added that this fusion into one whole of the organic and genealogical development of human thought does partly depend, also, on whether the notions used are strongly or weakly structured (see also section 11, subsection 6). Most mathematical notions are strongly structured, which makes possible their complete integration, whatever the genealogical development that characterizes the series of historical inventions that provoked their construction. In the case of notions that can only be slightly or weakly structured, as is the case with disciplines of a descriptive or classifying kind, it goes without saying that integration must be less complete. It is highly likely that, as far as biology itself is concerned, the weak integration noted above, which occurs in units of the higher "types" such as genus, families, orders, etc., is connected with considerations of a similar nature, because it is where slightly structured classes are involved that the law of inverse proportion applies, between "comprehension" and "extension," which means also between differentiation and integration. One must add forthwith that these considerations are dependent on what we know at the present moment; when we are better informed about the hereditary mechanism (about which nothing is known now), as it concerns the characteristics of these genera, families, orders, classes, and branches, obviously their integration will be seen to be superior to what it is now. Nevertheless, there are good reasons for believing that this integration will still be inferior to that which occurs in specific units, especially in the ontogenesis of individuals.

of two types of development into one whole is, so far as human thought is concerned, attributable to social life, which brings individuals together in a unique system of interactions from the very earliest stage of their development. We shall be coming back to this problem in section 22, subsection 5.

2. *The Evolution of Life*

First among the diachronic notions arising from genealogical development is that of evolution. Now, as everyone knows, this notion is of comparatively recent development in the history of biology, and it has taken a lengthy process of thought for us to graduate from the idea of a fixed state to evolutionism. In fact, although the notion of evolution, understood as development in time, was not discovered until Lamarck and Darwin, the way for it was well prepared by concepts which implied genealogical connections, although at that time they still had a notional form, with no sense of unfolding over time and, therefore, without "development."

The earliest of these concepts is the finalist hierarchy of "forms" that we find in Aristotle. For him, indeed, there are three kinds of soul: the vegetative one which accounts for vegetable life; the motor soul which helps us to understand the organization and movements of animals; and, finally, the spiritual soul which is both the "form" of the body and the guiding principle behind human thought. But instead of seeing them as arising one out of the other from the lowest level by means of development in time, Aristotle shows them as suspended from each other in an order of perfection, so that the ideal on the highest or final level is used to interpret the lower levels by a sort of conceptual downgrading, the ideal being an end in itself and not merely the termination of a series. This is supposed to correspond to the relationship between man himself and God, who is conceived of as the Ideal Form.

The next concept is that of creationism, which opens up the possibility of creation by stages as opposed to timeless "forms" (compare the revolutions of the globe in Cuvier's work). But if, according to the book of Genesis, vegetable life was created on the third day, fish and birds on the fifth, land creatures at the beginning of the sixth, and man right at the end, it still remains clear that they did not each grow out of the other, and that the only temporal thing about it is the carrying out of a preestablished plan, not the plan itself, which might have been eternal order conceived of in stages.

The third concept, whose historical role cannot be denied any more than can the preceding one, but which this time really has some scientific importance, is the idea of classification. Henri Daudin, in a remarkable study,[4] demonstrates the way in which classification, initially based on the simple, logical coordination of resemblances and differences chosen quite arbitrarily, finally reaches the stage at which it aspires to place things in "natural" classes based on observable characteristics. Since the latter are infinite in number, classification (exemplified by Blainville and others) has sought to bring out "essential" characteristics, which leads to the idea that outstanding similarity—a principle of logical interconnections—is an indication of some "community in Nature." It is from this theory that Cuvier gets his idea, however static and "prerevolutionary" it may be, of a "common plan of organization."

So we see that evolution, for Lamarck, consists of transforming this classificatory and static hierarchy into a hierarchic series having an order in time. The genealogical tree thus comes to have a certain logic from the outset, even though it is still in search of those "natural things in common." It is also to be held responsible for later development: "the things in common" become kinship, and that, in its turn, becomes philogenetic filiation.

Independently from the search for a causal explanation in evolution, which is what Lamarck and then Darwin were after all along (see section 8), the idea of evolutionary or genealogical development has become increasingly acceptable by reason of the convergent results obtained by four very distinct disciplines: first, paleontology (the history of former stages of life); then comparative anatomy, which, by using the method of structural comparisons or homologies, was able to make a more far-reaching analysis of kinships than mere system-making could do; then, embryology, which throws light both on comparative anatomy and system-making as well as being the most likely ground, from the ontogenetic point of view, for direct analysis of development; and, finally, genetics or the experimental study of heredity and variation.

Genetics, however, by the emphasis it places on conservation in hereditary transmissions and on the relative isolation of the germinative system, has led certain theorists—from Weismann with his "anticipations," Bateson with his "conceptions," de Vries with his

---

4. H. Daudin, *Les classes zoologiques et l'idée de série animale en France à l'époque de Lamarck et de Cuvier (1780–1830)*, 2 vols. (Paris: Alcan, 1926).

ideas on "premutations," right on to a considerable number of modern geneticists—to insist on the possible preformation of all kinds of variation, and to reduce evolution to a combinatorial system. This system is supposed to be calculable, from the structure of desoxyribonucleic acid (DNA, the carrier of genetic information) onward, but it is such that any apparently new development in fact fits into the framework of preestablished possibilities.

This sort of negation of constructive evolution is in conflict today with a new school of thought, which has opened up a new line of research; in this the prime mover was Darlington who, in 1939, introduced the idea of an evolution of the "genetic system" in which he included the genome itself. In that connection molecular genetics (with all its implications) in conjunction with biophysics and biochemistry (and along with that, in recent times, quantum physics) all open up new perspectives on the intermediary states between unorganized and vital matter. This is true especially of the stages in the organization of the genetic system, which is both the source and the product of evolution.

3. The Evolution of Reasoning Power

We shall have to come back to the notion of development, which will need to be made clearer as far as its "organic," if no longer its "genealogical," form is concerned. But before doing so, we must point out how strongly this brief outline of the stages in evolutionary theory recalls, at least in its main lines, the problem of the evolution of the thought processes or reasoning power. Actually, such a problem was never raised at first and might long have seemed even more out of the question than the evolution of organized creatures, whereas nowadays it sems inescapable.

Nothing was further from Aristotle's mind than the idea of evolution in reasoning power, since his "forms," though not situated in a suprasensible world as were Plato's Ideas, gave assurance of a permanent harmony between their triple manifestations, which were the forms of objects, logical structures used by the intelligence, and the organic motor principle.

Some notion of reasoning is unavoidable in the creationist theory, and this can be reconciled as to its consequences with Aristotle's notion, but is quite distinct in its source. It is the notion of an intelligence-faculty, an essential constituent of human nature, endowed with its formal mechanism—logic—once and for all, but its contents, that is, knowledge itself, being acquired gradually, handed on and added to in the course of time. The intelligence-faculty concept excludes any idea of the genesis of intelligence; rather, intelligence constitutes a primary factor which can only be explained in terms of itself. This anti-evolutionary conception of reason has proved to be much more resistant than creationism has been in biology. It inspired Descartes, in his theory of innate ideas (which include information provided by the senses and factitious ideas, in other words, ideas arrived at by mathematical operational construction), Leibnitz, with his doctrine of preestablished harmony between monads and the exterior world, and Kant, with his a priori theory. Today it is still a force to be reckoned with among the many philosophers who know nothing about psychology, and even among vitalist biologists who try to place intelligence in the very source of life: indeed Cuénot wants to give it a place in the genome.

A number of works followed on the same lines in the field of cognitive mechanisms, laying the way clear for an evolutionist conception of these mechanisms, just as researches along the classification line of thought prepared the way for evolutionary biology. This comparison can prove instructive in more than one way. With respect to the mechanism of the act of knowing, introductory work of this kind can often be seen in historical perspective, which was never the case with biological classification before the idea of evolution was established. Here we must make one reservation, which is, moreover, of a kind to reinforce the parallelism we are dealing with. When a nonevolutionary systematizer tried to set up a classification, he thereby postulated the fixity of species. But within this unvarying framework there was, nevertheless, nothing to prevent his admitting the existence of "varieties" dependent on environment and the history of the species, nor even of Cuvier's great "revolutions of the globe," which were supposed to produce modifications in fauna and flora, without involving evolution as a formative process. Similarly, where reason is concerned, it may be said that Auguste Comte, setting up his law of the three stages (a thing we do not need to discuss here) ended up with a classification of types of cognitive organization or rational organization, seriated according to the order in which they made their appearance in time. This is because they were supposed to be "varieties" of reason, although Comte insisted on the fixed or permanent character of his formal structure (modes of reasoning remained constant for him, and so, therefore, did "natural logic" itself). In the same way, when a mathematician classified the different headings of his subject, although he could note the conditions and the order of succession in their historical constitution, he still thought he was concerned solely with classifying possible varieties of knowledge and never suspected that his classification would undergo a thorough revision at the hands of later writers on the operational genealogy of structures. We are referring to the "mother structures" of Bourbaki, with their differentiations and recombinations, and also to F. Klein's "Erlangen program," which showed how geometric structures must not be thought of as immobile from the point of view of static classifications, but each of which gives rise to its successor by means of transformation systems, just as a basic "group" determines its subgroups by successive differentiations.

Thus, the idea eventually caught on, if only among a handful of those who were working on the subject (but it is with this handful that the future lies), that reason itself is not an absolute invariable but is elaborated through a series of creative operational constructions, which introduce new features and are preceded by an uninterrupted series of preoperational constructions. These result from coordinations of actions and can be traced right back to morphogenetic organization and to biological organization in general.

Turning to cognitive mechanisms, we shall find, as in biology, the idea of evolution supported by the researches of four separate subjects:

1. The history of ideas (historic-critical method in epistemology) as well as the history of species confronts us with transformations of the thinking process which go far deeper than people used to imagine; for example, from Aristotle's physics, to classical mechanics, and on to quantum physics—almost everything is different. Aristotle would have thought that, from the logical point of view, the double nature of corpuscle and sound wave presented by the same object was a contradiction of the principle of complementarity or of the fact that a corpuscle is supposed to be able to pass from a position in space P_1 to a position P_2 without going through any intermediate positions. In this case we shall have to question whether it is only the thought content which has changed or whether the formal operational mechanism itself has evolved in terms very different from those used before. In fact, one might very well reach the conclusion that the notion of a formal principle that remains

identical to itself independently of radical changes in its application has lost all meaning for us today.

2. Comparative psychology, carried forward into ethology, confronts us with very many varied types of knowledge, in terms of the different kinds of social environment of human beings (cultural ethnology) the different ages of people in these different social settings, and, above all, the innumerable kinds of animal species. On this account, it becomes impossible to study human reasoning power as though it were a watertight compartment quite separate from the evolutionary processes of the other orders.

3. The psychogenetic data, which we dealt with in section 2, are enough in themselves to show why mental ontogenesis, the continuation of embryogenesis, presupposes some kind of constructive epigenesis that turns sensorimotor coordinations, among other things, into logico-mathematical operations. This throws interesting light on the data of comparative psychology and serves to corroborate the evolutionist interpretation.

4. Finally, genetics, although it does not yet furnish us with any insights into the mechanism of intelligence, cannot fail to be concerned with the philo- and ontogenetic processes of cerebralization —a very important biological mechanism, which is linked of necessity to the evolution of the intelligence.

This, of course, does not prevent each new fact discovered in this connection from raising anew the fundamental question of preformation or actual construction, but in many cases one can make a decisive reply as far as intelligence is concerned; in fact, in terms of strict, formal logic, Gödel's theorems supply impressive arguments in favor of constructivism (see section 30, subsection 4).

4. Ontogenetic Development

Ontogenetic or "organic" development, to which we turn now, will allow us to get a firmer grip on the whole notion of development (and thus to be in a better position to compare it with mental development), because it is in every way an exemplary prototype. There are two reasons for this.

In the first place, as has already been said, organic or individual development brings together, into one functional whole, the processes of differentiation and integration, whereas in genealogical growth these are relatively distinct.

But in the second place, and this is something fundamental,

biologists today, like Julian Huxley and Waddington with their "synthetic theory" of species, are making phylogenesis depend in part on ontogenesis, and not only the inverse. Indeed, genes are not actually static elements but, rather, factors identical or analogous to enzymes, whose nature is revealed by their activity, interdependently and subject to a whole set of regulations throughout the entire process of embryogenetic growth in interaction with the environment. The result of this is that the information supplied by the genotype is not only transmitted but also transformed in the course of all this development, so that the essential system is no longer the genotype in isolation but a total "epigenetic system" in Waddington's sense of the term (see, in section 2, the notion of the epigenetic area or landscape). Moreover, selection is no longer thought of as having a direct bearing on the genes (considered as corpuscles, some of which will be retained and others eliminated, as Waddington puts it rather scathingly, like various sieves in a quarry singling out stones). Selection does, however, have some influence on phenotypes insofar as it causes the genome as a whole to make "functional responses" to the stimuli and tensions of the environment. As a result, at every level of its development, the phenotype becomes an essential instrument of variation, a thing which tends once again to make evolution, in its philogenetic aspects, submit to the laws of embryogenetic development.[5] This being the case, what can organic or ontogenetic development be? From the beginning, it has always been seen (contrary to the notion of evolution which was discovered late) as implying, first, an ordered series of stages and a causality connection linking each stage to the next. It has also been seen that this ordered series of modifications in space contains a further, temporal dimension (since causality enters into it), and thus the suspicion has been raised, in view of the length of embryonic life in man, that this expanse of time in turn presupposes some constant—and irreversible—speed.

But not not one of these characteristics or all of them together can yet characterize organic development, for we meet them all in physics. Not only that, but the first theories about embryology contained no idea of development, just as general biology began by leaving out of account the notion of evolution. These initial theories were, indeed, limited to registering the quantitative modifica-

5. On all these points, see also section 19.

tions of the embryo as a whole, as though the adult were already fully formed in the egg or sperm, but reduced in size, and development were merely the increasing of this size.

After 1759, G. F. Wolff's idea about epigenesis or qualitative, not just quantitative, transformation was absorbed into the earlier theories, but not without some bitter argument. This idea[6] was soon translated into terms of differentiations and correlative integrations, which is as much as to say that development is a progressive organization implying, on that acount, the notion of a construction of total structures and a filiation of these structures, so that the structures of stage n are derived from those of stage $n - 1$.

Finally, after 1891, following H. Driesch (or rather, in spite of him, for the shock of his discovery provoked a kind of intellectual regression in his mind, and he reverted to Aristotelianism), and as a result of advances made in causal embryology and interdisciplinary ties with cybernetics, this construction of organized structures came to be seen as a sort of progressive equilibration due to an action of autoregulations, first structural (reconstitutions of the total structure built up from partial structures) and then functional[7] (activated by feedbacks). Thus, the stages of development have the appearance of graduated steps in a progressive equilibration with its dual aspects: the diachronic (homeorhesis, see section 2) and the synchronic (final homeostasis, see section 7).

Needless to say, this epigenesis and these regulations presuppose some indissoluble and continuous interaction with the environment, for the building up of structures demands nourishment, and if the organism under development is continually assimilating the energy foods necessary for its constructions, then this assimilation into internal structures contains an equally continuous accommodation of these two situations, whether favorable or unfavorable to the environment. It is in this respect that the construction of the phenotype is not entirely predetermined in the genotype, but contains a system of "epigenetic" exchanges.[8]

---

6. Before it triumphed, the idea of epigenesis needed the support of many others, notably Geoffroy Saint-Hilaire, who demonstrated the changes in ontogenesis brought about by the environment.

7. See section 3, subsection 3.

8. Mayr calls the phenotype an "epigenotype" in view of the fact that it is caused by hereditarily programmed growth and by the "epigenetic" system as expounded by Waddington.

5. *Psychogenetic Development*

A review of the stages through which the concept of organic development has been evolved leads inevitably to a comparison with the way in which psychogenetic research into the cognitive functions has evolved. This evolution has extended much farther than along the lines dealt with in section 2.

Let us take as our starting point the opening remarks in subsection 4 above: what they amount to is the statement that embryogenetic development is not a mere "recapitulation" of phylogenesis, which is what de Serres, F. Müller, and von Baer thought it was. (Their idea remains valid in the main, provided allowance is made for the influence of changes in speed and short circuits.) Rather, it is, at least partially, the source of phylogenesis, insofar as essential variations due to regroupings in the genome rather than to strict mutations are brought about, or selected, in terms of phenotypic developments by virtue of genetic responses to the tensions of environment.

The problem presents itself at two levels when it comes to cognitive functions. First, there is the stage of hereditary transmissions: we need to know whether a cognitive hereditary mechanism—such as certain perceptual animal reactions (whether or not allied to the instinct)—is entirely determined in the course of its individual growth by programming in the genome, or whether the stages of individual growth give proof of some effect on its formation. This is one particular instance of the general cyclic process just recalled. Second, there is a stage of social or educative transmissions (already present to some slight extent in birds and mammals). Does the human child, during its period of mental growth, only manifest characteristics that are transmitted to it by language, its family, and its school, or does the child itself provide spontaneous productions which may have had some influence, if generalized, on more primitive societies than our own? In a word: as to intellectual characteristics, does man explain the child, or the child explain man?

This problem has already been raised by J. M. Baldwin (and then again by Freud, although he only does so in connection with the affective life). According to the American psychologist, the general characteristics of the child's mental growth can be used to explain a number of adult reactions, both in the primitive and even in the civilized state, for the child has something predating the stage of primitive and even of prehistoric man. I myself have defended a similar point of view, and it seems to me to be of paramount importance in the genesis of the most elementary logico-mathematical structures, which are also the most essential ones. We need only take one example, from physical causality: it is possible to find modern children of from seven to nine years explaining the movement of projectiles in a way which conforms to the Aristotelian *autiperistasis* (the mobile being carried forward by the air which it displaces as it goes). No adult believes this in the social environment that we studied (in Geneva), and it is unthinkable that such a notion should have been handed down by heredity from Aristotle or the Greeks to the schoolboys of Geneva; therefore, the idea must be accountable to Greek common sense at the time of Aristotle, for they had no knowledge then of present-day mechanics and never suspected the principle of inertia. That common sense of theirs caused them (including Aristotle) to reason along the same lines as children do in this particular sphere.

It will be seen, then, that the history of the discovery of the notion of development runs almost exactly parallel, insofar as the formation of reason is concerned, to what was described in subsection 4 above. Likewise, it was originally believed that the adult's reason was ready-made in an innate form in the infant, so that one had only to furnish this formal container with appropriate pieces of knowledge, simply filling up the memory, for a final, adequate stage to be reached: only the quantitative differences were thus retained with no hint of any qualitative difference. Rousseau, in 1762[9] (three years after G. F. Wolff, of whose existence and medical thesis he probably knew nothing), was the first to contest the fact that a child was "an adult in miniature," to use the phrase which has become current since then. He was thus responsible for the theory of an epigenesis of the intelligence. But this theory was not fully demonstrated until the twentieth century, when various pieces of research showed that the development of intelligence involves certain aspects of progressive organization.

Today it is known that this organization consists of a construction of operational structures, beginning with the general coordination of actions, and that this construction is brought about by means of a series of reflective abstractions (or differentiations) and of reorgani-

9. Date of the publication of *Emile*.

zations (or integrations). Moreover, we are fairly certain that these processes are directed by a form of autoregulation or progressive equilibration, and that they naturally presuppose a continuous interaction between the subject and its objects, which means that there is a dual movement of assimilation to the structures and accommodation to the external world (see sections 1–2). Thus, an almost complete parallel can be drawn between the history of these ideas in biology and in developmental psychology.

Section 7. Synchronic Notions

Every kind of development, whether genealogical or organic, ends in a state of relative equilibrium and, indeed, is bound to do so because of its autoregulatory mechanisms. We ought, therefore, to remind ourselves what notions have helped us to grasp this static character of the states of equilibrium, and we should distinguish what their connection is with notions concerned with development.

1. The Idea of Space

Genealogical or collective development culminates in the setting up of more or less stable phyla (these are, in fact, so stable that it took centuries to discover the concept of evolution, and evolution, to our temporal scale of observations, may appear to have slowed down or even stopped).

In the days when the idea of evolution was unknown, and when organic or individual development was thought of as a mere increase in size, the idea of species and, along with it, the logical categories superior to species envisaged by the classifying biologists (the category of "genus," in any case) were thought of as being so many permanent totalities, given, as such, in the state of nature. In practice, this "realist" notion (as opposed to the "nominalist" one) of species, genus, etc., was sufficient to ensure adequation with the external world, since the great nonevolutionary classifiers, like Linnaeus, were generally successful in achieving their ends.

It is unnecessary to stress the truly remarkable convergence of elementary structures in classificatory logic—built up quite independently of any biological bias, and spontaneously (among children of seven to eight years can be found structures of classificatory "grouping" which obey the same principles of linking together classes of things in terms of resemblances and qualitative differences)—and the structures of biological organization. We shall revert to this point in chapter 4, and it will be one of the examples used to illustrate the partial isomorphisms that exist between organic and logical structures. For the moment, however, the problem is to see things from the standpoint of the biologist only and not to go into the relationship between the organism and the process of thinking. Consequently, we must attempt some analysis of the various ways in which the notion of species has been expressed during the historical development of biology.

While we are on this topic, the notion of species provides our first example of a triad such as is to be found in every branch of biological thought, which includes diachronic and synchronic notions (and applies also to psychology and sociology). It will be clearer, however, if we begin this analysis with the synchronic concepts and then follow it with the question of relationship with the environment (section 8). This particular triad is made up of concepts which show totality to be a self-sufficient reality capable of interpreting its component parts,[10] of atomistic ideas relating the whole in terms of its parts, (or in terms of an aggregate of its individual components), and of relational ideas which regard totality as consisting of amalgams, each separate element being subordinated to the totalizing relationship.

The concept of species that existed before the theory of evolution was formulated may certainly be connected with the first term of this triad: a species exists by virtue of being a static entity, with permanent totality, which imposes its "form" on individual members of the species.[11] There exist as many species as the Creator made—so said Linnaeus, which is as much as to say that there are as many species as there are totalities capable of interpreting the characteristics of their separate elements. As for "genus" and other totalities involved in classification, they are all the more real, the better they correspond to natural bonds of community or kinship, such kinship having nothing to do with filiation but expressing the

10. Farther on, mention will often be made, in this connection, of "transcausal totality," insofar as it contains a mood of causality overriding any observable, causal interactions and thus remaining unverifiable.

11. A totality in extension (all the individual members taken together as a group) but, above all, in comprehension (the stable characteristics taken together, Aristotle's "ousia," etc.).

stability of the objective similarities of various degrees—similarities which, by analogy, reflect the Creator's intentions.

In evolutionism, the notion of species inevitably changes its nature, as the example of Lamarck will immediately show. From his point of view, the organism is fashioned by its environment without any endogenous constructions or any resistance from internal structures. This being so, the reality of the species qua objective totality disappears. (The same is true for empiricism, which seeks to subordinate the subject to the actions of the object and in which the idea of realism in classifications is replaced by a kind of nominalism.) For Lamarck, individuals alone exist, their lineage subject to constant variations. To cut up this lineage into species is essentially artificial, because the collective entities suitable for classification thus become no more than "parts of art."[12] It is true that when two descendants from a solitary tree become sufficiently distant at a particular moment in evolution, T_2, their separateness allows us to speak of distinct species, but so long as their gradual dissociation is in progress, during T_1, they are still linked by all sorts of intermediaries, so that it is a matter of choice whether they should be treated as different species or simply as "varieties" within the same species.

In logical terms, species will thus cease to constitute a simple "class" and take part, instead, in the structure of "relationships." On one hand, the qualities characteristic of specific or generic classes are capable of greater or lesser variation, a thing which adds to the simple equivalences of the transitive, asymmetric relationships. On the other hand, once these properties have become relative, they can introduce transitions from a given species to the ones around it, so that the species itself becomes relative to a certain mode of splitting up. This can also be clearly seen in Darwin, who, as C. Nowinski has demonstrated, interprets the species as a class relationship that becomes solidary with structures of the higher "logical type,"[13] such as selection, and so on.

With Mendelian genetics and the mutationism of de Vries and then of Morgan, etc., the notion of species takes on a third aspect, which, after the complete or causal totality which was characteristic

12. *Philosophie zoologique* (ed. Schleicher), pp. 1–4.

13. The term "logical type" is applied to the degrees in a hierarchical order of concepts. For example, classes containing only individuals are of type 1, classes containing only type 1 classes are of type 2, etc.

of its early stages, followed by the atomistic stage (by which the concept was reduced to separate entities), and the nominalist stage, which was typical of the early evolutionist ideas of classification, is now tending toward a structure of relational totality.

Indeed, the discovery of the laws of heredity has made it possible to demonstrate the existence of "races" which remain more or less stable until the moment when a new race appears (or disappears) through mutation. There are two vital consequences of this: first, an objective criticism can once again (or for the first time, speaking from a scientific and not a creationist point of view) be applied to species: a species is a collection of races whose derivations can, in principle, be analyzed, and crossbreedings between which are, in principle, fertile; second, and more important, there is no longer any alternative between a fixed state without evolution, which would mean species were permanent, and an evolutive flux in perpetual motion, which would remove all objective significance from the notion of species. The fact would seem, rather, to be that there is a series of states of relative equilibrium, of disequilibrium, and re-equilibrium, which admits of classification among the former states, while subordinating the overall system to a relational one, consti-tuted by genetic laws.

From that time onward, the relational idea has gained increasing support. One of the fundamental gaps in the classical mutationism of thirty to fifty years ago was the radical opposition, still of a semiatomistic kind, between the genotype and the phenotype. "Genotypic" was the term applied to the entire range of character-istics in a "pure" lineage brought about (by progressive selection) under laboratory conditions. As against that (and using the same terminology invented by Johannsen) the term "phenotypic" was applied to lineages either pure or impure but produced in varying environmental conditions and without the new properties' becoming hereditarily fixed. Looked at in this light, the opposition has nothing antithetical about it, for, as I was emphasizing as far back as 1929,[14] the two notions of genotype and phenotype are in no way situated on the same plane. Only the phenotype can ever be observed directly, and, even in the laboratory, a "pure" lineage (or one that is said to be "pure," for this is only a limit-notion) furnishes characteristics

14. *Revue suisse de zoologie* 36 (1929): 339.

which, likewise, always remain relative to the environment chosen and not merely to the hereditary patrimony. Thus, the genotype becomes no more than something that all phenotypes produced by one "pure" lineage might have in common. And so we are dealing with a notion that has been set up and deduced, whereas phenotypes can be both described and measured directly.

The essential novelty about contemporary genetics, as it develops beyond classical or Mendelian genetics, is that it has reintegrated genotypes and phenotypes into a relational totality. The essential characteristic of a genotype is seen today to be its "reaction norm," that is, the entire range of phenotypes which it is capable of producing by means of single variations on the properties of the environment. On the other hand, alongside the reaction norm of a particular race, which is to say, of an artifically purified genotype, we find references to the reaction norm of a "population"—of a mixture of genotypes such as is the rule in nature, where the unit is the "genetic pool." More than this, since Hardy and Weinberg established constant relative frequency of an allelomorphic character in certain hypothetical populations, there are those who have gone so far as to set up some kind of "population genetics," which is supposed to have its own laws, and one of whose principles is that a gene can never act solo, that every phenotype is brought about by the action of the whole group of genes. An experiment that has come to be regarded as classic of its kind was carried out by Dobzhansky and Spassky, who placed fourteen races of an adaptive value from 0.3 to 0.8 in a breeding cage, keeping back only the homozygotes. At the completion of fifty generations, it was noticed that, under these conditions, there was a compensation process which made good any unfavorable mutations, for, out of fourteen races, three had entirely reestablished their adaptive value, eight had done so approximately, and only three had failed to do so to any sufficient extent.

To sum up, having first entertained a realist notion of species, and then an atomistic and nominalist one, biology today is turning toward a relational study of functional totalities in the framework of which the species is seen in nature, which leads one to believe in the primacy of the notions of equilibration and regulation by virtue of the fact that, conceptually, they go far beyond the antitheses originally presented.

2. The "Genetic System"

We have seen that at one end of the scale, species or genus are states of relative equilibrium forming the climax of genealogical or collective development, while, at the other, there is the structure of the individual organism, a state representing the completion of ontogenetic development. Between these two we must still record the successive conceptions of the genetic system, especially with respect to the genome—a meeting point, as it were, between these two kinds of development.

Ideas about the genetic system have evolved in accordance with the same law just illustrated, that is, from the idea of transcausal totality to atomism and from that to relational totality, relying on autoregulatory mechanisms.

Aristotle's view of reproduction was determined by his general view of four kinds of causality: efficient, formal, material, and final. According to him, fertilization resulted from the fact that the male supplied the "form" (specific, racial, or family) and the female supplied the "matter," the two together being enclosed between an efficiency and a finality. In other words, the genome is a causal "form," set up by means of division in complete isomorphism with the "form" of the adult body, explaining the way the body multiplies.

At the end of the nineteenth century a quite opposite view was taken by Weismann. For him there was a radical separation between germinative plasma, which is carried on from one generation to the next in a continuous and, one might almost say, immortal fashion, and vegetative plasma or soma, which is a sort of momentary and mortal excrescence, characteristic of a series of individual beings. But at the same time he gave an atomistic interpretation to the "germen," as a system of "determinants," present but in differing numbers in somatic and germinal cells, and whose function was to transmit hereditary characteristics one by one with no influence from the soma and still less from the environment.

This atomistic view was naturally strengthened by the discovery or rediscovery of Mendel's law and by the idea that "genes" were little particles situated in the chromosomes. The binomial character of Mendel's law of distribution, the discontinuous structure of forms scattered about in space during mitosis and meiosis, the apparent sharp and random jump characteristic of observed mutations—all

seemed to lead to that atomistic vision of life which long has dominated all interpretations of the genetic system. The view was further
strengthened by the dogma of nonintervention by the environment,
which made allowance only for the essentially disintegrating influence of certain radiations.

Ideas such as this, still current in many circles, were eventually
challenged by a series of new facts which are now inclining opinion
toward a third position—an interpretation of the genetic system and
the genome itself as relational totalities which are both the products
of a protracted growth and the center of coadaptations and varied
regulations. As Mayr has said, what the new theorists have done
is to replace "the thinking of bean-bag genetics," in which each
gene is supposed to determine one particular characteristic of the
adult organism in its own independent and unequivocal way, by a
relational idea of genetics (Mayr speaks of "relativity"), in which
the genome constitutes an aggregate organization inserted into what
Darlington in 1939 called "the genetic system"—a combination of
processes in reproduction, transmission, and variation, which performs as a system, that is, as a series of constant interactions.

Within the genome, alongside the structural genes, certain regulatory or modifying genes have been distinguished, where incen-
tives or aliment comes from outside the nucleus or even outside
the cell. The genes as a whole, which are often thought of today as
being structural and regulatory, simultaneously and without exception, do not exist in a fixed state but are continually breaking
down and making new formations, by some internal metabolism, in
the course of genetic transmission. They do, however, retain their
structure, which is one more proof of organization. As for their
activity, it is not merely a question of transmission or variation,
allowing for later generations, since there is some synthetic activity
during ontogenesis, as much as 80 percent at the beginning but
down to 1 or 0.1 percent toward the end of development.

Further, the idea is gaining ground today that the genetic unit is
not so much the genome itself as the "genetic pool" or aggregate of
genomes interacting in the center of a given "population." Now the
genetic pool is, in its turn, coadapted and integrated and becomes the
source of overall regulations and continuous reequilibrations, so
that it thus constitutes (or so the leading theorists say) the intermediary level of integration between the individual and the species.

As for the notion of the "genetic system," it is becoming more and more widely accepted in contemporary opinion. For example, M. D. White, in his *Animal Cytology and Evolution,* writes: "By the general term of 'genetic system' we mean the mode of reproduction of the species, the dynamic of population, . . . the chromosomal cycle, the index of recombinations, the presence or absence of different forms of genetic or cytological polymorphism in natural population, and, in short, all the factors which go to determine its hereditary behavior in the course of a passage of time sufficient to allow for evolutionary changes to appear." Stebbins and others have gone even further, so that the genetic system has tended to be assimilated into the whole body of internal factors, as opposed to the environment. (This, however, does not amount to excluding the interdependence of exogenous and endogenous actions, a fact now seen with increasing clarity.) Still, if the very notion of a genetic system thus tends to become a little vague, it still, along with all present-day relational theories, has the great virtue of emphasizing the fact that the most "natural" organic or biological systems (as we saw previously in the case of the "epigenetic system") represent both the source and the fruit of evolution.

On the whole, it will be seen that the development of ideas about the genetic system has observed the same laws as that of the notion of species, which will recur when we turn to individual organisms: there is a transfer from transcausal totality to an atomism which claims to express the whole in terms of isolable elements, and a return to the idea of a totality which is both relational and responsible for functional development. It will be said that these concepts are merely the reflection of knowledge acquired at the periods under discussion, which depend, in turn, upon the techniques of investigation used at these periods. Of course, this is true up to a point, but we must go further than that and realize that the concepts which are used to explain or describe certain facts are always more far-reaching than the facts themselves, because they adopt this or that form of systematization, and such forms inevitably acts as auxiliaries or obstacles during our attempts to analyze the exterior world. So we shall be left with the necessity of finding out the source of these systematizations. Here it would not be out of place, by reference to section 4, to put forward the hypothesis that what originally distorted the thinking in this area may have been a sort of spontaneous psychomorphism, which led to the uncritical adoption of such ideas as seemed simplest and most economical and which could be deduced from the physical world. It was only with the swinging back of the pendulum that models more adequate to a living organization were formed.

3. The Individual Organism

Opinions about individual organisms bear out this hypothesis in a more direct way. The only purpose such a hypothesis can have is to underline the dialectic character of the movement toward objectivity in biology. In fact, it seems that, in order to achieve the sort of synthetic orientation that the attempt to find a relational totality amounts to (a totality characterized by autoregulations), what we shall have to do is to start off from the thesis of a transcausal totality based on models from the higher levels that are apprehended as a whole on an introspective mode (a thesis which would render one service only, but that a real one: raise problems for discussion). From these models we shall proceed, by means of an antithesis, through an atomistic analysis based on models from the lower levels, which are really pre- or infravital (but which, in their turn, render a service by providing the beginnings of measurements and verification).

The individual organism is thus primarily thought of as a form imposed on matter by causality. This "formal causality," in Aristotle's sense of the word, is naturally backed by an "efficient causality," the principle of the "life force" conjured up by vitalists, as distinct from physico-chemical forces, though analogous to them, and "final causes," which are supposed to be self-explanatory and irreducible.

It is easy to see that these three separate opinions are each drawn from introspective experience.[15] Of course, the notion of "form" is common to organic forms, or to mathematical or logical structures, the latter being based on the classical presupposition that there is a distinction between "form"' and "matter," which is precisely the distinction made by Aristotle. However, if the "forms" of thought and of the ego, etc., are submitted in their aggregate and imprecise shape to introspection, so that they may thus be considered as being causal, then scientific analysis (which was introduced by Aristotle, but in his logic, not in his biology) will begin when these forms are translated into terms of relation—or operation

15. In other words—and this is self-evident—it has no connection with scientific, psychological analysis.

—structures, which is to say, into a language that deals in implication and has nothing causal about it. Organic forms, on the contrary, arise from essentially causal interactions, even if they are expressed in terms of mathematical or algebraic structures, so that they thus come to be "resultants" and not causes. To try to make out that "form," in an undifferentiated sense that is both cognitive and biological, is the "cause" of the unity of the individual organism is, therefore, to remain in the deceptive realm of introspection, for which the "ego," or thought, or what have you, becomes the motor of organic activity.

As far as the "life" force and finality seen as a "final cause" are concerned, their introspective origins are even more obvious. Of course, the reasons given for the resistance of the vitalists have always been based on the insufficiency of the mechanist explanation at the particular moment in history when the discussion may be taking place. The dual historical function of the vitalist ideas has thus been to present us with problems, which is an excellent thing, but it has also tried to stop up the holes, and that is of more debatable value. Only, why should we try to stop up a hole with an idea as bold as that of the "life force"? Because, of course, our inner experience provides us with a model for such a thing. On one hand, the "ego" seems to be, as it were, a "form" of forms (but is actually, as Kant has already pointed out, only a "form of perception" of the experience we have lived through and not in any way a causal or substantial principle). On the other hand, seen from the point of view of introspection, the ego seems to be the origin of forces, in the generally accepted use of the term, such as mental or muscular effort. Maine de Biran based his entire work on this introspective illusion arising from the feeling of effort. In the heart of effort he thought he could see some sort of intangible cause— the ego—and a material effect—the movement of the muscle! The reply of any scientific psychologist to this one would be, like Janet's, that the "action of effort" represented by effort actually constitutes a regulation of physiological forces utilized by action (the activation regulation or even the acceleration of action regulation). Furthermore, the "feeling" of effort produces no effect at all but is simply a subjective indication of this regulation or the consciousness of this activation conduct.

As for finality, we have already seen that although it may correspond to autoregulatory mechanisms, which are real and by no means negligible, nevertheless there is nothing of a "cause" about it, in the sense of a "final" cause. We are dealing again with an idea that suffers from insufficient analysis, because in it are lumped together as a heterogeneous whole both conscious implication (anticipatory deduction) and physiological causality (in the cybernetic sense), and this, once again, is a result of the shortcomings of introspection.

These notions of transcausal totality of psychomorphic origin were followed, as one would expect, by attempted physico-chemical explanations, or explanations which are based on the elementary unities of which the organism is formed (cells). In other words, as was suggested in section 4, whereas the earlier group projected data borrowed from the higher levels into the lower levels, the second group proceeded the other way round, tending toward a kind of reductionism aimed at interpreting the higher (in this case, the overall structure of the individual organism) in terms of the lower (cells, etc.), or even of infravital physics.

Now, as is almost always the case with reductionist tendencies, attempts at basing an analysis of the organization on elementary data inclined their ideas toward atomistic systems, for such attempts correspond to the simplest kind of thought operation, namely, additive ones. We are thinking here not only of "colonial" theories of the individuality of Metazoa, through agglomeration of cells, but also of the sum of anatomical and physiological research done on tissue after tissue or organ after organ, as though the morphological or functional totality of the organism were brought about by a progressive synthesis starting from isolable elements or subsystems, which are themselves groups that can be analyzed right to the cell, in those of its reactions which are thought to be permanent. One example of this will suffice; the nervous system, which seems to us now to be both the model of autoregulatory systems and the essential organ of cohesion among the higher organisms, was for a long time thought to be an aggregate of isolable reactions—reflexes. It was not until Karl Goldstein that the nervous system, probably for the first time, was seen as a network, in the commonly used sense of the word. Unfortunately Goldstein knew nothing about the algebraic theories of "networks" or "lattices," and he was thus so impressed by his inspired guess, as Heinrich Driesch had been when he discovered embryological regulation, that with "Gestalt" as a pretext he returned to the extraordinarily vague notion of transcausal totality (*Der Aufbau des Organismus*). It was only with McCulloch that the notion of the neuronic network was given a rational form, isomorphic to that of the logical operational networks.

Under the twofold influence of embryology, which highlights the correlative processes of differentiation and integration, and the discoveries made in physiology itself about interactions—as opposed to lineal causal series—and homeostatic regulations, the concept of organization came to be seen as the central notion of biology. This notion is both synchronic, in that it corresponds to the relational totality that is a feature of the completed organism, and diachronic insofar as it corresponds to the succession of reequilibrations which are an essential part of all development, whether genealogical or individual. This fundamental idea, on which the whole of present-day organicism is based, has a further development in a complementary notion, which in its turn is both synchronic (hierarchical stages) and diachronic (succeeding stages). This further notion concerns levels of organization, according to whether we are considering submolecular biochemical processes, macromolecular biophysics, the cell, or the entire individual organism (and that leaves out of consideration the questions of populations and species and does not even touch upon the concept of biocenosis).

4. Comparison with Cognitive Problems

This is the point at which a comparison must be made between these varied synchronic notions and the epistemological concepts to which they correspond in the field of cognitive functions.

Little can be said about the notion of species (see section 7, subsection 1) that has even the slightest bearing on the field of knowledge except on two counts. First, we may note in passing the discussions about "species" of knowledge, which are distinguished by their belonging either to human beings or to the various kinds of animals. According to the realist (and especially the creationist) conception of species, man alone possesses reasoning power, while animals either are mere machines, as Descartes maintained, or else work exclusively by a system of associative learning. This specific difference, at least insofar as sensorimotor intelligence is concerned, was dealt with once and for all by the remarkable work of Köhler and his followers on the intelligence of chimpanzees. In this sphere the ape shows itself to be superior to the human child, because it has a similar schematism of action (assimilation schemata and coordinations) and interindividual exchanges which takes it almost as far as formulating symbols. So we can no longer speak of a kind of intelligence peculiar to the human "species" except when we want to distinguish between the various stages of hominization (and this can only be in theory since most of them are still unknown). Second, even supposing that there are, phylogenetically and ontogenetically (and, in the latter case, the levels are known), a number of degrees of cognitive structuration, and that these are built up from what we know about the equally distinct levels pertaining to the various genera or species of primate studied in this connection, does this mean that we have to follow the sort of nominalist or atomistic interpretations of "species" and consider the many types of cognitive organization—differing as they do so very much from one society to another, or, in our own society, from one group of people to another —as so many phyla (epistemological and not necessarily genetic) that have evolved by divergent and continuous processes, without necessarily having any structures in common? This is approximately what L. Lévy-Bruhl thought, although he took it all back, and it still remains a possible hypothesis. The third interpretation, on the contrary, amounts to saying that if human reasoning power undergoes any evolution, it is never modified without "reason," which is as much as to say that there are degrees of equilibration and of vectors or directions rendered necessary by the internal laws of autoregulation which cause the transformations.

Although it will be seen that there is some analogy here with the three positions that we defined in connection with the notion of species, nothing can be said, as of now, about the heredity of various kinds of knowledge, and hence the genome cannot be discussed with respect to cognitive functions, since there is not enough information available (see subsection 2 above). On the other hand, if we take as a parallel (which is perfectly permissible, provided we simply view it from the angle of the types of notions utilized by biologists and psychologists) the evolution of ideas in the field of simple genetics or of population genetics, and the many doctrines about the part played by life in society in the development of reasoning power, then once again we shall come up against the triad. True, it is presented from the other way round, as far as the first two terms are concerned, for, society being superior to the individual, the latter at first considers no one but himself, so that at the outset he is atomistic. Society is only an aggregate of individuals, and the truth about society is merely a generalization of what is known about any one individual in it.[16] When we come to the Durkheim school of thought, we jump from this kind of atomist individualism to a conception truly typical of transcausal totality; society is supposed to be the origin of logical thought and of truth itself, and it imposes these on the minds of individuals by means of intellectual and moral "constraint"; otherwise minds would be reduced to mere sensorimotor functions. The tendency today is to think of the relationship between individuals and the social group as a relational totality in which individual operations and cooperation form one inseparable whole in such a way that the laws of the general coordination of actions are, in their functional nucleus, common to inter- and intra-individual actions and operations.

But it is with respect to the nature of the individual organization (see subsection 3 above) that the parallelism, historically a very close one, between biological concepts and the trend of ideas in psychology and epistemology is most striking. Indeed, it can be taken for granted that the notion of a causal totality, seen in the triple aspects of form, force, and finality, should correspond to the notion of intelligence, seen as a primary faculty, inherent from the first with complete powers. What is less to be taken for granted is that a new kind of scientific psychology should react against all these ideas and take a strictly atomist line, since nothing in the analysis of kinds of behavior or of concrete mental life seemed to render such a conclusion inescapable. Nevertheless, that is what happened in Europe about 1903 (resistance in the United States was quicker, thanks to James[17]). In fact, for a long time "associationism" represented intelligence as being the product of sensations, all of which were extended into "images" mingled together in a sort of combination of past images and present perceptions. It is only in the past twenty years, and even then only after a good deal of backsliding, that the notion of structures or relational totalities has increasingly carried

16. This was true at least in the seventeenth and eighteenth centuries, but not in the Middle Ages, because ideas then about organized society and collective reason are evidence of a totality point of view such as is found later to a certain extent in Comte and Durkheim.

17. On the other hand, associationism has cropped up more often in the United States (Hull, etc.), though usually in perspective-motor forms.

the day (see section 1) over mental atomism, which relied on old concepts of the nervous system which it had itself invented.

Section 8. The Organism and the Environment

The parallels noted so far between biological concepts and those pertaining to the analysis of cognitive functions have no other significance than to serve as an introduction to the central problem about knowledge by which we mean the relationship between subject and objects, this relationship corresponding directly (as was shown in section 5, subsection 1) to the biological problem of interactions between organism and environment.

1. Organism $\times$ Environment Relations and Subject $\times$ Object Relations

In a question such as this, which is, moreover, common to both the diachronic and the synchronic dimensions, we are dealing with a dialectic triad which has gone beyond the transcausal totality of atomism or relational systems. Added to it now is a further trisection: (1) environment takes control of the organism and molds it throughout its working existence, affecting even its hereditary structures, which easily submit to its influence; or (2) it is the organism that imposes certain independent hereditary structures on the environment, the environment merely eliminating such structures as prove unsuitable or nourishing those it finds congenial; or (3) there are interactions between organism and environment such that both factors remain on an equal footing of cooperation and importance. However, while the third type of solution is naturally bound up in notions of relational totality, each of the two preceding types may be combined, either with atomistic conceptions or, in the opposite way, with causal totalities.

It can be taken for granted that each of these three types of solution is capable of a number of variations and that, since the third is a synthesis of the first two though more far-reaching than either of them, variations on it become, ipso facto, intermediaries between the first two. It would, however, be a mistake to seriate all possible solutions in an ordered line or to envisage them as a kind of fan with direct and predominant action by environment (Lamarckism) at one end, the opposite idea (classical mutationism), at the other, and the middle occupied by interaction doctrines. In actual fact there is no single series, in that ways of thinking and the very ways used to express causality or explain it have undergone a change between the first two concepts and the third. Actually, the first two are closer to each other than to the third insofar as they make use of simple causal sequences of the insufficiently elaborated type, whereas the third by its very nature is more far-reaching in a dialectic sense, introducing new explicatory models, cybernetic rather than linear, so that the very question has to be posed anew.

Before we go any farther, we must once more point out that the triad just dealt with may be met with in almost identical terms in the field of cognitive functions, where relations between subject and objects are concerned. In making this comparison, however, as we shall have to do time and time again, in various ways, we must remember the terms in which the problem was posed in section 5, subsection 1. There are, in effect, three possible kinds of knowledge: (1) the kind that is linked with hereditary mechanisms (instinct, perception), which may or may not exist in man but which correspond in biological terms to the sphere of characteristics transmitted by the genome; (2) knowledge born of experience, which thus corresponds in biology to phenotypic accommodation; and (3) the logico-mathematical kind of knowledge which is brought about by operational coordinations (functions, etc.) and corresponds, in biology, to regulation systems of any scale, in the hypothesis that elementary logical operations (revisions, dissociations, order, etc.), with their "necessary" characteristic of coherence or noncontradiction, represent the fundamental regulatory organ of intelligence.[18]

If a comparison is to be made between biological notions about the relationships between organism and environment, and epistemological notions about the relations between subject and object,

---

18. Something must be pointed out at this juncture, which will have to be dealt with again later on: namely, that although logico-mathematical structures are allied to their subject's activities rather than to the physical properties of their object, one cannot, on that account only, link them to hereditary characteristics (genetic potentialities) because the latter are contingent and variable. On the contrary, insofar as logical or mathematical connections are "necessary," it is impossible to relate their biological origin otherwise than to necessary biological characteristics. Autoregulatory mechanisms are of just this kind, since life at every level (genome included) depends essentially on autoregulations (conservation of cyclic structures, etc.).

it is forms 1 and 3 that must be considered and not form 2, which corresponds with phenotypic accommodation. In fact, what biologists today consider in the aggregate as hereditary, when they are discussing the relations between heredity and environment, includes *both* the "genetic system" as supplier of information, that is to say, as an innate programming which regulates development *and* the same "system" as the seat of regulation. This much is self-evident, since the genome contains both regulatory genes and a system of autoregulation; but people have not shown much curiosity in whether or not the transmission of a hereditary morphological characteristic (even in the shape of a "potentiality") is the same as the transmission of a regulatory mechanism, when the latter is both a simple continuation or reactivation rather than a "transmission" and also, in itself, the necessary condition of the first transmission. But since the two transmissions are inextricably bound together, it will be provisionally necessary, in order to compare the cognitive relations between the activities of subject and object with the biological relations between organism (in its hereditary mechanisms) and environment, to consider the first and third ways of knowing as one whole, distinct from the second way of knowing.

This being so, we find ourselves, once more, up against the triad encountered earlier: either the object controls the subject, qua object, affecting even its logico-mathematical structures (the empirical origin, in the physical sense, of mathematics, as conceived by Herbert Spencer or by d'Alembert, who tried to prove that arithmetic and algebra were feelings and then found himself puzzled by zero and negative numbers, not to mention "imaginary" ones!); or else subject and object are inextricably linked throughout the performance of actions. In that case logico-mathematical structures will have to be thought of as expressing their most highly generalized coordinations.

But here again, the triad only corresponds to the triad of transcausal totalities, atomism, or relational totality, insofar as the third type of solution is concerned. Indeed, it is possible to admit a primacy of the object in relation to the subject from a strictly atomist position, and this is what the "associationist psychologists" do (from Spencer to Hull, etc.), but similar views can be reached from the transcausal totality standpoint, as is the case with a number of Gestalt psychologists, attributing "right forms" to physical reality (in terms of fields). For them, in this case, the subject and its nervous system are merely the seat or the theater, and not the actor or author, of these generalized structures from which mathematics and logic proceed.

And, yet again, the third type of solution (interactions between subject and object) is not just an intermediary between the first two but in fact oversteps them dialectically. This is seen to be the case, for in the first two instances logico-mathematical structures are to be taken as given virtually, or even actually, complete, whether in physical reality or in a priori mental states, whereas in the third they are seen to be the product of authentic and continuous construction.

2. Preestablished Harmony

We shall be returning to this parallelism in greater detail, but, before then, it is vital to examine once again, just briefly, how relations between organism and environment were explained in preevolutionist doctrine (and still, for that matter, in the vitalism of Driesch and Cuénot!). It is, in fact, clear that the triad of biological notions that were discussed in subsection 1 above forms part of a strictly evolutionist point of view, but ideas always have a history, though a history without any definite beginning, and in science even a revolutionary theory is always influenced by the ideas it attempts—often successfully—to overthrow. For this reason, we cannot avoid examining the explanation, given by original vitalism in its transcausal totality or holism forms, of the connection between organism and environment. This is all the more necessary because the same question arises every time finalism comes back into fashion.

At first glance, each of the various kinds of vitalism, whether creationist or integral with eternal "forms," as in Aristotle's theory, puts the stress on the organism, not on the environment. In the same way, the equivalent of vitalism with respect to mental life or cognitive organization—in other words, spiritualism (which we find in Maine de Biran, for example)—or the theory of intelligence seen as a primary fact or "faculty" seem to interpret everything in terms of activities of the subject.

However, when we go beyond the words and tackle the real problem—that of finding out what these organisms endowed with permanent "forms" and with life "force" and this intelligence furnished with full powers from the moment of its inception actually do or how they behave—we shall soon see that they have nothing to do with constructing since they do not evolve and, above all, because environment, for the organism, and the external world, for the intelligence, are themselves supposed to be arranged already by virtue of the same eternal "forms" or the same act of creation. In this way, the activity of the organism or of the intelligence is strictly limited to the utilization of the environment according to some pre-established plan or to the contemplation of it as an intellection.

The basic notion of preevolutionist doctrine, as far as the connections between organism and environment are concerned, is that of preestablished harmony rather than of harmony or adaptation gradually established. This idea presents itself in identical form in the theory of an intelligence-faculty, for here again we find mere discoveries or utilizations in preestablished harmony with surrounding objects. This explains the inevitable union between vitalism and finalism, since every finalist explanation thus boils down to the substitution of a simple affirmation of preestablished harmony for causal series (whether strictly mechanistic, random, or cybernetic). It is said, for example, that the visual organs are where they are because the eye is "made for" seeing, and the whole thing is explained in this way.

Now, preestablished harmony is no more, in reality, than the subordination of the organism or of the intelligence to a ready-made world, which does, in fact, amount to eliminating all constructive activity. So it is not for nothing that Aristotle in his epistemology, diverging to his own detriment from Plato's mathematicizing conceptions, ends up with a simple form of empiricism and no sort of construction of forms by the subject.

In the same way, the "vital force," although it gives verbal form to a principle of internal organization, is essentially a principle of a hereditary adjustment to all environmental situations, and this, in fact, presupposes a continuous action by the environment, either in the observable manifestations of nature or in the Creator's plan.

As for finalism, it is highly significant that its present-day champions, generally hostile to Lamarckism and utterly refuting the intervention of environment in hereditary mechanisms, hardly seem to suspect that every finalist explanation boils down to crediting the organism with the power to foresee external demands, in other words, conferring a wide field of action on the environment, but only by means of psychological or, rather, psychomorphic intermediaries and not by physico-chemical ones. This was seen in detail (section 4) when we were dealing with Cuénot, and the problem will arise again in connection with anticipations. For instance, when a callosity, which plays a functional part in helping the adult to adapt himself to his environment, starts to develop at a very early stage in the embryo, either it is simply a case of acquired heredity, or it is a case of pure chance, or else this anticipation must be due to earlier information obtained through some mechanism for which a cybernetic explanation may be expected (reequilibrations in the course of development, but with progressive short circuits and, finally, genetic assimilation, etc.). To say simply that there is finality means that the embryo can take the environment into account in advance, in other words, that it is subjected to its influence, as in the preceding solutions (except in the case of chance), but this is merely a bald statement with no explanation of the "how."

Obviously, within all these vitalist-oriented hypotheses about preestablished harmony, certain shades of meaning can be distinguished in which the accent is laid sometimes on the organism (a tendency toward preformism) and sometimes on the environment (a finalist tendency), while in others the balance remains equal.

3. Lamarckism and Empiricism

To return to positive solutions of the problem of relations between organism and environment, Lamarckism still holds much interest for us even if it is no longer acceptable in its historical form, for in the English-speaking countries there is undoubtedly a revival of Lamarckian influence.

A few introductory remarks may be useful here, for although they apply principally to the sociological aspects of knowledge, they do reveal the difficulties of achieving an objective position in biological epistemology. Lamarck was essentially a functionalist, and his emphasis on the unique formative role of the environment reminds us very closely of the epistemological empiricists. It is for these two reasons that his doctrine might have been specially designed to appeal to the English,[19] while the structuralism and innateness inherent in certain mutationist positions are more apt to suit the French. The chance of birth having decreed otherwise, Lamarckism

---

19. As evidence of this, we might refer to the fact that England has produced one Lamarckian who is even more of an empiricist than Lamarck himself, namely, Erasmus Darwin, grandfather of Charles. And, to take another instance, Lyell attacked Lamarck, not because of his insistence on environment, but because of his ideas about inevitable progress.

came to be a primarily Latin doctrine, until neo-Darwinism, backed by winning laboratory techniques, prevailed for a time.

Once the positions were reversed, the unfortunate Lamarck became the object of somewhat petty-minded criticism even in his own country (Cuénot, Guyénot, etc.), as if great work does not always contain some parts that are weak or even shaky. Lamarck's critics hammered away at the giraffe's neck and other amusing examples, whereas in their comments on the great Darwin, who, as a matter of fact, eventually incorporated the Lamarckian factors into his own doctrine, they carefully omitted any reference to the doubtful points (the theory of gemmules, etc.). Now, even if Lamarck was wrong to leave almost everything out of consideration except environment as a factor in transformism, and the organism's tendencies to choose a favorable environment, yet he was certainly right in attributing a necessary role to those factors, as is being increasingly realized nowadays.

Such swings in fashion would not matter if they did not, from time to time, become coercive. Here is a case in point. Around 1930 I happened to make two disquieting observations. A famous American biologist with whom I was exchanging ideas, as one may do, during an Atlantic crossing, finally brought himself to admit to his conviction that there is a large measure of truth in Lamarckism. He went on to say, however, that it was impossible for him to announce such views publicly (he was still a young man at the time) because of the uproar it would cause. At just about the same time I was having some protracted discussions on environment with the principal collaborator of a leading anti-Lamarckian geneticist. "I am absolutely certain," this chief assistant said to me, "that the old man is all wrong. But not a word about this: if an institute is to serve any purpose, everyone in it has got to think alike." The "old man" himself once made this very revealing remark to me: "I'm betting against it, myself." At that stage he was a believer in chance and selection; twenty years later he was a finalist, almost a vitalist. As for me, I would rather have sought what really remains true in Lamarck's theories, between chance and finality, which is exactly what people are at last trying to do.

The two central ideas in Lamarckism are the part played by the exercise of the organs during development and the fixation in heredity of the modifications thus brought about (heredity of "acquired" characteristics).

The first of these notions is generally accepted, but even if the second is not accepted in the form Lamarck gives it, the first has changed a good deal in meaning. In the long accepted hypothesis that there is a radical difference between the individual phenotype and the single hereditary genotype, the modifications effected by the exercise of the organs are merely accommodations and not hereditary; they may indeed modify the phenotype to a greater or lesser extent, but they bring about no fixation of these acquisitions.

For about thirty years now (covering the latter half of T. H. Morgan's working life), with all the advance in population genetics an increasing interest has been taken in phenotypes, looked at as the product of inseparable interactions between the genotype (or the mixed genotypes in any one population) and the environment. Thus to every genotype (or to every population) there is a corresponding "reaction norm," which expresses the production of possible phenotypes issuing from such lineage in terms of variations in such and such a property of the environment.

Within the framework of these reaction norms, the part played by the exercise of the organs during individual growth thus remains decisive, which is one point scored in favor of environment. Only it must be remembered that this role is just a partial one; what is lacking in the Lamarckian interpretation is the explicit recognition of the fact that the effects of these exercises are always relative, not only to the environment, but to the genotypic structure (pure or impure) of the lineages being studied. To sum up, where Lamarck sees nothing but the effect of environment (the organism, for him, makes no reaction except to acquire "habits" which are more or less forced upon it), there are really interactions between external factors and the genome.

This first gap in his theory is full of consequences in itself. If Lamarck was right, the organism ought to be infinitely malleable and constantly varying, whereas, as a general rule, the modifications it undergoes take place only within the "reaction norm" (except in certain cases where there is serious disequilibrium, which we shall discuss presently when examining "the heredity of acquired characteristics"). To put it another way, the organism is less passive than Lamarck supposed: it makes a positive reaction when it assimilates the environment to its structures instead of letting them give way in all directions through indeterminate accommodations. It is true, of course, that the organism is capable of learning: but every time it registers some piece of information from the outside, this process is linked up with assimilation structures. Moreover, even if it is not yet established, for example, that a recording takes place, in elementary cases, by means of fixation in RNA (ribonucleic acid), it does appear that the integrity of RNA is a necessary part of this individual fixation.

The second problem, that of truly hereditary fixation (heredity of the acquired) is much more complex. Lamarck believed in a direct action by the somatic modifications (effects of exercise) on the genetic system, either by adjunction or by the suppression of characteristics. A considerable number of control experiments have been carried out on this key question, and the results have been uniformly negative. So the matter seemed to be cleared up.

However, now that other interpretations may be put forward, even leaving out of account the idea that any action by the environment should necessarily be involved in the adjunction or suppression of genes, or in simple mutation, it seems to be the case that hereditary variations, linked with certain external influences, are becoming observable! Waddington, who claims to be a neo-Darwinian (even though he takes a strong third line between Lamarckism and mutationism), has been so bold as to start using the term "acquired heredity" again, citing it as a fact but without giving Lamarck's explanation of it. He quotes, as an instance of this, the wings of a species of Drosophila. Apparently the transversal vein in these wings was disconnected at the phenotype stage because of a change in environmental temperature and then remained fixed in this state after several generations, even when the temperature reverted to its earlier state. There is yet another example in the case of certain Drosophila larvae, when the anal papilla is enlarged by an increase in salinity and, once again, the condition becomes fixed in spite of a reversion to the former condition. There is an even more striking example in the appearance, among these same Drosophila, of a modification in the third segment of the body, which develops a resemblance to the second segment if the eggs are submitted to ether vapor. After twenty generations of selection, this characteristic became stable.[20]

In fact, the fundamental axiom on which all can agree (whether they call it "acquired heredity" or not) is to the effect that a phe-

20. C. H. Waddington, *The Nature of Life* (London and New York, 1962), chapter 4.

notypic variation allied in a precise experimental way to an environmental modification may, after several generations, become fixed in a genotypic form. Waddington speaks, in these cases, of "genetic assimilation," defining this concept as the appearance of a characteristic x, which is first linked to a change in environment but which persists henceforward as a hereditary characteristic after the environmental change has been suppressed.

But it must be repeated that to accept the second basic fact of the Lamarckian position does not involve acceptance of the Lamarckian explanation of it. In such cases there are two possible explanations, which have the advantage of not being incompatible: first, the selection of phenotypes by elimination under the influence of the environment and the reorganization of the genome in terms of the new proportions of the genes which have been thus modified; second, the direct reorganization of the genome in terms of selection (by which, this time, is meant modification of the proportions and of the overall restructurations) but in "response" to "tensions" in the environment produced during the individual growth of the phenotypes.

This is not yet the moment to pronounce between these two explanations (see below, section 19, subsections 4–7), but it should simply be noted that in both cases it is no longer, as with Lamarck, a question of passive registration in the "germen" of the somatic characteristics imposed by the environment. Rather, it is active reorganization in terms of selection, which itself does not consist of elimination pure and simple, but of changes in proportion within an organized "pluri-unit." In other words, where heredity is concerned, Lamarck was once again forgetting the necessity for an internal organization which reacts actively and does not merely submit to external events.[21]

21. Not wishing to be unjust to Lamarck, we must point out that passages can easily be found in his work in which environmental influences, sometimes even dubbed "irregular," are contrasted with internal factors consisting of an organizing "power" of life. However, if Lamarckism has constantly been interpreted in terms of morphogenetic actions of the environment, and if Lamarck himself stresses this far more than he does the notion of organization, it is because his doctrine betrays the same hesitations and the same ambiguities in this respect as can be found, for example, in Locke, who, though the father of empiricism and the precursor of Hume's thinking on the role of habit and the association of ideas, nevertheless attributed some role to the "operations of the soul," perceived through "reflection."

Now, for Locke, all knowledge comes from experience, the soul is a tabula rasa, the mind remains passive while receiving "simple ideas," and

A consideration of the possible parallelism between organism-environment relations and subject-object relations within cognitive functioning elicits extremely compelling analogies. The doctrine according to which the subject is supposed to be under the complete control of the object is nothing but empiricism of the purest kind—empiricism which makes even the most basic notions of the mind

---

the "operations of the soul" consist merely of "combining" these "simple ideas" without adding to them in any way. Thus, all that these "operations" do is to associate the "simple ideas" with one another, either in some "natural" way, that is, in accordance with experience, or by "custom," in which case they are just as firmly combined even though their connection is subjective or formed by habit. So it is understandable that this seemingly internal factor of the "operations of the soul" should subsequently have been translated into a language of pure associations, and that Leibnitz, even during Locke's lifetime, should have reacted against such empiricism by pointing out that even if the whole range of experiential notions reaches us by means of our senses, the same cannot possibly be said of the "ipse intellectus," whose role is to provide structures and not simply to submit the mind to experience, receiving its structuration from experience alone.

Similarly, all attempts to analyze what Lamarck means by the "organizing power" that he sometimes refers to in his writing point to the conclusion that what he has in mind is essentially a "composition," lacking a composing structure and drawing its "force" only from the nature and the association of its compounds. In the psychological domain, Lamarck does, indeed, contrast "physical facts" with "moral facts" or "mathematical truths" perceived "by the intelligence and not by the senses" (*Philosophie zoologique*, note to Preface), but he later shows (ibid., Introduction), "how the force that stimulates organic movements can, in the most imperfect creatures, be outside them and yet animate them; how this force was transferred into the creature itself and made permanent there; and how it became the source of sensibility in the creature and, finally, the source of acts of the intelligence." Lamarck, then, is speaking, not of a process of interiorization of actions that are first material and external though partially endogenous and are then carried out internally, but of a purely exogenous mechanism that is subsequently extended to internal reactions.

On the organic plane, Lamarck explains in chapter 7 of his *Philosophie zoologique* what the "acts of organization" that stimulate the actions of animals consist in: "the affluence of subtle fluids (nerve fluid) which become [in the organs] the determining cause of the movements in question." But he immediately adds: "If I cared to review all classes, all orders, all genera, and all species of animal that exist, I could show that the conformation of individuals and of their parts, their organs, faculties, etc., are everywhere uniquely [!] the result of the circumstances to which each species is subjected and of the habits that the individuals that make up the species have had to adopt, and that animals are not the product of a primevally existing form which forced them into the habits that are now seen as characteristic of them."

Lamarck does say, in chapter 11, stressing the "irregular gradation" of evolution, that "the state in which all animals now exist is, on the one hand, the product of the growing composition of the organization, which tends to

attributable to the repeated lessons of experience and to habits acquired by the subject under the pressure of circumstances.

One has only to compare, for example, Hume's explanation of the way the idea of causality was formed with Lamarck's considerations on the part played by exercise and habit in morphological adaptations (remembering that Lamarck, though younger than

---

form a regular gradation, and, on the other, the product of the influence of a multitude of very different circumstances, which tend continually to destroy the regularity in the gradation of the growing composition of the organization." But the rest of the chapter shows that Lamarck is not contrasting an endogenous organization with the influences of environment, for in dealing with his two fundamental laws (use of the organs and heredity of acquired characteristics) he emphasizes that, if "habits form a second nature," the first nature is a prior habit, and in this connection he recalls a key passage from his *Recherches sur les corps vivants:* "It is not the organs, that is, the nature and the shape of the parts of an animal's body, that have determined its habits and its particular faculties, but, on the contrary, the animal's habits, its way of life, and circumstances . . . have, over time, constituted the shape of its body, the number and state of its organs, and ultimately the faculties with which it is endowed."

It would be impossible to be more categorical as to the exogenous origins of "the organization" as a regular "composition" (if the environment does not change suddenly) and an irregular one (if the environment makes sudden changes). Between 1815 and 1822, in his *Histoire naturelle des animaux sans vertèbres* (*Philosophie zoologique* was published in 1809), Lamarck returns to the organizing "power," which he then identifies with the great "general power" of the whole of "nature," nature being conceived as the sum total, not of bodies, but of movements and actions. This "power is limited, fully dependent, and . . . incapable of doing anything other than what it does," being of a "somewhat mechanical" nature. This "power" is, in particular, devoid of all finality, even in "living bodies." "Indeed, in each particular organization of these bodies, an order of things, prepared for by the causes which gradually established that order, has brought about, through progressive development of the various parts, controlled by circumstances [!], what appears to us to be a goal but what is in reality merely a necessity." Lamarck goes on to further elaborate the role of "climates," "situations," "dwelling environments," etc., in the formation of habits and, hence in the formation of "the organs of the individual."

In short, it is no exaggeration to see, in the "composition" that Lamarck deems to be the source of organization, a process essentially associationist in nature and not an endogenous structure as the reading of a few passages taken out of context might lead us to believe. The reason for the exclusion of all endogenous structuration is probably that, in terms of the physicochemical knowledge of the day, such structuration might have seemed imbued with finalist vitalism—as it was, in effect, in the thinking of the anti-evolutionists. Thus, Lamarck's antifinalist mechanism (failing to master the problems of interactions, feedback causality, etc.) was bound to overestimate the influences of the environment, just as Hume's rejection of innate ideas inevitably led him to an associationist conception of the supposedly exclusive role of "experience" or action of the environment.

Hume, was his contemporary for thirty years) to find exactly the same reasoning and the same gaps. For Hume, as for Lamarck, these sequences are manifested in the subject by the formation of associations or habits, which, however, are no more than a replica of external sequences. According to Lamarck this replica is extended into the organism by a material change of form, and according to Hume it is extended into the subject by means of a change of mental forms or ideas. This is because, for Hume, the various notions of causality (varied, that is, in their concrete contents although they obey the same formative law which constitutes the abstract idea of cause) are merely the subjective manifestation of associations or habits thus acquired. In both cases there is the same lack of reference to any structuring activity by the organism or the subject. In Lamarck's case environmental pressure is accepted, no more, no less, without being assimilated into a genotypic structure with which it might interact. In Hume's case it is the regular external sequence which is registered, no more, no less, without being assimilated into such deductive structures as might have made it intelligible, so that the "necessity" we attribute to the idea of causal connection becomes nothing but an illusion due to the force of association or habit.

It will be said that such a parallelism lacks the extension of acquired associations into hereditary acquisition. Maybe it does, in Hume, but when we come to Spencer's view, such is no longer the case, because for him, even if there are no "innate ideas," there is at least a possible genesis, both biological and psychological, of the intelligence as a cerebral aptitude arising from acquired associations.

On the other hand, if we once again consider mathematics and logic within the framework that we examined in subsection 1 above, it will be clear enough how classical empiricism (d'Alembert and others), conceiving of these forms of knowledge as being simply the product of experience and even of "sensations," could miss the problem as we see it today, which so closely recalls the question of fixation and, as is often said, of "imitation" of a phenotype by a genotype ("phenocopy"). When, for example, in mathematical physics, a body of laws arrived at by experiment (that is, phenotypically), is translated into a deductive theory that embraces the laws and goes beyond their various outlines, such a translation cannot simply be characterized as the passage of fact into norm—which would just be going back to Hume—but the subject, thanks to its autonomous deductive structures, must be said to have reconstructed and even imitated the system by experience, though it has done so in what is really an internal (subjective) way.

4. Mutationism

In his sixth edition of *The Origin of Species,* Darwin finally integrated the essence of Lamarckism into his conception of evolution,[22] the leitmotif of which was, nevertheless, founded on the two notions of small variations and their progressive selection. Once the Mendelian laws were rediscovered and mutations had been discovered for the first time, there followed a neo-Darwinian or mutationist phase, which we shall designate as classical to distinguish it from the considerably altered guise in which it appears today. The classical mutationists eliminated every trace of Lamarckism from their doctrine and substituted an emphasis on endogenous variations. For them, only variations of internal origin (mutations), produced within the framework of otherwise invariable genotypes, can be hereditary; environment merely comes into play at a later stage by selecting the variations thus produced (leaving out of account phenotypic variations, which are certainly due to environment but have no evolutive importance because they are not hereditary).

Such a doctrine must be entered under the second heading in our triad of notions set out in subsection 1 above (primacy of environment, or of the organism, or of some interaction between the two), for it stresses exclusively the internal structures of the organism. But it also belongs, and quite strictly, to the second part of our preceding triad (see section 7): causal totality, atomism, or relational totality. And, where the genetic system is involved, this atomism will go so far as to see in the genome an aggregate of discontinuous and independent genes, each of them forming its own isolable characteristics and in some other cases causing sharp mutations, as discontinuous as itself and having no connection with the soma or the environment (section 7, subsection 2). On the other hand, selection ends up by singling out individual genes as if they were adult or complete units, disregarding ontogenetic development when the phenotype is being built up by means of functional selections rather than by simple elimination as was formerly the case.

It may be of interest to proceed with a critical examination of

22. He retained the influence of environment and exercise but rejected the ideas of integral continuity, nominalism, and progress, etc.

these lines of thought in the light of contemporary findings, since, by shifting all the theoretical stress from the environment to the internal structures of the organism, classical mutationism embarked on a course which inevitably led to the setting up of explanatory models, fairly general in scope, which crop up, even in the field of cognitive functions, whenever the respective parts played by internal and by external factors have to be analyzed in any given system.

It is certainly not by chance that neo-Darwinism, in its desire to burn its bridges with respect to the influence of environment, has taken the atomist line, for every attempt to get at an organism or a genome by itself, or a subject (of knowledge) by itself—to consider it in isolation from external factors such as environment or objects—deprives it ipso facto of its functioning, so that only particles, or isolated organs, or categories of isolable and abstract thought can then be found. In other words, such an attempt leads to a kind of atomism which is not only inadequate but actually distorts the truth.

The great discovery that has changed our perspective and has rendered classical neo-Darwinism obsolete (though its influence still permeates the common sense of biologists) is that the genetic pool and the genomes constitute organized systems, that is, systems which (a) contain their own regulators, and (b) are brought about by an evolution within the genetic system as such—an evolution peculiar to the system and differentiated, which is both the origin and the product of general evolution. (Of course, the notion that a reality can be both an origin and a product implies some revision of the concept of causality along cybernetic lines.)

If the genome contains regulatory genes and a system of auto-regulations, it becomes a contradiction in terms to suppose that all connection with the soma or the environment can be cut off. As long as the genetic system is thought of as a sort of package of little boxes, each of which, as it opens, lets loose some ready-made characteristic or, occasionally, a surprise mutation and then shuts up again to get back to the job of manufacturing just such another little characteristic ready for the next generation, it can be said that the genome is cut off from external influences. But as soon as it is seen as an organization equipped with regulations, some function has to be assigned to these regulations. This function is obviously to preserve the system; so much is clear. But if the system has to be preserved, there must be obstacles in its way, or disturbing influences, etc. These will be said to come from the external world, the internal metabolism of the genome being perpetually threatened by instability. But where does this potential instability come from, and how can one conceive of a metabolism without aliment, which can be as much a cause of disturbance as of preservation? And if genes are not a series of motionless little balls but essentially processes at work throughout the whole of ontogenetic development, does this functioning take place without any external interference, and can it only be threatened from inside? It is the property of a regulation, in every sphere, to feed information to the system in action about the results of its actions, and to correct them in terms of the results obtained. If this genome contains regulations, that must mean that it is at work, and that it achieves its preservation by means of learning from the results of its work.

This being the logic of the system, it is easy to understand why, when regulatory genes were discovered, the idea of a radical break between the soma, or environment, and the genome immediately came under attack, so that new concepts had to be set up, directed, like Waddington's, toward a synthesis of all the work done on causal embryology and genetics. That was the first gap in the old kind of neo-Darwinism, which is now well on the way to being filled.

But there is more to it than that. The genome is an organized structure brought about by an evolution. This organization has been ignored by the mutationists, who have paid attention only to its contents and its static final condition. From this point of view, it can easily be said that every new change can be reduced to a random mutation, and that selection in itself will suffice to retain the good and reject the bad, the essential thing still being the conservation of the genes and their hereditary transmission. The mutationists are only forgetting that the (internal) conditions necessary for this transmission are the organization of the genome and the transmission or conservation of this organization, which is quite another thing from the transmission of individual characteristics by the genes. And, supposing this organization to be an autoregulation, it still needs to be explained how the conservation, transmission, or reactivation of this autoregulation from one generation to the next is achieved. This underlines the problem of conservation as such, and not merely that of the individual genes, which are the only things involved in a combinatorial system such as the Mendelian laws.

If we want to solve this problem, it will not be enough to remind ourselves that general heredity exists alongside special heredity or to cite cytoplasmic mechanisms alongside chromosomes and the DNA spirals. General heredity raises the same problem as the organization of the genome, and at every level, too.

It will be said, in reply to this, as we ourselves shall do later, that there is no transmission, properly speaking, from organization and autoregulation. What there is amounts to continuation in the form of dynamism, surviving as such because it never stops functioning. If this seems obvious, however, it is because there is a functioning which constitutes the necessary condition for the individual structures—a theory loaded with consequences because it implies functioning rather than static and atomistic structures. In this case, functioning implies continuous exercise, and to speak of exercise necessitates going beyond the idea of hereditary programming. In fact, the logical conclusion is that three factors are necessary to the make-up of a complete system: hereditary programming, which controls the detail of structures; environment, which begins interacting with structures during ontogenetic development and thus reacts to the regulations of the genome; and equilibration, or autoregulation, which controls functions. This is carried through from one generation to the next and coordinates the two preceding factors.

Thus, classical mutationism does not only leave out of account the soma or environment as cause of, or reaction to, the regulations of the genome throughout development; it also leaves out of account, in its very own field of internal structures, the functional and permanent organization which is the necessary condition of every hereditary transmission as soon as the genome is seen as a dynamic entity and no longer as a little collection of motionless particles.[23]

But the notion of selection itself inevitably requires the same dialectic revisions. In the case of mutationism, selection is a one-way process; the organism survives or undergoes variation, and the environment only intervenes insofar as the organization makes a once-and-for-all choice among the complete results offered by it.

---

23. In other words, if there are two distinct problems of interaction—interaction between the parts and the whole, and interaction between endogenetic factors and environment—it will sooner or later become impossible to keep them apart. We shall be returning to this in section 19, subsections 4–9.

In fact, as Waddington has demonstrated by referring back to Lamarck on this point, organisms make choices and transform their environment in terms of their behavior patterns, and in this respect it is the environment that is selected by the organism, which gives us the reverse of the previous process. More than that, the organism selects its aliment, and, in the initial metabolism of the genome and the choice by the regulatory genes of their external inductors to the nucleus, aliment is being selected by internal structures. Selection, therefore, is not just a one-way process, and the choice of endogenetic variations by the environment is simply another link in the vast circuit involved in the notion of interactions.

To sum up, mutationist interpretations founded merely on the two factors of chance and selection have all the symmetry of the Lamarckian interpretations, but, by reversing the Lamarckian, they simply complement them without destroying them, leaving the same kind of gaps as those they were supposed to fill. It thus goes without saying that a synthesis had to be made, not, of course, in the sense of reconciling the irreconcilables, but going beyond them by means of new ideas about growth and organization, and biological causality in general. Hereditary series in the environment-organism series, or vice versa, had to be replaced by circular interactions or cybernetic causality that would take into account both the original activity of the structures and their mutual dependence when in contact with environment.

5. Apriorism and Conventionalism

The translation of classical neo-Darwinian mutationism into terms of cognitive functions is of great interest, first, because it was suggested by certain biologists themselves, and, second, because the theoretical shakiness evidenced by the school which vacillates between preformation and chance in the realm of variations of the organism is just as apparent in the psychological and epistemological theories which, centering on the subject, vacillate in their turn between apriorist preformation and the conventional idea of chance.

Classical mutationism sees the genome as a collection of little particles, containing the whole future but disturbed sometimes by sudden variations which have unforeseeable results. Genes remain normal; so they are naturally seen from the preformist angle. Having no regulatory activities, they are still not thought to be renewing themselves constantly and preserving themselves by autocorrection throughout a number of transformations; they are simply there, and in them are to be found all the static characteristics of future generations. As for variations, they are supposed to be either nocuous and thus the result of chance, or else adaptive, and here there are various lines of thought: most writers still say that variations are adaptive by chance, or, if they are successful, it is because they were an original part of the genome's virtualities and are an extension of the normal characteristics, which simply takes us back to preformation. In a word, either classical neo-Darwinism attributes every new phenomenon to chance (including, by way of generalization from that, the entire past, though that has been crystallized into future preformation schemata if it still persists after selection) or it ends up by denying evolution in favor of preformism (Bateson, etc.).

The knowledge and intelligence theories which accentuate the subject as opposed to objects undergo exactly the same oscillations. Pure, generalized performation is Kantian apriorism: the subject is equipped with categories or varied "forms" (causality, space, etc.), which make their impression on experience by virtue of being previously established conditions. Even if the subject discovers or becomes conscious of them only through experience (a process which permits of ontogenetic development of variable duration) it does not draw this experience from them but organizes it by means of certain structures, previously virtual. The proof put forward by Kant is that such structures are "necessary," whereas an experimental fact is simply given "for what it is" (to use a famous phrase) and is not necessary at all.

We saw (in section 5, subsection 1) that Konrad Lorenz, who is both neo-Darwinian and Kantian (a consistent position in principle) believes, in his field of the instincts and the "hereditary sign-stimuli" (IRM = innate releasing mechanism), in the existence of innate knowledge. Being a neo-Darwinian, he interprets these as having an endogenous origin without acquired heredity (as Lamarck and Waddington understand it). So he tells us that they are a priori forms in the Kantian sense and comparable to the a priori categories that are to be found, according to him and Kant, in human thought. We are presented here, then, with an example of explicit translation, furnished by the biologist himself, from mutationism into terms of Kantian apriorism.

There is, however, one difficulty, which the neo-Kantians have certainly recognized where scientific thinking is concerned: the question of necessity. In the biological field there is nothing biologically necessary about instincts, since they vary from one species to another, and there are no instincts common to all the species except, maybe, the preservation of life, which, lacking special organs, has nothing specifically instinctive about it, whatever people say, and is merely a functional continuation. In the field of scientific knowledge, some kinds of reasoning are logically necessary at any given level, but no structure category is necessary, since causality, space, time, etc., have all been modified in the course of history.

Lorenz gets out of this problem by giving a very interesting interpretation (but one which would certainly have scandalized Kant himself—his old Königsberg colleague, as he used to call him when he was living in that city): slipping over, without seeming to realize it, from apriorism to conventionalism, Lorenz simply suggests that a priori forms are "hereditary work hypotheses," which means that they are innate but not necessary! So there is one variety of epistemological theory to find its place in the collection of solutions that have fanned out from the apriorist notion of preformation.

The next stage is conventionalism, which is the formal counterpart of the notion of chance mutations (in other words, endogenous but still not necessary). The proof of the epistemological relationship between conventionalism and apriorism is that there are some scholars who actually support both theories, according to the contents or fields under consideration. It was in this way that the great mathematician Henri Poincaré saw the notion of "group," notably in geometry, as being the expression of a synthetic a priori judgment in the Kantian sense. But the question of knowing if physical space is Euclidian or not remained a pure question of convention for him. It is true that the reasons for this choice between possible conventions were not, in Poincaré's case, purely arbitrary or haphazard:[24] for him, they were dependent on questions of convenience, which is an argument halfway between the work hypothesis, as Lorenz understands it, and pure convention.

In the case of Rougier, on the other hand, logic itself is nothing but a linguistic convention—a forced convention, since no other choice is available, but not a rationally necessary one, rather as

24. It should be remembered that it was probably his conventionalism that caused Poincaré to miss discovering the theory of relativity, a thing he came near to doing.

though nature had imposed this particular mutation on mankind by chance, as she does the color of hair and eyes. For Rougier, of course, there is nothing innate about logic. But, to extend the lines laid down by mutationists in their ideas about chance, it is clear that our brain, our logic, and mutationism itself are the products of random combinations selected more or less roughly in terms of the success obtained.

However, although there may be some parallelism between the range of solutions contained in the mutationist approach—between the ideas of preformation and random variation and the series of epistemological solutions that lead us, in the field of knowledge analysis, from integral apriorism to pure conventionalism—the interesting aspect of this parallelism is not that it is complete. The main interest lies in the fact that the convergence between analogous modes of thought and modes of posing a problem leads to similar difficulties, and for the same reasons. In both cases, the first reason is that the organism or subject cannot be dissociated absolutely from the environment or objects, and the second reason is that the essential endogenous factors consist, not of ready-made or static structures, but of an organizing and constructive function which is revealed by the elaboration of certain structures of a variable kind (and which, as we shall see, are perpetually outstripping themselves by means of certain vections).

Now in the field of knowledge, where analysis bearing only on the stages of postnatal development and on the historic (not prehistoric) stages of collective thought, these two reasons become one and the same. Logico-mathematical structures, for example, are neither preformed to the point of being completed structures within the subject, nor drawn from the surrounding objects. In their initial stages they presuppose a whole phase of actions upon objects and of experiences in the course of which objects are indispensable. However, this does not mean that such structures are drawn from the objects themselves, for they are built up by means of operational abstract elements from the actions of the subject upon objects, not from objects themselves, as well as from coordinations among actions, which are progressive and necessary from the outset. In this way we are presented with an organizing and regulatory function, which apriorism wrongly tried to translate into instantly complete structures, forgetting that their construction cannot be realized without a whole complex of interactions between subject and objects, during which the reactions of the objects constitute the opportunity for (but not the cause of) formatory regulations.

As for the part played by random or haphazard convention, it goes without saying that, as development proceeds, it is proportionately reduced as the stages are passed in which trial and error (on the model of chance variations and selection after the event) constitute the normal method, and the stages are reached in which deductive coordination predominates.

6. Waddington's Tertium Quid and "Progress" according to Julian Huxley

Opinions about the relations between organism and environment are at the present time in a state of crisis. New ways of thinking brought about by cybernetics are at war with the weighty traditions of atomist and preformist mutationism. However, beneath all the hesitancy, the retreats, the leaps forward, certain tendencies may be discerned which are highly instructive for us in our attempts to draw some parallel between biological problems and solutions and epistemological interpretations.

Striking, at this juncture, is the fact that no alternative presents itself: it is not a question of choosing between purely endogenous variations (from preformation to haphazard mutation) and selection after the event on the one hand, and environmental influence and automatic hereditary fixation on the other. On the contrary, there is actually an attempt to find a tertium quid such as may bypass the two antithetic terms. This tertium quid would consist, not of verbal solutions such as finalism and the many forms of vitalism, but of an attempt to set up intelligible models, all founded on the notions of organization or relational totality and of regulations or cybernetic causality.

Cybernetics itself is based on two central notions about information and direction, or autocontrol. Schmalhausen, in his 1960 book on the foundations of the evolutionary process by which cybernetics has been brought to light, speaks of autoregulation in connection with all the problems of the original forms of this evolution, the strongest section of the book being that concerned with these initial organizations. But in every case relating to the ulterior relations between environment and organism and the main factors of evolution, he is thinking essentially in terms of "information," and one might even say that his position is one of systematic atomism, with mutations unshakably conceived as random, and environmental influence on development conceived as mere "noises"!

Waddington, on the other hand, was the first to offer what one can really call a synthesis, when he distinguished, within the evolutionary system, four main subsystems, each of which contains its own regulations which are, nevertheless, inextricably linked to one another by an overall system of cybernetic circuits: (1) the genetic system, (2) the epigenetic system, (3) the utilization of environment, and (4) the actions of natural selection.

The genetic system, with its characteristics of organized totality and autoregulation which need not be further elaborated here, is linked to the epigenetic system by a collection of feedback circuits. Though the first is the source of the second and directs its course throughout development, nevertheless the second reacts upon the first, at the core of the normal period,[25] but also in proportion as reinforcements or obstacles arising from environment during ontogenesis have the effect of activating or inhibiting any particular aspect of this development. The epigenetic system, in its turn, controls the utilization of the environment, but it is also partially dependent on it, since environment necessarily intervenes in the formation of the phenotype. The phenotype, for its part, controls the utilization of the environment as long as it is dependent on it, since the organism chooses its environment and transforms it simultaneously. Last, we have the action of selection, but this is directed exclusively to phenotypes insofar as the latter represent "responses" made by the genotype to the instigations of its environment. Since selection never acts in an exclusive way but normally has the effect of producing changes in proportion and restructurations in the factors of the genetic pool and then of the genomes, the latter will react in the course of succeeding generations by means of genetic regrouping (much more important than simple mutations), and so the whole cycle goes on.

To put it another way, whereas Lamarckism saw in the germen an instrument which simply registered somatic modifications with a view to hereditary transmission, and mutationism considered this genome the sole source of preformation or chance variations, Dob-

---

25. See in this connection figure 6 in *The Strategy of the Genes*, where the substance X produced by the *as, cs,* and *es* is seen to be activating in its turn the gene b, which itself produces the substance Y with a and d, and in which the substance P is seen to be produced by f and g and itself to activate h, etc.

zhansky and then Waddington finally came to see it as an active system of "responses" and reorganizations, confronting the environment but not influenced by it, yet utilizing the information it offers rather than ignoring it or imposing its own program on it. This, then, is the novelty of Waddington's tertium quid, bypassing theses which had previously been considered antithetic, and this is why we can henceforth think of the three main currents in evolutionary thinking as Lamarckism, neo-Darwinism, and the new ideas emerging from cybernetics.

Another novelty not to be overlooked in present-day thought, one which originated not with Waddington but with Julian Huxley in his "synthetic theory,"[26] is the recurrence of the notion of progress in the scientific study of evolution. The early generations of evolutionists were naturally inclined to consider the succession of phylogenetic stages as characterizing a "progression" up to the human species, but they could not see clearly enough those objective elements which would have made it possible to speak of vection or direction (in the mathematical sense of the word and with no sense of finality) and of the subjective or anthropomorphic values which confer upon this idea of vection a significance that is purely relative to human evaluations. It was this sort of reasoning that made one present-day biologist say that if a bird could give an account of evolution, evolution would be a very different tale. So of course there was a reaction, allied to mutationism, in the shape of theories that attributed evolution to pure chance, with selection of the fittest, but with the higher types of mammal in no way regarded as better adapted to their environment than the Coelentera or parasitic worms are to theirs. Now, with Huxley, Simpson, and the rest, we are once again having to face the problem of setting up such degrees of organization as will enable us to establish some objective and independent hierarchy, untainted by any value judgment. Huxley and some others talk, in this connection, of "progress," whereas Haldane still holds the view that such a notion is unacceptable and subjective. It is purely a question of definition, but definition of a genuine problem, and it seems preferable in what follows to do as Haldane does

---

26. J. Huxley, *Evolution, the Modern Synthesis* (London, 1942), and *Evolution in Action* (London, 1953). See also I. I. Schmalhausen, *Factors in Evolution* (Philadelphia, 1949), chap. 4, etc.; G. G. Simpson, *The Meaning of Evolution* (New Haven, 1950), chap. 15; and F. Meyer, *Problématique de l'évolution* (Paris, 1954), p. 155, etc.

and avoid this ambiguous word "progress." We shall therefore speak only of "vection," for, if one agrees with Huxley that biological progress is both "inevitable" and "unpredictable," it is precisely these two qualities which characterize what has been called "vection" (since Lalande introduced the term) in the domain of the evolution of reasoning power.

This being understood, the problem is to find some objective criteria for a hierarchy of types of organization, in other words, for evolutive vection. Simpson's idea is increase in mass, but that is obviously inadequate when one considers how many species have become extinct by reason of their huge size. Huxley then invokes the idea of "dominant" groups at a particular paleontological period and interprets the succession of dominant features as a criterion of progress. But, if adaptation is to be defined as the survival of the fittest, it is begging the question to rely on numerical dominance as a criterion of the best kind of adaptation. The analysis must be carried much farther, into the internal criteria of adaptation. Huxley makes a notable advance in analysis by suggesting a two-way process: increasing control by the organism over its environment, and gradual independence of the organism from its environment. Claude Bernard had already demonstrated the progressive independence which arises from stability of internal environment, and in this connection we must not forget the very interesting "biochemical orthogeneses" pointed to by Florkin (*L'évolution bio-chimique*). But undoubtedly the best criterion is that of increasing "opening," an idea first put forth by Rensch. This "opening" is taken to mean an increase in the possibilities acquired by the organism in the course of evolution, and from this standpoint analyses in biological progress naturally end up, without any recourse to value judgments, by regarding knowledge a necessary final achievement, in that it multiplies the field of these possibilities.

However, good method demands that the study of criteria not be left hanging in the air but be based firmly on the study of their formatory mechanisms; that criteria be studied in their internal evolution, not as suprahistorical factors (to use C. Nowinski's perceptive expression when he speaks of the comprehensive usage of the notion of selection in early Darwinian thinking). If, as in current thinking, all the central mechanisms of evolution are regarded as both the cause and the effect of evolution (the genetic system, the epigenetic system, etc., up to and including selection itself and not forgetting environment, which is as much shaped by the organism as the organism is determined and directed by the environment), and if, like Waddington, we are to envisage every biological subsystem as being both autoregulatory and allied to all other subsystems by cybernetic circuits, then it is self-evident that this "vection," the criteria of which are gradually emerging, must be seen within the framework of progressive equilibration.

The problem thus takes shape, so that we can separate the contradictory elements, some apparent, some real, in what we might be tempted to use as criteria, and in what, in actual fact, are accounted for by the varying models that have been set up of the succession of disequilibria and reequilibrations. With a physical model, or a thermodynamic one, or even a quantum one in mind, we speak of an aging process in life or a progressive arrest in evolution, the mutations diminishing in something like quantum "leaps." But if we choose mobile equilibrium models and equilibrium displacements, with autoregulatory models that make opening and relative stability compatible, a slowing-down in genetic variability, such as seems to be the case with man, is seen to be not at all incompatible with the opening of behaviors, this opening being solidary with an anterior vection in cerebralization.

The main questions, then, which confront us when dealing with these original and exciting new concepts in biology, fram Waddington's cybernetics in the field of environment-organism interactions, to Huxley's "synthetic" theories about vection problems, are how to reconcile them with psychogenetic and epistemological data.

But, in dealing with questions like this, we are no longer faced with a simple parallelism between historical and partly outmoded points of view; we are in the front line, or at least in the marching wing, of continuing research. So we must leave until chapters 4 and 6 the discussion in depth, not only of the relations between types of biological, psychological, or epistemological knowledge, but also of the connections between the organism as source of the subject, and intelligence or the thinking subject in general.

Nevertheless, there are two comments which must be made, even at this stage, on the first of these two topics (thus working along the lines of chapter 3), which will serve as a sort of introduction to the full examination in chapters 4 and 6.

The first is the striking analogy between the ways of thought and of posing problems exemplified by a man like Waddington and the tentative interpretations now given by researchers in psychology and so-called genetic epistemology (genetic insofar as related to ontogenetic and historical growth generally[27]). There are, in effect, two dominant ideas in Waddington's style of biology, which draws heavily on "population genetics." The first is the idea of a relational totality, in which none of the concepts or subsystems contemplated may intervene in any independent or absolute way, since they are constantly thought of as being interdependent. The second is a historicism so radical that neither the environment (which is "chosen" and constantly modified by the organism, so much so that it sets up "ecological niches" dependent on it as well as on the external world) nor selection of various types (such as have a bearing on phenotypes at every stage in their growth) can avoid this combined movement, any more than can the epigenotype or the genome itself. Now, these are in the very forms of conceptualism that appertain to research in the development of knowledge; the object is supposed to be enriched by the subject, as the environment is by the organism, at the same time as the subject is supposed to be elaborating its own structures while producing reactions in the objects, with the result that their interactions preclude any idea of either empiricism or apriorism and favor that of a continuous construction embracing the two aspects of inseparable relational totalities and historical development. The formation of knowledge is thus seen as the history of a progressive organization; so by eliminating any kind of fixity from both object and subject, the explanation of it necessarily lies in the direction of equilibration and autoregulation mechanism, as much in order to link the respective contributions made by subject and objects into one functional totality as to give some meaning to a historicism which, though not radical, is nevertheless peculiar to a construction of norms.

However, if there is a complete parallelism between biogenetic and psychological or epistemogenetic conceptualizations, and if both of them, by reason of the stress they lay on equilibration, are eventually bound to raise the problem of vections, the question then arises whether it is possible to make a comparison between biological and epistemic vections, and this is certainly a question to which we shall have to return (section 22, subsection 3).

27. The term "genetic" was used in this general sense by "genetic psychologists" long before its meaning was restricted to biology.

Section 9. Conclusions: Biological Causality

In recapitulating the entire range of parallelisms or corresponding features between problem and problem, doctrine and doctrine, that we have met in the fields of synchronic notions, diachronic concepts, or interpretations of the relations between organism and environment, we are at once struck by the fact that these parallelisms are becoming closer and closer as research goes on. This is not in the least because of the overlapping that there tends to be between various fields of research—these, on the contrary, are getting more highly differentiated—but because the methods of explanation and the very way in which the problems are now posed are converging ever more closely by virtue of the kinship of the problems.

1. Ways in Which the Problems Are Converging

Of course, if we confine ourselves to the content and form of these notions as such, taking them as static, as it were, and independently of any analysis in depth, we may get the impression that the biological and the cognitive or mental fields used to be much closer to the prescientific or elementary scientific stages than they are now. We may even think there was the same distance between them at every period and that they simply grew closer or farther apart according to the opinions of the day. But the reason for this impression is that primitive biological theories were all psychomorphic or had their origin halfway between animism and spiritualism, giving the illusion of a complete initial union between the cognitive and the biological. Now if there really was a union, it was certainly brought about in a way that distorted both the terms it united. When, at a later stage, biological theories were elaborated on a strictly mechanistic model, the same thing took place with regard to psychogenetic notions and explanations about the formation and functioning of the intelligence, which accounts for the seeming parallelism that is being pushed so far today.

We have only to look at these ideas—taking into account (as was not done before) their degree of adequacy to experience and their transformations in the direction of a power of assimilation constantly being extended toward factual data of which there is a steady accretion—to see at once that biology, always confining itself to its own technical field, and the study of knowledge, working away along its own lines, no doubt in less ignorance of biology than is usually the reverse case but still working quite independently, moved closer together without realizing it. This, let me repeat, was brought about, not by any gradual interpenetration of the two fields or even of any particular concepts, but by a convergence of methods in their broadest application and of ways of conceptualizing in their overall intellectual strategy in the face of what are, in effect, parallel problems.

To put it briefly, biological causality has evolved gradually—"causality" here meaning the whole range of explanatory ideas used by the biologist in his search for the reason behind the laws he is observing—and this causality has evolved, unconsciously and, above all, unintentionally, in a direction that constantly increases the possibility of isomorphism between structures discovered in the course of observation or ways in which these are transformed, and the structures or transformations identified in their own fields by specialists in those problems which concern the elaboration and organization of intellectual development. To put it another way, by working on interactions, regulations, and cybernetic mechanisms, biologists have singled out certain structures and explanatory methods, which, in increasingly specialized fields and—as far as subject matter is concerned—lacking any contact with the experimentation or theoretical analysis of studies of intelligence or knowledge, have nevertheless converged with ideas current, though often very differently expressed, in those very fields.

The reason for this increasing convergence is one of central interest to our argument: in effect, if cognitive mechanisms do constitute the actual organs of regulation during exchanges with environment, which was the hypothesis put forward in section 3 of this book, then it is obvious that any biological interpretation which posits the intervention of autoregulatory processes or cybernetic circuits will eventually establish possible isomorphisms with cognitive structures. We might put it in a more familiar and less precise way by saying that if cybernetic models alone permit us to envisage the possibility of some artificial reconstitution or mechanical and causal imitation of the intelligence at work, then it is obvious that any attempt to use such models in interpreting biological circuits is certain, for that very reason, to establish some analogies between the biological and the cognitive.

It may therefore be useful, by way of conclusion to this chapter, to seek some better understanding of the reasons behind the historical sequences or dialectic triads set out in sections 6–8 in both the biological and the cognitive fields, so as to prepare the way for subsequent discussions concerning the isomorphisms themselves and, above all, concerning the explanation of the cognitive, starting with organic mechanism.

2. Precausality, Chance, and Regulation

The main triad is thus seen to be the one which leads us from those initial explanations, which we shall name precausal, to causal explanations pure and simple, relying on mechanism and the intervention of chance, and finally to those explanations which depend on regulatory interactions.

The term precausal may be applied to any explanation which is merely conceptual and which cannot possibly be based on any algebraic calculation of a general kind (symbolic logic, etc.) or on any experimental verification that involves measurement in the widest sense (ordinal, hyperordinal, or metric). In this sense, the appeal to vital force is precausal, insofar as it obeys none of these criteria, whereas the hypothesis that there is a direct influence exerted by environment, in the Lamarckian sense, has a causal nature, even though it may have been falsified by seemingly reliable statistics.

So it goes without saying that all the early explanations given by biology in its elementary stages could only be precausal, seeing that calculation and actual experiment were then so difficult. It is true that Aristotle's notion of "form" did give rise to some kind of algebraic structure, but this was in terms of logic and the syllogism. As applied to biology, however, the notion merely amounted to an affirmation that any individual carries within himself not only his own differentiated characteristics but also those of his species, type, etc. As for the organization of these various characteristics into an organic whole, an individualized organism functioning as a unified and total system, at that stage the notion of "form" could only supply either the simple statement of this fact or (and this is what Aristotle was working on and where the explanation became precausal) the hypothesis of there being some analogy with the ego, conceived as a "soul" supplied with some kind of unifying and motor power. Precausal explanations, then, are called forth by the need to fill in gaps in calculation or in possible experiment, by means of psychomorphic assimilations.

As progress was made in scientific biology, which was bound to develop at a later stage than deductive and experimental physics, the next attempts to provide causal explanations were naturally based on models drawn from physics. At that stage even Descartes was theoretically generalizing his mechanism concept to apply to the whole field of biology. That the continued search for a mechanistic explanation should have been conducted in Descartes' tradition even by the vitalists when tackling some ill-defined problem (as, for instance, when, according to Canguilhem, they came to study reflexes) has meant that causal biology was bound to evolve along mechanistic lines.

However, the inevitable conflict that was to arise between the needs of the biologist and the mechanistic approach of old-fashioned physics can be explained by the fact that the latter approach is a product of intelligence at grips with problems that are relatively simpler than those of real life, whereas the living organization is much more nearly comparable to the processes which formed intelligence than to the very general structures constructed by intelligence. Consequently, life, under the influence of the classic mechanistic analysis, has lost its functional verity in the minds of many biologists, and organic causality has been split up into an endless multitude of causal sequences seen as both independent of one another and yet all the time interfering with one another. Now interference by independent causal series is nothing but chance, so that eventually these biologists found themselves faced with the paradoxical result that the mechanistic explanation in biology simply amounted to attributing everything to chance—chance in variations, an idea terminating in mutationism, but also chance in selection, in terms of encounters said to be random (rather than "picked" as Waddington is so often right in thinking) between organism and environment.

Thus it became increasingly likely that this mechanistic model, diluted in certain essential points into a sort of integral stochastic one, should give way to other forms of causality which did not leave probabilist preoccupations out of account but included them in more far-reaching models. Physiology, for one thing, and causal embryology, for another, have prepared the way for a rethinking of causality along the lines since followed by cybernetics. This development of causality may be described, by the very details of the phenomena under examination, as an extension of the general idea of organization, seen as a system of transformations arising from one or another cyclic order. In other words, mere lineal causality (even allowing for all those interferences that can be ascribed to chance) has taken a circular path, predictable as soon as autoregulatory systems were discovered.

In physiology, for example, hyperglycemia and hypoglycemia have both now been seen as manifestations of a break in equilibrium between production and consumption of sugar. In the normal state, in fact, the amount of sugar in blood varies neither under the effect of intestinal absorption of sugar containing matter nor during the muscular activity that consumes carbohydrates, nor throughout the fasting period, during which the reserves of glycogen are used up. From this it has been concluded that there is a regulatory mechanism in normal glycemia, which is disturbed by illness, and this hypothesis, though formulated long before it was possible to give any detailed justification of its causal cycle, nevertheless gave rise to the idea of circular structures or feedbacks. In embryology, Driesch's discovery, in 1891, of autonomous growth in separated blastomeres, by extension to partial mechanisms of the general idea of organization originally seen in terms of a single whole, also led to the concept of regulation.

Two developments then became possible: a return to precausal notions, which is what happened in the case of Driesch, or a reelaboration of biological causality in the direction of cyclic order rather than a linear one, of interactions rather than isolable sequences, and finally in the direction of regulations seen as permanent systems and no longer as sporadic events accounted for by mere "displacements in equilibrium." Such displacements certainly occur in physics—for example, in the case of a gas under pressure which catches fire as a result, thus bringing about a change in the original conditions and setting up a new equilibrium. Le Châtelier's principle, to the effect that such displacements tend toward a moderation of the original disturbance, provided the beginnings of a compensation model. But Cannon, when he put forward the notion of homeostasis, went much farther, making the equilibrium of internal environment responsible for cycles, properly so called and hence permanent, which led to a recasting of causal biology.

Thanks to developments in physical and mathematical techniques a significant meeting point was reached when the new biological theories were seen to correspond to servo-mechanisms and autoregulatory machines. In other words, just at the time when biology was freeing itself from its restricting mechanistic ideas, and when some thinkers, confronted with this deficiency in traditional physical causality, were toying with the idea of a return to vitalism and finality, a complete reelaboration of the mechanistic approach opened up new perspectives along lines which corresponded exactly to those notions of circular or feedback systems or of cyclic rather than linear causality. It is well known how, at this juncture, a kind of mechanophysiology was introduced in order to unite the purely biological trend of thought with the new cybernetic one. But what has not been noticed so often is that this linking up of two separate schools of thought thereby made it possible and, sooner or later, even necessary that there should be a convergence between purely biological research, or cybernetic biology, and psychogenetic or epistemological researches into development, since these were already partly logico-cybernetic.

3. Finalism

The evolution of causality in terms of the triad precausality, lineal causality, and cyclic or feedback causality, is comprehensive of each of the other triads that we met with in sections 6–8.

Naturally, the first reaction to them was a development in ideas about finality. The former type of precausal finalism presented two drawbacks from the point of view of intelligibility. First, it explained nothing, for it is not enough to say that a need or an end exists if we are to understand the causal mechanism of the process which allows us to reach a given end; so finality presupposes causality, and is not self-sufficient. Second, to speak of an end as if it implied its own realization without any causal complement leaves the nature of this end undecided; it may be internal, as in the case of the preservation of the individual or the species, or external, as when we talk of conformity with a preestablished plan. Here again, only knowledge of the corresponding causal mechanism will permit us to define the nature of the relationship under consideration: adaptation, functional utility, and so on.

Thus, it is natural that finalism in the sphere of research based on mechanical and physical models should have been ruled out as being an illusory explanation. But the only intelligible response to the particular problems raised by this kind of finalism long consisted merely of notions about chance variations and selection after the event. This was so, at least, among biologists who did not believe in the direct influence of environment on inherited characteristics. Since it is hardly possible to supply calculations on the probability of the occurrence of random formation in an organ that is both differentiated and adapted, and since selection is the explanation of the choice made between given characteristics, but not of their appearance, this explanation remained an academic one, even though the notions employed were clearer than that of a "final cause." Moreover, since the whole strength of the finalists, like that of the vitalists in general, lay in their way of denouncing the doctrinal insufficiencies of their opponents and underlining the gaps in established theories (which allowed them to fill these gaps in some illusory fashion), they found themselves up against the same blank wall as was met with in causality (subsection 2 above).

One reason why autoregulation models were so successful was precisely because they furnished a reply to this annoying problem of finality. Cybernetics, while retaining everything valid in the finalist "description" (we use the term description because, although it made a correct analysis of the questions involved, all explanation of them was lacking), for the time offered a causal explanation—under the title "teleonomy"—of processes that were both set in a certain direction and capable of self-correction, sometimes able to anticipate what was coming and playing a useful part in an organized system, so that they could be summed up as what are recognized by common consent to be finalized systems. To put it another way, we can today retain all that is positive in the idea of finality but at the same time replace the notion of a "final cause" by an intelligible feedback causality.

4. Structure and Genesis

However, it is not solely in synchronic fields that this transformation of opinion in biological causality has made such a deep impression. The change from the concept of transcausal totality (one may now call it precausal) to that of atomism and thence to relational totalities represents thinking that is relative to the various kinds of development studied in biology and to such of their factors as have undergone fundamental modifications.

Taken all together, these ideas (sections 7–8) fluctuated in fact between what might be called a sort of structuralism without genesis and a geneticism without structure, until the two terms of genesis, or development, and structure, in the sense of general structure or relational totality, came finally to be seen as interdependent, that is to say, the one involving the other in a cyclic process.

Structuralism without genesis is the point of view common to all those concepts which preceded the idea of evolution. From Aristotle's "forms" to Cuvier's correlation of organs, all the emphasis is on structures, since transformism is entirely absent. In those fields where there is an obvious development, as, for example, in embryology, the notion of preformation cancels out any idea of genesis that may be contained in a temporal evolution of this kind. All this is self-evident, and we do not need to go back over it again. But what is remarkable and bespeaks the nature of the causality schemata involved is that, even when the idea of evolution had been accepted, various new forms of this static structuralism reappeared alternately with the antithesis of a structureless geneticism. This shows how hard it is to accept the idea that a structure might evolve of its own accord or, to put it more precisely, that an organization might involve two correlative principles, one of preservation throughout a series of transformations and the other of a transformatory construction linked with the very equilibration that assures conservation.

If we are to understand these swings and oscillations in opinion, we must first remember how Lamarckism constitutes the very antithesis of structuralism without genesis, for Lamarck admits a kind of genesis in the shape of some undefined evolution in organisms when subjected to environmental pressure, but does not recognize structures in the sense of organizations of the germen which resist these external influences or else assimilate them by submitting them to previously established internal conditions. In this way, the acceptance of evolution brings about a complete reversal in concepts of causality by introducing a continuous series of transformations, which are guided according to an indicated lapse of time, whereas the sort of causality which comes under the heading of structuralism is centered on notions of compensation and conservation. Indeed, the noteworthy characteristic of Lamarckian causality is that nothing in it is conserved, in biological terms, which certainly does constitute a kind of structureless geneticism (in keeping with the internal logic of all kinds of empiricism). The situation is unchanged with Darwin, for, though adding selection and slight chance variations to the list of inherited characteristics acquired by experience, Darwinian transformism is still nothing but an infinite series of modifications aimed in a certain direction but not necessarily for the purpose of conservation (unless it be for the approximate conservation of species by virtue of occasional and temporary results brought about by acts of selection that can always be modified).[28]

Thus, an underlying conflict opened up between two kinds of causality: one akin to structuralism and satisfactory to traditional thinking because of its emphasis on conservation, the other tending more toward geneticism, which is the kind of meat for dialectic minds because it brings out the historic dimension with given time limits, even though it abandons the rational standpoint taken by the opposite camp. Starting then, there dawned a period during which two diametrically opposed postulates eventually reached some kind of reconciliation, either by simultaneous affirmation accompanied by a demarcation of their respective roles or else by various oscillations. Weismann followed the first method with impeccably rigorous logic: the "soma" is drawn into Lamarckian development, where it evinces the two correlative characteristics of being variable and mortal, whereas the germen is conserved by dint of its permanent structure, its only variations being in the nature of amphimixic combinations according to a combinatorial that does not rule out preformation or conservation of structural elements.

Mutationism, on the other hand, is torn between these two tendencies without ever being able to make a synthesis of them. Theoretically, the genome conserves itself, and even in the atomistic form suggested by the first Mendelian law we find a structure quite independent of environment, which is to say, structuralism without genesis. But mutations are brought about by chance during states of internal disequilibrium or disintegrations caused by radiation. For a long time the sole principle of variation recognized was characterized by a kind of structureless geneticism, since mutation was a matter of chance and amounted to no more than an antistructure.

The crisis brought about by this opposition between structuralism and geneticism as an inevitable outcome of constructive development could only get worse, for conciliation in the form of allowing that there are structures which both conserve themselves and destroy

28. It is true that Darwin often stresses (in his "Notebooks") the "fixed organization" of the adult, but he does this to contrast it with the fact that the environment brings about "permanent" changes (= hereditary ones) in infants because they are still malleable.

themselves would evidence so unstable an equilibrium, not only in the genome but above all in its conceptualization by the theorists, that the conciliation would constitute no real advance in the sense of a synthesis transcending the antitheses.

At last, however, the advance was made, and in the most natural way imaginable—not by invoking, in the abstract, some structuralist geneticism or a developmental structuralism, but by making a root-and-branch generalization, based on the facts themselves, of the double notions of structure or organization and of genesis or development, so as to include the recognition that all development is an organization, and all organization, a development.

The idea that all development is a kind of organization became obvious from the moment that phylogenetic evolution was seen to be partly dependent on embryogenetic growth and on the ontogenetic formation of phenotypes, and not simply the inverse. It took a great embryologist turned geneticist, like Waddington, to make clear, at last, how out of the question it is to explain evolutive variation simply in terms of preformation or chance, ruling out any idea of intervention by environment. As soon as it is recognized that selection is brought to bear only on phenotypes and that, throughout their period of development, all phenotypes continue to be a series of "responses" made by the genome to the tensions set up by the environment, or that the environment is just as much organized by the organism as phenotypic variation is directed by the environment, then it becomes possible to speak of the "cybernetic circuits" discussed in section 8, and development can be seen as a series of organizational ladders, all different and all perpetually subject to cyclic causality.

If we look at the other side of the picture, the fact that any kind of organization is a form of development in itself stands out not only from the ontogenetic and embryological point of view, which is bound to dominate modern biology sooner or later, but also from the fact that the kind of conservation characteristic of an organization is not merely the permanence of a static structure but, more than that, the product of a continuous equilibrium. The genome itself is not merely the fruit of a long history in the course of which it undergoes a thorough transformation, but by reason of its being a synchronic structure it is also the fruit of a metabolic reconstitution which has been uninterrupted throughout successive generations. Above all, the genome is the fountainhead of formatory activities (epigenetic) just as it is of transmissions. The adult organism is in a state of relative equilibrium, but this equilibrium is brought about by regulations which never stop working, and these regulations do not differ fundamentally in their functional nature (independently of all that is involved in the physico-chemical actions coordinated by them) from those which are present in every kind of development.

Thus, the synthesis of structuralism and geneticism toward which we are now moving is brought about by an internal evolution in ideas about biological causality—a coordination between the two demands of conservation and transformation: conservation of structures as a whole, such as may be transformed without losing their identity because these transformations are reequilibrations and because transforming structures are capable (in theory and sometimes in reality) of being integrated into transformed structures derived from them and adding to them.

It is difficult to study the way in which all this has evolved—first structuralism without genesis, then geneticism without structures, and finally structuralist geneticism—without thinking of the growing convergence in various psychogenetic examinations of the intelligence. The first of the three terms corresponds naturally to the concept of intelligence as being given, not developing; the second corresponds to the sort of causality employed by empiricism; and the third corresponds to present-day doctrines about the filiation of structures.

One cannot even retrace the historical evolution of the various forms taken by biological causality without comparing them to the succession of ideas, not only about causality, but about implication itself, or to the connection between propositions and theorems as revealed by the history of mathematical epistemology, in which, however, the accent is all on structure and not on genesis. It is nonetheless true, following the static structuralism of the Greeks, Descartes' theories about "fabricated" ideas (as opposed to innate ones), born of some free operational combination, or again the concepts of the eighteenth century about the empirical origin of mathematics, are all directed toward a discreet sort of geneticism which still contrives to keep integral structuralism in check. The great movement set afoot by Galois and culminating in our present ideas of a genealogy of "structures" (Bourbaki) or in "categories" (McLane, Eisenberg) supplies us, on the contrary—though on a deductive and nontemporal level—with the model of what might be, in terms of the development of intelligence structures, the genetic structuralism toward which all views are tending today.

But we must now leave these historical analogies relative to the knowledge of the biologist and of the epistemologist and get to grips with more direct comparisons between the organism as source of the subject, and the subject of knowledge in general in terms of any one subject and its psychogenetic development.

4 Corresponding Functions and Partial Structural Isomorphisms between the Organism and the Subject of Knowledge

In what follows we shall no longer be dealing with biologists or psychologists vis-à-vis epistemologists, and the question of whether there is any convergence between their ways of working and thinking. Instead, we turn our attention to the organism in the various guises it has assumed currently, although we shall make no prophecies as to what may subsequently be discovered about it. We shall also deal with cognitive functions in such light as experimental research and formalizing analysis may have thrown on them in recent times. This fourth chapter will be seen to be specially relevant to the use of methods 2 and 3, as described in section 5.

Section 10. Functions and Structures

In biology, particular attention is paid to the organs of a function. These may include several different structures according to the group they belong to. Thus, we can speak of the function of breathing and point out that it can be carried out by very different organs (gills, lungs, swimming bladder, or even by some organ that is not differentiated at all) which contain numerous structures. Such a distinction would be meaningless in mathematics, where a function is a structure to itself (that is, the most general sense of the

term, and not in the Bourbakist sense) or in physics, where a structure is described or explained in terms of functions. The distinction
between functions and structures does, on the other hand, occur in
all the psycho-sociological fields in the same sense as in biology,
particularly in the concrete development of intelligence or knowledge. For instance, one can speak of an explanation function,
applicable at all levels of thought, while at the same time noting
that the various conceptual organs, or structures, used to this end
vary considerably from one level to another (from magical or
animist causality to the many forms of scientific causality, including
statistical or probabilistic ones). The very posing of the problem
in view of the comparisons that will follow—in other words, the
distinguishing of functions and structures in the study of possible
isomorphisms between organism and subject of knowledge—will
of itself constitute a primary kind of "formal homology," hence an
early isomorphism of a very general kind seem as the framework
for more specific isomorphisms.

But in this case it behooves us to make clear exactly what this
distinction is and to supply such definitions as will enable us to
carry out a satisfactory analysis.

1. Definition of Structures

A structure contains, in the first place, certain unifying elements and
connections, but these elements cannot be singled out or defined
independently of the connections involved. Even in the case of
simple aggregates, looked at as structures of atomist composition,
their elements cannot be taken as given independently of their connections (meeting place, spatial disposition); otherwise there would
be no structure. Such elements may be of very different kinds: chemical bodies, energy quantities, kinematic or dynamic processes in the
case of biological structures; and perceptions, memories, concepts,
operations, etc., in the case of cognitive ones. The connections may,
in the same way, consist of all kinds of links: spatio-temporal,
causal, implicatory, etc., according to whether the structures are
organic or cognitive, and, even more important, according to
whether they are static or dynamic (for example, anatomic or figurative, regulatory or homeorhesic, and so on).

In the second place, structures defined in this way may be considered independently of the elements that go to make them up.
That is not to say that they can exist in such a condition (except

in the case of the "abstract" structures of a mathematician); but, while abstracting the composite elements, one can still have a picture of the structure as a "form" or system of connections, and the recognition of this fact is essential to our comparisons because it is the principle underlying every isomorphism.

In the third place, there exist some structures of various logical "types"; that is to say, one must be prepared to envisage structures of structures, and so forth. For example, one can start from the structure of the skeleton in each vertebrate class, which will give us five structures in what we shall call type 1. But one can also, like Etienne Geoffroy Saint-Hilaire, single out "connections" between the organs, which will lead to what Owen called "homologies" and, thus, to a type 2 structure of a more general kind than the first (by homologically combining the wings and hind members or the coracoid bone of the bird with the coracoid process fused to the human scapula, or the hyoid bone of the fish with the ossicle from the inner ear of a mammal, and so forth). In the same way, turning to the cognitive domain, one can look at some particular classifications as a type 1, build up from that the general structure of qualitative classifications (type 2), and, by comparing this structure to seriations, etc., deduce from that an even more general structure of "grouping" (type 3), and so on. It is, of course, the higher "type" of structures that we shall attempt to compare, as between the organic and the cognitive domains, for isomorphism would not amount to anything with respect to the countless lower "types."

In the fourth place, it will be stated that an isomorphism does exist between two structures if some bi-univocal connection can be established between their elements, as well as between the links that bind them together, which retains the significance of those links. Since an abstraction can be made of these elements and their nature, any isomorphism between two structures therefore amounts to recognizing the existence of one structure, but a structure pertaining to two different collections of elements.

As for the notion of partial isomorphism, this was discussed in section 5, subsection 3, and it is therefore unnecessary to reiterate the precautions to be taken against it.

In the fifth place, we shall give the name substructure to any sector or part of an organized whole which may or may not present some isomorphism with the total structure: for example, the structure of the stomach by relation to that of the digestive tract, or the structure of the inverse operation by relation to a "group" structure. So it is important not to confuse a substructure (using this terminology) with a structure of some lower "type" or with one of the structures involved in an isomorphism (although a substructure may be, in some cases, isomorphic to a total structure, as a "subgroup" by relation to a mathematical "group").

2. Functioning and Function

Since structures may be static or dynamic, it is possible, in the latter case, to speak of the activation or of the activity of a structure. We shall use the term "functioning" to describe such activity.

As for the term "function," it is often used in the sense of an organized group of structures together with their functioning. It is according to this common usage that we speak of "cognitive function" or that the term "symbolic function," etc., is used. Elsewhere the term is taken in a sense that is almost synonymous with that of functioning. On the other hand, in the expression "the function creates the organ," the word takes on a significance which is both more specialized and more distinct from that of structure, since function and structure may then be opposed.

Taken in this precise sense, in which we shall be using the term in this chapter, function is the action exerted by the functioning of a substructure on that of a total structure, whether the latter be itself a substructure containing the former or the structure of the entire organism. We shall be speaking, for example, of the function of gastric juice in the process of digestion; or of the function of breathing as common to all living creatures, which will lead us to inquire whether creatures capable of assimilation (a still wider function) but not of breathing, such as viruses, still belong to the class of living creatures.

Three complements must be added to this definition, however. First, the action of functioning in a substructure will only correspond to a function if such action is "normal," that is, useful in preserving or maintaining the structure of which the substructure is a part; for example, when an excess of gastric juice or its pathological alteration are no longer playing a functional role in their effect on the total structure.

Second, if the term function is no longer applied to a specified substructure such as gastric juice but to a collection of possible substructures, all differing, as when one speaks of the "function of breathing," function here refers not only to one particular group of actions but to a whole class of analogous actions, virtual as well as actual and all equally subordinate to the criterion of what is normal or useful as concerns the conservation of the total structure.

Third, if the condition of what is normal or useful is attached to the idea of function, this means that function can have meaning only within an organization context.[1] Thus, one may speak of the organization "function" (as opposed to particular organization structures or to those general laws of which we are still ignorant, which are characteristic of every organization structure). But since, in biology, there is no such thing as action without interaction, one can extend the preceding definition by saying that, if specialized functions consist of actions exerted by the function of a substructure on that of a total structure, then the organization function in its turn is the action (or the class of actions) exerted by the functioning of the total structure on that of the substructures contained in it.

The distinction between function and structure may seem, at first, to be faint, since there is no function without a structure—the fact on which we base our definition. To say, as Lamarck did, that the function creates the organ (which does, at least, remain true at the phenotypic level) is to underline the fact that a functioning reinforces development and, at the early stages, the very differentiation of an organ, though always on the basis of an earlier structure. So we may ask ourselves what makes the distinction necessary, especially in connection with the comparisons which we shall be drawing.

The decisive reason is, as everyone knows, that one and the same organ—hence, a substructure—may change its function (as witness the swimming bladder of dipnoans, which assumes the role of a lung,[2] and, moreover, as has just been said, the same function may be carried out by a great number of different organs. This is, in fact, the general rule: one large function corresponding to a multiplicity of structures. So the notion of function is theoretically as wide as that of structure, and there are cleavages between the two notions which are followed immediately by readjustments.

1. In the current sense of the term, function is used to designate the class of useful actions in a substructure, the class described as "comprehension" by reference to an organized system.

2. Modern biochemistry, moreover, stresses the fact that one and the same structure may fulfill very different functions.

The difficulty, however, is to determine how functions may be compared to one another, and whether the term functional isomorphism can be used in an analogous sense to the way it is used in defining an isomorphism between structures. In one sense it can, but the "elements" of a function are the structures it uses, and, in the case of a common function carried out by different organs, there is no term-by-term parallel between the elements, for they present no structural isomorphism at all. So we must support the theory that functional correspondence—to abandon the word isomorphism—rests solely on the term-by-term correspondence between the dynamic relationships characteristic of the "role" of the organ, that is to say, its functioning as a substructure in relation to the functioning of the total structure.

We are thus admitting that in a comparison between total structure B_1 and total structure B_2 there is a "correspondence" between the function of the substructure A_1 in relation to B_1 and the function of the substructure A_2 in relation to B_2, if the relations intervening in the functioning of A_1 and A_2 correspond to each other term by term in their action on the functioning of B_1 and B_2. In this very general sense we may therefore make a functional comparison of the part played by the two regulatory mechanisms in widely different structures, insofar as they both have the final effect of reinforcing or inhibiting some activity in proportion to the result immediately preceding. In this case, the structures may well be distinct, not only with regard to their content or their elements (such as a regulation of blood plasma or a sensorimotor activity with gropings and retroactive control) but also with regard to their structural relations (the difference between the various feedbacks of the system), though the possibility of some functional analogy or "correspondence" is not thereby ruled out.

Biologists, in fact, often find it useful to use such functional comparisons. When, for example, they talk of "memory" in order to designate the conservation of information in some elementary organism, it is clear that this comparison is primarily of a functional kind such as is bound to precede any attempt to establish a structural isomorphism with the memory of invertebrates equipped with a nervous system and, to an even greater extent, with that of vertebrates with developed cerebrums. And yet it is clear that the terms involved in "conservation of some former experience modifying subsequent behavior" have a meaning, but it is a meaning that is instructive insofar as it is very much wider than that of structural homologies and may determine what direction the latter take.

There are two reasons of a purely biological kind for comparing functions before proceeding to structural correspondences. First, as the example of memory shows once again, function may be much more general than structures, since a series of structures of growing complexity may fulfill the same invariant function. This very invariance of the more general functions constitutes one of the most remarkable phenomena of life, in view of the continuous and irreversible flow of evolutive processes. The existence of invariants is actually less surprising in physics, since time has less effect on it than on causal sequences. It is true that these invariants do sometimes take a surprising form, such as the conservation of energy in spite of its degradation in thermodynamics, or the conservation of impulsive force (not to mention the more "empirical" conservations of quantal numbers, such as charge, spin, or even "strangeness coefficient"!) in spite of periodic disintegration in microphysics. But such degradations or disintegrations are merely partial processes which leave other structures unchanged, whereas in life everything is perpetual movement, including those very structures which follow one another irreversibly during evolution while their main functions remain unchanged—a fact which constitutes their central interest. In the second place, the distinctiveness of biological structures lies in their being dynamic in themselves, which is to say that they contain a "functioning," an idea that would have little meaning in physics. So much so that present-day anatomists study everything within the framework of these very functions.[3] Bertalanffy, in his essays on general biology, is constantly insisting on the fact that, where living things are concerned, there are no "rigid forms" independent of processes: "We must therefore look for some primary order in organic processes, not within preestablished structures, but within these processes themselves" (*Les problèmes de la vie* [Gallimard, 1961], p. 35). In another context he says that the forms of organization are not the origin of functional processes but only their support; thus, he conceives of a sort of "dynamic morphology" (*Probleme einer dynamischen Morphologie, IV: Biologia generalis*, 15, 1941), which is a generalization in some ways of old Lamarckian concepts such as Cope's "kinetogenesis." It is enough

3. For example, Benninghoff starts off from "functional systems" such as locomotion with bones, muscles, nerves, etc.

to say that, even without going so far as the old "function creates the organ" formula, in the sense that functions without supports could be envisaged, functional analysis represents the essential framework which must be set up before any structural analysis.

In our problem, a fortiori, there can be no question of investigating structural isomorphisms until we have examined the functional correspondences which alone can endow them with an acceptable meaning.

3. General and Special Functions of Knowledge

If, in the structural sphere, we are already aware that the isomorphisms will only be "partial" (section 5, subsection 3), in the sense that a more primitive structure only possesses some features in common with any more highly evolved one that may arise from it, this will be all the more true when we come to functional correspondences, although in a different way.

It is, in fact, obvious that if the functions characterizing cognitive mechanisms were exactly the same as the main functions of the organism in general, knowledge would contain no particular function of its own, which, in turn, would have two equally ridiculous consequences: either intelligence is already present at every level of organic life, or else it introduces nothing new and so contains no functional reason for development.

In the master hypothesis developed in section 3 we put forward the contrary supposition: that cognitive mechanisms constitute both the resultant of general autoregulatory processes in the living organization and are also specialized regulatory organs in exchanges with environment. If there is a good foundation for this hypothesis, as we shall seek to prove in the present and following chapters, it will mean that, from the functional point of view, certain general functions common to both organic and cognitive mechanisms do exist, but that, in the case of cognitive mechanisms, a progressive specialization of functions also exists.

The lines along which our research will proceed are thus clearly laid out. Where function is concerned, it will be a question, in each sector, or deciding which functions are common to both organic and cognitive mechanisms, and what the specific functions and specializations are that belong to the latter. After which, and keeping within such a functional framework as alone is likely to bring out the significance of the structures under comparison, we shall have to undertake the study of structural correspondence, guided by the following considerations, which are the direct outcome of findings with respect to the invariance of the main functions and the variability of structures.

In comparing an elementary organic structure such as an "anticipation" during morphogenesis (for example, the appearance of some callosity in an ostrich embryo well before its coming into contact with the environment or before it can have made any functional use of it), and the corresponding cognitive structures (deductive foresight of what will be the consequences of an event before it happens), one finds, first, all sorts of intermediary stages between these two extremes. For example, there are morphological anticipations during the development of a phenotype (the growth of an adventitious root on the branch of a plant while the branch is still in the air and has not touched the ground or broken away from the parent plant); or there are sensorimotor anticipations (adjustment of bodily position when balance is slightly disturbed, anticipating the fall that would result should the unbalance increase), etc. Second, in examining what there is in common between these different reactions, one finds a certain number of mechanisms which are more or less general: anticipation depends on information previously supplied which alone can explain its happening. Such information is usually part of a schema or organization such as may transfer itself from one situation to another (by some hereditary means, by transfer of an organism from one area to another, or by generalization, etc.).

Thus, two possibilities arise concerning the parenthood or filiation of such partially isomorphic structures: either there is a direct, lineal descent such as will, for example, permit the cognitive processes to draw from the organism certain ready-made anticipatory mechanisms and translate these into behavior of an intentional and conscious kind; or else there is a series of reconstructions such as allow anticipatory mechanisms to be set up at every level of development according to analogous formation processes. It can be seen at once that in this particular case only the second solution can possibly stand.

This interpretation, whereby a necessary reconstruction takes place from one level to the next in partially isomorphic structures, is certainly not without interest, for at the very least it expresses a certain affinity in functioning, having to do with the general laws governing organization, the conservation of previous information, the way in which it is applied, and its eventual generalization.

More especially (as we shall see in section 20, subsection 6), this stage-by-stage reconstruction, with extension and increasing mobility at every one of these stages by relation to those preceding it, indicates some highly generalized laws of development. The ontogenetic formation of the intelligence includes a series of stages (see section 2), each one of which has its origin in a reconstruction, on a new level, of structures built up during the preceding one, and this reconstruction is necessary to the later constructions which will advance beyond the former level. In biological terms, each generation repeats the development of the preceding one, and new phylogenetic variations, as they appear during ontogenesis, extend this reconstruction of the past. The fact that there are points of convergence (the eye of cephalopods resembling that of vertebrates, etc.) shows just how far these reconstructions, on which progressions are dependent, can go, and in those cases where one family comes to occupy all the "ecological niches" in some new and isolated territory such convergencies reach an amazing kind of isomorphism in differentiations; various related branches of the bird family Drepanididae, in the Hawaiian islands, produce beaks of very varied forms corresponding to those that are a distinctive feature of very different families on the nearby mainland.

Briefly then, while these functional correspondences we are going to talk about will supply some indication of effective continuity in functioning, the structural isomorphisms that we may single out will not necessarily be a proof of direct or lineal filiation. Rather, they are likely to be a disjointed series of convergent reconstructions, which will, moreover, be much more interesting as far as relations between life and the cognitive functions are concerned.

Section 11. Functions and Structures of the Organization

All manifestations of life, whatever they may be and at whatever level, give evidence of the existence of organizations. The adult organism is far from being alone in this. Embryological development is a progressive organization; the processes of fertilization bear witness to an amazing organization; the genome is an organized system and in no sense of the word a mere collection of assembled elements;

reactions to environment are relative to organization, and evolution itself makes use of chance only as it is manifested in progressive organizations. These cells are organized; living bodies of the most elementary kind are, too; and when macromolecules are submitted to subjacent biochemical processes, the stages of another organization are manifested.

So we can speak of an organization function, but only at the risk of its being confused with life itself. Nevertheless we have to express it thus when contrasting the continuity of organizing functioning with the endless diversity of structural organization forms. To keep within the terms of our original definition (section 10, subsection 2) we might then say that the organization function is the functioning of a structure, even a total structure, but one which we are taking as a substructure in relation to the one which immediately follows it, including the case where there is continuity and complete automorphism between them. Or, to put it more simply still, if a function may be said to be the action exerted by the functioning of a substructure on that of the total structure, it can be maintained, as has been seen, that, by reciprocation, organization as a function is the action of the entire functioning on that of the substructures.

1. Continuity and Conservation

The essential fact concerning this functioning is, in effect, its absolute continuity. As we emphasized earlier (section 8, subsection 4), the transmission of hereditary characteristics from the genome upward presupposes, as a preliminary condition, that this genome is organized and this organization is conserved and extended without interruption, not only during the transition from one generation to the next, but also during the guiding of embryonic development from the moment the genes become active. In this sense, the organization qua functioning is not transmitted by heredity as are characteristics such as shape, color, etc.; it continues and succeeds itself qua functioning as *a condition necessary to every transmission and as a transmitted content.* Any epistemologist reading these lines will recognize the language of Kant (except that in this case the a priori is a development in itself!), but this phraseology is just such as may render comprehensible the functional correspondences with the intelligence (to which we shall be returning shortly) and yet it remains in a strict sense the language of biology, or so it seems to me.

1. The first characteristic of this organization function is that it is

a conservation function. Whereas a chemical body decomposes when combined with another, and only its elements are conserved intact, it is the essential reaction of every organized being to conserve its essential overall shape and thus to go on living as an organized whole. But there is nothing of the inert about this kind of self-conservation, and even though, in talking about the continuity of this functioning, we have used terms like "succeeds itself" and "extends itself," it was in the context of establishing the result. On the contrary, the essential fact is that activities and transformations are occurring continuously, and that conservation is an invariant throughout the covariations and transformations. This invariant is, of course, only approximate, not fixed, but it nonetheless exists as a fundamental tendency.

The whole that is conserved is thus a relational totality. This means that in every organization there exist partial processes which are relative to each other in essentials, in other words, which are only seen to exist because of their makeup. These elements taken as processes are thus interdependent, and their whole is no more than the system set up by their assembled parts. Since the partial processes have no existence apart from one another, their whole is not to be considered an aggregate of elements existing previously. But neither is it an entity distinct from its elements if its elements are relationships or composition processes.

2. The second characteristic of the organization function is, therefore, the interaction of differentiated parts. If there were no parts and no processes, partial or differentiated, there would be not an organization but a homogenous totality playing an inert role in its own conservation. If there were no interactions or solidarity between the component parts, there would be no organization either but a mere collection of atomistic elements.

3. These two properties do not, however, suffice to define what an organization is as opposed to physical systems that move. One fundamental fact must be added, namely, that the contents of the organization are perpetually renewed by means of reconstructions (metabolism). This amounts to saying that the conservation of the whole is the conservation of a form and not of its contents, and that the interacting processes require aliment in the form of energy drawn from sources outside the system.

However general these characteristics may be (and one dare not say more than that about them until one has examined their structures), it will be noticed at once that these characteristics are also those of the most highly evolved forms of knowledge, in addition to being those of the various modes of knowledge at every level. In other words, knowledge comprises first and foremost an organization function, and that is our first fundamental analogy with life.

1. Any act of the intelligence presupposes the continuity and conservation of a certain functioning. Leibnitz's reply to empiricism, which described intelligence as merely a collection of elements produced by the senses, was to produce the famous formula *nisi ipse intellectus*. When A. G. E. Müller maintained that perception was nothing but associated sensations, W. Köhler might have replied similarly, *nisi ipsa perceptio*. And so on and so forth. To put it another way, there is no cognitive impression without the intervention of some organizing functioning, conserved from previous situations, which can be traced back to innate reactions. This does not mean that such previous conservation is complete, which would mean preformation, for functioning modifies structure by its very exercise, but it does show that there is a tendency to conservation that is increasingly successful as development goes on and becomes decisive on reaching a certain level.

It is, indeed, worth noting that in every domain cognitive functions constitute invariants which are vital to their functioning, even in situations where immediate experience does not seem to make them necessary. These invariants do not concern merely the cognitive instruments used by the subject; they are projected into reality in the form of notions of conservation applied to objects themselves. In the domain of sensorimotor acquisitions, for example, actions become generalized as "schemata," the organization of which crystallyzes in a relatively constant form, and this relative constancy in schemata is translated into the construction of invariants in the real world, such as the schema of the "permanent object," which postulates the existence of substances behind perceptual configurations—a schema that is established progressively toward the end of the first year of a human child's life, after only three months in a kitten (but this in elementary form: Gruber), and at corresponding ages in the young baboon (Paillard and Mme Flament). In the field of perception, in addition to the formation of schemata like those just mentioned, the construction of well-known "perceptual constancies" can be cited, whose functional role in the organization of perception is very clear but which do not always come about for reasons of practical utility. For example, the constant of size may be replaced by inferential corrections, as happens when a certain distance is reached, at which point the intelligence will adjust any apparent dwindling in size.

But it is in the domain of intelligence itself that the need for invariants is most striking. On one hand, the whole of logic consists in establishing invariant schemata aimed at organizing into thought form the irreversible stream of external happenings and the continuous development of the stream of internal consciousness. Concepts, both as classes and as relationships, are a good example of this; and the principle of identity, although it is always challenged by the environment at some stage or another, expresses this demand for invariance as a norm of the thinking subject, as long as thought is to remain coherent. On the other hand, the intelligence does impose on reality a series of conservation notions, which, as can be observed, are necessarily formed in the course of the first twelve years of a child's development: conservation of the quantity of matter, in the pouring of liquid from one vessel into another (about 7 years), or in changing the shape of a solid body (about 8 years); conservation of weight in unchanging conditions (9–10 years) or of physical volume (11–12 years); conservation of lengths and surfaces of sets (7–9 years), etc.; to say nothing of the scientific elaboration of "conservation principles," which are known to occur in a different form at every level (including relativity and microphysics) when previous forms become ineffective in organizing the lessons taught by experience.

2. Needless to say, these cognitive organizations are constantly aiming, as biological organizations are, at differentiation and complementary integration, since all cognitive systems (perception, sensorimotor schemata, and conceptual ones above all) always develop in the twin direction of differentiating refinement and growing cohesion. This fact was challenged, nevertheless, by A. Lalande, who set the principle of identity, the supreme norm of the homogeneity characteristic of thought, in opposition to biological organization, the source of differentiation, and by E. Meyerson, who, in every cognitive progression, set identification—the sole cognitive function—in opposition to the diversification imposed solely by reality. Lalande, however, was forgetting that biological organization is as much the source of variance as it is of differentiation, and both men were leaving out of account the fundamental fact that

thought itself is always differentiating its structures, as in mathematics, and is not trapped in a sterile and never-ending tautology from which it can be extricated only by the external world.

3. The most remarkable analogy, however, between a living organization and one pertaining to cognitive functions lies in the fact that in the latter case, similarly, the organized content is being modified unceasingly, with the result that organization here too is dynamic in essence and can be said to integrate into permanent forms the continuous stream of objects and changing happenings. One and the same perceptual "right form" applies to very different kinds of objects: from a grain of lead to a full moon, where roundness is concerned, etc. The essence of a sensorimotor schema is that it generalizes itself in relation to new situations. All concept systems at all intelligence levels function effectively, when thought is being put into action, only by reference to new circumstances or problems, which assure constant change in the content of these ideas.

2. Cognitive Forms and Conservations

But if this is so where living thought is concerned, that is to say, thought in its concrete and effective functioning, then it will be seen at once that there are not only fundamental analogies of this kind but also differences, which are no less significant, between "forms" belonging to the higher cognitive functions and those on which organic morphology is based. Here we are confronted by the first of several systematic functional differences such as may help us understand the profound specificity and originality that are an essential part of knowledge despite the common ground linking it to the living organization.

Two interdependent differences are involved: the first connected with the degree of approximation or of success in the invariables or conservation forms, the second with the degree of dissociation of the "form" and the content.

To start with the second difference, because it controls the first, it is clear that the "forms" belonging to the organization of living creatures and therefore to organic morphology, in its twin guises of morphogenesis and of forms in equilibrium, are inseparable from their material and energetic content. This inseparability is carried so far that no one has yet succeeded in formulating a satisfactory mathematical or algebraic theory of biological organization in general; and certain minds, whose speculative tendencies are rather retrograde, however progressive their experimental work—I refer to Driesch and K. Goldstein—believe they can only conceive of an organization in terms of entelechy or transintellectual intuition. We shall be returning to this when discussing structure, but, with respect to functioning, the dynamic solidarity between "forms" and their content is still more obvious, for if functioning ceases, the "form" is destroyed, which means that it dies and returns to physico-chemical structures of a "nonorganized" kind. On the other hand, the outstanding characteristic of cognitive organizations is the progressive dissociation of form and content.

In the domain of instinct, sensorimotor functions, and perception, a dissociation of this kind can barely be observed, which goes to show the kinship between their "forms" and those of organic morphogenesis; instinct is often no more than the functional extension of the "form" of the organs, and the same thing is true of many reflexes and behavior of an acquired elementary sensorimotor kind associated with prehension, locomotion, etc. Perception is inseparable from sensory excitement, etc.

With intelligence, on the other hand, we can see in the human child a progressive dissociation of forms and content. Though still weak at the preoperational thought level, where, thanks to the use of language, conceptual schemata tend to leap ahead of the experience of the moment to some extent, this dissociation in the child can be clearly seen to develop at the "concrete operations" level (section 2, subsection 2). At this level certain elementary deductions (transitivity, etc.) become possible and are already accompanied by a feeling of inferential "necessity," which thus clearly exceeds the content. But even in this case, dissociation is still only relative, because transitivity, for instance, will not be applied outright to weights and measures, although it will be in evidence when it comes to simple quantities. On the level of propositional operations, on the other hand, an assembly of forms are sufficiently detached from their contents to set up "formal" or independent hypothetico-deductive operations, to the extent that a certain autonomous logic can be developed. It is this same "natural" formal logic which has made it possible, therefore, in the realm of scientific thought, to establish both a reflective or axiomatizing logic and a "pure" mathematics—"pure," that is, insofar as it is independent of content or object.

Whatever their biological origin may be, the "pure forms" of intelligence thus bear witness to a power of dissociating form and content, a power which is unattainable in the organic domain and presupposes the power of thought. Thus, there is a primary specialized function belonging to knowledge at the higher level contained within a functional organization framework of a much more general kind.

The consequence of this difference is another difference in the domain of invariables or conservation notions. Whereas functional invariables or the conservation of the organizing functioning, with its attendant general "forms," can only be said to be approximate at the organic level, being always under the threat of variation or death for the very good reason that their forms and contents cannot be dissociated, cognitive forms, by virtue of their increasing independence with respect to contents, can achieve strict conservation structures, as in all the advanced deductive fields. So there would seem to be a second function, peculiar to cognitive mechanisms of the highly evolved type, but, as can be seen, this second function is much more like an end or a completion, in relation to the general conservation function found in all organizations, than a discontinuous and specific innovation.

3. Organization and "Open System"

These considerations bring us to the examination of structures within the organization. There is no doubt that the man who has given the deepest thought to this subject is Ludwig von Bertalanffy. Whatever Cuénot may say, along with many others who are hostile to modern cybernetic modes of thought, there is nothing of the vitalist or finalist about Bertalanffy. The great merit of his "organicism" is, in fact, that even back in 1926 (*Roux' Archiv.*, 108) it showed some realization that there was a place for some intelligible theory of totality between the two extreme alternatives of mechanism and vitalism. To be sure, it owed much to the Gestalt[4] psychologists (Köhler and Wertheimer from 1912 on), but, to an even greater extent than Gestalt psychology, Bertalanffy's functional and relational concept of totality goes beyond the notions of "emergence" (Lloyd Morgan), which are essentially phenomenological and irrational. It goes beyond holism, too, which simply takes cognizance of innovations at every stage and attributes them to "precausal"

4. Bertalanffy, it is true, remained too attached to the nonfunctionalist concept in psychology, although he certainly outgrew it in biology.

totalities, not relational ones. In fact, Bertalanffy strove to supply a theoretic elaboration of the idea of organization, and the current of opinion in cybernetics since then has shown how fruitful was the line he took.

In Bertalanffy's view, if we leave out of account the fundamental fact of historicity and limit our considerations to the organization in terms of result, we can hazard the following definition: "A living organism is a hierarchical order of open systems, the permanence of which is assured by the intervention of the exchange movement of the components, achieved by virtue of its system conditions" (*Les problèmes de la vie*, p. 173). The structure of the organization thus contains three characteristics: an open system, dynamism in exchanges, and "primary activity" as opposed to the reactivity interpretation in which reactivity is thought of as primitive. Something else should be noted here, namely, that the notion of totality implied in the notion of an open system is actually of a relational nature, that is, neither atomistic nor Gestaltist in the strict sense (because it is too near to the idea of totalities as self-explanatory); thus, Bertalanffy says that the whole cannot be reduced to the sum of the *"parts taken in isolation.* All the same, if we know the sum of the parts and the *relationships existing between them*, then we can deduce the upper levels of the elements from which they are constituted" (p. 198).

We do, however, lack one essential here if we are to see in this description a satisfactory analysis of the structure of the organization, and that is the reference to a cyclic order, whereas the property of a hierarchical order may be thought of as derived by differentiation, though always present in known organization.

The central ambiguity is that of the "open system," for, if system exists, then something like a closure intervenes, which has to be reconciled with the "opening." The opening is certainly justified and is founded on the basic idea that "in biology, there is no rigid organic form carrying out vital processes but a stream of processes which are revealed as forms of a seemingly persistent kind" (p. 186). The opening, then, is the system of exchanges with environment, but this in no way excludes a closure, in the sense of a cyclic rather than a lineal order. This cyclic closure and the opening of the exchanges are, therefore, not on the same plane, and they can be reconciled in the following way, which may be entirely abstract but will suffice for a structural analysis of a very general kind.

The material or dynamic elements of a structure with cyclic order we shall call $A, B, C, \ldots, Z$, and the material or energetic elements necessary for their maintenance, $A', B', C', \ldots, Z'$. We shall then have the following figure, the sign $\times$ representing the interaction of the terms of the first range with those of the second, and the sign $\rightarrow$ representing the end point of these interactions:

$$(A \times A') \rightarrow (B \times B') \rightarrow (C \times C') \rightarrow \ldots$$
$$(Z \times Z') \rightarrow (A \times A') \rightarrow \text{etc.} \tag{1}$$

In a case like this we are confronted by a closed cycle qua cycle, which expresses the permanent reconstitution of the elements $A, B, C, \ldots, Z, A,$ and which is characteristic of the organism;[5] but each interaction $(A \times A')$, $(B \times B')$, etc., at the same time represents an opening into the environment as a source of aliment.

Of course, it may be supposed that each element in the structure, whether $A, B, C, \ldots, Z$, contains within itself substructures of the same forms as (1), which brings in the hierarchical order put forward by Bertalanffy, but for the moment we do not need to make this differentiation, as we are keeping to the abstract. Moreover, one might presuppose more complex combinations, such as $(B + M) \times (B' + M')$ etc., in which the sign $+$ will designate conjoint actions. But, here again, simplification is possible in the abstract. On the other hand, the notion of a cyclic order seems indispensable to the permanence of the open system; otherwise such a permanence could not possibly contain regulatory mechanisms (as Bertalanffy has since pointed out) and would be reduced to an equilibrium in the shape of a balance of opposing forces, a thing no longer peculiar to the organization.

The cyclic character of the system becomes particularly necessary as soon as the organization is extended by adaptation and assimilation, a point to which we shall be returning at a later stage.[6]

Meanwhile, the first essential is to demonstrate in what way this necessarily circular, not merely hierarchical, character of the system (by differentiation of the structure into possible substructures)

5. Without forming any prejudgment about the kind of frontier or absence of frontier between A and A', etc.

6. It is only right here to point out that C. Nowinski has the theory that every characterization of an organization cycle and its exchanges with environment presupposes the condition "in normal circumstances" and that this of necessity is related to development and to history itself. Moreover, this is the case in every biological equilibrium.

is as much characteristic of the spontaneous cognitive organization as of the biological. A conceptual system, in fact (and a fortiori, a sensorimotor one, etc.), is a system such that its elements are inevitably supported by one another, while at the same time it is open to exchanges with the outer world. Let us suppose, against all possibility, the construction of a single concept A, considered as a starting point for a classification, etc. If this is indeed a concept, that is to say, if it has any kind of meaning, then it is opposed to the concept non-A, which will at once set up a total and circular system. In the case of a multiconceptual system, which alone corresponds to reality, it is impossible to describe any concept without making use of the others in a process which is of necessity circular also.

The circles we are talking of here are dialectic, an inherent part of thought in its functioning. As soon as there is any need to demonstrate or deduce, however, thought takes a lineal, or hierarchical, or single-track order, so as to avoid making circles which would, by relation to such justificatory or didactic intentions, become "vicious." The purest form of such lineal orders is axiomatization, either logical or mathematical. But in such cases the conventional or "constructed" character of the lineal order is immediately apparent. One is compelled, in order to avoid making an explicit circle, to begin by positing "indefinable" notions in such a way as to define those one needs to use, and axioms or propositions such as "cannot be demonstrated" in order to demonstrate those that are to be classed as "theorems." Now the choice of indefinables and undemonstrables must of necessity remain arbitrary, in terms of the intentions of the system. In effect, there is thus no lineal order except by means of a process freely adopted in order to widen the circular order and to cut from within it the lineal series—still having no absolute starting point—that will be required if we are to demonstrate (relatively speaking) this or that consequence.

But supposing we abandon logic and return to psychology and epistemology, every system of things known is, in reality, circular, and from that standpoint the extension of knowledge simply amounts to widening as far as possible the sphere contained within its limits. As has been shown elsewhere, classification of the sciences in themselves[7] presents just such a structure, and progress in its development amounts to transforming this circle into a spiral by an

---

7. In *Logique et connaissances scientifiques,* Encyclopédie de la Pléiade.

infinite series of similar widenings in scope. This circular character is thus very general and bears witness, if it does nothing more, to the organizing nature of all forms of knowledge in contrast to the merely additive or linear character attributed to it by a falsely pedagogic common sense.

4. *Inclusions* [Emboîtements]

We must now return to the hierarchical order which occurs in every differentiation of an organization. The most general "form" found in a hierarchy is the inclusion [emboîtement] of a part, or substructure, into one whole, or a total structure.[8] Now, this "form" or elementary inclusion structure is of very special interest in the context of our discussion because it happens to be the principle in common to the fundamental logical operations which constitute classification and the no less fundamental biological structures which arise, not only in those hierarchical connections revealed by systematic zoology or botany, but also in the organization of the genetic system, in the succession of embryonic stages, in the processes of physiological assimilation in its widest sense, and finally throughout the whole range of behavior.

α. It is at once obvious that the classification used in systematics corresponds to something in the distribution of organized beings. Of course, it is by no means certain that the bonds which have been established will always be successful in expressing "natural" kinships. No more is it certain that the various degrees under consideration (species, genera, families, orders, etc.) will always have the same value where their position on the scale is concerned. But what is clear, and that is sufficient to our purpose, is that if one compares individuals whose characteristics are more or less similar or progressively dissimilar, one will find: (*a*) common characteristics relatively peculiar to a small number of these individuals, which will then be grouped as belonging to the same species A; (*b*) characteristics of a less specialized kind, common to a slightly larger number of individuals, including the former group; in this case they will be called "genus" B, if all A are B, and, generally speaking, if all B are not A, from which we form the figure $A + A' = B$ where $A' =$ the

---

8. Of course, Bertalanffy is thinking of many other kinds of hierarchies, especially physiological ones, in his definition of the organism. But we are going to confine ourselves here to simple inclusion, which has a special significance in relation to our argument.

species B which are not A; (c) characteristics which are still fairly special but are more widely distributed than the former groups; the individuals possessing these characteristics will then be grouped into one "family" (so that $C = B + B'$ where B' are genera other than B belonging to the same family C and where the B and B' are themselves divided up into species; (d) and so on right up to "subkingdoms" and "kingdoms."

Independently, then, of the absolute values of grades A, B, C', etc., and this is something that remains constant in any zoological or botanical classification, a series of inclusions is thus arrived at:[9]

$$A + A' = B; B + B' = C; C + C' = D; \text{etc.} \qquad (2)$$
$$\text{where } A \times A' = 0; B \times B = 0; \text{etc.}$$

Thus, classification corresponds to certain objective inclusions as between generalized groups of individuals. Now these groups A, B, C, etc., comprise individuals, all of which bear characteristics of the a order for the groups of type A, of the b order for the groups of type B, etc. But the result of this is that one and the same individual, belonging to species A, will itself bear both characteristics a (specific), b (generic), c (common to his family), etc., since all A are B, all B, C, etc.

In this way, it can be said that every inclusion of individual groups (for example, the species "domestic cat" A included in the genus cat B, which in turn is included in the feline family C, etc.) corresponds, in each individual case, to an inclusion of characteristics such that, for example, any domestic cat possesses, first of all, every characteristic common to living creatures, then those of animals, then those of vertebrates, mammals, etc., right up to the characteristics c of the Felides, b of cats, and a of domestic cats. Agreed, provided the sign $<$ here simply designates the inclusion:

$$a < b < c < \ldots \text{corresponding to } A < B < C < \ldots \qquad (3)$$

The inclusion connection applied to the characteristics themselves simply means that characteristics of the higher order are more general than the lower ones and that, for example, the characteristics c are differentiated into b and those in b are differentiated into a.

β. This proposition (3), introducing an inclusion among characteristics as such, might appear questionable as much from the bio-

9. For greater clarity, we are using $+$ signs for union ($\cup$) and $\times$ for intersection (determination of the common part or $\cap$).

logical as from the logical point of view.[10] It does acquire, however, one very concrete meaning—though it still contains a number of mysteries from the point of view of causality—throughout its successive and necessary stages. In fact, even if ontogenesis is not an exact and detailed recapitulation of phylogenesis, because of differences in speeds and possible short circuits, not to mention neoformations, it is nonetheless true that, within certain main outlines, the embryo of a cat at first evinces only the characteristics of a living, even unicellular, creature, then those of an animal, then only those of a vertebrate, etc., and finally those of a felid and a cat. Even if the series (3) is not found in full detail, it remains unchallengeable that, at least in the main stages, there is a progressive differentiation of characteristics, such that the more general come before the more specific and swallow them up, just as a whole is organized of its parts. The basic inclusion connection thus exists in the same individual creature with respect to its characteristics, and is translated in embryo by gradual stages from the general to the differentiated.

10. From this logical point of view, the question cannot possibly be resolved until more detailed knowledge is acquired of the logico-mathematical structure of the "organization." This Woodger tried to do, but his logical positivism led him to offer reductionist solutions of an excessively simple kind. The essence of his construction rests on a modular trellis, which thus contains hierarchical inclusions, but in which everything is reduced to what is observable, whereas what ought to happen is that the accent should be laid upon the operators, the supposed network of which would be merely a resultant. As for inclusions, Woodger introduces, where they are concerned, a relationship S which he calls "sum," distinct from inclusion, which seems to us to be the same thing as what we have called (in the psychogenesis of logical operations) partitive addition in apposition to the addition or mingling of classes or groups. But this relationship does no more than join a part (cell, collection of cells, etc.) to a whole, in a hierarchy like a tree. At the same time, it allows for the possibility of a subgroup that reflects the totality set up by this "group of parts." It is not out of the question that, by completing these static analyses by the introduction of operators, one might again come up against inclusions like those in our proposition (3). Woodger sets about this in his analysis of reproduction, by introducing fusion operations Fs and division operations Dv and by imagining that there is a sort of equilibrium between Fs and Dv. $U = Fs \cup Dv$ in the modular trellis. However, we must note that, in addition to its reduction to the merely observable, without any sufficient operator, the great gap remaining in Woodger's attempt at analysis is that it allows no place for processes of the historical kind, since his relationship t is only an antecedence in time ($x \, t \, y$ is limited to expressing the fact that there is no instant common to both x and y). Now we probably ought to make use, in this case, of operators such that the resultant would be partly a function of the ground covered (which would imply a systematic limitation of associativity).

The characteristics *a*, *b*, *c*, etc. (prop. [3]) corresponding to classification in species, genus, etc. (prop. [2]) are all hereditary. More and more information is forthcoming about "special" heredity, meaning heredity of characteristics that are below the level of the species as a whole or which only sometimes come up to it. On the other hand, little is known about "general" heredity, concerning characteristics of a supraspecific type. This does not mean that they are not hereditary. Indeed, it is heredity, both general and specific, that determines the genetic program achieved during the growth of the embryo, although it is helped in this way by epigenetic reactions.

This hereditary nature of all types of characteristics—those of race, variety, or species, right up to the most general types—allows us to assume, surely, that the structural inclusions (2) and (3) are not foreign to the genetic system, whatever form they may take in the genome or plasma.

δ. But if these inclusions, particularly in the form of proposition (3), thus recur at every rung of the hereditary ladder, isomorphically with those characteristic of classification, then surely this means that the whole range of assimilatory processes which are physiologically typical of metabolism and material exchanges with environment also must include a classificatory system. In fact, specific and generic characteristics, etc., of types *a*, *b*, *c*, etc., as presented by any living creature, determine a certain choice from among the substances and energies of the environment in order to constitute or reconstitute themselves perpetually throughout metabolism: a green plant needs light; a certain cell needs proteins, fats, carbohydrates, minerals, etc.; and, even if its choice of chemical and energy aliment may not correspond in every detail to characteristics *a*, *b*, *c*, etc., it is not the same for a vegetable as for an animal, for an earthworm as for a dragonfly, etc. As a result, the physiological behavior of each group necessarily presupposes a series of discriminations of a type not unlike classificatory inclusion. This means first that, on one hand, organisms absorb certain substances and reject others and, on the other, the substances so absorbed divide themselves into those retained and those rejected. The next step is that the assimilated ones are transformed and shared out in endless different ways. Their final stage always involves the retention of a certain number of characteristic properties, not merely those of life in general, but also organizations of increasingly restricted types, extending from branch to genus, to species, and farther on still.

In a word, and without making any sort of pronouncement in detail about correspondences, it does seem clear that the classificatory, embryological, and genetic inclusion of characteristics is extended into what might be called a classification at work in the very mechanism of physiological exchanges with the environment, as a direct function of the diversity of the structures and specialized forms of assimilation that maintain those exchanges. It may not, of course, be the same kind of classification, and, in particular, it must be admitted that the exchange mechanism involves something more than a classification, but if there is choice, and hierarchy in that choice (a hierarchy dependent either closely or distantly on the hierarchy of types of organization in general systematic classification), at the very least there must intervene some inclusion structures in the very method by which an organism appropriates one category of aliment and not another and, from this one category, chooses one subcategory rather than another.

Perhaps it will be objected that this sort of talk is purely metaphorical and that it could just as well be said that if a chemical body N is combined with others, of category B, and in a different manner according to whether members of A or A' are involved, it is then choosing members of B as against those of C and is including members of A within B; in short, classification is taking place in terms of the body N. But three kinds of differences are to be found between these selective chemical reactions by which the body N is combined with body B (A or A') and the embryonic forms of classification that I believe can be perceived in the interplay of biological assimilations. The first is that the living body conserves its organized structure as it assimilates aliment from outside, whereas N undergoes modification as it is combined with B. Insofar as it is an organization conserving itself during assimilation, the living body is indeed a starting point for what later becomes the "subject" of knowledge, to which we shall return in section 12. In the second place, assimilation is not merely some kind of reaction but an activity which varies according to the types of organization, including specific or even racial types. It will be said that this is also the case with chemical reactions, which are differentiated ad infinitum according to the chemical species or particular components. But what we are here calling "activity" means much more than that: it is a process which is both functional, in relation to the conservation of the organization, and historical, in relation to the progressive and phylogenetic differentiation of the types of organization. Viewed in this way, the assimilatory activity may be said to be, in quite a different way from ordinary chemical reactions, a field for choice, and consequently to be a classification in action. In the third place, and most important of all, physiological or organic assimilation prepares the way for assimilation that is purely functional or relative to actions—a passing from the physiological to the "behavioral" scale.

Indeed, insofar as the organism chooses its material and energy aliments, it must sooner or later undertake an active search for them, which certainly gives evidence of the kind of activity presented by the assimilatory function in relation to the organization. This search is one of the central motivating forces of behavior, the basis of cognitive functions. A green plant will turn toward the light, which is a tropism and an elementary kind of behavior. In the animal world there is a scale of behavior at every stage of evolution.

Now there can be no behavior without some elementary form of classification. Every act of perception is "categorical," as J. Bruner has demonstrated; this means that it tends to identify the object perceived in relation to previous action schemata, and this presupposes some classification. The exercise of instinct likewise presupposes classification: choice of food, of building material, of sexual partners, etc. The elaboration of habits leads to the formation of schemata which are to a greater or lesser extent included within one another, and evidence of this inclusion is what Hull calls a "hierarchical family of habits."

In the end comes representation or thought, and the classifications constructed by this activity at every level of its development have the novelty of being more or less deliberate but, above all, reflexive; that is, they constitute systems that have ceased to be immanent to a functioning but are produced and sought after by the functioning insofar as it is conscious. On this order are prescientific classifications (as in infants and primitive societies, or inherent in language, etc.) and scientific classifications (including those of the systematic biology which was our starting point in α).

Thus, the classificatory function seems to be found in every organization structure, and this fact constitutes a remarkable structural isomorphism between biological and cognitive organizations. Of course, we are not talking of the same kinds of classification;

sometimes the inclusions of the subclasses or substructures within classes or structures are, as it were, incorporated in a material organization (α, β, and γ), sometimes they are an immanent part of a functioning (δ and ϵ), sometimes they arise out of it (ϕ), but the difference between α-γ and δ-ϵ is only one of degree, and the only two actual poles are those of classifying inclusion structures inherent in the functions (α-ϵ) and those arising out of them (ϕ). But this bipolarity will be found again in every structural isomorphism that we try to analyze, and its explanation is always the same: thought starts in structures that are immanent to the living organization, but by reconstructing them at its own level it extends and enriches them in endless ways.

5. Order Structures

Everything we have just said about inclusion structures can be found again in similar terms with respect to relational structures and particularly to "order" structures. Here again we discover structures inherent in functioning (any functioning in time presupposes order relationships) and structures produced by a functioning (order seen as a thought structure). However, in order relationships, even more than in inclusions, the construction of an order structure by the thought process clearly presupposes a thought to which some order has already been given as it functions (although that will be a more elementary type of thought). There is thus something to be gained in this particular case by starting from the higher or cognitive levels before coming down to the lower or organic levels.

Order structures are essential to the mechanism of thinking. In pure mathematics, if the inclusion structure is necessary to the set theory, the order structure is equally necessary to ordered wholes, networks, and so on. Among the primary operational structures set up by a child, that of seriation (inclusion of transitive asymmetric relationships) is the corollary of that of classification, and their synthesis is necessary to the construction of number.

The notion of order cannot possibly be found in experience. Helmholtz, in his analyses of the formation of number, assumed that we could find order in the ordered succession of states of consciousness (memory, etc.), but we only find order in our memories or successive states of consciousness if we introduce it ourselves by some reflective or reasoned reconstruction. As for such order as a young child may discover in some configuration or other which it perceives (the uprights in a banister) or registers in some sensori-motor way (a regular succession leading to a series of associated reactions), he will only discover it by means of ordered conduct: successive, orderly movements of the eyes or hands, for the banister, the construction of a schema of linked articulations for the formation of a habit. D. Berlyne, who made a study in my own laboratory of the discovery of an order of succession in children, reached the conclusion that this kind of apprenticeship presupposes a "counting agent" [compteur], which is what we shall be calling an ordinatory[11] activity (and this in spite of Berlyne's leanings toward American behaviorism).

But the kind of "order" that is made use of on the sensorimotor level (which can be seen so clearly in the ordering of means and ends in any articulated act of practical intelligence) is itself preceded by a broad group of order relationships involved in nervous and physiological mechanisms generally, and these are of a hereditary nature. A reflex presupposes an ordered succession of stimuli and motor reactions; a hormonal regulation includes an order or succession; and so on.

As for ontogenetic development, it does not consist solely of a succession of stages, which is to say, an ordered series of states or momentary organization forms. To say that would be to argue as though ontogenetic development underwent this condition of order like some physical process. But there is much more to it than this in the sense that the epigenotype itself controls the order by means of a series of regulations, arising from both the genome and a number of interactions, of such a kind that they succeed one another by what Waddington calls a "time tally." Thus, in the successive stages of a caterpillar, the metamorphosis of the chrysalis, and the adult state of the butterfly, the different parts of the genome can be seen to intervene in turn, imposing a sort of ordered rhythm. As for the genome itself, it is well known that the DNA code is based on sequences or, in other words, on order (Watson and Crick).

Finally, phylogenesis itself can certainly be interpreted as a series

11. See D. Berlyne and J. Piaget, *Théorie du comportement et opérations,* Études d'epistémologie génétique (Paris: Presses Universitaires de France), vol. 13.

of chances, in which case the order in which the stages of evolution succeed each other will simply be something the organism undergoes without any analogy with the order of a function but, on the contrary, in conformity with the succession of states in a thermodynamic system. But, here again, the question is whether the order structures intervene as instruments of the function, in which case the situation may be compared to the various degrees of the order implied in a development such as that of embryogenesis, or as the result of blind and fortuitous circumstance, in which case the evolutionary order will have no connection with the cognitive order and will have no existence except in the mind of the biologist who is reconstructing the phylogenesis.

To sum up, order structures do seem at the outset (from the DNA stage) to be inherent in every biological organization and in its functioning. At the other end, order structures are produced by thought, but a thought which also is ordered in its functioning. Between these two extremes are found all the intermediary stages, and the parallelism between these and inclusion structures could be described in greater detail. Here again we are confronted with a fundamental isomorphism between biological and cognitive structures.

6. Multiplicative Structures, "Strongly Structured" Classes, and Endomorphisms

These three examples of structures—cyclic (subsection 3 above), inclusion (subsection 4), and order in general (subsection 5)—are mere samples of what it will be possible to say about isomorphisms between living organizations and cognitive ones when enough progress has been made in mathematical knowledge (especially of the algebraic and topological kind) about the former.

Commenting on the interesting geometric descriptions by means of which d'Arcy Thompson analyzes the evolutionary transformations of mollusks and fish, or the gradual change from the eohippus to the present-day equus, Bertalanffy says rightly: "What we would like to know is not merely a few equations of measurable vectors but the law which integrates them. . . . As far as we can see, questions of this type belong in part to the domain of topology. . . . Others are allied to the theory of groups, since the question of invariance in the transformation of equation systems arises" (loc. cit., p. 211). But this organization mathematics has yet to be established, and, when it is, it will have to take the form of some qualitative algebra, like that concerned with networks and groups,[12] making allowance for the dynamism which is an essential part of all regulatory systems.

Before returning, in section 14, to this last point, we must make some further remarks about the structural properties of the living organization and their partial isomorphisms with certain cognitive structures.

1. Inclusion or order structures of the kind dealt with thus far correspond mainly—in their elementary forms, such as are found in thought processes at the psychogenetic stage—to purely additive operations. The inclusions of propositions (2) and (3), and seriation as well, thus only constitute additive "groupings." But there also exists an equivalent number of others taking a multiplicative form, and their elements belong to several classifications or seriations at one and the same time. The distinctive characteristic of these multiplicative groupings is, then, the intervention of "connections" (either bi-univocal or co-univocal).

The correspondence structure plays a fundamental role in the living organization, again a role that may truly be called functional, which means that it appertains not merely to the description of phenomena by the observer but also to the very activity of the organized entity or, in other words, to the organizing process itself. The simplest example is "multiplication" generally, meaning that a species or a variety is represented not by a single individual but by a multiplicity brought about by reproduction, such that each individual corresponds to each of the others in the detail of its specific characteristics considered term by term. In this case we are dealing with a correspondence that might be called "qualified" (as opposed to numerical or "indeterminate" correspondence), in the sense that a

12. In connection with the "group" notion, Ashby holds that the only systems of which a scientific study can be made are those whose pertinent variations allow of their being described as "absolute systems"; their main characteristic is that in action they have the structure of a function, in the strictly mathematical sense. He goes on to demonstrate (*Design for a Brain*) that the absolute system offers us a "group structure" by reference to its transformations in time; the composing elements in the functions which describe the subsequent state and, failing that, the subsequent output of the system, have a "group structure." According to G. Cellérier the notion of an "absolute system" is certainly reducible to that of a finite automaton.

It must also be remembered that Sommerhof (*Analytical Biology*) has found the equivalent of a regulator in his analysis of the structure of an organism in exchanges with environment.

certain characteristic or organ in one individual corresponds, in another individual, to a characteristic or an organ presenting the same qualitative distinctions. Now this qualified correspondence, which in the reflective or cognitive state forms part of the elementary operations of logic, intervenes here as a constitutive structure in biological reproduction or multiplication.

Thus, it would be easy to reiterate the developments described in subsection 4 above concerning hierarchical or classifying inclusions, but in this case to apply them to the correspondence structure. In the first place, if individuals of the same species have characteristics corresponding to one another in every particular, their genomes must correspond in the same way (and multiply themselves in an infinite series of duplications while preserving the connection between all their multiple amplifications). In the second place, the DNA of the genome projects its characteristics into the RNA (with its various subsequent forms of transfer, etc.) by means of new correspondences which last throughout the development period of each individual. In the same way, innumerable qualified correspondences will be found in physiological or nervous functioning as well as in behavior (perception, imitation, etc.) right up to the time when the structure ceases to be a component part of the functioning and breaks away as an instrumental product involved in the thinking process.

We must also point out that, even if the correspondences just referred to are no more than semimultiplicative structures, as it were, insofar as the same characteristic of inclusion is multiplied or reproduced to the nth degree, nevertheless we can find, in comparative anatomy, structures analogous to true products on the Cartesian model or multiplicative matrices complete in themselves by means of intersections between different structures. For example, if the scapula girdle in the entire vertebrate species is considered an autonomous system, and all the types of organization belonging to the different classes are considered another system, the product of the two systems will then illustrate the fact that two homologous elements may cease to have the same function (this much has already been said when dealing with the coracoid bone): in such a case, the intersection of the correspondences is an effective translation of the objective structural modifications and does not merely constitute a descriptive instrument for the comparative scientist.

2. If multiplicative correspondences thus form a bridge between

logical and mathematical ideas, what we now have to say will take us nearer still to mathematical structures proper. A logical class of any kind, such as "furniture," may be considered "weakly structured" insofar as the properties of one of its subclasses—let us say, "tables"—do not allow of reconstruction of the subclasses either of other parts or of the whole (except, in the latter case, by abstraction or dissociation of the characteristics and not by construction). A mathematical class, such as a "group" and its subgroups, is, on the contrary, "strongly structured" insofar as it is based on a system of transformations such as allows each of its subclasses to be reconstructed by reference to any of the others. This applies also to the class as a whole in terms of an organized system, not merely of a whole with generalized and weakened characteristics.

This difference between weakly and strongly structured classes would seem to be essential to the argument, for it corresponds to two sorts of generalization: one of them merely inclusive, in which the whole is less than the parts and does not engender them but is merely comprised of what they have in common; the other constructive, in which the whole is seen to be a system of possible transformations whose parts constitute so many realizations by means of specialization. Thus, in the realm of weakly structured classes one can verify the well-known law according to which the extension of any class (in quantity of individual types) is in inverse ratio to its comprehension (the number of characteristics or predicates), whereas this law becomes meaningless in the case of strongly structured classes: it is impossible to tell whether the laws governing a subgroup are more or less rich than those of the group as a whole, for their specialization can as well be considered a limitation as an enrichment.

In view of all this, it is remarkable that the same problem recurs in connection with biological classes. If a genus and a species are considered in terms of assemblies of individual adults (cf. proposition [2]), it is clear that weakly structured classes are involved: the species, if less numerous than the genus, plus its specific differences. But in the case of the included characteristics of the genome and the epigenotype, do we have to admit that specific differentiation during embryogenesis is, in relation to its generic characteristics, what an algebraic subgroup is to its "group," or what the characteristics of a wooden table are in relation to furniture as a whole? Of course the atomist mutation attitude would incline toward this

second solution, with the implication that the specific characteristics
a are a collection of accidents superimposed on the characteristics
b of the genus, and in turn, those of the genus on the characteristics
c of the family. But such a way of thinking has become unacceptable
to us today, at any rate in its exclusive form, because of new perspectives opened up by organicists and cybernetics. Just as the
genome in part determines the formation of the phenotype (only
in part, for there is some interaction with the environment as far as
history and chance are concerned), so, in the same way, the generic
characteristics of the genetic system no doubt determine, in part,
the specific characteristics (although allowance must once again
be made for the part played by history and chance); and so on
and so forth.

In other words, from the point of view of the inclusion of characteristics of life in general, of the animal kingdom, of subkingdoms,
etc., right up to those of species, etc., an organized structure would
seem to bear the same relation to its substructures as the properties
of a mathematical transformation group bear to those of its subgroups, but with two differences. The first is that the sort of structures involved have a history and are partly brought about by it,
which means that at least some of the group transformations are
dependent, as in algebra, on the path they follow (limitation of
"associativity" in the group). The second is the part played by
chance in the incidents occurring along these paths. But if we combine algebra with cybernetics, we shall certainly achieve sooner or
later the kind of algebraic topology of the living being that Bertalanffy dreamed of.

3. Meanwhile, when we seek to make comparisons between organic and cognitive structures, we shall have to content ourselves
with the partial isomorphisms which we are sketching out here.
One especially interesting connection in this respect, from the point
of view particularly of analogies with the theory of groups, is that
evinced by the structural regulations at the outset of embryogenesis.
With regard to the multiplicative inclusions discussed in subsection
1 above, it has been noticeable, ever since the classic experiment
carried out by Driesch, that one part of the embryo (a blastomere)
can reconstitute a whole that is isomorphic to the initial totality.
Thus, some kind of "endomorphism" intervenes at this point, at
least in a limited sense. Endomorphism is the name given to a
univocal connection between a whole, *B,* and its part, *A,* which is

included in it, whereas the other morphisms are homomorphism (noninclusion and univocal connection), isomorphism (noninclusion and connection of a bi-univocal kind), and automorphism (equivalence or mutual inclusion and bi-univocal connection). An endomorphism is the kind of morphism which is characteristic, in particular, of a group and its subgroups.

To carry these analogies between "groups" and the living organization any farther entails turning to the realm of the nervous system, for among networks found there is that of the Boolean functions, which also include a quaternality group (see section 15, subsection 3).

Section 12. Functions and Structures of Adaptation

It is impossible to dissociate organization from adaptation, because an organized system is open to the environment, and its functioning therefore entails exchanges with the external world, the stability of which defines the adapted character of the system. From the formal point of view, this means that in proposition (1) (section 11, subsection 3) it is vital to distinguish between the elements $A, B, C, \ldots$, appertaining to the organism, and the elements $A', B', C', \ldots$, furnished by the environment; the cyclic form taken by the system is thus characteristic of its organization, whereas the permanence of the interactions $A \times A'$, etc., is characteristic of its adaptation.

Then again, we must distinguish between adaptation as a state, just defined, and adaptation as a process, which raises a further problem that must now be considered. The adaptation process intervenes inevitably as soon as the environment undergoes any modification, and where the life of the phenotype is concerned it is perpetually undergoing modification, at varying speeds according to its place on the evolutionary ladder.

Let us suppose, by reference to this first proposition, that the environment is modified in such a way as to replace the element (or group of elements) B' by B'', slightly differing from B'. One of two things happens: either the cycle is interrupted and the organization is destroyed through failure to adapt, or else the cycle maintains itself as before or modifies itself by substituting, for example, C_2 for C, but still without losing its cyclic form. It will then be said that an adaptation has taken place in the sense of a process:

If, in

$$(A \times A') \to (B \times B') \to (C \times C') \to \dots$$
$$(Z \times Z') \to (A \times A') \dots$$

(prop. [1]), B' is modified into B'' and C into C_2, then, when adaptation takes place:

$$(A \times A') \times (B \times B'') \to (C_2 \times C') \to (D \times D') \to$$
$$\dots (Z \times Z') \to (A \times A') \dots \qquad (4)$$

We must therefore try to make clear what are the conditions of such a process.

1. Assimilation and Accommodation

The constant functional conditions of the process are two in number—assimilation and accommodation—and their rather close solidarity must now be determined.

We might say, in a very general way, that assimilation has taken place between the new element B'' and the established organization (under proposition [1]), if this organization, while integrating B″ into its cycle, still remains the organized structure that it was. In a more general way still, it might be said that the external elements A', B', C', . . . (prop. [1]) are assimilated into the organism under discussion insofar as they are integrated into its cycle. But in the case of the new element B'', assimilation occurs if it is integrated, in its turn, into the organization's cycle without destroying it.

But if the new element does not destroy the cycles, it may modify it. In this case we shall say that there has been an accommodation in the assimilation cycle if this cycle (proposition [1]), while assimilating B'', is itself modified by this new element in such a way that, for example, one of its elements (C) is transformed by it into C_2 (proposition [4]). The accommodation is thus inseparable from the assimilation, and it might be said by reciprocation that every assimilation is accompanied by accommodation. If the assimilation of the new element B'' did not cause modification of C into C_2, this would simply mean that the previous accommodations in the cycle had been sufficient, but the assimilatory cycle would, nonetheless, have undergone accommodation.

Thus, adaptation, seen as a complement or a consequence of proposition (4), may be defined as an equilibrium between assimilation and accommodation. But two things should be noted. First of all, it is necessary to explain why we do not define adaptation simply as accommodation, as one might be tempted to do. The reason we do not is that, without assimilation, there is no adaptation in the biological sense; for example, it could be said that, metaphorically speaking, a liquid adapts its shape to that of its receptacle, but this is not a case of biological adaptation at all, for the new shape is merely an accident of the moment and will not stay the same if the water is put into something else, precisely because there has been no assimilation into any permanent organization. Therefore, adaptation presupposes an equilibrium between assimilation and accommodation and not merely an accommodation alone. If there is accommodation without lasting assimilation, the word *accommodats* may be used, meaning temporary phenotypic variations. Second, we must emphasize the indissociable nature of assimilation and accommodation, which are constitutive conditions—at once necessary and inseparable—of adaptation. In fact, in biological terms, accommodation can be nothing but the accommodation of an organized structure, and so it can only be produced, under the influence of some external factor or element, according to whether there is temporary or lasting assimilation of such element or of its extension within the structure that it modifies. This is by no means the equivalent, as we shall see in a subsequent example, of postulating the heredity of acquired characteristics in the Lamarckian sense of the term. It is simply a matter of affirming the fact that no exogenous variation is possible in a general conservation of the structure that varies on this point—in other words, without some assimilation of the elements involved, or of the effects produced by them, into the structure undergoing the variation.

To sum up, assimilation and accommodation are not two separate functions but the two functional poles, set in opposition to each other, of any adaptation. So it is only by abstraction that one can speak of assimilation alone, as we have done and shall do again, as constituting a function of essential importance; but it must always be remembered that there can be no assimilation of anything into the organism or its functioning without a corresponding accommodation and without such assimilation's becoming part of an adaptation context.

This having been said, it must now be recalled that the basic functions of adaptation and assimilation, embodied in the most diverse structures, are to be found at every hierarchical level, from the genome and epigenotype up to the cognitive mechanisms of the higher orders.

2. *Adaptation and the Genome*

To take the genome, or genetic system generally, first: Lamarck saw it as unconditionally pliable under the influence of environment, which was as much as to attribute to it an indefinite power of accommodation, though without assimilation into unchangeable structures as far as the (cyclic) conditions of their organization are concerned. To put it another way, the hereditary organization, as in our recent example, was compared to a liquid which assumes the shapes of all receptacles without stabilizing itself and even without any sort of historic irreversibility. In the case of mutationism, the positions are reversed, and the genetic system is supposed to have assimilation without accommodation insofar as it lives off the somatic organization but undergoes no variation as a result of this; even the effects of radiation are seen as setting off endogenous mutations, which means that they are not supposed to influence their form, and that again is a case of assimilation without accommodation, despite variation. On the other hand, phenotypic *accommodats* were certainly considered to be attempts at individual adaptation, but without the possibility of heredity. This radically antithetical situation, which, in mutationism, set phenotypic variation against stability and genotypic mutation, caused Cuénot, Caullery, and others to say that characteristics were of two kinds, one kind being adaptive and not hereditary, and the other hereditary but not adaptive. And this attitude continued among biologists for a good fifty years because of the amorphous doctrine of anti-Lamarckism or the negation of any kind of influence of the environment except by selection (this was at the cost of setting up a perpetual vicious circle: selection is based on "useful" characteristics, but utility, for lack of any clear notion of adaptation to environment, is defined by selection) or because biologists took refuge in finalism (which, as we have seen, is a way of implying the intervention of environment).

A third solution at last appeared in the form of Waddington's synthesis; now the genetic system is seen as being adaptive in itself, in the precise sense that there is an equilibrium between assimilation and accommodation. A phenotypic variation, resulting from an interaction between the genetic pool, or genome, and the environment, is explicitly seen as a "response" made by the genome to external stimuli. There is thus an accommodation in the very sense we have given it, an accommodation to the circumstances imposed by the environment and assimilation of the effects of this accommodation into the structures of the genome. The variation thus produced may be fixed in heredity by "genetic assimilation" (the term is Waddington's own and not one that we are putting into his mouth) conceived as being caused by selection, but in the strict sense of a modification in the proportions of the genes by means of development and the survival of the fittest phenotypes, that is, the best responses to the environment that the genotype can make. There is no denying that Waddington's views waver a little, perhaps by reason of that circumspection in wording things which any innovator has to observe in an atmosphere still essentially neo-Darwinian, or perhaps because a theorist who is, in other respects, an experimentalist is unwilling to affirm anything that he cannot prove. This problem will be dealt with again in chapter 6.

However, for the selection exerted on the genetic system (in the sense of a modification of the proportions inherent in the genome) to be achieved solely by the death or survival of the adult phenotypes, or by regroupings imposed on it during the development of the epigenotype, there must of necessity be both accommodation and "genetic assimilation" within the genome itself as soon as we escape from the blind alley alternative of accommodation in the neo-Darwinian sense. Insofar as the term "response" has any special meaning, this meaning cannot be other than that of an adaptive response; otherwise we are back again with the random variation theory. Waddington rightly shows this to be both mathematically and biologically insufficient to take account of the evolutionary processes. It is therefore of great interest for the study of the isomorphisms that we intend to single out in this chapter to note that the three aspects of adaptation, assimilation, and accommodation quickly recur in an analysis of genetic structures when it is undertaken with an open mind by one of those rare scholars who combines in his work the twin qualities of a gift for synthesis and the caution proper to an experimentalist.

3. Phenotypic Adaptation

In the field of individual development (embryogenesis and growth), however, adaptation is recognized by most scholars apart from those who are in the process of changing their minds, as happens from time to time, in favor of preformation models and who see environmental influence during embryogenesis as merely a feeding process entirely assimilated into the genetic program without any accommodations other than quite temporary ones. On the other hand, in Waddington's conception of homeorhesis and chreods (see section 2, subsections 3–4) and, generally speaking, in those interpretations according to which ontogenesis determines phylogenesis just as much as the reverse, it is taken for granted that epigenesis is the result of a collaboration between the synthetic activity of the genome and the environment. This inevitably implies an equilibration of a progressive kind between assimilation and accommodation, and that means adaptation.

In those cases where development adheres to its customary channeling or normal chreods, this collaboration manifests itself in the kind of equilibrium of movement or homeorhesic equilibrium in which subsequent assimilations and correlative accommodations keep the organs under formation in their normal channels. But, starting from the functional stages, an increasing role is given to exercise in cooperation with maturation. In the case of some new or disturbing influence, a certain formation may be conducted out of its normal chreod and made to adopt another, slightly different or very different; when this happens there is phenotypic variation, harmful or adaptive according to whether the accommodation thus imposed either does not or does find a new equilibrium with the assimilating cycle. This adaptation may remain individual or may subsequently be fixed by "genetic assimilation," which presupposes, even at this level, a distinction between two kinds of adaptation, the one individual or even merely temporary, and the other hereditary.

As for the adult phenotype, both its physiological and its morphological adaptations obey the same principle of an equilibrium between assimilation and accommodation. It must, however, be understood that such a description must remain for the moment essentially functional, despite the tentative structural analysis contained in proposition (4). In fact, proposition (4) does no more than explain "a displacement of equilibrium" in relation to proposition (1), but, being relative to a process of cyclical order, both this displacement and, generally speaking, the equilibrium between assimilation and accommodation presuppose the existence of differentiated and more or less refined mechanisms of equilibration. These are, in fact, regulations, a subject to which we shall be returning in section 14 and which, even in their details, present striking isomorphisms between the organic and the cognitive domains. Moreover, physiological or morphological equilibrium between assimilation and accommodation presupposes some conservation of the past, or "memory," and leads to various anticipations widening the field of accommodation; section 13 will attempt an analysis which should be useful as an introduction to the understanding of autoregulations.

4. Adaptation and Behavior

To turn from organic to behavioral organizations, exactly the same functional relationships are found, though applied to very different structures. But as we shall be devoting chapter 5 to the examination of the stages in the formation of cognitive functions throughout the animal kingdom, we may confine ourselves here to a few introductory remarks, designed merely to show what meanings, analogous to those discussed in subsections 1–3 above, the terms assimilation, accommodation, and adaptation can have in the field of elementary cognitive functions allied to behavior forms at the prerepresentation stage.

Instincts and reflexes, in the first place, form the transition between what we have called assimilation "cycles" from the point of view of organization or of adaptation, depending on whether only the elements $A, B, C, \ldots, Z$ are considered or also the elements $A', B', C', \ldots, Z'$ (propositions [1]–[4]), and what we shall later call "schemata." I prefer to speak of "cycles" when the elements $A, B \ldots$ or A', B' are substances or energies and the processes $\times$ or $\rightarrow$ are physico-chemical and the resultant "forms" essentially material. On the other hand, I prefer to speak of "schemata" when the elements A, B or A', B' are considered on the scale of organs or external objects and the $\times$ or $\rightarrow$ processes are considered on the scale of behavior—actions of the organism on the environment described in a generalized way as constituting functional forms. For example, the digestion of food from the moment of its ingestion will form part of an assimilation "cycle," whereas the search for it, the handling and taking hold of it, will represent behavior "schemata."

It will be seen at once that "schemata" also have "forms," but these are of a functional nature since they are concerned with actions. Schemata also contain a cyclic order, since the different movements $A, B, C, \ldots$, affecting the objects A', B', C', are linked to one another up to some final term Z, whereupon they begin all over again ($Z \times Z' \to A \times A'$ etc.). But the return from Z to A may be relatively fast (feeding, etc.), or it may be deferred (modification, etc.). The speed of this rhythm is of slight importance here; what matters is the fact that the rhythm is there, and that the behavior schema thus becomes the equivalent of a cycle.

Hence, it is obvious that an essential function of adaptation in behavior schemata or subschemata is an adaptation or readaptation of a continuous kind, and that this adaptation obeys the same laws as do the cycles previously spoken of.

It is important, first, to underline the fundamental part played by assimilation, and it is especially in this respect that instincts and reflexes make the transition between physiological or epigenotypic cycles and behavior schemata. Just as the substances x, y, etc. are foods which will be assimilated in the form of A', B', etc. in a physiological cycle in the course of which they will contribute toward the production of the elements B, C, etc. in the cycle, so the objects X, Y, etc., containing these substances, constitute functional food (and may already be "perceived" simply as food), stimulating and maintaining the behavior involved in searching, taking hold, etc., which will lead to ingestion of the objects. Thus, they are "assimilated" into forms of behavior in the same sense—that is, of incorporation or integration into a schema—as they will later be assimilated into the physiological cycle. And, just as in this example the division into schema and cycle is entirely relative to what is considered to be the scale underlying the whole cycle, including the behavior leading to ingestion, followed by digestion, so assimilation into the schema and then into the cycle are merely the two phases of one whole process.

In the same way, to say that a sparrow needs pieces of straw and other materials to build its nest and to say that a snail needs calcium, etc., to make its shell are both expressions of the necessity for incorporating external elements into a construction of organized forms. But in the second case an organic form is involved, and the assimilation is physico-chemical and therefore related to a "cycle." In the first case, on the other hand, we are talking about forms of behavior or forms imposed by the sparrow on a small section of the external environment; the assimilation of the pieces of straw into the forms of the nest-making activity is, at that stage, merely functional, and so we speak of it as assimilation into a schema. But in both cases there is an assimilation of the environment into a form constructed by the organism, so that there is assimilation in a general sense.[13]

There is nothing artificial or metaphorical in giving a generalized sense to the term "assimilation" by applying it to behavior as distinct from the subject. The essential thing is to be clear from the outset as to what we mean by form and to understand that if form has any meaning in the fields of material morphology, anatomy (including histology), and even physiology, by the same token it also has meaning in the field of behavior; and, since the form of instincts and reflexes is often an extension of the organs, the analogy is all the more obvious. If we distinguish between cycles and schemata only insofar as their respective scales are concerned, then the assimilation of an object into an action or behavior schema becomes simple, the direct and natural extension of its assimilation into the organic cycles.

We are now left with the problem of habit or of sensorimotor acquisitions of an individual rather than a hereditary type. We must first remember that all transitions link these acquisitions to reflexes by means of conditioned reflexes. When food reaches a dog's stomach, the mechancial and chemical action of the foodstuff on the mucous membranes of the stomach sets off a secretion of some extremely acid gastric juice (whereas, if the stomach has been without food for twenty-four hours, it will produce no juice, and the moisture of the mucous membrane will remain more or less neutral or alkaline). The assimilation of food is thus characterized at this level by stable reactions which are a part of a normal cycle (which in a purely formal way conforms to the cycle of proposition [1]). In the event of visual and olfactory contact with food before ingestion, there is, by analogy, a salivary secretion, and one can likewise speak of an incipient assimilation, except that assimilation into the digestive "cycle" is in this case accompanied by another assimilation into the perceptual schemata, the latter being integrated, as subschemata, into a reflex schema. If, on the other hand,

---

13. One intermediate stage between snails and sparrows is that of the hermit crab, whose borrowed shell, although organic, is only an external object assimilated as part of a behavior pattern.

food is associated with a sound, and the sound alone will set off the salivary reflex, this new behavior is no longer hereditary and constitutes what Pavlov sometimes called "psychic" salivation. What does that mean? First, that the sound has been assimilated into the schema of the reflex, and here it will be seen that the notion of assimilation represents simply an extension of what we were just now calling assimilation of the piece of straw into the schema of the sparrow's nest-making instinct; only here it is a question of the setting up of a habit and not of a pure reflex. Second, that the sound has been assimilated into the food, not in the sense of what we should discover if we were to speculate about the dog's consciousness, of which we know nothing, but in the sense of a substitution of behavior or its effect. Thus, it will be seen that the assimilation which pertains to conditioning or to habit extends the assimilation of the reflex, but outstrips it in the sense that it "generalizes" reactions and even stimuli.

In the same way, we can say that when an infant has formed the habit of making objects hung in front of it swing backward and forward (by pushing them without grasping them), and when it applies this behavior to some new object that it has not seen before, there has been assimilation of this new object or situation into the swinging schema. Thus, it can be seen that the term sensorimotor assimilation is not at all artificial.

Now, if instincts, reflexes, conditioning, and sensorimotor habits include perpetual assimilation of objects into their schemata, it is self-evident that schemata, in their turn, are continually obliged to accommodate themselves to passing circumstances and to the peculiar nature of the objects assimilated. The kind of adaptation that forms part of behavior, whether hereditary or acquired (or both, through "genetic assimilation") thus constitutes yet again an equilibrium between assimilation and accommodation.

5. Cognitive Adaptations

Finally we must deal with adaptation in the sphere of thought and the higher cognitive functions. Adaptation of the subject to the objects of its knowledge does exist and is merely a particular example of the organism's adaptation to its environment. In both cases the criterion of adaptation is success of this adaptation, whether it be a matter of survival or of comprehension. For instance, it might be said that the theory of oxydization is better adapted to the phenomena of combustion than was the phlogistic doctrine, or, to take two approximations of one thought process, that Einstein's theory of gravitation is better adapted than Newton's. One might even say that between the survival of an adapted organ and the success of a comprehensive theory there are mechanisms in common, for the survival of the best theory also depends on choices dictated by experience, and these are not unconnected with selection imposed by environment, etc.

But if the comparison of these two widely different terms seems purely verbal or metaphorical, the question takes on an entirely different aspect as soon as transitions are looked at as a whole between elementary types of behavior (see subsection 4 above), and as soon as higher cognitive mechanisms are considered collectively, in particular when the intermediary stages are examined from the perspective of assimilation and accommodation.

First it should be asked what "form" is, in the functioning of thought, and whether the term "schemata" as applied to conceptual and operational schemata is used in the same sense as it is in behavior schemata and, hence, in the cycles which make up any organic "form." The difficulty arises mainly from the fact that a conceptual schema is rather closely linked to language, whereas the latter does not intervene at all in behavior schemata prior to the establishing of the semiotic or symbolic function and even less in organic cycles. But language is not thought, nor is it the source or the sufficient condition of thought. The roots of thought must thus be sought in action, and operational schemata derive directly from action schemata: the operation of addition proceeds from the action of joining things together, and so on (see section 1, subsections 2 and 3). Generally speaking, logico-mathematical structures are extracted from the general coordination of actions long before they make any use of language, either natural or artificial.

If one can pass from schemata made up of forms that are both organic and sensorimotor, such as reflex and instinct schemata, to schemata that are sensorimotor, properly speaking, such as "habit" schemata, it becomes clear that such a transition is equally natural if made between habit schemata and schemata of representational intelligence. The intervening stages are supplied in this case by the many schemata of sensorimotor intelligence which are initially mere coordinations of habit schemata but which eventually set up schemata atsonishingly isomorphic to those of representational intelligence. For example, a certain number of partial displacements, each one of which can correspond to one habit schema only, finally coordinate into a wider system, corresponding to a "displacement group," though remaining purely practical and functioning only approximately without any image of the whole. Now this sensorimotory "group" schema, however limited it may be in its functioning, nonetheless constitutes a substructure on which, at some time between seven and twelve years, the thinking will build a corresponding operational structure—a structure that is still unreflective, in the sense that it remains internal to the functioning of the intelligence (but as a representation now, no longer merely as an action) and is not an object of the intelligence. After this, reflective abstraction of a mathematical kind will build up a structure qua object of reflection, in the same way that it builds up all other elementary operational structures (groupings, intersections, orders, connections, etc.) from structures inherent in the functioning of thought and action.

In similar fashion, the schema of the permanence of objects, constructed by the sensorimotor intelligence, marks the starting point for operational conservation schemata in thought such as are elaborated in the eighth and ninth years. Thus, it is impossible, if one recognizes the existence of more or less generalized schemata on the behavioral level, from reflexes and habit formation up to the many constructions set up by the sensorimotor intelligence, not to consider imagination and thought schemata as adaptive schemata in the biological sense of the word. There is, therefore, such a thing as conceptual assimilation in the sense of sensorimotor assimilation of objects into the action schemata of the subject, since these actions are extended into operations. And at every level these schemata are constantly differentiated by continuous accommodation to new conditions, an adaptation resulting from the equilibrium between the accommodation and the assimilation.

6. Adaptation and Operations

This does not take away from the fact that, although intelligence is adaptive and assimilatory in origin just as organic and sensorimotor structures are, yet the sort of cognitive adaptation which occurs at the higher levels achieves much more complete results and much more stable structures. Organic adaptation has constantly to be readjusted under the pressure from the changing environment and new accommodations. Individual adaptation usually ends in failure or extinction, while phyletic adaptation goes on, but in such unsatisfactory forms that new evolutionary modifications in abundance have had to take place afterward. It is true that something similar is to be found in the numerous forms of human thought, and one would have to be an optimist indeed to see only stable cognitive adaptations among them. However, in the field of technology and science it is hard to deny that there has been some progress, for if science is in a perpetual state of adaptive reorganization, Oppenheimer is surely right in saying that science does not make the same mistake twice in the same way, something which can hardly be said to be true of biological evolution.

The essential difference between intellectual and organic adaptation is that thought forms, when applied to increasing distances in space and time (with progressive differentiation of the scales) leads to the setting up of an "environment" which is infinitely more extensive and therefore more stable, whereas operational instruments, for their part, being dependent on semiotic auxiliaries (language and writing), retain their own past and acquire some continuity and reversible mobility (by means of thought); they acquire dynamic stability, which is unattainable by the biological organization.

One result of this is that conceptual or operational assimilation is much more "conserving" than is assimilation in the realm of organic forms. From Euclid's elements up to contemporary theories on "structures" and "categories," mathematics has undergone countless revolutions, which, however, have not resulted in a mere amalgam of rejects from Euclidian geometry and arithmetic, but have continuously integrated the past into the present. And, even if the same cannot be said of the experimental sciences, at least the successive approximations characterizing such sciences give evidence of the same sort of constant effort toward integration and continuity, particularly on account of the possibilities for distinguishing and coordinating found in the various categories of phenomena.

On the other hand, while accommodation to new experiences has a certain irreducible quality of the unforeseen which is constantly threatening the new adaptations all over again, yet such accommodation made by intellectual assimilation schemata to the unforeseeable data of environment does have two remarkable characteristics that confer on it a greater degree of compatibility with assimilation than in the case of organic accommodations.

The first of these characteristics is the existence of certain accommodation forms which are, so to speak, permanent. A theory in biology or physics is in no sense of the term permanently accommodated, since it only needs the intervention of some new factor to be checkmated. (It is well known that no experiment can ever be made that will exactly confirm any theory, but experiment can invalidate a theory.) On the other hand, not only will no experiment ever disprove logical or mathematical theorems, a fact which is self-evident because of their hypothetico-deductive nature, but also one can rest assured that any fact arrived at by means of experimentation will lend itself, not to an integral deduction (history cannot be deduced), but to a logico-mathematical treatment, carried out in greater or lesser depth, which the fact will not contradict. In this way, the isomorphic juggling, the order structures, and so on, which present-day mathematics are applying to anything and everything, are evidence of some kind of permanent accommodation within the most generalized thought structures. Now this fact is not unconnected with what is found in biology, for although no particular organic form undergoes a once-and-for-all accommodation, yet accommodation of the most generalized forms of living organization merges into life itself and thus lasts as long as life does. This will be one among several reasons put forward to justify the interpretation attempted in chapter 6, namely, that the reasons for the remarkable accord between logico-mathematical structures and reality are to be sought within the very laws governing the functioning of the living organization in its permanent continuity.

The second striking characteristic of intellectual accommodation is its capacity for anticipation. If adaptation in the intelligence were limited to the field of the immediate present and the reconstruction of the past, it would be found wanting, in the domain of experience, much more often than is the case. But there are a great many happenings that can be foreseen by the exercise of thought, and the mere fact that the object of mathematics is to discover the sum of all possible transformations, and not merely that part of them which can actually be realized, is sufficient proof of this deductive power of the human mind. Even in the sphere of chance, which is constantly interfering with what has already been determined, particularly where history is concerned, logico-mathematical operations allow for calculation of every kind of probability, which constitutes yet another instrument of anticipatory accommodation.

Here again, anticipation is not confined to cognitive mechanisms, as we shall be recalling in section 13. But these anticipations as well as the permanent accommodations on which they are based are infinitely richer in the cognitive than in the organic domain. The conclusion to be drawn from the present section is, therefore, that cognitive adaptation is an extension of general biological adaptation but that its proper function is to attain such adaptive forms as are unattainable on the organic level owing to their infinite power of assimilation and accommodation and to the stability of equilibrium between these two subfunctions.

Section 13. Conservation of Information Acquired Previously, and Anticipation

Anticipation, to which a general allusion has just been made, is something much greater than an extension of accommodation; it makes possible the formation of anticipatory accommodations, but, in its general form, it derives from a capacity for inference or transfer, based on information previously acquired—based, that is, on the conservation of their assimilation schemata. We thus find ourselves confronted by two new functions (possibly with generalized structural characteristics) which are common to life and to knowledge: a conservation-of-information function, or "memory," and an anticipation function.

1. Memory

The notion of "memory" as the conservation of information raises two important problems, one of them related to learning, or the acquisition of information, and the other to its conservation as such. These problems are interdependent, for it is impossible to speak of learning or acquiring information if what is learned is not conserved, and, on the contrary, one can only use the term "memory" where information from an external source is conserved (otherwise anything to do with heredity would be mixed up with memory); but these problems are, nevertheless, distinct, for learning and conservation correspond to two successive phases in a complete process.

The organism has often, and quite rightly, been regarded as a machine for learning, just as essential a capacity in the organism as those of assimilation and reproduction. Indeed, if a careful distinction must be made between learning and development— although all kinds of learning are partly dependent on environment, and, moreover, there is such a thing as development in all forms of knowledge, including learning—it is nonetheless true that various kinds of learning are to be found at every level of the evolutionary scale and at all the stages, at least the functional ones, of individual development. But what do these forms of learning consist of? The organism may be seen as a "black box" from which the "outputs" provide nothing more than the "inputs."[14] Or again, the organism may be seen as a center in which all the information supplied will be subjected to transformation, or, at least, to organization such that the output is rendered much richer than the input. Now it is obvious that the kind of conservation involved will not be the same in both cases, and that if every acquisition is responsible for an assimilation, the conservation of information is, in its turn, dependent on assimilation schemata.

This is why the notion of "memory" is, in fact, a rather equivocal one. In terms of human psychology, it covers a certain number of processes, of which the two extremes are as follows. The most elementary form is simple recognition in the presence of the object perceived but without evocation of it in its absence. Perceptual recognition is a function of a sensorimotor schema which can be set up only when a previously perceived object reappears (which marks the beginning of a habit) but which is, generally speaking, a habit schema in the proper sense of the word. In fact, every habit presupposes recognition of indices and situations, which is what gives it its close relationship to recognition and its partly mnemic character (again, motor memory or habit memory are terms which are used in this connection).

At the other extreme, there is the term "evocation" memory, used to designate the capacity for evoking objects or events that are not actually present by means of perception and in the form of picture memories. Evocation is something of a much higher order than recognition and presupposes a symbolic function (mental

14. This is as much as to say that the only activities involved would be encoding and decoding, without any transformation, properly speaking, or any other mechanism, apart from translation or actualization.

images or language, as in "story-telling behavior," which P. Janet sees as being the root of evocation memory) as well as the processes of inference and logical organization necessary for the mental reconstruction of the past. This does not, incidentally, exclude the possibility of unconscious registerings. Penfield produced some proof of such a possibility by exciting electrically the temporal lobes, but it is not yet known how far-reaching the unconscious registering is in relation to parts of it which have been decoded, nor how reliable it may be in relation to the reconstructions presupposed by such decoding.) It is therefore clear that evocation, too, presupposes certain schemata, but these are conceptual or operational, and necessary either for the organization or for the reconstruction or merely for the decoding of memory or even for all these mechanisms at once.

Thus it can be seen how complex memory is, which takes us rather far from the concept formulated by Semon about what he called the "mneme." Instead of an automatic recording by "engrammes" and a direct and exhaustive decoding by "ekphoria," we are confronted by encoding or decoding that is linked up with assimilation schemata, which is to say, action and operational schemata. This presupposes transformations between the two in the shape of organization, if no more. From that point, leaving on one side the question of how memory and learning are acquired, the problem of their conservation has two distinct aspects: the conservation of schemata qua schemata and the actualizing of memory (or decoding) by means of recognition or evocation.

The problem of the conservation of schemata is not, properly speaking, a problem of memory, unless the meaning of the term is extended in an unwarranted way, for the schema of an action, being the transferable or generalizable quality in the action, is self-conserving; the memory of a schema is thus nothing more or less than the schema itself, and so there is no need to talk of "memory" in connection with it except insofar as to show the schema to be an instrument of memory. On the other hand, memory in the strict sense of the term, which is to say recognition or evocation (including evocation touched off by experiments such as Penfield's), is simply the figurative aspect of this conservation of schemata—figurative in the sense of something perceived (recognition) or imagined (evocation by a memory-image).

In the following pages, therefore, it will be not so much memory in the strict sense that interests us but the conservation of previous information in the widest sense, that is, everything acquired or learned in terms of the external world. So we shall be talking mainly about conservation and transference of schemata insofar as such schemata are elaborated in conjunction with environment. (That is why we have used the term memory, until the beginning of the present section, only in quotation marks, for its usage in biology is much closer to notions of learning, of conditioning, of habit, etc., than to memory in the psychological sense of recognition and, more important, of evocation, the latter being incontrovertibly a human property or, at least, a property of the higher primates.)

The great difficulty, however, in dealing with schemata themselves, is to draw the demarcation line between what is innate and what is acquired, since every transition takes place between two things, as, for example, between the reflex and the earliest habits (whether conditioned or simply instrumental). Between a hereditary system and some acquisition imposed on the subject by the environment and its regular sequences, there does, in fact, exist a tertium quid, which is exercise. Thus, it seems almost certain by now that maturation of such and such a sector of the nervous system is allied to some functional exercise, and, if one studies the manifestations of the sucking reflexes in a newborn human infant (as I have, indeed, done), one can observe increasing consolidation and adaptability during the earliest days (ability to find the nipple again after it has been moved slightly, etc.). But this exercise, though at first it teaches the subject nothing outside its hereditary programming, does, nevertheless, constitute a functional acquisition and presupposes some intervention by the environment. Now a functional acquisition may be extended into a structural organization. Thus, Hebb admits the part played by exercise even in the formation of perceptual "Gestalts"; Lehrmann similarly argues against the purely innate character of instinct, in favor of some early kind of exercise in the embryo. One might even go so far as to wonder whether the neurobiotaxia described by Kappers as existing in the embryonic organization of the nervous system from neuroblasts upward does not, even at that stage, show an effect of the same kind.

2. Elementary Forms of Learning

The object of the present chapter is simply to pick out the general isomorphisms between organic and cognitive functions or structures, not, as we do in chapter 5, to define the epistemology of cognitive ones, that is, to find out their necessary and sufficient conditions qua knowledge. From the isomorphic angle, we need only point out that, with regard to conservation of previously acquired information, this essential function is common both to organic life and to knowledge, and that within these two fields the same initial difficulty of dissociating acquired from hereditary information recurs as well as the same necessity for taking account of an exercise factor between the actions of both.

These problems present themselves as early as the molecular stage in biology. For example, it has been possible to look at immunity as a kind of "memory." But, with the study of bacteria and the formation of antibodies set up specifically to combat antigens, two sorts of possibilities presented themselves, and the choice between them has not been determined. According to the first, the antigen constitutes a sort of matrix, which the antibody enters and takes shape in. This would constitute a piece of information acquired from the external world, implying that immunity was a memory, in the sense that it was conserved. According to the second possibility, which seems to be prevailing, the specific adaptation of the antibody to the antigen is supposed to be the result of selection within the genetic information already established, so that "memory" can no longer be spoken of. But such a selection cannot possibly be translated into terms of the survival or the elimination (death) of individuals, since it is essentially a matter of choice and regrouping on the basis of predetermined information that still has to be regrouped and adjusted. The kind of selection involved here is much more like learning by trial and error than an all-or-nothing process. We are dealing, then, with a "response" in Waddington's sense, and the conservation of this response can certainly be seen within the framework of the conservation of newly acquired structures, even if such acquisition presupposes a close interaction between external conditions and that which is endogenous and predetermined. Even if the term "morphopoietic genes" is used, it still remains true that, although morphopoiesis brings about a succession of choices, these choices are oriented by their successes or their failures, in other words, by the overall situation. The famous question of the Michigan planarians (whose information acquired by means of conditioning is supposed to be retained in cases of regeneration after artificial divisions of the creature or even after absorption by an unconditioned creature of the fragments of a trained individual) does seem, on the contrary, to be losing its effect. So long as sufficient precautions are not taken about genetic characteristics in the strains that are being used, the question arises whether the effects observed, which have not been corroborated by other experimenters in this field, are not due to an initial selection rather than to "memory."[15]

On the other hand, the problem that has been set remains intact: the localization of acquired information in the RNA or the necessity for a functionally intact RNA if such acquisitions are to be conserved. This problem is of enormous theoretical interest, since RNA is closely dependent on DNA, which would seem to mean that acquired information is retained by virtue of activities requiring the action of a hereditary framework. Hyden, for example, has demonstrated, in his experiments on rats, that any further learning involves an increase in RNA, and the reply to this has been in the form of an alternative question: Is this the effect of learning as such, or of the activity expended? But if it is the activity, this may nonetheless be the result of the exercise itself, which is inherent in learning, independent of its content, and this, as we have seen, represents an intermediary factor between the innate and that which is acquired from outside.

Whatever may be the truth of the matter as regards such conservation of information at the macromolecular level, it does seem obvious that at the intervertebrate level there is already some acquiring of information from outside, even before there is any differentiated nervous system. In the Protozoa, for example, learning curves among paramecia have been established by making them turn about in a narrow tube in order to get out; the statistical improvement in the averages prevents any talk of instinct in this case. Positive results were obtained, even, by conditioning infusorians to

15. On the other hand, experiments which may prove decisive have recently been published by F. R. Babich, A. L. Jacobson, S. Bubash and A. Jacobson (see *Science*, 149, 656 [1965], and *Proceedings Nat. Acad. of Science* 54 [1965] no. 5, 1299). After submitting rats to a learning process in which they were guided toward food by means of a sound, the authors killed the animals they had trained, removed a piece of the brain, and injected RNA from it into a new group of rats; they then noticed that the latter did, in fact, show themselves capable of learning much more quickly. This experiment was repeated for control by E. F. Fjerdingstad, Th. Nissen and H. H. Roigeerd Petersen (*Scand. J. Physiology*, 6; 1; 1965) with positive results, whereas Gh. G. Gross and F. M. Carey (*Science*, 150 [1965], 3704, 1749) failed to discover any such facts. These latter authors are collaborating at the moment with the Babich team in order to try to discover why there should be this divergence.

associate light with food. Unfortunately, the possibility of the persistence of chemical traces left by the infusorians in the liquid does not altogether preclude the intervention of actual stimuli in what would generally seem to constitute the conservation of this association. We shall be returning to this problem in section 18.

As soon as any sort of nervous system, even a noncentralized one, appears, it follows inevitably that acquisitions become current and capable of being conserved in terms both of the many factors analyzed by theories of learning and of the structures identified either by experimentation or by the intermediary of the learning "machines" constructed by cyberneticians. In this way all the transitions between conservation of acquired information on the organic plane and on the plane of cognitive functions come into being, conditioned reactions occupying a specially privileged place in this respect because of their dual aspect of simply vegetative or visceral conditioning and conditioning relative to exteroceptive stimuli.

3. Cognitive Anticipation

Conservation of information previously acquired does, moreover, cause anticipatory reactions at all the higher cognitive levels, to the extent that one of the essential functions of knowing is to bring about foresight. In the realm of scientific thought, the establishing of any law presupposes foresight, for in order to verify hypotheses relative to the law being investigated it is necessary to organize the experiment, that is, to orient it in terms of certain anticipations and not to allow events to run on in haphazard fashion. On the other hand, since the essential quality of a law is its generality, it applies to the future as much as to the present and the past, which is the same thing as saying that it not only permits foresight but actually makes it necessary. Auguste Comte, whose aim it was to confine science to the mere quest for laws, totally leaving out of account the need for explanation or understanding, was thus handing over to scientific knowledge the central function of foresight—an incomplete summary of Comte's thinking, perhaps, yet accurate in what is affirmed.

However, this anticipatory function is very far from being exclusive to scientific thought, and it is to be found over and over again at every level of the cognitive mechanisms and at the very heart of the most elementary habits, even of perception. Indeed, consideration of the future does not belong to thought alone, although thought, being theoretically unlimited in scope, naturally extends its foresight or its projects much farther into the future than sensorimotor action or perception can. Nevertheless, to distinguish between the immediate future and the distant future that is accessible to imagination or deduction, it remains true that any habit, by the very fact that it conserves acquired information, has some application to the immediate future. That is why Tolman, whose theory of learning is much more comprehensive than Hull's associationism, asserted that an essential factor is expectation, by virtue of which every sensorimotor organization is oriented, even when based on "sign Gestalts" or significant configurations, for these very significations are relative to expectations.

In the domain of perception, it is known, for example, that the weight illusion, according to which the larger of two boxes of equal weight will seem to be the lighter, presupposes the anticipation of an approximate proportionality between weight and volume. Mental defectives or very young children, who do not exercise this foresight, give evidence of no such illusion when they weigh the boxes in their hands, so that even if anticipation does not explain everything, it certainly does play a part as a necessary factor, though not a sufficient one. A Russian psychologist, Usnadze, has constructed a visual equivalent of this weight illusion in such a way as to eliminate the muscular factors involved when the box is actually weighed in the hand; two unequal circles of 20 and 28 mm. are shown to the subject several times in succession in the space of 1/10 second, and are then replaced in the same location by two equal circles, 24 mm. in diameter. What then happens is that circle A in the place of the 20mm. circle is seen as bigger than circle B, having the same diameter but being substituted for the 28mm. circle. To put it another way, the initial presentation has brought about an effect of succession in time which has modified the previous perception. Now, since this effect increases with age, and the rapidity with which it is suppressed increases in the same way (so that error in juvenile subjects is weaker but longer lasting), we clearly have here a case of an anticipatory activity and not merely of aftereffects such as W. Köhler and Wallach talk about.[16]

Finally, the conditioned reflex itself is surely also anticipatory as

16. See J. Piaget, *Les mécanismes perceptifs* (Presses Universitaires de France).

well as, and on account of, being an instrument for repetition and generalization. The sound of a bell or a whistle releases the salivary reflex only as long as it is the herald of food, and if this food is never again forthcoming, the conditioning will fade away for lack of "confirmation" of this anticipation.

Thus, the function of anticipation is common to cognitive mechanisms at all levels. But the essential point to be noted in the comparisons we are now going to make is that at each of these levels, even the highest, anticipation presupposes no "final cause," deriving solely from previous information, whether by inferential means (scientific deduction or representation of some kind or other), by motor transfer, or by perceptual transposition.

The ambiguous character of the notion of final causes has, indeed, already been stressed—an ambiguity which is the psychological out-

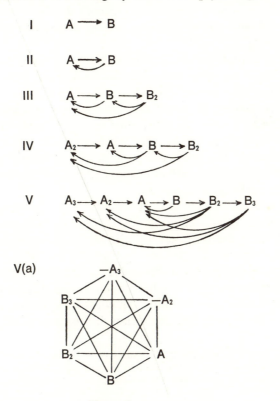

Figure 1

come of a confusion between the physical or physiological relationship of causality (cause *a* produces effect *b*) and logical, or consciousness-connected, relationships of implication (the use of *A* implies the result *B*) or of instrumentality (to reach *B*, *A* must be used).[17] But although it does consist of a kind of bastard complex, finality as final cause embraces elementary notions, each one of which, if kept distinct, is both clear and capable of causal or logical interpretation; of such a kind are the notions of fundamental utility, adaptation, direction, and, most important here, anticipation. In this connection, the latter characteristic can be explained in full by processes of transfer or inference based on previous information, in other words, on the application or generalization of schemata which were originally nothing but simple causal series and feedbacks, leading back from the result obtained to the initial action, but without any help, at first, from the anticipations that become possible later on, although any schema may become anticipatory once it is constructed.

Let us try to set up the simplest kind of model of such a process. A child of eleven or twelve months, accidentally pulling at a tablecloth or some support (action *A*), sets off a slight movement in the object lying on it (result *B*): result *B* is immediately linked by feedback to action *A*, which then starts over again (passage from I to II in figure 1); in other words, a chance act has become a schema. At this point two sorts of extensions are possible, one forward, which we shall call extrapolation, and the other backward, which we shall call recurrence.

Extrapolation consists of extending the previously obtained movement *B* into different positions, B_2 or B_3, each new result being fed back to the initial action *A* (III and IV in figure 1). Recurrence, for its part, means that action *A* may be set off by indices which preceded those of the original situation in figure 1; for example, the subject, not seeing at first that the object is placed on a solid support, discovers this when he notices the edges of the surface against which the object is perceived and realizes that, because of the difference in

17. J.-B. Grize, who has made a study of these three relationships from the point of view of logistic calculation, demonstrates in the same way that the relationship of "final cause" is an illogical concept because it mixes the real relationships of language (instrumentality and causality) with isomorphic relationships belonging to "metalanguage" used in order to relate causality $a \rightarrow b$ with instrumentality $B \rightarrow A$.

level of those edges, there must be some solid support which can be pulled, etc. In other words, action A will be set off by the recurrent indices $-A_2$ or $-A_3$, etc.

It is, then, the sum of the feedbacks linking B or B_2 or B_3, etc. to A or $-A_2$ or $-A_3$, etc., that makes anticipation possible, and anticipation is nothing other than a transfer or application of the schema (V or V[a]) to a new situation before it actually happens, the temporal order of terms A and B being immaterial since each can be linked to all the others (V[a]). To put it more precisely, schema AB, though not anticipatory at the outset, has become so by its double extension backward and forward. Either of these extensions would be sufficient in itself, but that is because each may be broken down into extrapolations and recurrences according to how much it is schematized.

4. *Organic Anticipation*

Looked at in this way, the function of anticipation is one of the most widely generalized in organic life as well as in cognitive mechanisms, by reason of the very fact that it is an extension of all forms of conserved information, whether genetic or acquired.

In the genetic and the epigenotypic domains, conservation, which we saw in section 11 to be implicit in every organization, is necessarily extended in anticipation as soon as reproduction is involved, since the subsequent generation carries on the genetic program transmitted by the preceding one, and the stages by which this is carried out must, then, be anticipatory by reference to the final adult state. So it goes without saying that the various organs will first appear in the form of a series of outlines before reaching their functional state. Cuénot deduced from this something that he calls "the law of anticipation in development," by virtue of which mechanisms are supposed to be set up in the embryo well before the organism needs them (preparation for the future, for example, callosities, plantar pads, hooves [see *Invention et finalité en biologie*, p. 21]). Guyénot, in his turn, talks in the same way of "the prophetic functioning of the organism."

To see anticipatory processes in facts such as these is perfectly permissible, provided one begins by characterizing anticipation causally as being the outcome of the transfer or generalization of information previously organized into schemata or cycles and preserved as such throughout the process (section 11). In this case the previous information is clear, and its organization with autocon-servation is clear too, since the genetic program conserved by the organization of the genome is what is involved. The transfer and generalization are clear also, since hereditary transmission during the "reproduction," or multiplication, of the original model is in-volved. So there is no particular reason to introduce a finalist argu-ment here, unless it is insisted on as part and parcel of any living mechanism.

If two scholars like Cuénot and Guyénot feel that there is some-thing mysterious about elementary callosities and hooves in em-bryonic life, it is for a very different reason from the one applicable to anticipation, since there is no problem about anticipation as such. It is because, as they fiercely deny all environmental influence al-though callosities and hooves have clearly no meaning except to be made use of in an environment, they cannot possibly see anything in this embryonic preformation but some preestablished harmony, and it is from this standpoint and only from this standpoint, there-fore, that they regard anticipation, as a kind of prophecy with an inescapable odor of finalism about it. But ever since Waddington exorcised the effect of environment and made it compatible with the endogenous reorganizations of the genome, and since cyberne-ticians did the same for finalism, making anticipation and even regulation independent, there has been no reason for confusing anticipation with prophecy or for attributing a psychoid to the genome, thus basing morphogenetic anticipations on some intelli-gent and conscious deduction; regulations and organic transfers are all that is necessary to this end.

Still to be reviewed is the vast collection of anticipatory processes which go to make up instinct, that is, in the field of anticipations that depend on the genetic program and not, or not exclusively, on acquired information. This subject was not dealt with in subsection 3 above because, although behaviors are involved, they are not of the kind in which learning predominates. It is true that the younger generation of ethologists, who have given thought to the inseparable interactions between the genetic program and envi-ronmental influence demonstrated in every phenotypic process, are refusing to consider instinct as something entirely innate (they speak of "behavior such as used to be called innate"), and Lehrmann, in particular, underlines the part that exercise or acquisition can play at every level. This does not take away from the fact that the unleashing of an instinct does not follow the same laws as an act of learning based on information acquired from the external world. From that point, instinct is the model for behavior which is both preestablished, since it rests on genetic information to a large extent, and yet also remarkably anticipatory, since it adjusts itself to external environment as though it had both knowledge of the end in view and instrumental relationships subordinating to this end a series of successive and connected means in a soundly adapted manner.

In reality, the knowledge involved in instinct is merely reactions to "significant stimuli" to which the organism is sensitized by its hormones (appetitive behavior), leading to "consummatory actions" which succeed one another in a series of elementary reactions. It is nonetheless true that, from the point of view of the biological cycle that is maintained by means of this hierarchical behavior pattern, the instincts present a commonplace yet extremely impressive example of anticipations based on previous information that is largely genetic and, in varying proportion, also acquired.

5. An Example of Morphogenetic Anticipation in the Plant Kingdom

I have been planning for some years now to make a closer examination of one particular case of morphogenetic anticipation in the field of phenotypic reactions among organized entities lacking a nervous system, such as plants. The development of a flower or of the plant's essential organs provides, in a natural way, examples of anticipation as Cuénot understands it. These instances of anticipation, however, though closely dependent on external factors such as light and temperature, are too well programmed, genetically, to provide a field for easy analysis of how previous information is put to use. On the other hand, in plant reproduction there are enough variations between one species and the next and, sometimes, from one variety to the next, for more or less random comparisons to be made. For example, a species of lily, *Lilium bulbiferum* L., produces axillary bulblets, while the subspecies *L. croceum* produces none; in this case the formation of the bulblets surely has some anticipatory significance where reproduction is concerned, and this anticipation would seem to be due to the transfer to an above-ground level of processes which normally take place underground, such as the division of the bulb into bulblets.[18]

As a testing ground for my analysis, I therefore selected a case which is analogous but of wider application: that of the shedding of sterile secondary branches from the *Sedum,* a genus of thick-leaved plants (Crassulacae) whose branches often fall without dying (because of their fleshiness) and give birth to new plants by putting down adventitious roots that automatically take root. We raised, over a period of years, about 150 species of *Sedum,* the European, the Asiatic, the African, and the American kind, some indoors and some outdoors, and at varying altitudes. We also did a series of close studies of the same species or varieties in their natural conditions in varying environments.

The interesting fact with respect to anticipation, and that is what concerns us here, is that the shedding of these branches varies a great deal from one species to another (among those that have such branches) and even from one environment to another in the

18. In any attempt to describe the general characteristics of reactional processes, without limiting oneself to the cases in which these processes are subject to the activity of the nervous system, they will be seen to fall into two categories. The first kind of reaction (one higher form of which is the reflex action) has the two following characteristics: (a) the periodic trigger-ing off of a hereditary apparatus, which then goes forward in ne varietur fashion; (b) this trigger action is provoked by external stimuli of a specific kind. Now the distinguishing factor about all plant growth, as compared with animal growth, is that there is a periodic recurrence of these triggered devel-opments. Whereas an animal has one genital system, which always remains the same, and an invariable number of paws, etc. a plant loses its flowers every year only to see them bloom again, thanks to some specific stimulus (light, etc.) or never to bloom again, for lack of such stimulus. It also produces a number of stems, but this number may vary from one year to the next, and so on. The second class of reactions includes, on the contrary, processes which are variable in terms of exchanges with external surroundings. It is characteristic of this class to have transfer and generalization processes (generalization of the response, or of the stimulus or both). In the animal kingdom, the examples we can cite are the conditioning and formation of habits. In the plant kingdom, not much study has been made of transfer processes (except by Corner, Miège, and Agnès Aber), because they are only becoming acceptable again, no doubt, in an epigenetic context and have no meaning if looked at from the purely genotypic preformation point of view. The facts such as we shall describe them in the present section do seem to provide quite a clear example (for further details see J. Piaget, *Observations sur le mode d'insertion et la chute des rameaux secondaires chez les Sedum, Candollea,* 1966), but it is possible that these notions about functional gen-eralization and transfer will throw some light on certain quite vital questions such as those of the flower's connection with the other parts of the plant (Goethe's theories, etc.),

same species, and sometimes even in one particular plant. Now, in those cases where shedding is frequent or even systematic (as in the *Sedum nicaeene* All. in the Mediterranean basin and also in several American species), this shedding seems to have been prepared for by a fairly distinct morphological device, consisting of a circular groove (or channel) at the point where the branch is inserted (figure 2*B*), or a groove which allows of some shrinkage so that abscission can be made (figure 2*C*). The branches which are

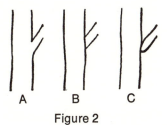

Figure 2

not going to be shed are usually of type *A* insertion. Moreover, it sometimes happens, not necessarily or even very frequently, that adventitious roots sprout near the insertion even before the branch is shed. These characteristics taken together would seem to constitute a morphogenetic anticipation of the shedding, and, indeed, in the case of those species where the *C* type insertions predominate, it is difficult to touch one tuft of a plant or transplant it without abscission's resulting from the slightest shake. In its natural state, all that is needed is a fall of rain or gust of air or a swarm of grasshoppers for fallen branches to be seen.

We must now point out that this anticipation is linked on to a definitely reactional process, which, in extreme cases, recalls the sort of autonomous reflex often found in crabs, lizards, dormice, and so on, although in this case the branch that has been shed engenders a completely new individual growth (which recalls a regeneration mechanism as in the shedding of leaves in the *Sedum stahlii Solms*) and does not break away in order to protect the parent plant. Of course, this reactional process is linked to genetic conditions, in the sense that not every species evinces it, at least not with the same frequency. There does exist one group of hardy species such as the *Sedum acre* L. in Europe or the *Sedum moranese* H.B. in Mexico, which only show infrequent shedding and have but few of the *B-C* insertions, and this is the case with nearly all the annual species whose reproduction is almost entirely sexual rather than vegetative. But in those species where shedding is frequent, its reactional character is typified by variations according to environment: the *Sedum album* L., for example, shows shedding and insertions of the *B-C* type, occurring much more frequently in the Alps at 2000 meters than at 1000 meters (in the case of the *Sedum montanum* the reverse is true). Some American species raised in Geneva alternately indoors and outdoors regularly changed the frequency of shedding and the modes of insertion as they went from one situation to the other.

It may be replied, at this point, that such shedding and insertion methods are constantly being subjected to a precise form of determinism: the part played by desiccation, aliment, light, and so on. This goes without saying, and I would expect such determinism to be recognized, although that is certainly not the case in this particular sector. However, the external factors do nothing to explain why there should be abscission, shedding, and vegetative reproduction rather than simple growth or necrosis; these factors must therefore be on a different plane from the overall process of separation—a process that remains anticipatory in nature (just as the flower is anticipated in the bud, and the stages of its development are not brought about simply by light or other factors that accelerate or inhibit its flowering).

This reactional and phenotypic anticipation calls for an explanation, and we shall therefore seek to account for it by starting off, in accordance with the rule, from previously acquired information.

In the first place it is possible to group the species in distinct categories according to whether they do, or do not, possess secondary sterile branches and whether they are attached to twigs or shoots growing along the ground or entirely off the ground. There is no point in going into detail about these categories or subcategories, which, moreover, do not correspond entirely to the phyletic subdivisions. Next, an exact statistical statement should be made about the methods of insertion (*A, B,* or *C,* with subdivisions that are of no interest in this context), by categories and species, and insertion methods in underground branches (roots, rhizomes, underground suckers) should be examined.

It will quickly be noticed that the separation processes begin in the parts underground and then extend throughout the ground shoots. Now, at these two levels there is nothing anticipatory about the process, which is simply a causal chain of events: (α) growth of the branch; (β) putting down of adventitious roots at its base but level with the top of the earth; (γ) gradual independence of the branch fed by its own roots as well as by the twig supporting it; (δ) beginning of separation (insertion A turns into form B or C); (ϵ) complete separation.

It will further be noticed that each of these links in the chain has caused a reaction in the one preceding it and has strengthened it, so that the lineal chain becomes a feedback system and, hence, a kind of schema whose parts become interdependent during the growth process.[19] Thus, all that is needed to account for the anticipatory nature of the process while the branches remain strictly above ground level is to recognize a transfer of the schema, from underground to above-ground level, as in the case of the *Lilium* to which we referred earlier.

The best indication of the fact that transfer takes place is that the process is gradual. By comparing the statistics of insertion methods in two successive categories, a clear correlation will be found between the connections $(B + C)/A$ and C/B, which steadily increase in importance, and this shows a slow progression in the direction of insertion (form C) and abscission of branches.

In sum, we can confirm that in simple plant forms there are reactional processes which, acting as a schema, become anticipatory by the transfer of this schema from one level of the anatomo-physiological organization to another. The anticipatory function evident in every habit and every conditioning thus recurs both in phenotypic plant adaptations and in animal behavior.

Section 14. Regulations and Equilibration

There is another major domain in which isomorphisms are apparent between the functions or structures of the organism and the functions or structures of cognitive mechanisms: the domain of regulations themselves, of particular importance for our main hypothesis (section 3) since we are trying to interpret the instru-

19. Compare figure 1 under V and V(2), the feedback system in this case being due to the fact that the causal actions are accompanied by return actions.

ments of the learning process as specialized regulation organs within the functional exchange that takes place between the organism and its environment. However, we aim to go further than this, attempting to show that cognitive regulations are an extension of organic regulations. Now, if it is true that they are such an extension as well as constituting specialized organs in exchanges with the external world, this must mean that organic regulations are not sufficient for everything, and that, in addition to the partial isomorphisms that are easy to distinguish, cognitive regulations also present original features which will now be described.

This originality may have two different explanations. The first could be simply that the domains of organic and cognitive regulations are different because the latter include exchanges with environment extended in ever-increasing distances into space and time (so that they can even reach infinity in logic or mathematics) and, by this very fact, exert an influence on "forms" or structures which at this stage are no longer exclusively material but functional or "formal," in the sense of conceptual or representational. The second explanation will, on the contrary, appertain to the very mechanism of the regulations involved.

1. Regulation and Construction

Let us start off, then, by analyzing the domains of regulation. If we are to understand the common nature of organic and cognitive regulations (and we must proceed from this common nature if we are to bring out the difference between them), we must first stress the fact that regulation is not something over and above the construction of forms and exchanges, but that it plays a part in this construction as a prime instrument, in the sense that the construction not only arises out of it but is in itself an autoregulation.

The physicist Lippmann used to say that the difference between living creatures and unorganized matter is that the latter only produces "phenomena," whereas the former produce "apparatus" or organs. The psycho-zoologist Uexküll went even farther, adding that the cell is not only a machine but a machinist. These two formulae mean that processes of organization, adaptation, "memory" or conservation, anticipation, etc., do not have a prior existence to regulatory mechanisms aimed at refining them or correcting their errors, but that each of these mechanisms forms part of a constructive mechanism, which can function only on condition that it is autoregulatory. Without autoregulation the mechanism would lose its identity and continuity, which means that it would disintegrate into a multitude of changes without self-conservation and so without "life."

To identify the two most essential characteristics of life, one can say, with all other writers, that life is "the creator of forms" (Borachet) or that it is "invention" (Cuénot), which incorporates, as a necessary condition or consequence, the idea that it is always extending its conquest over environment. It should quickly be noted that these are also the two most central characteristics of every kind of cognition and that they epitomize the mechanisms common to life and to knowledge that were analyzed in sections 10–13.

Starting with the construction of forms, it might be thought that there is construction on one side (organization, embryonic morphogenesis, etc.) and regulation or correction on the other, in the sense that the constructing process goes first and regulation would constitute the return process as a control. However, the proactive and retroactive effects are inseparable, because a construction without conservation is no longer an organic growth but merely some kind of change. Moreover, the construction of new forms does not arise from an irrational principle of "life impulse"; it becomes intelligible only if seen as a new equilibrium, that is to say, a product of a reequilibration in response to some tension in the environment. Now reequilibration simply means regulation insofar as there is continuous and obligatory conservation of some previous functioning, such as occurs in any "upsetting of the equilibrium" throughout the realm of living matter.

As for exchanges with environment, these are implicit in reequilibration, and inasmuch as the evolution of organized creatures confronts us with a sort of "progress," as understood by Huxley and, more particularly, by Rensch, with an ever larger "opening" in the possibilities of adaptation, it would seem necessary to admit that the creation of forms is made manifest, during material exchanges and especially in behavior, by a cumulative conquest of the environment.[20] Whether one accepts von Uexküll's definition of environment as the overall sum of sensory stimuli affecting behavior, or H. Weber's, as the overall sum of influences, irrespective of

20. Except in certain cases, where we find the reverse strategy of closing up or shrinking the environment. This is what happens with parasites or forms that have failed to evolve beyond the primary era (*Lingula*, etc.).

their stimulating quality, it remains clear that there is a wider environment corresponding to the more "open" systems, not only as involved in exchanges but to an even greater extent in potential exchanges. Here again, the increasing extension—it is better not to say the "regular" extension—of environment inevitably entails regulation systems, from which it cannot be dissociated. Indeed, either extension will be lethal to the individual or the entire species or it will prove adaptive, and adaptation is a kind of equilibration. Now, since this growing equilibration is quite different from the molding process in the adaptation of a liquid to a vessel or a simple balancing of the forces involved, but presupposes some adjustment of a parmanent kind between accommodation to situation and an assimilation that conserves functioning, it must be pointed out anew that regulatory mechanisms are inherent, not merely added to these exchanges with a constantly expanding environment.

Everything that has just been said can be equally well applied to cognitive as to organic mechanisms and will in no sense be modified by an examination of the following differences. Such differences do indeed exist, and they concern transformation of forms and transformation of environment, particularly where human thought is involved.

To take environment first: although life, at whatever level, shows a continual "tendency" to extend itself (dissemination of seeds, movement in animals, etc.), this tendency is even more marked (and here it needs no quotation marks) in the realm of knowing, where the coordinative nature of all forms of knowledge inclines them to generalization and application to new objects and the exploration of fields as yet little known. These numerous widenings of scope thus correspond to an extension of the "environment." But we are using "environment" in the same sense here as in biology? Von Uexküll says no, opposing "Merkwelt" to "Umwelt." Bertalanffy agrees, but adds that the notion of "Umwelt" ceases to be valid in the case of human behavior. But even if language and social life permit the creation of a culture which may be handed on by means of education, not heredity, and if the objects of knowledge are extended indefinitely in time and space, this does not take away from the fact that the sum of these objects continues to be, biologically speaking, a collection of "stimuli" and, therefore, an "environment." That these stimuli then cease to be purely "sensory" goes without saying, but, since at all levels a perceptual

reaction presupposes assimilation into frames or endogenous structures, the fact that objects of knowledge in the external world are
integrated into logico-mathematical or verbal or social frameworks
is no reason why they should cease to play any part in environment.
Moreover, since the relationship between organism and environment
is an exchange relationship and not merely an act of subjection,
cognitive exchanges are no less biological. There is one overriding
difference between the two, however, and that is that the cognitive
"environment" is constantly expanding, at a much greater speed
and with infinite possibilities, and this brings us up against the
first likelihood of difference in regulations.

Hence, the second difference between the respective domains:
organic regulations react on material processes, whereas the regulation of an act of pure mathematical reasoning bears on "forms"
dissociated from all actual content, which therefore become entirely
functional in their abstract conceptualization. But, although the
difference is a striking one and involves, as we shall see, a differentiation of mechanisms within the regulations, we cannot rest content
with such a confrontation, concerned, as it is, with two extreme
cases, for it is possible to find all kinds of transitions in between
organic "morphopoiesis" and the construction of cognitive "forms."
As has been seen above (section 11) in the case of the inclusion of
classes, order relationships, and the like, behavior "forms" are often
only an extension of organic ones (instincts, prehension habits,
etc.), and concepts formed by the intelligence are themselves an
extension of sensorimotor schemata in acquired behavior. Having
said this much, we must now try to bring out the analogies and the
differences between organic and cognitive regulations.

2. Organic and Cognitive Regulations

In its most general form, a regulation is a retroactive control which
maintains the relative equilibrium of an organized structure or an
organization in process of construction. But since the construction of
a structure is inseparable from its regulation (see subsection 1
above), it must be added that this retroactive control, although
retaining its role as a control, also makes a valuable addition to the
organization itself. At the elementary level of organization it even
becomes a part of it, an expression of the interplay of reactions,
sometimes equilibrated and sometimes not. In the case of a structure
in process of construction, the retroactive control adds something

to the construction in the sense that it cooperates in the construction.

That being so, the general nature of strictly organic regulations and of cybernetic regulations in the current usage of the term is to supply, by means of retroactive control, corrections or modifications in case of error. Either the regulation will bear on the outcome of a process and so amount to accepting the normal working or success of that process, or else it will compensate for deviation and correct any errors. Otherwise the regulatory mechanism must have an effect on the process as it takes place, or on the action itself, not on its result, and thus it must contain some anticipatory dimension and consist of a guiding power which again serves to confirm useful tendencies and to correct, or compensate for, bad ones.

Earlier, in section 3, we singled out structural regulations, which have a modifying effect on certain anatomical or histological characteristics, and functional regulations, which effect the exercise of the organs. Further, we singled out situations in which regulation is fused with the very interactions of the system and the formation of specialized regulatory organs, as in the case of the endocrine system, which is the origin of regulations, particularly of the structural kind, and the nervous system, which superimposes on structural regulations (neurosecretion, etc.) whole networks of functional regulations.

Now all these forms of organic regulation conform to the general characteristic of the correcting or moderating of error, a characteristic not inconsistent with the constructive aspect of regulation, since the correcting aspect is an expression of reequilibration or equilibration. When the term regulation is used in embryology in the sense of structural regulations such as may cause an artificially isolated blastomere to reconstitute a complete embryo, the "error" which the regulation compensates for is precisely this separation made by an external agent. Regulations in the genome—where regulatory genes or "repressors" either activate or prevent the functioning of other genes—present a case of bipolarity found at every level of organic organization: facilitation or reinforcement on one hand, and inhibition on the other (a dual role also found in the logical field with affirmation and negation, although then, as we shall see, it has other characteristics as well). Now this bipolarity, on the organic plane, has no meaning unless it is looked at from the point of view of adaptation, that is, the correction of errors and the registering of successes.

As soon as there is any differentiation in the regulatory organs, as with the endocrine and nervous systems, this characteristic of control, now correcting and now activating, becomes even more marked and is manifested in every domain by reequilibrations or the maintenance of an approximate equilibrium. Moreover, on all forms of feedbacks, feedforwards are superimposed, and these remedy slowness or excess in the feedbacks by constituting, as it were, regulations to the second power or controls of the regulation itself.

These classic models of regulation are found yet again, in this same role of correcting or anticipating error, on the level of elementary cognitive structures. Learning by groping or trial and error is simply the progressive construction of a schema, but in stages of successive regulations, such that the result of each action has a modifying effect, either positive or negative, on the following one. All sorts of models of groping have been offered, from the purely random, with selection after the event (Thorndike), to the "unfolding of a melody," or dynamic Gestalt, by means of progressive equilibration. However, as soon as the subject is no longer regarded as a mere theater in which chance occurrences take place, or as an equilibrium on the physical mode, and is seen again as a progressive organization making active attempts at discovery, then it will be obvious that groping is a succession of regulations following the line of an equilibration by means of assimilations and corrections brought about by the subject itself.

One even more striking example of equilibration brought about by regulations is perceptual learning, where the subject does not know what the ensuing results will be. For example, if the subject is presented, twenty to forty times in succession, with a Müller-Lyer figure or a diamond shape with the major diagonal sketched in (which will always cause it to be underestimated), then the illusion will decrease gradually as the presentations continue, until, with some adults, it even fades out altogether. Now it has been demonstrated in my own laboratory, by G. Noelting and Gonheim, that this kind of learning only occurs from about the age of seven onward, whereas in younger subjects error oscillates around a constant average. So there we have a regulation that develops with age, independently of any knowledge of measurement—two reasons why it might be called anticipatory: the acts of exploration are progressive and groping, and they correct, by means of a gradual decentering, the distorting effects of centering (that these are a source of error can be shown by experiment and even calculated).

3. Regulations and Operations[21]

Whereas elementary cognitive regulations can thus be shown to be of the same type as organic ones, the higher kinds of regulation, which are in fact operations, are of a different form, though they constitute the result of a complete transition from ordinary regulations (a similar transition as that from probabilistic induction to necessary deduction).

Before going any farther, we should point out that there is nothing sudden about this transition and that the earliest representational, though preoperational, regulations make a transition between sensorimotor regulations and operations. For example, a child of five or six years will maintain that a meatball rolled into a sausage contains more meat because it is longer, but if one continues rolling that sausage out, the child will then think it contains less because it has become "thin." In this case the error is reversed by means of a regulation based on the very exaggeration of the error. The reversal will, in turn, lead to the idea of interdependence between the lengthening and the thinning down and so finally to an operational compensation "longer $\times$ thinner $=$ same quantity." Thus it can be seen how a reversible operation, followed by conservation, may be derived in an absolutely continuous fashion from the interplay of regulations.

But we must go even farther and see a higher form of regulation in the operation as such—regulation in which retroactive control has become complete, rigorous reversibility. The example just given illustrates reversibility by reciprocity within a multiplication of relations. But a simpler example can be taken, the biological isomorphisms of which were seen in section 11: the inclusion of classes expressed as the result of an additive operation $A + A' = B$; $B + B' = C$, etc.

First, this A plus $A' = B$ operation, whose primary effect must be proactive, since it leads to the construction of B, is found to include a retroactive effect, since A is enriched, logically speaking, by some new characteristics as soon as it is joined to A' and integrated into

21. In connection with several points raised in this subsection, see the fine study by G. Cellérier, *Modèles cybernétiques et adaptation*, Etudes d'épistémologie génétique (Presses Universitaires de France).

class B (the statement "All A are B, or have the b characteristics of B," could not have been affirmed before B was constructed). But this retroactive effect is also found to have a control character, since what it finally does is to conserve A, in spite of its integration into B, and even to make sure A is conserved, since, if B is placed beneath the figure $A + A' = B$, A can be found again by means of the inverse operation, $B - A' = A$. So it is this inverse operation $(-)$ which plays the part of regulation in this case (retroactive control) in relation to the construction (additive operation $+$), and it can be seen that the control is one and the same thing as the construction, since operations $(+)$ and $(-)$ are the same operation extended in opposite directions.

It may be said that such a regulation presupposes conservation. But that is not true at all, for it is precisely the reversibility which brings about the conservation, as can easily be demonstrated in the psychological field: reversibility is the very process from which conservation is produced, and this process varies in degrees of approximation as long as it remains in the state of a regulation in the usual sense of the word. This explains the intermediary responses obtained between nonconservation and conservation. On the other hand, the child's arguments when he is trying to justify some conservation that may have become self-evident to him are of the reversibility type ("You can turn the sausage back into a round shape") or of the identity type ("It's the same paste," "All you've done is make it longer," "Nothing has been taken away or added," etc.). Identity teaches the child nothing new; he knew all the time, whatever his age, that nothing had been added, but that did not prevent his concluding that there was nonconservation. In fact, identity actually becomes an argument in itself as soon as it is subjected to reversibility ($+P - P = 0$, or 0 or $P^0 =$ the identifying operation in the system). Thus, it is certainly reversibility that entails conservation and not the reverse, as E. Meyerson believed.

Will it be said that this reversibility presupposes, if nothing else, some sort of "memory"? On the contrary, and this is true of any regulation system, it is retroaction and, in this case, reversibility, that gives rise to this "memory" as a simple conservation of schemata constructed by proactive and retroactive action (see section 13).

The reply to this will be, at the very least, that in this case reversibility must be adjusted if it is not to be either too "long" or too "short" but to reach the exact target. And, in effect, the construction of a model would presuppose that such an adjustment was being thought of. But two possibilities present themselves in this context: either a unit system, which would, however, be out of the question here, since the construction is not numerical (if it were, that would presuppose the synthesis of the inclusions and a serial order A A' B', etc.), or else a consolidation of the inclusions themselves. Now they are, in fact, consolidated or controlled by the bi-univocal correspondence between the direct and inverse operations: $-A$ corresponds only to $+A$; $-A'$ to $+A'$; $-B$ to $+B$, and so on.

However, since this interpretation consists of viewing operations as regulations of the higher type, hence, as the final state that can be reached by ordinary regulations when their approximating retroactions lead to complete reversibility, it truly holds a deep biological significance, going much farther than the limited scope of formal isomorphisms. If regulation of the lower or ordinary type is a process for correcting or modifying errors, then operational regulation is seen as a process for precorrecting, avoiding, or eliminating errors, which is something much greater.[22] Indeed, an operational deduc-

22. W. R. Ashby, in his *Introduction to Cybernetics*, gives a nice example of a regulator based on the games theory, which he claims is the commonest and easiest to construct and maintain, biologically speaking. It concerns a game between the regulator R and the source of a disturbance P (environment, perhaps). These are introduced into organism T, which is trying to conserve certain essential variable constants E. Now in a model of this type, regulation cannot possibly be perfect since the information needed by R, if it is to function, must come out of E, and the result once produced in E can produce an approximate regulation. If this regulation is to be perfect, what is needed, therefore, is the intervention of the regulator before P has produced any result in E. This sort of thing seems to us characteristic of the

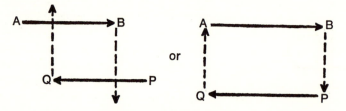

kind of operation in which the regulation does not affect the result but the action itself, and in which the action allows the result to be foreseen and either to be used or to be canceled out by means of a reverse operation. This would seem to be the deductive course of actions as operations, leading to perfect regulation both by anticipation of the results and their possible

tion is not subject to any error if it is in conformity with the laws of its structure ("groupings," "groups," "networks," etc.). An error in logic or in mathematics is the result of an individual slip, of factors of attention, memory, and the like, which have nothing to do with the structure being used, whereas a perceptual structure, for example, has a probabilistic aspect that excludes any kind of composition other than by approximate regulations.

Thus, it can be seen that during the gradual extension of the knowledge "environment," that is, the sum total of external objects on which the intelligence is brought to bear, and during the gradual dissociation of forms and their contents, that is, the elaboration of abstract and conceptual "forms" as opposed to perceptual or sensorimotor forms and, a fortiori, as opposed to the material forms of the organism, the regulations whose task it is to control cognitive exchanges with this environment, that is, to organize experience in terms of deductive frames, will reach a level of precision never found in elementary regulations. Instead of being restricted to corrections after the event that bear only on the results of processes or behaviors, or to an approximate guidance of anticipations that are never more than probabilistic, they carry out a function of precorrection in the proper sense of the word. The exercise itself of this function remains, of necessity, approximate where inductive methods are concerned, since the content of experience does not yield to any all-embracing prevision. Nevertheless, it is a function that is completely fulfilled in the domain of the deductive or logico-mathematical structures of the intelligence. If one were to take

---

canceling out or inversion. Furthermore, between the elementary model with a single feedback starting off from the result of the action, and the reversible operation, one can think of models with a double feedback (*BP* and *QA* in the figure set out in this footnote). This becomes possible as soon as the regulation affects the actions and not their results, for example in the case where some empirical seriation in a child's mind, having an ascendant order ($< \ldots$) entails a later seriation in descending order ($> \ldots$) or again, where the lengthening of a clay sausage causes the child to notice that it has got thinner, etc. In this case, what was at first merely a succession of regulations (at different stages in the action, as will be seen by consulting the two figures) will become a system of direct and reverse operations as soon as the two actions *AB* and *PQ* are coordinated into one whole instead of being adjusted from without by a succession of progressive regulations. Here again we must notice that, if we are introducing two distinct actions *AB* and *PQ*, then the action *PQ* also may only have been a feedback in the first instance in relation to *AB*, which would make *BP* and *QA* regulations to the second power.

mathematical entities as external to the subject, what has just been said would still be valid in essence, insofar as the intelligence would have to adapt itself to them. But it goes without saying that if we look at logico-mathematical structures, as we shall be led to do in chapter 6, as being the product of the broadest functionings of action and of the living organization itself, then to attribute to intellectual operations the nature of higher types of regulation will take on an even more profoundly biological significance.

4. Conclusions

The overall conclusions to be drawn from this chapter and, particularly, from the present section (14) seem both simple and restrictive.

In the first place, the more generalized functions of the organism —organization, adaptation, and assimilation—are all found once more when we turn to the cognitive domain, where all of them play the same essential part. Only reproduction has not been mentioned under this head, but if we dissociate in it its two main components of conservation or repetition, and regrouping of transmitted characteristics, it will be self-evident that these two aspects also are anything but foreign to the mechanisms of repetition and combinatorial interferences evinced by individual intelligences when interacting. Even the relations between the individual genome and the "population" are partially isomorphic to the relations between the individual and human societies. Of course, the basic unit is the population or society, but this does not alter the fact that each individual contains within himself an inextricable knot of social interferences and thus constitutes a sort of microcosm reflecting a sector, be it large or small, of the main group to which he belongs. Nor does this alter the fact that it is within the individual, especially during his period of ontogenesis, that genetic or social regroupings are effected, causing new syntheses to be made. As soon as atomism is rejected in favor of dialectic constructionism, it becomes apparent that the problem of deciding whether it is the individuals that give the social group or "genetic pool" their characteristic stamp, or the reverse, is analogous to the fruitless question of which comes first, the chicken or the egg—a question, incidentally, which I would much rather put in terms of the hen and the chick, since the egg is merely a transition stage in development.

In a reciprocal way, the essential characteristics of knowledge present us with obvious organic points of correspondence. The two main functions of the intelligence are to invent and to understand, and morphological and physiological invention are as much the basis for this as is organic assimilation, which is what brings about the progressive discovery, or infinite extension, of the environment.

But although partial isomorphisms such as we have tried to bring out would seem to prove that there are certainly mechanisms in common, only partial correspondence is involved, basically because knowledge, however much it may draw on the living organization for its functional framework, is always much more far-reaching in that it sets up more delicate structures, though in a direction determined from the outset. From the point of view of organization, intelligence succeeds in making structures that are both more stable and more highly differentiated, for although it would be possible to conceive of the mathematization of all biological structures, all mathematical structures could not be realized on the organic plane. In adaptation, intelligence achieves equilibrium forms between assimilation and accommodation which are carried forward and rendered coherent quite otherwise than in organic approximations. Conservation of the past and anticipation of the future will give rise to similar statements. But it is in the domain of regulations that the advance in cognitive functions, by comparison with the approximate equilibria achieved by the organism, is most striking.

The analyses we have striven to make throughout this chapter remain, nevertheless, incomplete and fragile, for partial isomorphisms have no meaning, as has been said, unless transformation laws can be produced such as will allow a transition from one of the compared terms to the other, and unless proof is furnished that these transformations can actually—and in this case biologically—be realized. Now, there is a way, not to bridge the immense gaps in theory, but to do something to that end, and that is to examine the levels of "behavior" which are the median term between organic life and knowledge and to try to find out the necessary and sufficient conditions for these sucessive forms of behavior from the angle of their adaptive success or knowledge value. This will be our object in the following chapter.

5

The Epistemology of Elementary Levels of Behavior

The epistemological analysis of any kind of knowledge involves finding out what are its necessary and sufficient conditions, not only from the formal or logical point of view, but from the angle of the relations between the cognitive instruments of the subject and the characteristics of the object insofar as it is accessible to the subject's experience (with eventual reference to how it appears when seen from the vantage point of subjects at a higher level, that is, as an observer would see it).

The classic method has been for the epistemologist to ask himself how any science is possible, in other words, what the necessary and sufficient conditions are that will take account of how far our intellectual equipment is adequate to the world around us. Solutions to this question have been many and contradictory, but it is our hope to make some progress toward a positive solution by making a combined study of the constituent conditions, from a rational basis on one hand, and from historico-critical and psycho-genetic points of view on the other.

Similarly, there is nothing to prevent one's asking how instinctive knowledge is possible and making use of more or less comparable methods. It will be said in reply that instinct is not a kind of knowledge but a behavior, and that practically nothing is known about

how it is in fact formed. As to the first point, this is simply a mis-
understanding: we may not know anything about animal consciousness, but we can analyze (1) its perceptions and reactions and (2)
what it "knows how to do" in response to stimuli perceived in the
external environment. "To know how to" [*savoir faire*] is a kind of
knowledge [*connaissance*] or ability or [*savoir*] like any other, and
in the human child it precedes conceptual knowledge by a wide margin. The second objection is much more serious, but it is precisely
because we do not know what is the genesis of the instincts that we
shall have to confine ourselves to an epistemological analysis which
may well be incomplete for lack of data on the development of instincts but will still be possible, up to a point, by comparison with
the genesis of acquired knowledge and intelligence.

So we shall be asking the same questions, respectively, about perception, learning, and animal intelligence. But first a few points must
be made concerning the nervous system as the necessary intermediary between the living organization and its knowledge and as the
seat of the most elementary hereditary reactions or reflexes whose
transitional character is such that we do not know whether they are
the source of "pieces of knowledge" or simply of reactions.[1]

Section 15. The Nervous System and the Reflexes

Outside the biological field, wherever intelligence and thought are
put forward as self-explanatory prime facts or, ultimately, as the
source of facts, which is the idealist thesis, the function of the nerv-

1. For the general question of behavior as it applies to the main problems
in biology, see the collection *Behavior and Evolution,* edited by Anne Roe and
G. G. Simpson (Yale University press, 1958). Simpson's article demonstrates
that behavior is not merely a resultant but a determinant of evolution.
E. Caspari talks about the genetic bases of behavior (genetic selection such
as modifies the rat's speed of learning, etc.). R. U. Sperry stresses the fact
that there are unknown bases in the ontogenesis of behavior, and F. A.
Beach underlines the evolution in the use of hormones whose chemical
structure varies very little. Thomas H. Bullock, a specialist in the basic
mechanisms of behavior in invertebrates, believes that they have a functional
unity at every level, even the higher ones, but recognizes that his views are
only hypotheses. R. A. Hinde and N. Tinbergen make a comparative study
of specific behaviors, in species, and E. Mayr brings out the relations between
behavior and systems in zoology. C. S. Pittendrigh tackles the problems of
adaptation and selection, and S. L. Washburn, in collaboration with V. Avis,
those of human behavior.

ous system cannot be understood. For if the body is necessary in order to incarnate thought, then this body ought to be enough in itself, and introspection ought to provide us with our information, not only about the condition and functioning of every organ and every cell, but also about the biochemical and biophysical processes within each of the macromolecules of which we are made. Thus, the presence of the nervous system cannot be understood, all the more so because, being of ectodermic origin, it gives far more information about the external environment than it does about what goes on inside the body, even in cases where it has developed the role of regulatory organ for the whole of the organism. This is why, in Bergsonian spiritualism, the nervous system vis-à-vis the mind is reduced to the modest role of a hook with a coat hung upon it. But even the hook presents a problem, for from this point of view it is the coat itself which is the fount of life, and that renders the hook useless.

1. The Nervous System and Assimilation

If, on the other hand, we consider life to precede knowledge, and knowledge, while retaining the essential characteristics of the living organization, to exceed and extend it in such a way that its mastery of the environment is more far-reaching than that which any physiological exchange can achieve, we then see the nervous system as having a dual capacity: as the most direct and perfected expression of the body's organization, controlling all the workings of that organization, but also as the cognitive and, at the same time, organic instrument by means of which it achieves that functional mastery of the environment which extends the physiological mastery.

This joint organizing and adapting function in the nervous system makes it, in fact, both the most highly evolved and perfected of living things and the most highly differentiated instrument for the functional assimilation of environment. Two things, in particular, give evidence of this.

With respect to the organization and its regulations, Bertalanffy points out something which it is essential we bear in mind. In the course of embryonic development, the "regulability" (as Driesch uses the term) decreases in inverse ratio to the setting up of successive differentiations. There is, however, a single exception,[2] and that

2. Aside from the pacemaker system, which can be supplied by the atrioventricular node and by His's bundle, though plainly under the control of the nervous system.

is the nervous system, which is capable, right up to the adult state, of regulation in the embryological sense, that is, of reconstituting the total system from any part that is left in place. For example, beetles and crabs, if one or more of their claws are cut of, will set up fresh circuits modifying the central function: "The nervous system evinces a regulability which it owes to its original equipotentiality. The latter may have been inhibited during development, but it has not disappeared completely" (*Les problèmes de la vie*, p. 159).

One could go farther than this. The three main phases of embryonic development may be considered as initial segmentation (with possible regulation, endomorphism, and reconstruction of the whole from one part), determination or differentiation, and functional "reintegration," as Weiss has rightly called it, which is to say the phase in which functional unity is reestablished under the influence of hormonal and nervous regulations. It thus seems that this functional unity, guaranteed in the last resort by the nervous system, represents the extension of that morphogenetic dynamism which we saw in the second phase (determinations) and, once reunion has taken place, of the regulability or basic mechanism of the first phase.

As for the adaptive aspect of the nervous system, the essential problem, as far as we are concerned, if adaptation is indeed an equilibrium between assimilation and accommodation, is to understand the part played by nervous activity during the change from the material assimilation of substances and energies that constitutes physiological assimilation, to the functional assimilation of information from the external world that is characteristic of cognitive assimilation. What we have just said about regulability in the nervous system and its role during embryogenesis has already demonstrated that its action primarily consists in extending material forms into "functional" forms or dynamic structures which ensure the working of organic structures. But then what are we to say about assimilation —the question that arises as soon as both the acquired and the innate nature of cognitive assimilations are taken into account? The adaptive function of the nervous system is, in fact, aimed at accommodating each individual to the ceaseless and countless changes in environment, whether on a small scale or at the widest and hereditary level. So what is to be said about assimilation's part in this?

The hypothesis is that nervous reactivity (exciting and effecting) does, in fact, assure the transition between physiological assimilation, or integration of external substances and energies into the structure and functioning of the organism, and cognitive assimilation or integration of objects or situations into action schemata and eventually into operational or conceptual schemata.

We must first remember that reactivity to external stimuli is not a primary process. Not only is one of the two essential functions of the nervous system the internal regulation of the organism, as we saw earlier, but there are also such things as spontaneous and endogenous nervous activities. Adrian has demonstrated this in connection with animal kinetics, and it has also been proved by means of electrographic recordings.[3] Thus, reactivity is first and foremost an assimilation, taking into account these functional forms and internal activities.

Next, we must remember that, although there is differentiation within the nervous system from the Coelentera upward, yet the functions carried out by it, including reactivity with its acquired modulations as well as its innate ones, are present even at the level of Protozoa. Some very instructive observation by Scheffer, for example, showed that the amoeba is affected by acquired experience; it will at first refuse particles of tyrosin, but then, having accepted and absorbed particles of globulin, it will eventually accept the tyrosin which it at first rejected. Here, then, is a fine example, not only of prenervous adaptive modification in the sense of a reactivity of an acquired type, but also of an assimilation which, remarkably, is an intermediary between physiological assimilation (absorption of substance) and nervous assimilation, in the form of the integration of a new element into a previous schema as a form of experience. When an amoeba pursues a paramecium for twenty minutes, as Grassé has observed it doing, or when a lacrymarium stretches out its "neck" (by means of a sort of functional cephalization) toward food, then, in the same way, there is both physiological assimilation and assimilation into an action schema.

But once the nervous system has been set up, reactivity can be considered in general terms (stimulus-reaction) as a form of transition between the two types of physiological and cognitive assimilation. It is no longer a case of assimilation in the sense of a simple absorption of a substance or energy, because the stimulus is not the ingredient but the thing which sparks off the internal activity and so

3. Hamburger found that the chicken embryo shows some spontaneous and rhythmic motility, although this is not integral and so must be random. It is evinced before any sensorial input occurs.

is assimilated simply as a functional element. But it is not yet a cognitive assimilation, because this sparking-off process is still only causal rather than being perceived as significant, whereas it will become cognitive as this perceptual significance becomes differentiated. The very term "sensitivity," used to characterize the way in which stimulus is received, is sufficient evidence of the continuity of the transition, for this sensitivity may well not lead to any perception, properly speaking, and yet be a source of perceptivity. And is reaction merely a movement, so that it cannot be called a cognitive function, or is it an action schema, which is a kind of behavior in that it involves some practical knowledge or "knowing how to do" in the proper sense of the terms "doing" and practical "knowing"? Thus, it can be clearly seen that the question is insoluble, which goes to show that there is a continuity between assimilation into a physiological functioning and assimilation into action schemata, which may be as elementary as the innate mechanics of locomotion but still give evidence of this kind of practical knowledge.

2. Reflexes and Assimilation

Any examination of reflexes, in the strict sense, and of their relation to instincts will bring out even more clearly the intermediary character of nervous reactions between physiological assimilation and cognitive assimilation. According to Viaud (*Les instincts* [Presses Universitaires de France] pp. 105–9), reflexes in the higher animals are to be seen as "reactions in the form of muscle contraction or glandular secretion, set off by some well-defined stimulation applied to some more or less localized point on the surface of the skin or in some organ of sensation and having a sufficient intensity" (p. 105). Reaction is thus seen to be a glandular function, which means it is not behavioral, or a muscular one, which is, on the contrary, capable of embracing any kind of transition, from an isolated movement to one which contributes to a protracted action. In Viaud's opinion, the first of these alternatives is the correct one, and his general interpretation is that a reflex is neither a form of behavior nor an integral part of instinct. This needs further discussion.

Let us first remember that, according to current views on the subject, a reflex is the product of a differentiation touched off by spontaneous centralized activities. Embryologists such as Coghill have demonstrated clearly that specialization is progressive, and Graham Brown, in his study of the reflexes involved in locomotion, reaches the conclusion that the overall rhythm does not spring from some coordination between previously established isolated reflexes, but that the reflexes splinter off as a result of the rhythm. It is true that these activities or coordinating rhythms are not forms of "conduct": rather, they are the outcome of the internal functioning of the nervous system, but, as instinct itself is the result of an endogenous apparatus, it was worth recalling the wholeness of this functioning that precedes its differentiation.

The problem, then, is not so much the nature of reaction, for, although it may have its origin in some internal function, reaction may evince quite a varying power of adaptability to environment, as, for example, in locomotion. Furthermore, this adaptation can be perfected with experience without, nevertheless, stepping outside the bounds of its hereditary programming, except when there is conditioning. Some time ago, as has already been mentioned, I made a study of the gradual consolidation of sucking reflexes during the first few days of the human baby's life. It is known that a calf that is spoon-fed will not be able to suck so well. Experiments carried out long ago by Spalding on the importance of experience in the flying powers of young swallows have since been confirmed by Dennis, working on nocturnal birds of prey. Thus, reaction may become partly behavioral, with all that this implies in terms of action schemata, even if it is only a question here of "reflex schemata," which are, however, evidence of some history.

But an examination of the nature of stimulation does raise the problem of cognitive or physiological assimilation. Rabaud, attempting to demonstrate the graduated character of reflexes and the transition from segmented responses to an overall response, made the edge of a spider's web vibrate with the hum of a tuning fork, producing the kind of stimulus aroused by the trapping of an insect in the web. If the vibration was weak, the spider raised only one or two legs; as it increased, all the legs reacted; and, when it reached a certain point, the spider came running. However, when this was repeated, the spider no longer responded. So there we have a fine example of a variable reflex carried forward into action.

Viaud's reply is that this is no reflex. His argument, which is of interest in our study of this problem of assimilation, is that the stimulant here is a kind of perception, whereas a reflex does not react to "signs" (in the sense, of course, of signals or indices, not the sort of sign which occurs in semiotic functions). Furthermore, Viaud goes on to say that in the case of true reflexes the physical stimuli "do not need to be seen, that is, recognized" (p. 106). The first thing to be said here is that any act of perception is a long way from implying recognition, and that sights which are entirely novel are nonetheless perceived. But the real question is the significance or nonsignificance of the stimuli of a reflex, for, if they are significant, there must be cognitive assimilation, and if they are not, assimilation is something more like an energetic or physiological integration.

The noteworthy thing about reflexes, in the fields both of stimulation and of reaction, is precisely that they supply us with examples of the whole range of transitions from nonsignificance to significance and, hence, from physiological to cognitive kinds of assimilation. Nobody can deny the significance in a reflex of the conditioned type: the sound of a bell is assimilated by Pavlov's dog into a food signal. But in the case of an absolute reflex, when the smell and sight of food actually set off a salivating reflex, could it be said that these sensory stimulants have no significance, are not "perceptions," and are not "recognized"? Only by a peculiarly hidebound theorist. Moreover, this example of cognitive assimilation is all the more remarkable in that reaction here is not an action schema in the strict sense but a physiological process: salivation. What connects it with behavior is, on the other hand, the anticipation of salivation in relation to ingestion. Will it then be objected that a reflex only begins when contact is made between the food and the mucous membranes of the mouth? But perception is at play here too—and a perception of marked significance, to judge by the differential reactions of the dog to the food he prefers, the food he is just prepared to accept, and the food he refuses. So we find ourselves in a sort of frontier zone between physiological assimilation (meaning the initiating of digestion by the saliva) and cognitive assimilation, or recognition, by means of a reflex. This frontier zone is plainly a very restricted one.

On the whole, it is no exaggeration, nor even a mere figure of speech, to say that nervous reactivity is what assures the continuous transition between physiological assimilation in the wide sense, and cognitive assimilation in its sensorimotor form.

3. McCulloch's Logical Network

The nervous system is something much greater than the aggregate of reflexes it was formerly thought to be. McCulloch and Pitts showed it to be a "network,"[4] not in the somewhat vague sense of the term given it by K. Goldstein, but in the precise sense of an algebraic structure (lattice). This discovery is not only of fundamental importance for the study of the nervous system, but it gives hope that it may be possible to apply a logico-mathematical treatment to the whole organism, of which the nervous system is both a reflection and a regulator.

In effect, McCulloch and Pitts, by a detailed analysis of the neuronal connections, have found isomorphic links with the sixteen functors of the bivalent logic of propositions, in other words, with the binary combinations of a Boolean network of values 0 and 1. What, then, will be the meaning of this isomorphism with the logical operations which in our societies are established in a child only between twelve and fifteen years of age?

The first question to ask is whether this is indeed a case of "logic" or of a cognitive mechanism. One can certainly speak of some kind of logic, but only on condition that a careful distinction be made, as we did in section 11, between the structures inherent in a function, which thus intervene as factors in its internal mechanism, and the structures produced by the function, which inaugurate functioning of a higher order, that is, "behavior." Now the logic of neurons, though it may constitute a structure produced by organic functioning of a general kind (which leads one to hope that the structure of the organism may at least be dependent on some Boolean equation), naturally remains inherent in nervous functioning, which cannot of itself constitute a cognitive mechanism.

McCulloch and Pitts entitle their paper "From immanent ideas to nervous functioning." This is, no doubt, a figure of speech, but its concrete sense is that such ideas are "immanent" and thus inherent in the functioning. As for the "ideas," it goes without saying that McCulloch has no intention of attributing to the nervous system any unconscious operations or even any concepts in the sense that the intelligence has concepts. These immanent ideas are like those used by an electronic brain, which is to say, they are a causal mechanism isomorphic with conscious implications (see section 4, subsection 4), but they remain causal, although the programming of the machine may include the handling of very advanced kinds of reasoning, whereas neurons cannot reason at all, simply because their connections are isomorphic to operations.

4. *Bull. Math. Biophys.*, 5, 115, 135, and 7, 89.

This does not take away from the vital nature of McCulloch's discovery; on the contrary, it adds to it in that it reveals the possibilities opened up by nervous functioning. But it is still only a question of possibilities, not yet of realization. So, starting from the structures inherent in an elementary functioning, an investigation of the filiations that will lead to higher structures produced by a series of successive functionings—such as the natural logic of the propositions used by human adolescents and by ourselves—should begin with the following considerations. The nervous system permits, in the early stages, the construction of reaction and sensorimotor schemata, and although there is a logic about these schemata, they contain only relationships of inclusion, of order, and of correspondence that are very undifferentiated and, on the whole, elementary by comparison with the "logic of neurons." At the same time, they may achieve endogenous structures for which they draw on the functioning of the coordination of actions itself, which is to say, the functioning of the nervous system. Next, at about seven to eight years, concrete operations begin to be elaborated, still making use of this nervous functioning but drawing their substance from sensorimotor schemata, after a series of regroupings and decenterings in relation to action proper and to external perceptual configurations. Only then, between twelve and fifteen years, do propositional operations occur, becoming increasingly elaborated by means of the nervous functioning, though they draw their substance from concrete operations, with new modifications and combinations. Thus, it is not by any direct reference to the logic of neurons that the logic of propositional operations—admittedly isomorphic—will be built up, but rather by an uninterrupted series of constructions that may have been oriented by structures inherent in the nervous functioning but which nevertheless presupposes a series of new instruments.

As for these successive elaborations, we shall see, when we come to the instincts, to what conditions of reconstruction and of progress they submit in terms of actual behavior.

Section 16. The Conditions for Instinctive "Knowing"

As was said in the introduction to this chapter, it would be possible to attempt some sort of epistemology of the instinct even without knowing anything about animal consciousness, for "knowing how" is a kind of knowing just like any other; it does, in fact, obtain observable results which modify the exterior environment (inanimate objects, the sexual partner, the aggressor, and so on), and in this it starts off from stimuli belonging to the same environment, whatever may be the conditions of internal drive and the endogenous patterns which inevitably intervene between the stimuli and the final or consummatory actions. Supposing the problem to be simply one of determining the necessary and sufficient conditions of such a "knowing how," as in any epistemological question, and then of assessing its value as to efficacy or operational success, then the admirable analyses made by Lorenz and Tinbergen and their objectivist collaborators, or by scholars like Grassé, Deleurance, etc. will suffice to provide us with the elements of a reply, even though nothing is known of the origins of instinct.

Of course, to know the genesis of instincts would really be the only certain basis from which to conduct such an analysis. Indeed, it is on such territory and on no other—territory on which instinctive behavior has its phyletic formation—that the sort of "genetic epistemology" that I have been championing for so long might come to real fruition where instinct, that special branch of cognition, is concerned. But though we do not yet have the data vital to the solution of this problem of formation,[5] it still remains possible to make a static or structural comparison of the mechanisms of instinct with those of acquired behavior (conditioning and habit) and, above all, with those of the intelligence.

1. The Problem is Posed

We must first seek to pose the problem in its right context. Comparisons between instinct and intelligence have been made since time immemorial, but very often from an angle that falsified the data from the outset because the comparisons were conducted, either explicitly or implicitly, with a view to throwing light on the very genesis of the instincts, which were then conceived of either as a sort of intelligence fixed by heredity or, on the contrary, as working against intelligent understanding right from the start. And since human intelligence develops in the individual in terms of social

5. Ethologists do study (and as one of their central concerns) the filiations of forms of behavior between neighboring species in order to identify their common roots, but no general interpretations other than the neo-Darwinian ones (random selection) have yet emerged.

interactions—too often disregarded, but which, even if given due emphasis, are dependent on transmission by learning or external means, not on hereditary transmission—it therefore follows that comparisons between instinct and intelligence have nearly always been conducted as if instinctive forms of behavior were of an individual nature, established by heredity but individual in origin and exercise. This point of view brings one up against insurmountable difficulties when the comparison is attempted. Indeed, it is only too obvious that if one restricts oneself to the plane of individual forms of behavior, instinctive behavior is so different from the sort of intelligence which constructs its own instruments or schemata little by little as it coordinates acquired experience (even allowing for the endogenous factors of functioning within the general coordination of actions), that it is easy to demonstrate the impossibility of an individual intelligence's mastering such problems of cognitive adaptation as are solved by the instinct. As soon as it is remembered that instinctive organization spills far over the limits of each individual life, being seated in species or rather in "populations," biologically speaking, then comparisons between instinct and intelligence, untrammeled by any preoccupation with explaining the origins of instinct, can be carried out much more objectively and, in short, throw more light on the formation of the intelligence than on the formation of instinct. In a word, the illusion which has hampered so many comparisons between these two extreme types of cognitive function is the undying preconception that leads to the projecting of higher forms of knowledge or organization into lower forms, or merely to the comparison of heterogeneous levels by treating them as though they were on the same plane, ignoring the question of development.

To set our problem more squarely, it is essential to take certain precautions and to recall at least three preliminary ideas.

1. In the first place, in order to make a fruitful comparison between the cognitive mechanisms of the instinct and those of acquired reactions—particularly of structures of the intelligence that are closely dependent on the activities of the individual subject—it must above all be noted that the structure of the instinct goes far beyond the bounds of individual activity. This is not because instinct is something "supraindividual," meaning either an individual form of behavior made general by hereditary fixation, or a result of social rather than hereditary interactions, which nevertheless place upon

the individual the constraint of external transmissions. If one takes into account only observable and well-established facts, then, on the contrary, instinct is to be seen as "preindividual," or, even better, as "transindividual," in the sense of a structure imposed on the individuals from within, not on individuals as being all similar to one another and presenting the same characteristics (as in the case of reflexes), but as coordinated into organized and differentiated totalities within which any individual may play a different part from that of the others. The most generalized and instructive instance in this respect is the sexual instinct, which involves an organized overall structure within which the male individual evinces instinctive behavior different from, and complementary to, that of the female. Another typical case, though less general, is the instinctive relationship between parents and their progeny, within which three complementary roles can be played: that of the mother, that of the father, and that of the young, which react instinctively to the mother, to the father, and to both. This, to be accurate, is a case, not of three distinct instincts, but of a total structure with differentiated substructures. The same will naturally apply to social instincts (as in insects, etc.), where individual roles are not, or not entirely, learned but conform to an overall hereditary programming.

2. In such conditions, the comparison between instinct and acquired or intelligent forms of behavior must be carried out quite independently of any discussion about the genesis of instincts. If we knew what this genesis were of course, it would throw light on the comparison we are seeking to make, but in the absence of any factual data a valid discussion of the subject can be carried on only after structural comparisons have been made and must not be allowed to influence them. The essential reason for this—and one vital to the method used—is that instinctive structures and acquired cognitive structures or, to put it more precisely, structures opening up the possibility of individual acquisitions, are not all on the same level of development. There are, of course, points at every stage of evolution where learning takes place. But if, as we shall be maintaining later on in this book, learning presupposes some genetic or endogenous preliminary, it must therefore be true that behavior controlled essentially by some hereditary programming belongs to an earlier stage of development, both biologically and epistemologically. Insofar as any comparison between instinctive and intelligence structures can be attempted, the comparison must be made

between two different levels (as, for example, the mechanisms common to, and the differences between, sensorimotor and conceptual intelligence can be investigated) and not between two kinds of behavior at the same level of development. It follows that, although an analysis of the intelligence may clarify an analysis of instinct, in the sense that knowledge of the terminal point of a development helps set the beginnings in perspective, yet information is more likely to flow in the opposite direction: significant things can be learned about intelligence itself from an analysis of common mechanisms at the level of a cognitive structure pertaining to a species or genetic pool rather than to individual acquisitions.

3. However, there is a third point to be made, which seems to me of fundamental importance if we are to get these questions of development levels in perspective. The higher types of acquired behavior,[6] especially those classified as intelligent, manifest something much more than purely linear developments or filiations, by which each stage is a direct extension of the preceding one by means of cumulative or additive acquisitions. On the contrary, as we have seen in section 10, subsection 3, we find a series of stages, and, on each of these, development begins by reconstructing structures acquired at the preceding level, which have to be reelaborated so that they may be integrated into these new structures, which enrich and extend them. To recall, for a moment, the three periods *A, B,* and *C* in the development of a child's intelligence (see section 2, subsection 2): we are here confronted with three kinds of intelligence. The first, being sensorimotor, only makes use of perceptions and movements, with no symbolizing or semiotic evocations; the second, leading up to "concrete operations," makes use of the semiotic function but constructs adequate structures only at the handling level (classification, seriation, or comparison of objects); the third, which attains "propositional operations," is capable of working on spoken hypotheses. It follows that the same structure which was elaborated at the sensorimotor level, in action, must be reconstructed in terms of concepts in order to be utilized in thought, even where it is simply a matter of handling objects: for example, the "displacement group" which allows a child of between eighteen

6. Here we must note, once and for all, that this elliptical expression always means "behavior which, although it includes necessary innate conditions (the nervous system, etc.) does open up possibilities of acquisition by the individual."

months and two years old to find his way about his own yard must be reconstructed mentally if he is to picture in his mind the known routes he has to take, and it is only when he is about seven or eight years old that rotations or translations will be correctly composed in his mind, even though the objects he has to look out for are there before him. In the same way, a whole reconstruction process has to be gone through in order to translate concrete structures into manipulatable hypotheses by means of abstract or hypothetico-deductive reasoning. For example, only at eleven to twelve years will a child be able to "reflect" about displacement sufficiently well to be able to solve the problems aroused by two displacements in relation to each other.

These reconstructions of structures from one level to the next, with widening scope and innovations at each new level, naturally rule out, in consequence, the possibility of an absolute beginning. Thus, sensorimotor structures can only be called an initial stage in relation to what follows them, themselves constituting a reconstruction of previous structures recorded in nervous coordinations, and so on. It will at once be seen, therefore, that instinctive structures are part of these previous structures, although this does not imply any direct filiations, of course, for various kinds of collateral relationship may be supposed, either by ramification from a common trunk or by simple convergences between instinct and structures previous to those of sensorimotor intelligence.

2. Analogies in Functioning

In section 20, subsection 6, point 3, we shall be calling the process just illustrated a "convergent reconstruction with overtaking." As this is very general in scope, it may well be called a law (and I have given a number of examples of it elsewhere under the name "vertical translations"). For the moment, while in the domain of cognitive functions, we might formulate this law as follows: "When new instruments are put at the disposal of a cognitive development, the progress made on their account starts off from a reconstruction, analogous in form but resulting from these new instruments, of the structures elaborated at the previous stage."

The hypothesis that we shall attempt to justify on the basis of this law is that some analogies, at least functional ones, are to be found between the coordination of schemata on the genetic or epigenetic plane of the organization pertaining to instinct and the individual coordination of schemata in the domain of intelligence, at least sensorimotor intelligence, although the latter comes at a later, not an earlier, stage than instinct. The point of this hypothesis, taken in conjunction with the whole book, is not to lead to an interpretation of how instincts originate, which would be impossible as yet, nor even to arrive at some conjectures about the filiation of intelligence from instinct. Our aim is simply to provide, in the field of behavior, authentic cases of transition between organic structures (insofar as instinct is hereditary, which it certainly is for the most part) and cognitive structures (insofar as certain instinctive coordinations are analogous to intelligent coordinations, a thing which has yet to be confirmed).

It now seems undeniable that, in the domain of instinctive organization, successive inclusions are to be found between action schemata and order relationships, both of which give grounds for supporting Tinbergen's theory of a "logic of instinct." Thus, our starting-off ground can be the table of hierarchical connections that Tinbergen drew up in 1951 when working on the behavior of the three-spined stickleback.

First, however, some agreement must be reached about the significance of what follows. In fact, Tinbergen did not confine himself to setting up a table of the hierarchy of behavior; he quickly proceeded to formulate some theories about the subjacent nervous mechanisms, and he put forward all sorts of hypotheses, not as actually verified but at least as plausible, about the hierarchy of "centers" and the details of subordinations. This side of his work has been much argued about, and we shall be making no use of it here, nor shall we take any stand on the neurophysiological questions raised by instinct. That is why we shall attempt only to establish an epistemology; in other words, we shall investigate the necessary and sufficient conditions of instinctive behavior insofar as this may be a form of practical knowledge, and we shall not concern ourselves with its causal functioning.

However, even in the field of behavior, Grassé has declared against the idea of hierarchy ("Zoologie I," *Encycl. Pléiade,* pp. 261–65), maintaining that it is not so much a question of subordination as of sequences, coordinations, and switches. He and Deleurance talk of "behavior units" that are more or less independent. Grassé thus raises an interesting problem, which must be taken up, and that is the epistemological nature of the connections involved: inclusions (because if there is any hierarchy there must be inclusions of the more specialized into the more generalized forms of behavior) or order relationships, subordinations or coordinations between schemata, and so on. The sort of epistemology we are concerned with is not that of the biologists, Tinbergen and Grassé (as in chapter 4); it is an epistemology of the instinct or even of the creature itself, whether stickleback or termite, so that we can determine the conditions of its "knowing how" when building a nest or a termitarium (a more modest form of knowledge than that of the biologist, but in our case much more instructive).

Be that as it may; without touching on Tinbergen's neurophysiology (however excellent or debatable that may be), the four levels of behavior that he distinguishes in the stickleback seem indisputable, at least with respect to their being distinct from one another. The first is a general appetitive behavior (as Craig expresses it), which serves as a framework for the entire range of behavior that follows it, and which makes the creature react to significant universal stimuli (IRM = innate releasing mechanisms).[7] The second stage is made up of substructures which correspond to specialized instinctive forms of behavior and to a differentiation in indices: fighting, nest-making, and pairing. At the third stage, each of these substructures is differentiated into "consummatory actions" peculiar to each; in nest-making, for example, these actions would be finding and choosing the materials, hollowing out a hole, and so on. At the fourth stage, every one of these consummatory actions differentiates itself into elementary movements.[8]

So there we have a table of levels (that should not yet be called

7. In point of fact, we shall not be able to find out to what extent these IRM, or RM for short, are innate, as long as we do not know anything about their detailed ontogenetic development.

8. If a more complete logic of instincts could be established, it would take account not only of the connections between the different levels that may exist within the same instinct, but also of the connections between differing instincts in the animals: for example, the interconnections between the sexual instinct, aggressiveness, and the flight drive. These relationships find expression in positive or negative correspondences (or correlations) among all the instinctive acts which can activate or inhibit each other. G. P. Baerends (1956) and W. Heiligenberg (1963) have each brought out this sort of pluridimensional system. They may be compared, from the logical point of view, to multiplicative structures, not just to additive ones, as was the case with the earlier hierarchies.

hierarchical), and we can try to determine whether it has, as it were, a logical character in the sense that a subject may have logic (insofar as it is a subject of behavior, quite independently of any consciousness, which we do not deny but of which we know nothing), in exactly the same way that we attempted to bring out the logical structure of behavior schemata or schemata of the sensorimotor intelligence in the human infant between birth and the time it begins to speak. This then is our problem.

3. Schemata of the Instinct

The right modus operandi will be to establish, first of all, the fact that behavior at these levels corresponds to "schemata," that is, to units of behavior that can be repeated in a virtually unchanging way and applied to situations or objects of varying kinds. The second step will be to distinguish between the various modes of connection between these schemata, whether in the context of coordination between successive schemata or internal connections between one particular schema and its subschemata.

Thus, the main question to decide is whether appetitive behavior is a schema in itself, and at first sight it would seem not; in this case the table would be heterogeneous, for where appetency is concerned, impulses and hormones are spoken of, whereas with other forms of conduct it is a question of perception and emotional reaction. But before we go any farther, it should be noted that any kind of behavior will always have an energetic or affective aspect to it as well as a structural or cognitive aspect. To say that appetitive behavior arises from a hormonal impulse and shows itself by a tendency or *Trieb* is simply to classify it under the first of these aspects, and the second remains to be characterized.

The structural aspect of appetitive behavior has been subjected to a masterly analysis by Grassé, who reduces it to the two following essentials, a fusion of which is exactly what we have already called an "assimilation schema" in the context of the forms of behavior and the sensorimotor intelligence of a babe in arms (with the difference, of course, that in the case of instinct the schema is endogenous, and that in the infant's case it is an expression of the child's need for movement and exploration, so that it is both endogenous and exogenous).

1. First there is a "search" activity, which takes the form of kineses: the hamster sets off on its exploration without having

caught any scent of the female, the wasp starts to hunt its prey without having seen any, and so on.

2. On the other hand, and correlatively, the organism is sensitized to stimulating situations to which it has been indifferent so far. In particular, it will from now on be excited or roused to specific activities by certain significant stimuli (IRM, although Grassé thinks them wider still in application than the objectivists do) which formerly caused no reaction.

Thus, it will be seen that an overall sensorimotor schema is certainly involved, though a largely innate one. It is, in fact, made up of movements, not of operations or mental images. As for its cognitive aspect, this consists of conferring meanings on significant stimuli, in other words, to objects which, when seen, will set off the secondary type of behavior. Once the details of these objects and their significance have been differentiated, they become related to the particular instincts or subinstincts of this second stage, but, insofar as they are significant, they constitute a sort of class (as relative to the general assimilation schema corresponding to appetitive behavior), which distinguishes them from other objects that have little or no significance even though they are perceived. It may be true that this class, for lack of any instrument of evocation (symbolic function), contains no "extension" from the point of view of the subject. But, in "comprehension," each perceived object is perceived whether or not it affects the behavior, and this itself involves a series of perceptual assimilations that must already have been schematized. The best proof of this is that before the well-differentiated significant stimuli of the second stage come into play, those belonging to the first stage (and thus to the appetitive schema) remain more generalized: at this stage they are simply the choice of territory with its overall conditions—temperature, vegetation on sandy soil, and average depth of water. There is, then, a kind of class of affecting objects, the extension of which remains entirely perceptual or spatial.

This cognitive character, indicating the relationship between a behavior and the object it perceives as significant, becomes even more marked when we turn to instinctive behavior of the differentiated kind, found at the second stage. In nest making, for instance, it is obvious that the stickleback, when choosing its materials, assimilates them into a particular schema consisting of the whole organized group of movements necessary for the construction of the nest. There we are dealing with a sensorimotor assimilation

schema, but an innate one, effectuated by means of organized movements and triggered by objects (or stimuli) that are significant
precisely in proportion as they are assimilated into the schema, that
is to say, as they can be used in the making of the nest.

The third stage is where "consummatory" actions take place.
These are simply differentiations of the preceding schemata, but
differentiations of a very far-reaching kind. For example, Grassé,
writing of termite behavior, uses the term "stigmergia" [*stigmergies*]
to describe the termites' response to signals that are made in terms
of the act of construction as it proceeds; when the balls of earth
have been worked to a certain size, the very sight of them sets the
termites to building a pillar or shafts, which themselves act as stimuli
directing the further course of the work. Thus, the nature of this
work is all the more remarkable for having not a single order of
succession but a sum of interdependent acts, which still lead to the
same result, whatever the order followed.

One interesting phenomenon attests to the fact that behavior at
this third stage is characterized by well-closed schemata. I described
this, some time ago, in an article about reflex schemata in the
young infant, which goes on sucking when there is nothing more
to suck. Lorenz has called this kind of conduct "vacuum activities":
for example, geese will hunt around on the bottom of a pond that
has nothing growing in it when they have seen plenty of food put
down for them just a little way off, and the starling will go through
all the motions of catching a fly when there is no fly there, and so
on.

Last of all, we come to the movements of individual subjects, each
of which can be repeated and thus set up a subschema, although this
will always be included within those which precede it.

4. The Logic of Instincts

Having defined the nature of each of these schemata, we must now
find the logic in them. The main quality of this logic is that it
contains several structures, but tangled up together and relatively
undifferentiated.

1. First, what may properly be called inclusion structures can
be discerned, that is to say, structures whose raison d'être comes
from the overall structure of which they are part.[9] In this

9. These inclusions may be additive but they can also be multiplicative,
as we saw in subsection 2, n. 8, above.

way, the red belly of the male stickleback (which only turns red in the nest-making season) constitutes, as do all meaningful stimuli, a perception schema functioning qua schema, since it allows those subjects perceiving it to apply it to a whole group of separate individuals, perceived one after the other, and brings about instant recognition. This perception schema is, however, only a subschema in relation to the overall schema that gives it its special significance: a combat schema for the male and a mating schema for the female.

In the same way, a specialized instinct schema on level II is normally included in a generalized appetitive schema, but it may be momentarily detached from it, since an instinct may be roused without actual need by some stimulus, which seems meaningful at the time.

2. On the other hand, order relationships can be discerned, which arise automatically, since instinctive behavior evolves over time. But such seriations, whether backward or forward, may be relatively constant, as in the case of the stickleback and his nest building, or it may follow some vicarious order, as in the case of the "stigmergia" which intervene during the building of a termitarium (in which case inclusion is more important than order).

3. Furthermore, correspondences can be noted between one inclusion and the next and between one series and the next (a serial correspondence). We must first remember that the overall schemata found in instinct have the very remarkable property that they extend far beyond any individual behavior and join a number of complementary behaviors into one functional whole, for the behaviors of sexual partners, of two males fighting, of workers in a termitarium or a hive, all arise from one total structure which embraces both male and female, and so on. A variation in individual color, for instance, such as the red of the stickleback caused by the contraction of melanophores only at the nest-making season, has no meaning at all except for the female and its rivals, so that it forms a part, not of an individual schema, but of what might very well be called a transindividual schema. As a result, corresponding, or (in the logical sense of the word) multiplicative, relationships occur between the movements of one partner and the other. These corresponding relationships may be part of a hereditary programming and thus belong to the logic of the instinct. But they may also merely

be inserted into the hereditary framework as individual acts, such as imitation: when the male stickleback assumes an upside-down position, head down and tail up, in front of another male (replacement or derivation behavior, avoiding a fight on the outskirts of its territory), this is merely a case of individual imitation. Tinbergen achieved this effect by putting a mirror in front of a male stickleback.[10] There is nonetheless a correspondence between the positions of the animals.

4. But all these relationships do not occur at the same time. The general schema of appetitive behavior precedes the putting into action of forms of behavior at levels II to IV. Inclusions and order relationships thus fit into an overall structure comparable to a sort of genealogical tree, on which schemata are created, or set in motion, one after the other, according to a law of filiation inherent in the behavior itself and not by means of any multiplicative structure.

These, then, are the main kinds of structure involved. If it can be said that the logic of the organs is instinct, not intelligence, which constructs its sensorimotor and conceptual forms in a much freer way, considering the organic conditions from which they start, then it can be seen that the expression we are using, "logic of the organs," is not just a metaphor, but does in fact contain the basic structures of inclusion and relationship—in a form both additive and multiplicative—that occur in the logic of acquired sensorimotor schemata and, better still, in operational logic. The fact that these same structures can be discerned in a largely innate form does not at all take away from their logical nature, and the partial isomorphisms studied in section 11 will explain why this is so. On the other hand, the largely hereditary nature of the logical structure of the instinct raises a problem which is capital to the very processes of construction, coordination, generalization, etc. from which the structure emerged.

5. Coordination of Schemata

As for intelligence schemata, which are sensorimotor and mainly operational to start with, their coordination and subordination to collective structures—not always stable at first but becoming in-

10. Should this be seen as an active response rather than as an imitation, then the imitative conduct of ducks or other satiated birds can be cited, which, although they have had all they want to eat, will return to the pecking ground if they see other birds feeding.

creasingly equilibrated—are the result of continuous assimilatory activity, which eventually becomes a truly operational activity. This active assimilation, while engendering schemata by means of generalization, at the same time submits them to various reciprocal forms of assimilation, either partial (inclusion) or total (forming of relationships and correspondences). The schemata are thus constructed step by step, and there is no problem about their logic, because it is produced by a progressive individual activity that can be analyzed directly with relative ease. The difference between these and the logical structures of instinct can be seen right away, the latter producing a result that can be analyzed, but being constructed in a way that cannot be perceived, because it is brought about by genetic or hereditary mechanisms.

It by no means follows that everything in so-called instinctive behavior is hereditary. Even ethologists of the old school, such as Lorenz, recognize that the content or minutiae of reactions to significant stimuli or of consummatory actions are constantly dependent on environment and may occasion temporary adjustments, depending on the various stages of an acquisition (from learning to intelligence). The new generation of ethologists no longer talk about innate mechanisms, except with a certain amount of caution, for they know that instinct is a phenotypic kind of conduct and that any phenotype is the outcome of some undecipherable interaction between environment and the workings of heredity. To this Lorenz has made an impassioned reply,[11] rather indignant but not very convincing, one must admit, especially if one has just read Waddington. On the other side, W. H. Thorpe, D. S. Lehrman, and even Tinbergen have stressed the inevitable learning or exercise factor which comes into play from the embryonic state onward and continues to influence such acts of the intelligence proper as can be noted even in insects and are often involved fairly closely with the workings of instinctive behavior. Viaud rightly concludes from this that "pure instinct, such as Lorenz has described is . . . a sort of extreme case" (L'instinct, p. 159); in other words, instinct never occurs in its pure form.

This does not take away from the fact that, even if it never occurs in any homogenous or "pure" form, there is still a hereditary framework to instinctive behavior. We should not say—and the

11. K. Lorenz. "Phylogenetische Anpassung und adaptive Modifikation des Verhaltens," *Zeitsch. f. Tierpsychol.,* vol. 18 (1961), pp. 139–87.

nuance must be finely observed—that such a framework is simply written into the genotype, although it is closely involved with it. What we should say (and here we must be content with a prudent supposition) is that this framework is inherent at least in the "epigenetic system" as Waddington understands it; that is, it is set up during the development of the embryo according to extremely stable "chreods," which, while manifesting interaction between genome and environment, still contain a genetic component and, hence, some hereditary programming, the actualization of which presupposes the assimilation of elements from the environment.[12]

Instinct, then, looked at analytically from the point of view of necessary conditions, would seem to belong to an earlier stage than learning or intelligence, even if the genetic conditions are not sufficient. The problem is to understand the functioning of the schemata that we have just described as being constitutive of the logic of instinct, or, to put it another way, to find out what the assimilatory activity is that engenders and coordinates them.

Where intelligence is concerned, the very way in which the schemata are exercised and constructed presupposes continual interaction between subject and object. In any case of adapted physical knowledge, whether sensorimotor (for example, in the schema of a permanent object) or operational (any kind of conservation), some account must be taken of the data provided by the experiences and the coordinating activity of the subject. Even at the level of logico-mathematical schemata as such, experience is necessary, for while extracting these schemata from the general coordination of his actions, the subject must act in order to make the abstraction, and must act on these objects.

In the same way, one of the fundamental characteristics of instinctive schemata is their adaptation to environment; this is something on which everyone is agreed. This kind of adaptation is carried much farther in the morphological field, for it is not a mere approximation but has to allow for a series of individual occurrences. More than that, there is something anticipatory about

12. As has already been said in connection with the IRM, we shall not really get on top of ethological problems until we have developed an ontogenetic ethology which will extend, in animal psychology, as far as what has been achieved in human psychology with respect to the study of psychogenesis. It is in order to set up such a new branch of study that G. Richard is working in Rennes, and A. Etienne in my own laboratory.

it in almost every case; when the cuckoo lays its eggs in another bird's nest (and all eighty species of cuckoo do this) it certainly knows nothing, as an individual, about what will happen to those eggs, but the epigenetic schemata in its instinct are possible if the following conditions obtain: first, that species of nest-building birds exist and that failure to make a nest is not general among birds or animals, and second, that these nest-building species have such instincts as enable them to take care of the young, even a young cuckoo.

This being so, there are only three possible explanations, not only in the range of known theories, but by means of logical deduction (and even, if need be, formal deduction or calculation): either there is some preestablished harmony or else it is a matter of chance or an interaction of some kind which supplies the epigenetic system with information about the external environment (interaction being conceived in the light of any number of explanations, even including the Lamarckian, but explanations infinitely richer in possibilities in the perspective of present-day cybernetics).

Preestablished harmony is logically possible, but all it means is either that the Creator has organized everything in advance or else that there is some sort of combinatorial intelligence in the genome, as Cuénot interprets it. This, however, is merely a verbal solution, for the problem is precisely to analyze how instinctive schemata are set up and function. To decide to call the system as a whole an "intelligence" merely amounts to saying that it works well. This we already knew, but we still have to explain how it comes about.

Chance mutation and selection after the fact is the umbrella solution that is tirelessly repeated with the same persistence, as Bertalanffy points out, and the lack of concern with detailed proof as a Tibetan prayer wheel. Now if this theory is untenable in the field of morphological and physiological adaptations, it is even more sadly inadequate in the field of instinct, in which the transindividual nature of adaptations presupposes the convergence of fortunate chances in the widely different yet complementary behaviors of a number of individuals at one and the same time. Where random variation is concerned, there would therefore be some sort of probability, decreasing as time went on. Where selection is concerned, which only applies (as we now know) to phenotypes, these being so many "responses" made by the genome to environmental circumstances, the real problem is to know how these "responses" are formed, not how they survive. We are now reaching the point where mutation is yielding ground to "regroupings," and random variations to regulations. If there is one field in which the finalists excel in showing up the shortcomings of traditional neo-Darwinism, it is that of instinct—so much so that the new solutions are no longer to be found in oversimplified models of chance and selection, which did serve their turn but are now outdated, but rather in the direction of regulatory interactions.

Having said this, let us attempt not to enunciate a new theory but simply to draw together the various factual data and the possibilities arising from them.

1. Instinctive structures consist of schemata coordinated in a manner very like what we find in the field of sensorimotor acquisitions and sensorimotor intelligence. In particular, the instinct makes use of instruments, apparatus, or "tools" (beaks, burrowing feet, glands that secrete filaments, and so on) which are both organic and programmed by heredity, whereas sensorimotor or fabricating intelligence finds such instruments in the external world, or designs and constructs them (from the chimpanzee upward).

2. In these latter fields, the schemata are solidary with continuous assimilations and accommodations which generalize or differentiate them, relate them or include them in one another hierarchically.

3. Where instinct is concerned, analogous individual activities play only a restricted part, and if the individual possessed of an instinct could foresee the entire scope of its workings and their outcome, that would presuppose some intelligence of a very much higher kind that what we have seen in chimpanzees, for instance, with regard both to their limitations and to their achievements.

4. On the other hand, the structures of instinct are ranged on a scale that is both epigenetic and transindividual—a scale in which the cognitive capacities of the individual count for almost nothing but in which the entire organization profits from regulatory systems originating either in the genome or, more especially, in development (ontogenetic development, but more or less common to all individuals).

5. It may be true that schemata in acquired behavior are transformed and coordinated between themselves, acquired behavior being much less well organized at the elementary stage than is the epigenetic evolution working with the genome, but that is no reason why we should refuse to allow that instinctive schemata, being both

epigenetic and transindividual, have the capacity, in their turn, to be coordinated and differentiated. In particular, one capacity of animal intelligence is to make a functional whole of segmented forms of behavior. Why, then, should elementary instinctive schemata not be coordinated by means of some reciprocal assimilation into fuller schemata, which can be differentiated by some other means? This is no atomist argument but simply the recognition of the fact that many inventions have been produced by the conjunction of two formerly separate components.

To take one very simple example of possible schema assimilations: the edible snail *Helix pomatia* L. lays its eggs in the ground a few centimeters below the surface. Not having much intelligence, it is doubtless incapable of foreseeing the advantages of behaving in this way; so we cannot point to any anticipation in what it does. However, (a) it takes shelter from the sun and cold beneath stones, etc.; (b) it is capable of generalizing this protection schema in times of intense cold to the point where it will even bury itself in winter; (c) it has a tendency, no doubt hereditary, to hibernation, and shuts itself up into its shell, blocking the entrance with some epiphragmatic secretion (accumulated mucus); (d) moreover, it lays eggs, and one can well imagine that it will never confuse them with any excretion, so that, however rudimentary its perceptions may be (proprioceptive as well as exteroceptive), it takes these eggs into its sphere of conservation as soon as it lays them. Thus, the tendency to lay eggs below the ground could be seen as the result of coordination or assimilation of the laying schema into the schema for self-protection or sheltering in the ground.

The description just given is in terms of individual behavior, but if everything went on at this level there would be no question of instinct but of individual invention repeated with each new generation. On the contrary, if the burrowing schemata in each individual, and the temporary preoccupation with laying eggs, were hereditary, the same hypothesis would amount to the supposition that all these schemata achieved coordination between themselves, at the genome or epigenotype level, by virtue of their similarity in structure or functional significance. Indeed, at the sensorimotor level, an act of intelligence consists merely of this sort of coordination of schemata (for example, as between the schemata of "placing upon" and of "pulling"), purely as a result of their tendency to mutual assimilation, with no need of an intervening "intelligence" to connect the two of them, like some deus ex machina. Nor is there any need of an intelligence concealed within the epigenetic system to enable these two instinctive schemata, if that is in fact what they are, to connect with each other. Of course, the name "intelligence" might be given to the sort of spontaneous coordination of schemata at the level of sensorimotor acquisitions, but as instinctive schemata are obviously of quite a different nature insofar as they originate in the epigenetic system, written into the subsystems of the genes on which the creature's nervous organization depends, we would do well not to baptize epigenetic and transindividual activities with such a name.

6. *Instinct and Hereditary Adaptation*

The whole of contemporary ethology leads us to believe that the genetic reequilibrations which modify any particular organ also modify the behavior associated with the organ.[13] Thus, it is becoming more widely accepted that behaviors are an integral part of life and that the epigenotype is responsible as much for their hereditary frameworks as for their morphogenesis.

It might be as well, however, since behavior belongs on a different scale from localized morphological characteristics and is only to be found at the functional level of organogenesis, to stop referring simply to "genes" but to apply the provisional title "schemata or cycles programmed by the instincts" to epigenetic correspondents of the behavior schemata examined in subsections 3 and 4 above. We must remember, in fact, that an overall instinctive cycle is transindividual, that is to say, it derives from the genes of two or more distinct individuals, from two or more separate embryogeneses (sex or social role), from two or more sorts of organs and hormonal activations, and from two or more specialized and complementary kinds of behavior, with their separate categories of significant indices and their separate categories of motor responses, capable of bringing forth further indices. This highly complex cycle is at once largely hereditary and yet possessed of an individual shape in space (sex or social role) and time, (parents and progeniture). Nevertheless, the overall cycle contains not only individual be-

13. In a reciprocal way, the evolution of some type of behavior may influence morphogenesis. For example, many birds at mating time show off their chests or crests, and certain species, though only a few, have morphological structures or specially vivid colorings in those parts.

haviors but also logical structures of inclusion, order, correspondence (between complementary individuals), and genealogical filiation with respect to the development and chronological evolution of those behaviors.

The interpretation put forward in subsection 4 above would thus amount to a supposition that the cycle, or total system, of instinctive schemata is brought about, not by some hereditary fixation, an individual act of learning, but by spontaneous exercise or combinations and recombinations of the schemata at the level of their formation and development, hence, the level of the epigenotype. An act of individual learning that might explain instinct in its whole transindividual cycle is not something very likely to occur, in view of the intelligence and long-term powers of anticipation such learning would demand. On the other hand, that the exercise or spontaneous combinations of schemata at the level of the overall transindividual cycle should be written into the programming of the epigenotype is not at all unlikely. For one thing, in the study of variations today the accent is less and less on random mutations, which are conceived of as "noises"; the emphasis now is on genetic recombinations within a genotype or pool having a number of regulations (a multiregulated pool). So that if it is admitted that the transindividual cycle of the instinct is linked to certain individual systems or subsystems in the genes to which the instinctive schemata are attached as functional units, then the recombinations of these subsystems among themselves (with possible modifications within each subsystem) can be taken for granted. The only new element in this, which will therefore have to be discussed, is that these combinations of schemata conform to their own inner logic, that is, to the possible inclusions, order, correspondence, etc. described in subsection 4 above and not only to the morphological and physiological characteristics contained within the genetic information. In other words, if an elementary instinct schema A were attached to a gene system a, and a schema B to a gene system b, the combination of a and b would not produce a new whole ab taking no account of the functional characteristics of A and B, but would be determined by the form of A and B and by their conformity insofar as they could be included within one another or put in order or correspondence. It would thus seem to be the "logic" of these schemata that determined their combination, and this would explain why the whole transindividual instinct cycle may resemble an act of intelligence (brought about, similarly, by coordination of the schemata through reciprocal assimilation). To say that this logic exists does not mean that intangible characteristics are involved, any more than the circuits of a computer are intangible. All that is necessary is that the initial schemata, like so many "forms" written into the epigenotype, should combine through direct assimilations and accommodations by virtue of the formal characteristics in them that are isomorphic to those of a sort of logic, and not by virtue of any kind of characteristics.

However, insofar as these new instinctive groups, brought about genetically or at the epigenetic growth level, make some allowance for environment, there must surely be reequilibrations of which the genome is informed, whether by selection of the phenotypes thus modified or by the interaction of the formatory regulations during epigenetic development.

In this connection, let us consider cases in which instinct causes foreign material to be introduced into the subject's organism: crickets for the *Sphex,* nests, termitaria, and so on. Two cases are possible: (1) the organ is adjusted to its function: the slender tube by which the mosquito is able to suck blood; stings; burrowing paws; and the like; (2) one of the organs carries out some task unrelated to its condition.

In the first case it would be difficult to think of separate formations of the organ and of the instinctive conduct, although many examples could be produced to prove the possibility of some dissociation, though perhaps only of a secondary kind, between the two aspects. If these two go together, one might indeed say that instinct is the logic of the organ, but one would have to add that the organ is the materialization of the behavior; this is the line Bertalanffy takes when he speaks of "dynamic morphology," which, in a way, is a generalized application of Cope's "kinetogenesis." But the problems this raises from the point of view of heredity can quickly be seen. This is why I have had a detailed study made of one case in which the creature's reactions effected a notable transformation on the normal morphology of the species (*Limnaea stagnalis* L.). Here the fixation was carried out by means of what Waddington calls "genetic assimilation," and at the same time the new variety was making a definite choice of a suitable environment by modifying the usual specific behavior (see below, section 19, subsection 7).

In the second case it is even harder to see how an instinct can adapt itself exactly to the environment without some information from the environment. But the difficulty is that in many cases (not general ones) the individual subject remains indifferent to the success or failure of its instinctive actions,[14] even though, lacking evidence of direct action by the environment, one would have to postulate at least some sort of feedback system triggered by the results of the action. Even allowing for the differences in scale, however, one can conceive of information which emanates from the environment at the level of the transindividual instinctive cycle, without acquired adaptation in the individual. We shall be returning to this problem in connection with the origin of the instruments of hereditary knowledge (chapter 6, section 19, subsections 4–6).

Section 17. Perception

All transitional levels can be found between general and, later, nervous sensitivity of the organism toward external stimuli and sensory or perceptual sensitivity. Suffice it to say that for a long time perceptions are controlled by hereditary structures. This is particularly true in the case of the perceptual recordings of all those "significant stimuli" which play such an important part in the mechanism of the instincts. "Nativists" such as Hering, to name only one, made long drawn-out attempts, during the nineteenth century, to explain spatial perceptions in man as being innate mechanisms. The "empiricists," such as Helmholtz, opposed this with the thesis that only acquired experiences were involved and that these were linked together by association, or even by subconscious inference. In section 1, subsection 4, we cited the opinion of Holst, who attributes perceptual constancies to a hereditary mechanism of feedback or re-afferences (or even, of efference copies), which correct apparent size in terms of distance, whereas, for my part, I allow that there might be a mechanism of this kind but believe it to be an acquired one. Although there is still uncertainty about the part played by innate structurations in man, it is hard to deny that in the less highly evolved kind of animals innate structurations always preponderate. The dragonfly larvae, for instance, that Ariane Etienne is studying in our laboratory after having worked with Lorenz and

14. The larva of the *Phrygana* setting to work over and over again on its cocoon every time it is destroyed, without seeming to learn anything.

Mittelstaedt, responded in such a regular way to the various parameters of a moving imitation of food that it would be hard to distinguish any learning in this case.

1. Gestalts

Thus, perception presents us with yet another case of transition between organic and cognitive structures, and this is what gives it its epistemological interest, as being the most immediate point of cognitive contact between the subject and the data provided by its environment.

When Lamarckians or empiricists observed some organism undergoing influence from the environment, they first interpreted these acts of perception in an associationist or atomistic way, seeing perception as an assembly of sensations joined together by amnesic associations. The nativist reply to this was in the Kantian tradition (indeed, Müller explicitly referred to Kant) to the effect that the part played by acquired experience was indeed undeniable but, due allowance having been made for previous conditions, took the form of spatial frameworks, either a priori or innate.

The problem of the relations between perception and the organism took a much more definite turn once Wertheimer and Köhler had evolved, between them, the Gestalt psychology of 1912. According to this, perceptible structures were interpreted by means of field models applicable alike to perception, to the nervous system, to the organism, and even to an agglomeration of physical phenomena made up by Köhler—a physicist by training—and given the name *physische Gestalten*. So it will be worth our while to give some thought to the reasons why this attempt had partial success but eventually failed, because the Gestalt notion (which is still perfectly viable once it is let loose from its purely Gestalt chains!) did meet with great success and was taken up even by embryologists, and because Bertalanffy, who was mainly responsible for propagating "organicist" ideas, based them on Gestalt ideas and said, in that connection, that it was in modern psychology (meaning the work of the Gestaltists) "that a scientific approach to the problem of totality was first attempted" (*Les problèmes de la vie*, p. 249).

The idea underlying this doctrine is that perception is not brought about by a joining together of already existing elements, supposedly sensations, but that perception constitutes from the outset an organized totality in which certain characteristics or elementary units are to be found but only by means of analysis and in terms of constituted elements, not constituent ones. As early as 1890 Ehrenfels was saying that a melody can be "transposed" in such a way that all its notes are changed (and so, therefore, its "sensations"), but this does not prevent its being recognized at once as a Gestalt. Ehrenfels, however, saw in the total "form" a property added to sensations, whereas Gestalt psychologists consider the form as primary.

What the Gestalt psychologists did first, then, was to establish the laws governing form, the two most important of which will now be recalled, their significance being both biological and psychological. The first is the law of "good form": a form or Gestalt gains in significance according to how much "better" it is in the light of criteria analyzed separately by definite experience. The qualities which make a form "good" are simplicity, regularity, symmetry, order, closeness of the elements, continuity, and so on. The second law complements this analysis of the totalities: every "form" stands out against a "background," so that even an isolated dot is still a totality insofar as it stands out against a neutral background. Numerous other properties have been discovered and studied: the laws of frontiers, kinetic Gestalts (stroboscopic motions), and static Gestalts, to name only a few.

The Gestalt psychologists gathered an impressive collection of experimental work in the field of perception, which they had thus revived, and then generalized the system, applying it to motivity, to memory, and even to the practical or sensorimotor intelligence of chimpanzees (see section 18). Wertheimer went so far as to try to see Gestalt laws at work within the structures of the syllogism and mathematical operations.

When it came to the interpretation of these multiple facts, the originality of the early Gestalt position lay in their attempt to reduce them to equilibrium models in physical fields, applicable to innate mechanisms as well as to acquired ones. This went far beyond the usual alternative, even at that stage. Every Gestalt that imposes itself on the consciousness, perception, etc.) is isomorphic to an organization or particular nervous Gestalt. Now nervous mechanisms (polysynaptic fields, etc.) are dependent on electro-magnetic fields, and as soon as there is a field, in physics or anywhere else, the observable forms are caused by a group of actions and their equilibrium. There is a double consequence of this: (a) the field action implies the formation of a nonadditive totality, meaning one in which the whole differs from the sum of its parts and is imposed on those parts at every stage or modification: this is the definition of a Gestalt; (b) this totality is brought about by the effects of the slightest action, and the "best" form, toward which the totality is tending, is simply the best-equilibrated one.

It will be seen right away that these considerations are as important for the organism and neurology as for the study of perception. They prompted the fine work done by Lashley on the effects of mass in the brain. K. Goldstein then applied them generally to the entire organism (*Der Aufbau des Organismus*) but with a slightly different emphasis, as in A. Gelb's case also: for these scholars the principle of form and background is specifically biological in the sense that the background is, in essence, a behavioral context (the signal for a conditioning, for example, is a sort of form standing out against a background of waiting).

Theoretic interpretations of this kind therefore lead to a sort of integral reduction of the cognitive to the organic, although in a way that is indubitably too comprehensive, since the vital at once becomes reduced to the physical, or at least to the sort of physical phenomena which depend on the field effects (as opposed to mechanics, etc., whose strictly additive compositions remain irreducible to Gestalt models).

But the great interest in such bold theories, provided they are well thought out (and such is certainly the case with the founders of the Gestalt school, although here we have done no more than sketch out their main points), is that even their shortcomings can prove very instructive, and any critical examination of them will bring to light new connections between them. The weak side of the theory is that, when the subject or organism is irrevocably subordinated to field or equilibrium laws, thus constrained from without as well as from within, there can no longer be any constructive activity, any development, any organization, even, in the sense of the endogenous regulations which it is the glory of modern biology to have discovered. Gestaltism, then, can be criticized mainly for the shortcomings of the notion of equilibrium that it was content with, a notion that makes no allowance for progressive equilibration by means of autoregulation but is a mere balance between forces in the usual sense of equilibrium in physics.

Before returning to perception, let us point out that it is precisely this absence of ideas about equilibrium by means of active and progressive compensations which explains, on one hand, the insufficient role accorded to development and, on the other, the unjustifiable reduction of the higher totalities, such as the operational structures of the intelligence, to perceptual or motor Gestalts.

In the case of development, supposing the Gestalt to be regulated by highly generalized laws of the equilibrium of fields, then by definition it must be superior to any kind of development and, in consequence, either suprahistorical or ahistorical. However, neither biology nor the psychology of cognitive functions can be limited to "forms" of given and unchanging kind, since the central problem, in both cases, concerns the origin of forms and their elaboration from the functioning stage upward. According to Gestalt structuralism, structures are prior to any kind of functioning. In fact, they seem to eliminate functioning altogether by absorbing it into ahistorical structures. But the most convincing evidence that cognitive development takes place and is dependent on an equilibration that is distinct from normal physical equilibrium is precisely that the operational structures of the intelligence are irreducible to perceptual "Gestalts." Although they do constitute authentic totalities insofar as they possess their laws as systems independently of the properties of the elements, these totalities are built up in a strictly additive way (2 plus 2 makes exactly 4) and, more important still, are reversible, unlike perceptual Gestalts, which are neither reversible nor additive. Now, as we saw in section 14, subsection 3, this reversibility represents the culminating point of regulation equilibration, whereas perceptual regulations are only capable of achieving a very approximate sort of reversibility.

To get back, at last, to perception: its organization proper corresponds most faithfully to a Gestalt structure, if taken as a description and divorced from its explanation by means of any effect the physical field may have upon it. It is, in fact, much closer to organic structures than to the overgeneralized physical laws to which Gestalt psychology claims it is subject. Indeed, perception might be characterized as a direct contact made between (1) perceptual activities carried out by the subject through an extension of assimilatory action schemata (relating and so on), and (2) objects in the environment which are reached by the intermediary of sense data in figurative form. Contact with the object takes the form, at this stage, of a sort of probability sampling—something like selection but only in the sense that an organism may choose its environment, and not vice versa—and thus brings about centering effects and the likelihood of "encounters."[15] The activity aspect, on the other hand, brings about all the acts of relating, from "couplings" between encounters right up to the relationships set up by exploration, transport, transposition, anticipation, referring, and so on. In these cases, the Gestalt is brought about by equilibrium, not of the physical field as such, but of the organizing activities of the subject and of the data provided by the object, which is one particular instance of equilibrium between organism and environment.

Such forms of equilibrium are only statistical or probabilistic and are always at the mercy of the tide of events and of the situation. This is what gives Gestalts their doubly irreversible and entirely nonadditive character as perceptual compositions, whereas the higher forms of intelligence reach a complete and mobile equilibrium, which is what gives them their operational reversibility. An analogy with physics may not be out of place here: this opposition between perceptual irreversibility and operational reversibility calls to mind the opposition between irreversible physical phenomena (thermodynamics, etc.) and the sort of reversibility found in mechanics.

2. Perceptual Regulations

Insofar as perceptual Gestalts are the result of an equilibrium that is both dynamic and probabilistic, in which the active compensations made by the subject in response to a disturbance from outside can override the simple balance of forces within any given field, it goes without saying that perception is a collection of organic regulations and not confined to the sort of changes in equilibrium governed by Le Châtelier's principle.

The most elementary of these regulations, if we leave out of account the possibility of hereditary regulatory mechanisms of the type conceived by Holst, are to be found as soon as any brake is put upon centering. This kind of coordination is, in fact, regulatory because, as the centerings are successive, the corrections put out by the act of decentering are continually retroactive as well as proactive. Examples can be given here in the shape of the astonishing results in

15. I made an analysis of the effects of centering which appeared in *Les mécanismes perceptifs* (Paris, Presses Universitaires de France). This was in terms of the likelihood of "encounters" between the elements of the figure and the elements of the perceptual organs and of the likelihood of connections or "couplings" between encounters within one sector of a figure and encounters in another sector.

perceptual learning without external help that begins at about seven years of age, which was described briefly in section 14, subsection 2.

Another remarkable case of perceptual regulation is that of "superconstancies," such as when a normal adult frequently sees a vertical rod, at a distance of 3 or 4 meters, as being equal to a 10-centimeter rod that is close up, when the one at a distance is only 9 or even 8 centimeters in length, thus making a correction of probable error ($>$ 10 cm) that goes so far as reversing the error to excess.

However, in this field of visual perceptions, the most spectacular case of acquired regulations is the celebrated example of the distorting spectacles utilized by Ehrismann and Ivo Köhler. The subjects were asked to wear mirror spectacles for a continuous period. These spectacles caused objects or people to be seen upside down so that in a fencing contest filmed by Köhler the normal subject hit Ehrismann's knee when he was aiming at his thorax. After a few days there was a complete reversal, however, and at the end of the film the same subject is seen to cycle round the streets of Innsbruck with those same spectacles on. In this case, regulation has been effected by means of reafferences dictated by the habitual sensori-motor action schemata in such a way that visual positions are adjusted to tactilo-kinesthetic positions. While this superb experiment may uphold, in the teeth of the Gestalt theory, the subordination of perceptual activities to action schemata taken overall, it serves to define even more clearly the regulatory character of the perceptual organization.

On the whole, then, it can be said that, even on the perceptual plane, where the internal response is figurative (the forms or Gestalts perceived seem to supply an unadulterated copy of the real world with the maximum of purity and immediacy), knowledge does, in fact, amount to an assimilation and an organization, both of which are closer to vital mechanisms than at first seems the case, and this in their own special forms of equilibration and regulation. Since, on the other hand, perception can never be independent of action or, at the higher levels, free of the interiorized coordination of action schemata which makes up the intelligence, while at the lower levels it intervenes as a significant indicator in the instinct cycles even at the level of reflex schemata (for at this stage we have already seen how difficult it is to dissociate general sensitivity and significant sensitivity), it may truly be said of perception, as of all the other cognitive functions, that it is a direct extension of vital assimilation and organization.

Section 18. Learning and "Intelligence"

Our object in chapter 4 was simply to bring out the general isomorphisms between knowledge and life and in this regard we have already pointed out (section 13) that organic life involves problems of memory, or learning, and of anticipation. Our object in this present chapter, however, is to raise the epistemological problems involved (leaving an examination of their biological interpretation for chapter 6). What we have to do now, then, is to determine, in the case of elementary forms of knowledge allied to behavior, what are their necessary and sufficient conditions. We hope to demonstrate that these conditions always presuppose some biological component.

As long as we were dealing with the nervous system and the reflexes, either instinctive or perceptual, this component was axiomatic: reflexes and instincts are largely hereditary and, even when perceptions are applied to new objects which are not included among the significant stimuli attached to the instincts, they presuppose some hereditary sensory apparatus, even though they may not call upon its regulatory capacities. Now these capacities are either specific and innate (toads do not react to surgical intervention aimed at achieving I. Köhler's upside-down effect and thus they may die of hunger through failure to adapt their methods of catching flies) or they may be acquired under the influence of the higher functions.

As soon as one begins to examine these, one is confronted with a new problem: Does knowledge arising from a true acquisition, having no relationship with any hereditary programming, necessarily have a biological component? Perhaps it will be replied that even the highest type of act of the intelligence still presupposes brain activity in the same way that any act of perception presupposes a sensory organ; consequently, both acts are biological if looked at in this way. But there is still this difference, that the sensory organ may, indeed, vary only slightly under the influence of some new perception and still be able to complete its functioning by means of conditionings and reafferences, whereas the brain is capable of elaborating a great number of new circuits or acquired association channels on top of its hereditary circuits. Moreover, it is easy enough, in epistemology, to dissociate a piece of logical or mathematical knowledge from its neurological support, whereas an instinctive "knowing how" has no existence outside the biological cycle of which it is part and parcel. Is it true, then, that this kind of logico-mathematical knowledge alone, not in a formalized sense but its concrete psychological context, contains an irreducible biological component?

The reply that we shall be making in this chapter, and elaborating in the following one, is that every kind of knowledge at the higher level presupposes the intervention of such a component, whether as an innate framework or a starting point or, going back to the biological roots, as a necessary and continuous functioning, outside of which no sort of structuration is possible.

1. Elementary Kinds of Learning

Let us remember, before we go any further, that although acquired behavior may be described as higher in relation to instinctive behavior, this is only because, in those zoological groups that have a kind of cognitive privilege—that is, in primates and man—instinctive behavior is clearly inferior to acquired behavior by reason of the latter's considerable and highly progressive cerebralization, whose main stages of development are well known. In a general way, the capacity for learning increases noticeably at the successive echelons of the animal kingdom.

This does not take away from the fact that, as has already been said (section 13, subsection 2), some kind of learning has been induced by experiment in the Protozoa; this learning is similar to conditioning except for the fact that there is still no nervous system, and, hence, no reflexes either in the strict sense of the term. Bramstedt experimented with paramecia on these lines, putting some in a tank that was half lit up and half in darkness. The creatures swam round in it without showing any preference for light or darkness. Bramstedt then established that the creatures made some association between light and warmth and between darkness and cool water. When the temperature was restored evenly throughout the tank at the end of the training period, the paramecia were swimming only in the dark part of the tank. In the same way, H. Soest trained stylonichia to crawl on only the third of three parallel surfaces, this third surface being smooth while the others were rough. At first they crawled over rough or smooth without any distinction, but then the rough surfaces were fitted with an electric current so that the creatures learned to avoid them. When the current was turned off after the training period, they still confined themselves to the smooth surface.[16]

Having reminded our readers of this, we must next point out that elementary kinds of behavior such as may be designated variously as training, learning, conditioning, or habituation (and as opposed to intelligence proper, which is a direct derivative of these but which has, instead of their unchangeable rigidity, a reversible mobility constantly widening in scope) can take a whole range of forms, from the pole of activity, characterized by all sorts of discoveries made by spontaneous exploration, to the pole of passivity, in which the acquired association seems to be imposed by some regular external sequence. The development of the human infant offers contemporary examples of these two poles of behavior; from the second month onward, the child acquires the habit of sucking its thumb between feeds and is conditioned by the sounds of this very reflex of sucking.

These two poles interest us insofar as they demonstrate that behavior acquired by means of the assimilation of the new element (stimulus or response) into a previous schema that is largely innate and may be either a reflex schema (as witness the thumb and the conditioning by sucking) or else a more general appetitive schema, such as Craig's appetitive behavior, but without necessarily being connected with any particular, specialized instinct. From the epistemological point of view, we have here a fact of considerable general importance, according to which any information acquired from the external world (that is to say, from objects) is always so acquired in terms of a framework or internal schematism (subject) that is more or less structured and is, above all, functionally adaptable to each particular case. (The term "functional' is used here in a sense which does not exclude the necessary intervention of schemata that

16. We must, however, point out that some biologists have challenged this capacity for learning among the Protozoa on the grounds that one cannot exclude with certitude any physico-chemical indices, apart from the stimulus test, which would set off "learned" behavior without any conditioning. The essential fact for us to remember, though, is that there is a possibility that learning takes place before the intervention of any nervous system, whatever form that learning may take.

are simply more or less general, as was seen in section 16, sub-section 3, in connection with appetitive behavior.)

For an example of the activity pole in animal acquisitions, it would be well to start with what has so aptly been called "stimuli hunger." This is connected with Watson's significant pronouncement that animals seem to be guided more by indices that they have to find than by responses that they have to make. Blodgett's "latent learning" can be put under the same heading: a well-fed rat which is not really in need of food gets out of the maze just as quickly, after its "disinterested" exploration, as a hungry one does. Similarly, Kimble and Kendall have demonstrated with rats that monotonous repetition of stimuli brings about a higher extinction than that which results from the responses themselves. However, when Broadbent interprets "stimuli hunger" as meaning that stimuli are more impor-tant than responses, we must point out (and this applies equally to Watson's formula) that it is not just a matter of stimuli and re-sponses but of schemata into which stimuli are assimilated and which produce responses. Hunger for stimuli, then, is essentially an expression of the fact that, at a time when no particular schema is exerting any controlling action (or, in other words, when none is making itself felt by means of any actual and compelling need), the animal is not passive but remains in a constantly seeking state for functional stimuli such as may put one or other of these sche-mata into action. Thus, stimuli hunger is an expression of a double need that is general, not local: (a) to feed reaction schemata that are already in existence, and (b) to adjust them to the actual situ-ation taken in its entirety (unless there should be some partial or local adjustment, in the case of some overriding need). So there is no question here of any superior evaluation of stimuli as opposed to responses but, rather, a spontaneous and continuous need to feed schemata that are necessarily sources of responses. The search for stimuli as a form of spontaneous exploration behavior thus shows that acquired reactions in such a context relate to some general ap-petitive behavior, evidence of the necessary role of the previous schematism. The roots of such schematism are innate, whichever way you look at them.

Of course, this exploration behavior, one aspect of which more-over, corresponds to what Berlyne calls "curiosity" (see also Dar-chen and Montgomery) leads to a fairly wide extension of the en-vironment and thus multiplies the information received from the external world. This does not alter the fact that, from the very beginning, exploration behavior is an assimilation into an internal schematism.

2. Conditioning

Opposite this pole of activity in the subject searching for information, there seems to be a pole of passivity, wherein the subject is compelled to link up with the outside world and can make no response except through these links. Conditioned reflexes are on this order, but, however subordinate they may be to external conditions, they are nonetheless a case of assimilation of the new stimulus into a previous, innate schema.

It is well known that, alongside these classic examples of conditioning, which we may call the first type, there is a second type in which the response is no longer identical with the reflex reaction but consists of new reactions, either learned, as in the case of Miller and Konorski's dog holding out its paw, or "emitted," as in the case of Skinner's rats and pigeons, which learned to press a lever. Now this "instrumental" conditioning, as Hilgard and Marquis call it, is one more proof of activity, only this time in another sense; it is no longer a matter of assimilation into previous schemata, because there are no previous reactions or unconditioned stimuli, but of construction in the sense of the discovery and utilization of new relationships, in particular as between objects in the environment. So now we find ourselves in the field of discoveries bound to lead, sooner or later, to inventions which, by means of trial and error, will become more and more accurately adapted to the facts of the environment—the field of active combinations made by the subject itself.

The problem, then, is how to assess the part played by chance in the reading and recording of these external data and also to assess the method of recording. The empirical point of view, which usually predominates in explanations of learning, as it certainly predominates in Lamarckian biology, would be that all this reading and registering is obviously passive, any new elements being due to chance occurrences or circumstances imposed by the environment. But the other possible interpretation, which is the one I shall adopt, is that the relationships discovered are the outcome of active "introduction"; that is to say, they are directed by coordinations of schemata which, though differentiated by perpetual accommodations to the data, are nevertheless schemata brought about by assimilatory activity. In other words, chance plays a part only insofar as the subject (dog, pigeon, or rat) may confer some significance on chance events, and this significance can only emanate from an assimilation schema. Such assimilatory activity is not improvised but is brought about by previous assimilations and has no absolute beginning precisely because it is already at work during conditioning of the first type, as in the stimuli-seeking discussed in subsection 1 above.

To put it another way, with the earliest occurrence of the various forms of conditioning, we can see that, in order to turn "associations" or artificially isolated examples of chain reaction into a more functional and continuous process of "assimilation," we no longer have to make two heterogeneous categories: (1) the assimilation of the conditioned stimulus to the unconditioned stimulus; and (2) the assimilation observed in behavior of the second type. One and the same process leads from the first to the second and from there to the construction of schemata with an ever-increasing number of acquired elements, as opposed to the instinctive or reflex sources of this schematism.

Other noteworthy situations arise in which there is transition from assimilation into innate schemata to that kind of differentiated assimilation which makes for the invention of new reactions by means of coordination or recombinations. In situations of this kind, which we are getting to know more and more about nowadays, some lapse or unforeseen obstacle or conflict, in an instinctive context, will set up a reaction not allowed for in the hereditary programming, and this can be qualified as "intelligent." (It must of course be understood, as always in this book, that every kind of intermediate stage can be found between elementary acquisitions and higher forms of intelligence, any gap being partly a matter of chance.)

In illustration of this, Grassé cites the case of the Natal termites which immediately began to close up the queen's cell when he knocked heavily on the termitarium wall. Now, there was nothing planned about this closure as far as the instincts were concerned, but what was instinctive was the protection of the queens and also, no doubt, some fairly generalized schema for the shutting up of, or excluding the outside world from, the termitarium. Thus, the new reaction of closing up the royal cell might be caused by coordination or by the reciprocal assimilation of two or more previously existing schemata, according to the principle that any invention begins by some combination of existing elements. Here again, it seems, before we start trying to explain things by appealing to "faculties" of a higher kind, we ought to try starting off from some idea of functional continuity among types of behavior already in action, and here, too, we shall be giving the name assimilation to this sort of continuity in integration and coordination through integration.

3. *Sensorimotor Behavior in the Newborn Child*

In the development of sensorimotor behavior during the first twelve or eighteen months of the human child's life, before symbolic functioning and the use of language are established, absolutely continuous transitions can be observed between the first habits acquired and a completed "sensorimotor intelligence" that is almost at the level of that of the chimpanzee. The vital question which then arises is whether this continuity, so enlightening from the biological point of view, is due simply to the fact that man possesses, to an even greater extent than do primates, a hereditary intelligence of such a kind that it would seem that those unconscious transitions from elementary learning to a sensorimotor intelligence capable of spatial and temporal organization, of conservation of objects and of causality, must be the outcome of some sort of pull toward higher things (to say nothing of an even more marked pull toward representation and thought), or whether we are dealing with a functioning by means of successive assimilations such as was discussed in subsection 2 above.

There is undoubtedly a hereditary component in human intelligence, since man has created civilizations unknown to the apes, and since, as we are seeing more and more nowadays, there is such a diversity of individual aptitudes. It is virtually impossible to produce any modification in the intellectual level of a *minus habens*, for example. But to say that intelligence as an aptitude is hereditary is not at all the same thing as saying that structures of knowledge are hereditary, whereas the heredity of instinct implies the heredity of a relatively complete apparatus. Thus, the heredity of intelligence is both much wider and much narrower than that of the instinct; wider because it includes the transmission of a functioning that is capable of going far and learning almost limitlessly (at least, until now); but narrower because no particular structure is transmitted.

For the purposes of our discussion it is therefore pointless to attribute all the detailed stages of development in the sensorimotor intelligence of the infant to some hereditary intelligence in man or the primates (any more than it would be to attribute later progress to this). To be sure, this heredity explains the fact that man is capable of such progress but it does nothing to explain the forms of the functioning, and what we are after is the mechanism of this functioning. To speak of "intelligence" in connection with this mechanism is simply to use an umbrella classification that teaches us nothing about what kind of processes are at work.

So much being said, it will serve no purpose to go into detail about the continuous stages by which the infant passes from the early acquired schemata to sensorimotor intelligence.[17] We must, however, focus on two essential points in time to show that there is continuity and to understand what analogous filiations there may be between the corresponding levels in animal behavior, though observable only at very different phyletic stages, whereas what is so enlightening about the human infant's development is that it evinces ontogenetic filiation in behavior in the space of the six months between the ages of twelve and eighteen months.

The first of these points in time is the passage of elementary habit schemata, acquired through the utilization of chance events in the external world by reproductory or generalizing assimilation, to the first intelligence schemata proper, in which there is coordination of means and ends. For example, an infant of four or five months happens to pull a cord hanging from the head of his cradle; he pulls it simply because he has just learned to coordinate seeing and touching, so that he takes hold of everything that comes in his line of vision. In this particular case, this simple action (the generalization of a budding assimilation schema brought about by the reciprocal assimilation of visual schemata and the schema for taking hold of anything touched) happens to lead to very interesting results from the subject's point of view, although these were not anticipated: the hood shakes, the toys hanging from it swing backward and forward, all sorts of noises come out of the plastic balls because they contain grains of lead. As a result, the subject goes on and on repeating his action through a circular reaction or reproductive assimilation, but there is still no differentiation between ends and means; all we have is a simple habit schema taking place all of a piece. A few days later,

17. See J. Piaget, *La naissance de l'intelligence chez l'enfant,* and *La construction du réel chez l'enfant* (Delachaux et Niestlé).

it is enough to hang something on the otherwise unadorned hood for the child to feel about for the cord and pull it, staring at the object as it hangs there; this time there is a beginning of differentiation between means and end, and thus there is also a beginning of anticipation. Later on, one need only swing something from the end of a stick two meters away and the child will feel about for the cord and pull it as soon as the swinging stops. This time there really is some generalizing intelligence involved, though an inadequate one for lack of spatial contacts, and soon a great many similar actions can be observed, in which the means used will be borrowed from habitual schemata and then adapted to ends that are inherent in the new situations. It is this coordination of schemata by means of reciprocal assimilations that does, in fact, mark the beginnings of intelligence proper, if we take as an arbitrary criterion the anticipatory subordination of means to ends arising out of distinct normal assimilation schemata.

The second important point in time linking up two different stages of behavior is the passage of acts of intelligence that involve the discovery of new means, achieved by groping and by progressive differentiations starting off from familiar schemata, to acts of a higher type involving sudden comprehension or insights. W. Köhler certainly gives us the impression that his chimpanzees—all fully grown and working away like serious adults who have to earn their food—proceed directly by means of overall reorganizations and sudden understanding; they suddenly find out how to make use of a stick, for example, in a single, momentary intuition. The human child can accomplish the same sort of thing at about eighteen months old if he has never been given a stick before. But in the development which leads up to this, it is to be noted that these rapid and interiorized coordinations, made without any material external groping, can only be achieved when the assimilation schemata have acquired sufficient mobility in generalizing assimilation for them to become included within one another or set in order, simply upon inspection of external events. This mobility itself, however, is the product of a long period of learning, during which the same sorts of coordination were carried out by means of successive discoveries and not, at this stage, by any combinatorial invention. The ability to get an object to come toward oneself by pulling whatever it is lying on (tablecloth, cover, etc.) presupposes, in a child of ten to twelve months, a series of successive acts of relating, whose stages can be followed as the child gropes about. It is only then that such assimilation schemata are constructed in any significant number by means of new experiments carried out on previous schemata and by accommodating differentiation of the new schemata thus constructed; the latter then become capable of faster coordinations, which gives the impression that some sudden act of comprehension has taken place, quite independent of what has gone before, whereas really it is the final stage in a whole chain of preliminary processes.

To sum up, the study of an infant's sensorimotor achievements, right up to a sensorimotor intelligence capable of insights or new and sudden combinations, throws remarkable light on the continuity of the learning processes from the most elementary upward, and demonstrates the permanent part played by these assimilatory activities which seem to be common not only to animals and men but also to all levels of cognitive function.

4. Animal Intelligence

In the many kinds of animal behavior that animal psychologists hesitate to designate as intelligent, we should not be surprised to find common functional mechanisms that remain constant, and, at the same time, the perpetual and vexing problem of criteria and how to classify such behavior. For the most part, this is an artificial problem, or, rather, the line of demarcation between "intelligent" and "nonintelligent" is entirely a matter of convention and semantics, although it must be admitted that the question of hierarchial levels is an essential one.

Take, for example, the case of the wasp *Ammophila*, observed by the Peckhams and written up by Viaud (*Les instincts*, p. 158), which rams the topsoil above its nest with a little pebble held between its mandibles. Here we can certainly speak of an instrument's being used although there is no question of the polyvalence of the stick used by the chimpanzee. But whether or not this extraordinary discovery is made by the wasp's intelligence certainly pales in interest alongside the truly essential fact that here we have an insect constructing an action schema (ramming away at the earth with its mandibles) that is well enough "schematized" for it to be able to assimilate an object such as a pebble as a functional extension. Another example is the ant *Oecophylla*, which A. Ledoux observed sewing leaves from the coffee shrub together, using its larvae as shuttles and employing their silk. In wondering whether this was an instinctive act (since such automatisms are specific and, therefore, innate) or an intelligent one (since an instrument was used), Ledoux seems to me to forget the most interesting solution, which would be to maintain both these answers as correct. The extreme point of interest in such behavior is, in fact, that it constitutes what might be called an intelligent instinct, which is to say that it shows us the complete isomorphism attainable by an insect as between an instinctive coordination of schemata and the same mechanism of assimilatory coordination in the domain of progressive gropings, leading to individual intelligence. If there is any truth in what was said about instinct in section 16, it is clear that, although on a different plane, instinct works by means of the same logic in assimilation schemata, and so it follows naturally from this identity of functional process that the combinations of instinctive schemata should be capable of using instruments—an extension of the combinations of objects in the constructions and utilizations of organs. In creatures capable of engendering silk-making larvae and mastering a schema for uniting objects (the leaves of the coffee shrub) with a definite aim, the exercise of such a uniting schema will be extended into the search for elements that bring about union, extending the union resulting from the act itself; hence the assimilation of the silk of the larvae into the schema. As for the act of sewing when the leaves might simply be stuck together, a study is yet to be made of the stages in this development, which is certainly a mystery so far, and I shall not venture to say it is anything more. In principle, however, it might well be of the same order of behavior as that of the monkey, which progresses from the use of a single stick to the construction of a kind of fishing rod with several sticks.

Similarly, necrophores, among which Fabre had already noted a remarkable example of individual adaptation (cutting the string with which a dead mole was tied to the top of a stick), can estimate, according to Viaud, the width of cracks in dried-up soil in order to bury the dead moles in the widest cracks. Naturally enough, Fabre refuses to see any intelligence in necrophores, claiming that their action in cutting the string is merely assimilable to what they often do by way of cutting grasses or roots in which some dead animal gets caught up as they drag it along. He is, of course, right in giving this explanation of the behavior that he provoked experimentally by tying up the mole, but he does not seem to realize that this assimilatory generalization of an acquired schema does indeed constitute an act of intelligence, at least from the point of view of functional continuity, which is the one taken here. As for Viaud, he makes no pronouncement about their degree of intelligence, although he rightly observes incipient "detours" in the necrophore's behavior and admits that this is a sign of intelligence, but he says there is not enough evidence for "the interpretation of signs of intuitive thought" (p. 158). However, there is no need at all to be using the word "thought" in this case, for the processes of reproductory assimilation, recognition, and the generalization of schemata may be analyzed with sufficient accuracy in exploratory or control experiments, which invariably show the extent of the powers and the unattainable limits of these coordinations of schemata.

"Detour" behavior, in particular, fine examples of which have been pointed out by W. H. Thorpe in connection with the *Ammophila,* may be said to represent some criterion of intelligence (but alongside many others). But it is in connection with such criteria that a study of successive assimilations into previous schemata is particularly necessary. In those cases where detours are possible immediately and without restriction in a given field (without direct generalization outside that field), they show evidence of a well-structured spatial schema isomorphic to a "displacement group" in geometry, and it is this kind of thing which can be observed in a child, beginning at sixteen to eighteen months, from the strictly sensorimotor point of view, of course (which means without any overall representation such as might presuppose symbolic instruments). But we still have to establish by what successive assimilations this schema has been set up, and this is precisely what we shall learn from studying the first few months of a child's life. First comes the very laborious conquest of elementary reversibility (going back and forth on courses of varying complexity, without screens and then with them). Then we find various displacement compositions (course AB is coordinated with course BC into a single course ABC and then, after very gradual assimilations, into $AC,$ should ABC not be in one straight line). Next, there is progressive associativity (in the logical sense of the term: $AB + BC + CD$ breaking down into $AC + CD$ or into $AB + BD$), which will assume widely different forms according to whether the trajectories are rectilinear, or at various angles, or whatever. Detour behavior is thus very far from affording a simple criterion, and the real problem for us is that of the mechanism which assimilates the coordination of schemata: How does the subject arrive at the coordination of separate acts into one complicated piece of behavior by means of reciprocal assimilations? There is the problem in a nutshell, and, as will be seen, it epitomizes all the different problems at all the different levels which have been discussed in this chapter, because it is precisely the problem of coordination by reciprocal assimilation of action schemata.

It would be interesting to take a second look, from this angle, at the remarkable experiments of Köhler, of Guillaume and Meyerson, and of many others on chimpanzees. But all we need refer to here are those first-class studies of reasoning in rats made by N. R. F. Meier and T. C. Schneirla. (Laboratory rats, however degenerate, are intelligent enough to fault the associationist theories about learning.) These experiments were all about the same in principle: to make the animal achieve, in the course of its spontaneous explorations, a certain number of partial, horizontal courses (along little bridges joining one table to another) or vertical ones (up and down columns). Then the rat was put on a familiar table facing some food that it could see but not reach (transparent screen), or that, if it was to reach the food, it must make all sorts of horizontal and vertical detours over and under and up and down the other tables or bridges or columns. The result was that the rat always succeeded in coordinating all the separate courses known to him.

In this connection Meier and Schneirla actually mention reasoning on the part of the rat, and they are right to do so because, from the behavioral point of view, inferential conduct does, in fact, consist of drawing all possible conclusions from a schema by means of some anticipatory coordination. And it is legitimate to talk of anticipation, if it is remembered what feedbacks make anticipation possible from previous information and hence from the various links implicit in a schema. But to go on from there to talk of "ideational behavior" and to presuppose that there are representations in order to support these inferences or anticipation—all this is unverifiable and fruitless. It is very hard to conceive of any representation because the animal has no semiotic instruments (language or the like), and to call up "mental images" presupposes a capacity for evocation which is not only impossible to verify but is, moreover, superfluous, since there is, in this case, perception of the total field: the rat does not have to imagine the objects or events which are not perceptible at the time. All it has to do is to combine its motions and perceptions in assessing the indices more closely each time. It does not have to form a total picture as a draftsman or cartographer does. There is, of course, an overall system, but this is within the action schemata and not in representation. Now this should be sufficient to account for such acts of intelligence, just as it is for the cases of sensorimotor inference in infants of twelve to eighteen months (removing a screen behind which an object has been hidden and then suddenly removing a second screen, not previously seen and placed underneath the first one, because the object sought for, according to the child's understanding, cannot possibly be there).

I shall conclude this chapter, summary as it may seem yet sufficient, I hope, for the main purpose of the book, by putting forward the proposition that, although every kind of knowledge, including instinct, includes information about the external environment, it nevertheless presupposes, in learning as in everything else, some structuration imposed upon it as a previous and necessary condition by internal functioning allied to the subject's organization. This structuration, however, takes two forms, through remarkably isomorphic one to the other: first a hereditary form, innately programmed down to the last detail of the structures (but allowing, at the same time, for a good deal of acquisition). Of this kind is instinct, whose inner "logic" we have shown to be closely connected with the forms and schemata of sensorimotor intelligence. The second form, not programmed in detail by heredity, intervenes as a kind of assimilatory mechanism whenever learning, however elementary, is going on; this form leads, by means of progressive assimilations, to sensorimotor intelligence. This assimilatory activity —which is necessary in all kinds of learning, however empirical, just as it is in every act of intelligence—either works as a direct extension of some innate activity, as with conditioned reflexes, or opens out into constructions going far beyond what was innate, yet still containing an endogenous element, although this will be largely as part of a functioning.

Our problem then, is to distinguish, in these two kinds of acquired, or rather "constructed," knowledge, between the part which is acquired from outside, that is, from environment or experience, and the part which belongs to the subject's activity as a kind of endogenous functioning. The hypothesis is that the latter part, even at an early stage, is logico-mathematical in nature, just because it belongs to the coordinations of the subject's actions, not to objects as such.

This logico-mathematical nature is first seen clearly in perception, which, although it supplies a series of data about the empirical properties of things, includes some schematism and geometrization which do not pertain exclusively to the object. In every kind of learning and especially in the details of sensorimotor schemata of practical intelligence, the logic of the schemata becomes more and more important: inclusions, order, connections, and so forth. It is accompanied quite clearly by a sort of geometry that involves detour behavior (displacement groups) and refined spatial grouping, such Guillaume and Meyerson found in their chimpanzees.

Thus, we cannot avoid the supposition that there exist three main types of knowledge: (a) hereditary forms, of which the prototype is instinct and which even at an early stage include, as we have seen, a kind of logic, although this is crystallized into a rigid, innate program whose content refers back to largely innate information about the environment; (b) logico-mathematical forms constructed progressively, as in the case of the relatively superior levels characteristic of intelligence; and (c) forms acquired in terms of experience (from learning up to physical knowledge). At the levels that we have studied in this chapter, however, forms *b* and *c* are not dissociated as they are on the level of human thought, but this does not mean that they are reducible to each other. That is why the distinction has not been stressed in this chapter, but in the next chapter it will be returned to as part of the problem raised by innate forms, from the point of view of trying to explain hereditary adaptation in general but with particular attention to those types of knowledge best represented in man.

6   The Biological Interpretation of the Three Forms of Knowledge

From the point of view of the biological problems that they raise, we can distinguish three forms of knowledge that result from the exercise of the cognitive functions in man—at least when he reaches a certain level of civilization. In the first place, there is the vast category of knowledge acquired by means of physical experience of every type, that is, the experience of external objects or of whatever appertains to them, abstraction being made of objects as such. At once it will be seen that this means an infinite extension of learning behavior or practical intelligence, but there are all sorts of novel aspects to it which need explanation. In the second place, there is the extremely restricted category—in fact, it is debatable whether it has any real extension—of knowledge structured by hereditary programming, such as may be the case with certain perceptual structures (seeing colors and two or three dimensions in space). The limited nature of this second category at once raises a great biological problem, just because of the contrast between it and the great variety of instincts in animals. In the third place, there is the category of logico-mathematical knowledge, and this at least as extensive as the first. Such knowledge achieves independence of experience, and, even at the stage where it is still bound up with experience, it seems to spring not from objects as such but from the general coordinations of the actions exerted by the subject on the objects around it.

Biologically speaking, it is this latter category which raises the hardest problem. Do we, in fact, have to see it as part of the first category, reducing mathematics to some sort of generalized physics, or as part of the second, as Konrad Lorenz does, admitting that mathematics is based on synthetic, a priori judgments, in the Kantian sense of the term, but claiming that these a priori are to be seen as comparable to innate forms for the same reason as the instincts are? And if each of these solutions comes to distort the character of logico-mathematical structures, then would it be possible to conceive of a third type of formation from a biological point of view?

To put it shortly, this last is what I wish to do, but my solution will take the following form—the direct outcome of my conclusions in chapter 5: if all types of knowledge, innate or acquired, necessarily presuppose a certain permanent functioning, which gives rise to assimilatory schemata and their coordinations, then the hereditary forms of cognitive behavior, which predominate among animals (reflexes, instincts, and so on) as long as the field of adaptation or equilibrium is limited, will divide up in two complementary ways as soon as this field is extended by means of representation or thought. First, it will tend toward externalization or phenotypic accommodation to environment, in other words, to learning, to experiment, and to physical knowledge of the first category; then it will tend toward internalization or formal structuration through consciousness or, to put it more exactly, through reflective abstraction based on the internal conditions of each functioning (that is, on those general forms of organization which extend beyond cognitive assimilation and back into the common mechanisms, hence, to those processes which lie at the heart of any living organization). This would be my interpretation of knowledge in the third category, and so it would be impossible to reduce that knowledge to the first two categories although it would result indirectly from the splintering off of the second, since the seeming disappearance of instinctive knowledge in man would be typified (a) by a considerable extension of acquired knowledge, by dint of experiment in the physical world (first category), and (b) by a no less considerable extension of the logico-mathematical structures, insofar as these are already at work in some elementary or immanent form in every cognitive functioning. This would, however, become the object of reflective knowledge as soon as the emergence of thought made such reflection possible (third category).[1]

This hypothesis, advanced early in order to facilitate the reading of the present chapter, may appear to be mere speculation. However, it will be much less so once epistemological or logical and especially psychogenetic reasons for such an opinion are examined step by step, and that is what will be attempted now. The justification for this position must begin with a systematic examination of the central problem raised by any hypothesis about innate knowledge—in other words, about the problem of whatever relations there may be between environment and hereditary, morphological, or cognitive adaptation. Of course, we have already admitted that there is as yet no possible explanation of instinct, and the following section is not supposed to supply one. But, as soon as one begins to ask what could be hereditary in human knowledge, and that is certainly where one has to begin from a biological angle (especially where logico-mathematical structures are concerned, because these are universal and coercive and extraordinarily adaptive), one has to make a close examination of the biological conditions which would have to obtain if there were any knowledge that was both hereditary and adapted to environment. We shall devote section 19 to the making of this detailed examination, which is indispensable although hypothetical, and then in section 20 we shall be able to get back to human knowledge and thus situate the question of logical and mathematical knowledge in a much wider context.

Section 19. Innate Knowledge and the Hereditary Instruments of Knowledge

There are only a very small number of cognitive structures in man which can definitely be said to be innate. Nevertheless, such struc-

1. One further remark: we are omitting the modes of metaphysical and ideological knowledge because they are not kinds of knowledge in the strict sense but forms of wisdom or value coordinations, so that they represent a reflection of social life and cultural superstructures rather than any extension of biological adaptation. By this we do not mean to dispute their human importance; it is simply that the problems are quite different and are no longer the direct province of biological epistemology.

tures as there are present us with the central problem of all those structures which are either organic or dependent on behavior transmitted by heredity: that of their adaptation to the external environment. This will be especially the case if we include all the differentiated hereditary organs which play an essential part in the building up of knowledge (the brain, the eyes, the hands, and so on).

1. A Priori Concepts

There are no innate ideas, in the Cartesian sense. One can, of course, consider a priori categories, such as Kant talks about, to be innate by extension. The existence of a priori synthetic judgments in epistemology was admitted by H. Poincaré in connection with number intuition (meaning the iteration $n + 1$) and "displacement groups." In psychology, the same Kantian interpretation has been sustained by certain Gestalt psychologists such as W. Metzger and, above all, Konrad Lorenz, who judges notions of cause, space, etc., to be previous to any experience, just as horses' hooves and fishes' fins are present even in the embryo (and, as he goes on to point out, with adaptation to the environment or to experience and for the same reason, namely, selection).

From the psychogenetic point of view, however, such interpretations will not stand up to examination. The displacement "group" and the intuition of $n + 1$ that Poincaré points to would seem to be the ultimate term (necessary, just like the Kantian a priori, but still ultimate and not previous) of a progressive equilibration and not a prior condition of spatial or numerical development. General and necessary categories such as causality are never found in ready-made form, especially not at initial stages. There are a great many types of causality which succeed each other in regular stages, and what they have in common is not a form, which would have to be extremely weak if it were common to them all, but simply a function or a functional need for explanation, arising from the application of deduction to regular temporal sequences. Now, if the a priori is only a function or functioning, it is impossible to talk of "innate" ideas in any structural sense.

Still more hereditary apparatus are to be found in sensorimotor schemata, as, for instance, in the coordination of seeing and taking hold, due no doubt, to maturation of the pyramidal system. But there is still no question of thought or representative knowledge.

And, further, from the cognitive point of view, if this coordination were not hereditary and were only dependent on acquired habits or conditioning, it would not make much difference.

In the perceptual domain, on the other hand, it is reasonable to hypothesize the existence of certain innate structures. It is not certain whether three-dimensional vision is acquired or not (blind people whose sight is restored, the gradual evaluations made by infants, and so on), but the remarkable constancy in estimations of depth in terms of disparation and the independence of these estimations with respect to age would seem to the point to some innate mechanism.[2] Where the other two dimensions are concerned there would seem to be little doubt; the newborn child certainly does not perceive its universe as reduced to one little point which is later going to branch out in length and width. Now, if two-dimensional surfaces, if not volume, exist from the outset, this ought to mean that the visual organs impose from the outset some structure that makes it possible to make an adequate recording of experience in this respect.

Whether space has a Euclidian character or not, it does not seem to be hereditary, although Luneberg thought (and Jonckheere supported him in this) that he had discovered curves reminiscent of Riemann's theories in the perception of parallelism. On the other hand, it is remarkable that we never succeed in "seeing" or imagining in more than three dimensions (that is, in precise mental images, as opposed to thought, which remains sovereign). It is true that mathematicians such as Freudenthal speak of the supple way in which intuition "learns" to move in four or n dimensions; but this is an operational kind of intuition, not a perceptual one at all. From the purely visual point of view, limitation to three dimensions is still a remarkable thing and does seem, once again, to contain some innate structure, although this time in a limiting sense (as with so many biological characteristics).

Alongside these few remnants of innateness, striking in their paucity when compared to animal instincts, we must allow for some discussion of the hereditary organs of knowledge. It is true, of course, that brains, eyes, and hands are not pieces of knowledge, even in a virtual sense. But it is obvious that if our eyes were any different (if they had facets and were without focus) or if we had

2. According to research carried out by M. Lambercier but not yet published.

none and if we had neither the power of manipulating nor the power of moving, with our nervous system as perfected and cerebralized as it is, our cognitive universe would be very different. And, furthermore, if we were living with similar organs on a quite different scale such as that of the atom, then our fundamental concepts would be turned upside down, not just because of the way things appeared to us but because of our means of action.

2. The Traditional Solutions

So, then, our biological analysis of human thought must start off with a discussion of the problem central to knowledge, although it is the most difficult one from the biological point of view: that of adaptation or of the cognitive adequation of hereditary structures to the external environment. There is not a single instinct, in fact, which does not have well-differentiated cognitive adaptations to the environment (and here one must refer to instinct generally and not just to the only two manifestations of it which subsist in man[3]). Even in the case of sexual instinct—where the "object" is not a physical material or a landscape of some kind, as is the case in nest building or migrations, or a living creature, as with predation or the stinging of insects, but consists of an organism that is complementary to that of the subject and of the same species—what the subject has to do is make a perceptual discrimination of the object of its desire, and this again is a cognitive adaptation to external data. So we must try to understand how a hereditary mechanism, which is transmitted by internal, not external, means (training or imitation, which may be superimposed, as with the predatory instinct in kittens, according to Kuo, but which does not on that account constitute the whole of instinct), could acquire by any other means a whole range of anticipatory information about the environment.

1. The first reply comes from the Lamarckians, who say that instinct is only a habit fixed in heredity. Now this habit consists of a series of associations imposed on the subject by the environment, and all that is inherited is the memory of it, which is handed down to the descendants. As a result, the adaptation of the instinct to the environment simply consists of anticipations based upon pre-

---

3. These are the feeding and the sexual instincts, that is to say, the only ones which include some appetitive conduct and specialized organs. Attempts have often been made to draw up some sort of catalog of other series, but all they reveal is tendencies, and the hereditary character of these is dubious.

vious information transmitted from the environment to the germinative system.

As things actually stand now in relation to these problems, two
aspects of such a theory need to be pointed out: the general
processes, by which information from the environment is passed
to the genome or to the "genetic pool" and by which acquired
knowledge is inherited; and the causal mechanism of these
processes, that is to say, the way in which habits are acquired, the
homogeneity of the individual memory or habit and the memory
of the species or heredity, the essentially receptive character of the
germinative system, which is open to every kind of external influence, and so on.

Bitter and dogmatic argument has been going on for a good fifty
years between the neo-Lamarckians, who accept the system as a
whole, and the neo-Darwinians, who reject it outright. Now, leaving
out of account any heredity in acquired knowledge, we are beginning to see, nowadays, that the two general processes postulated
by Lamarck, and eventually agreed to by Darwin, are both acceptable but that we still need to reexamine, and in a fundamental way,
those causal mechanisms which were supposed to account for them.

The "heredity of the acquired," to take that first, had become
taboo, either as a notion or even as a problem, and those who made
so bold as to raise it were looked down on as intellectually inferior,
much as are seekers after the secret of perpetual motion in physics,
as though there were some sort of rational contradiction of inner
vice in the reasoning involved with admitting at one and the same
time the autoconservation of the germinative plasma and its power
to transmit through heredity other elements than those which it had
received from previous generations—a series of irregularities or dis-
organizations in the form of mutations! It took someone with the
courage of Waddington, as we saw in section 8, to use his authority
by speaking up once again for the "heredity of acquired characteristics." However, he did supply, in addition to the notion of "genetic
assimilation," one further causal model.

In the same way, the idea that information should be transmitted
from the environment to the germinative system long seemed to be
in contradiction to Mendelian discoveries about the mechanism of
heredity. But as soon as it was seen that the phenotype, instead of
being an uninteresting epiphenomenon, was in fact the outcome of
interaction between the genotype and the environment, and, even

more important, as soon as it was noted that selection influenced phenotypes by way of interaction, then the passing of information from the environment to the genome became intelligible as a kind of selection aimed at retaining the best-adapted phenotypes.

To sum up, the difficulties of the Lamarckian interpretation lie, not in the general processes postulated by him, but in his ignorance of endogenous variations. This means that the organism, instead of passively accepting pressures from the environment (Lamarck did go so far as to admit there was some active part taken by the living creature in the actual choice of environment), assimilates them into structures that are endowed with the power of autoconservation. Therefore, in what concerns the problem of hereditary cognitive adaptations to environment, the general processes of Lamarck are of little use to us and simply amount to a confirmation that such a problem exists; we still need to understand how, among all the details of the causal mechanism, the genome can acquire any information about the environment and, above all, how these modes of reaction—endogenous at root and at the same time containing external or exogenous information—are constituted. What Lamarck did was simply to subordinate the genetic system to acquired habits, and in this he was content with insufficient proof, so that he could offer no justification for the general principles inspired by his functionalism even though they cannot be doubted.

2. The second solution put forward to the problem of hereditary cognitive adaptation is the mutationist one. According to this theory, instinct owes its origin, just as morphological, anatomical, and physiological characteristics (including the human brain) do, to chance mutational variations, progressively sorted out and thus refined in the process of selection. As Herodotus said, "Given endless time, anything can happen." But if it is not considered in any way incompatible with survival that evolution should wait some thousands of centuries to endow a horse with a tail and a mane made of hairs and not feathers, it becomes rather difficult to envisage how long it would take to ingrain the instincts of reproduction, nest-building, and so on among species whose very existence depends on cognitive precision in relation to those instinctive mechanisms. We need only take one example: the eye in vertebrates. This is not indispensable as a means of acquiring knowledge but it is indubitably useful. Bleuler's calculations showed that if the mutations necessary for the formation of this organ had been brought about simulta-

neously or conjointly, they would have had a probability of only 1 in 10^{42}, in other words, practically none. On the other hand, if it had been a question of successive mutations, in which new ones were simply added to preceding mutations, so that a cumulative effect was achieved, then it would have taken as many generations as would correspond to the age of the world or even exceed it.[4]

Then again, when it comes to cognition proper, it would simply be impossible to believe an explanation of the development of logico-mathematical structures in man by a selection mechanism such as that used to account for the formation of hooves in horses or fins in fish. Biological selection is, in fact, related to survival, whereas the victory of one idea over another depends, in the final analysis, on the value of the truth contained in it. Now it may be beyond dispute that in any species a greater intelligence, allied with progress in cerebral development, is, by and large, a factor favorable to survival, but this explanation becomes meaningless as soon as cognitive adaptations are examined circumstantially. A precise application of logic presupposes, among other things, the constant obligation not to contradict—a program very hard to carry out and one that people not interested in accuracy or truth will not much care for. This lack of intellectual honesty may be of a certain practical use (it is usually more convenient to be able to contradict oneself) and, when scruples about truth finally triumph, it is certainly not because there has been competition or selection in terms of utility alone but rather because of certain choices dictated by the internal organization of thought. Thus, it is unthinkable that the human brain's capacity for constructing logico-mathematical structures that are so admirably adapted to physical reality should be explained away by mere selection, as the mutationists do, for factors of utility and survival would have led only to intellectual instruments of a crudely approximate kind, loosely sufficient for the life of the species and its individual members, and never to that precision and, above all, that intrinsic necessity which demand a much more penetrating explanation of adaptation by a posteriori selection within random variations.[5]

4. Needless to say, these calculations are based on the supposed age of the Earth, the rate of extrapolated mutation, the indices of regrouping, the number of DNA triplets considered necessary, the size of the populations under consideration, and so on.

5. The eminent biologist B. Rensch has seen this fundamental difficulty more

We can, then, attach no credence to the mutationist solution. And when we look more closely at the mutationist explanation of adaptation, there is one question it leaves wide open. Starting out from factual data and not axiomatically on the basis of deductively reconstituted origins, mutationism recognizes three groups of phenomena: (a) organized systems, such as the organism as a whole, or the germinative system, although this is seen as a "bean bag" (as Mayr flippantly puts it), which means as an aggregate of atomistic particles having, nevertheless, the power of self-conservation which represents at least one aspect of the organization; (b) chance in bringing about mutations; and (c) selection in the shape of mere survival or elimination of mutated individuals, both of these being brought about simply by random encounters with the elements or events in the environment. However, seeking to explain phenomenon *a* by means of *b* and *c,* instead of retaining all three with their interactions, the mutationists at once forget that chance variation either kills off the individual, that is, it suppresses the organization that fails to make sufficient assimilations in its encounters with the environment, or else it is integrated by the previously existing organization, which is to say, not only that chance has been at work here but that chance has been made use of by means of a prior organization (necessary, in particular, for later transmission by heredity). This theory, moreover, leaves out of account the fact that selection itself is not just a matter of sifting through a sieve, through which the mutated organization must either pass or fail to pass, but implies a reciprocal choice by the organism, of an environment which suits it and of elements which will assure its survival.

Briefly put, the mutationist interpretation, by refusing to recognize that the organization is a causal factor and by limiting causality to chance and to selection, blinds itself to the fact that it is only talking about chance as made use of by the organization and about reciprocal or controlled selections; thus, mutationism is led to attribute the organization to chances which are already partly orga-

---

clearly than anyone else, and so he does not adopt the mutationist approach of K. Lorenz but arrives at interpreting logico-mathematical structures as extrabiological and extramental. However, before we abandon the unequal struggle over them and the biological explanation of them, which would be to submit the biology of cognitive functions to the sway of Plato and Husserl, perhaps we ought first to think about improving biological conceptions of adaption.

nized and to selections which are themselves controlled, so that there is a perpetual vicious circle. As a result, when those who oppose this doctrine ask how a living being can emerge from a series of lotteries or random groupings based on unorganized matter, or how an organ or instinct can be adapted by chance mutations that usually succeed only in disrupting the living creature rather than enriching it, the mutationist claims to see chance and selection only as positive factors, because he is, without realizing it, setting them in an organization context.

It is as though we were to conclude that, because thought is constantly meeting with lucky or unlucky chances in its attempts to discover things, and because the hypotheses or gropings of this thought are necessarily selected as a result of experience, then not only are those hypotheses more or less endogenous but even the thought itself is entirely due to such chances and selections. This would be to forget, first, that it is only the lucky chances that the subject can make use of and, second, that the only effective selections of hypotheses are those which result from a good organization of experience. No doubt the organism is less active than thought is, and so our comparison is not quite symmetrical from the quantitative point of view, but the qualitative principle in it is correct, and this can clearly be seen in the domain of instinct, halfway between the organism and thought.

As far as instinct is concerned, the mutationist theory amounts to the supposition that all instinctive behavior has been brought about by motor or perceptual productions arising by chance, just as mutations arise, and that the environment has selected the successful productions after the fact. It might just as well be said that the bird kept heaping up material haphazardly until it began to make nests, that it laid its eggs anyplace before it took to laying them in those nests, that the males and females tried everything before they found how to coordinate their activities, and that of all those endless acts of aberrant behavior, the only ones conserved were those that were of advantage to the next generation. Here again, if the mutationist feels unconsciously protected from such ridiculous implications, it is only because random variations, such as may come about during the formation of the instincts, are, in fact, produced only in terms of some previous organization, and because selection, as it chooses among these variations, does not work solely on a survival or extinction basis, but in terms of those very survival mechanisms which, in the case of instinct, are primarily the failures or the practical or cognitive successes among the actions attempted.

It must be admitted that, in recalling the necessary part played by the organization in the utilization of chance, we might appear to be reasoning in a vitalist manner. But if the organization translated in terms of regulations, the lacunae in mutationism become even more obvious. It is known, at the present time, that the main sources of adaptive variation are not chance mutations but genetic recombinations and that two lethal mutations combining can produce a viable variation.[6] Furthermore, it is known that the organism chooses its environment and thus may be said to have selected it quite as much as it has itself been selected. From the point of view of instinct, the possibility is thus open for an explanation by means of coordinations of schemata in conjunction with genetic combinations and, more particularly, with epigenetic regulations during the formation of the phenotype, since it is phenotypes that are the object of selection.

3. The vitalist or finalist interpretation of instinct amounts to presupposing some preestablished harmony between the organism and the environment. The moment one attempts to find out how this harmony is established during development rather than preestablished before development, one is involved with causal explanations.

3. Population Genetics

Let us now examine what possible explanations of instinct or of the hereditary instruments of knowledge are being put forward by contemporary scientists in the field of population genetics: Darlington, Dobzhansky, Haldane, Julian Huxley, Lerner, Ludwig, Mather, Mayr, Stebbins, Waddington, and others.

Instinct, as we have seen, is based essentially on transindividual cycles, in the sense that the behavior of one individual—the male in relation to the female, the mother in relation to the offspring or vice versa, the worker in relation to his social group, and so forth—

6. See the important work on this done by Pontecorvo, already referred to in subsection 3, and also Coffron's book (*A "Book Model" of Genetic Information in Cells and Tissues*) in which he suggests that genetic processes are comparable, not to a machine that only acts as a compositor of letters, but rather to a machine that can make up new words or whole phrases.

is programmed by heredity, with respect both to significant perceptual schemata and to consummatory motions or actions, in terms of a totality containing a number of individual roles which are distinct and complementary rather than in terms of a single action common to all individuals. Now, although these transindividual cycles do not correspond, in any way, either in functional mechanisms or in structure, to what contemporary geneticists call a population, it is nevertheless interesting to note that the underlying idea of them is no longer a cross between two individuals whose purified genomes are supposed to constitute the basic elements of all genetic construction, which is seen as a combinatorial starting from these individual atoms, but that the perspective is also transindividual.

The prime concept is, in fact, population, but population viewed as a group of individuals, each pair of which possesses, in principle, the same chance of fertile coupling (panmixia) but each individual member of which shares a common "genetic pool," that is, a collective genetic system resulting from all possible crossings. This basic theory about the genetic pool is conceived of, not as an aggregate—and herein lies the main difference from mutationist theory—but as having all the characteristics of a "system"; its elements are co-adapted and integrated into a whole, which includes its "genetic homeostasia,"[7] just as in every genome there is polygenia[8] and also, frequently, pleiotropism,[9] taking the form of regulatory interactions. Where the genome is concerned, some theorists make a distinction between structural and regulatory genes, but others go no farther than the statement that each characteristic produced is influenced by the genes as a whole, interacting on one another, and that each gene is dependent on the total system. Corresponding to these relationships—which are, so to speak, established in "comprehension" (in the logical sense of the word) inside each individual genome—are, by extension, various integrating relationships between the individual and the species; but here the central concept is no longer the individual, or the species as an entity, but the population as a

7. This idea comes from Dobzhansky and Wallace (1953) and from Lerner (1955), and may be applied to the genotype, the population, or the entire species.

8. The intervention of two or more genes in the reproduction of a characteristic.

9. The production of two or more new characteristics after modification in one single gene.

dynamic system taking its character from its genetic pool and from the "reaction norms" which supply its phenotypic expression by interacting with the environment.[10]

From the point of view of variation, the change of perspective makes just as great a difference. It is no longer mutation but, rather, genetic recombination that is the main factor, and this produces new genotypes up to the point where a better equilibrium is achieved in the succeeding generations.[11] The first thing to notice here is that recombination can have no effect unless applied to the differences between the elements that are being reorganized. Now, unless we assume that there are perpetual neoformations in the genes, we have to say that new genes are engendered from their predecessors by means of the progressive addition of specific and limited mutations. There must, therefore, be a process of intragenetic variation at the DNA nucleotid level. In view of this, the way in which recombination exploits mutation by means of efficient combinatorial systems is of capital importance for the process of evolution. In fact, recombination is of longer and more universal application than meiosis, since it occurs even among bacteriophages. On the other hand, recombination provides an explanation for those vital initiatives taken by living creatures in the course of evolution, whereas chance or selection alone offer none (for selection only produces effects of immediate utility). Darlington even goes so far as to say that such initiatives are "anticipatory preadaptations."[12] But finally, and most important of all, recombinations bring about new forms of equilibrium. Heterozygotes evince, on the average, a higher genetic homeostasia than homeozygotes,[13] and the characteristics are no longer definitely dominant or recessive but can switch roles in this

10. The "reaction norms" may equally well be attributed to the genotype, to the population, or to the entire species (the notion of "reaction norm" was already known to Johannsen and Morgan and was reelaborated by Kühn).

11. On recombination, see Darlington, *Evolution of the Genetic System* (1939 and 1958), and Lewis and John, *The Matter of Mendelian Heredity* (1964). They calculate the recombination index in terms of the sum of the haploid number of chromosomes and the average number of crossings-over per cell.

12. For these preadaptations or "prospective adaptations," see Simpson, *The Major Features of Evolution* (1953, pp. 189–97). See also his book *The Study of Evolution* (Columbia University Press).

13. See R. C. Lewontin's study of homeostasia and heterozygotia in *The American Naturalist*, July-August 1956.

respect according to the new combinations. Generally speaking, and this is the main point, a new variation is no longer to be considered an isolated product brought about by the purest chance, but as an expression of a reequilibration following some loss of equilibrium. Thus, it is part and parcel of an overall equilibration that is manifested in the equilibrium of alleles (relational equilibrium), of different loci (epistatic equilibrium), and so on, in a mechanism that involves the entire genetic pool of the population.

As for selection, these new ideas, whose general tendency is to reduce the role of chance in favor of equilibrium, seem to be producing some modification in the interpretation of this too, replacing the idea of mechanical selection by that of progressive adjustment. In its framework, since selection has a bearing only on phenotypes and reaction norms that express the interactions of the genetic pool and the environment, selection is reciprocal from the outset insofar as organisms both choose their environment and are chosen by their environment. Selection is, in mechanism, a modification of the characteristic proportions of the genetic pool: the proportion of the various genes, the frequency of heterozygotes' increasing the genetic homeostasia,[14] and so forth. Looked at in this way, selection may be "dynamic" or it may again be an equilibration factor, but this time in direct interaction with environment. In this "stabilizing selection"[15] Waddington distinguishes a negative aspect of elimination of deviations (normalizing selection) and a positive aspect favoring the exercise of stabilizing mechanisms (channeling selection). But the main point is to recognize that there are two ways in which to look at selection: from the point of view of the present, concerning survival and genetic homeostasia, and from the point of view of the future of the pool, concerning its plasticity and the range of all possible responses. For example, recessive characteristics (and they may have become so after having first been dominant) may increase the likelihood of later adaptations. Selection, insofar as it modifies or maintains proportions, must therefore be seen from an essentially probabilistic angle. It is as relative to the probability of survival or of

14. See Pontecorvo, *Trends in Genetic Analysis*—a lecture published in 1956.

15. The idea and the expression "stabilizing selection" are Schmalhausen's. For the present state of ideas on selection, see W. Ludwig, "Die heutige Gestalt der Selektionstheorie," in *Hundert Jahre Evolutionsforschung* (Stuttgart: G. Fischer, 1960); and E. Mayr, *Animal Species and Evolution,* as well as J. M. Smith, *Theory of Evolution.*

adaptability in the descendants as it is to the actual state of genetic homeostasia, and thus it constitutes an equilibrium mechanism that is both dynamic and synchronic, since here, once again, the essential consideration is the population, not individuals as such.

In a consideration of how hereditary knowledge or instincts in their cognitive adaptation to environment are built up, this new thinking is of vital importance. In the first place, it makes possible a complete integration of Lamarck's two principal processes—information transmitted from the environment to the genome and the heredity of the characteristics acquired in this way—but by putting a new interpretation upon their causal mechanism. In effect, by moving the stress from the individual genome to the genetic pool, one abandons the notion of an individual organism in favor of the notion of a sort of collective organism, or at least a transindividual organization, with the twofold activity of constantly maintaining its equilibrium while adapting itself to the environment. In this case, selection must be a modification of the equilibrium in the genomes and the genetic pool. This modification will proceed in a manner comparable to Lamarck's conception of the action of an external factor upon the organism, but it will replace simple causal action by a probability form of action upon the proportions of a pluri-unit. So information is continuously transmitted from the environment to the genetic pool, and variations are fixed by "genetic assimilation," with heredity of acquired information again proceeding by means of selective stabilization or, in other words, by modification —now irreversible—of the proportions of the collective genome.

But, in the second place, and this for us is no doubt the most interesting point of contact between Lamarckian functionalism and population genetics, every stable genotype variation is a "response" made by the genotype to the tensions set up by the environment, as Dobzhansky and Waddington put it, not merely a random fluctuation, and thus there is continuity between phenotypic accommodations and genetic adaptation. Where the instinct is concerned, this notion of response, which has no meaning if not an adaptive one, suggests that there may be adjustment of hereditary behavior to the environment.

But that will not be the end of it, far from it, for if chemical, energetic, and other modifications in the environment can produce tensions and responses at all levels in the productions of the phenotypes that selection operates upon, then variations in behavior can only be possible at more advanced functional stages, and the genetic application of these interactions between behavior and environment can no longer immediately be understood. In other words, supposing the instinctive cycle to be transindividual and linked to the structure of the genetic pool, then behavior capable of introducing new features by means of acquisition in terms of the environment must be behavior attributable to individuals that are already partially formed insofar as their somatic structure goes. How, then, are we to view the relations between the individual and the population, and, more important still, between the behavior of this individual and the sector of the genetic pool which constitutes the individual's own genome? To put it still more precisely, the hereditary fixation of a new behavior seems to imply some transmission from the soma to the genome, whereas, following the neo-Darwinian tradition, the general opinion of population geneticists (except for Waddington, who does at least recognize the problem) is that there is a radical isolation of the genome, which they justify by instancing its regulatory mechanisms for autconservation.

4. Individual and Population

The relations between the individual and the group, a problem which presents itself in human sociology as well as in population genetics, can be conceived in any one of three ways: individualistically, "holistically," or relationally.

From the atomistic or individualistic point of view, the individual is the source of all new characteristics or transformations, so that the group or population is nothing but the additive outcome of such initiative by the individual. This is the line taken by mutationists, and it is one which excludes any possibility of a genetic pool but does allow for the individual genome's being seen in isolation from its environment.

From the holist or totalist point of view, everything happens at the population level, so that the individual is nothing but a passive reflection or, at best, a partial one, of processes which are quite independent of him and belong to a quite different genetic scale. So there is nothing to exclude the possibility of the individual's being isolated from the soma, since the individual genome is only a link in a chain and this chain is the only thing that counts, having laws unto itself.

From the interactionist point of view, again the individual is seen as not being an autonomous element or a primary source, because it is simply the product of a number of interactions, dependent upon the population as a whole. At the same time, the individual is the source and not the result of these interactions, for the population has now, in its turn, ceased to be a "force" or an "organism" pressing upon individuals from outside, and is, instead, a sort of system composed of all the interactions. Properly speaking, then, there are no longer any groups or any individuals, but simply a number of coordinated interactions, and whether these are described as being within the individual or within the group, taken as a unit (involving scales), they are still the same interactions. There are thus ways of analyzing them, but the same phenomena are being described, only from different angles, just as a complex object may be analyzed from without or from within, or a tunnel may be bored from both ends; the only important thing is not to lose sight of the overall plan.

In this third approach, which will be the one taken here, the individual becomes, not just an element or independent source, but a "population" in itself, although of course hemmed in, more or less, by the whole structure and, at the same time, essentially collective or interactive by nature. So one might say the individual is a sort of microcosm reflecting the population, since its genome is a composite which represents a sector, wide or narrow, of the genetic pool. (In the last resort the individual may even be a complete "representation," like an endomorphism as a univocal connecting link between the whole and the part.[16]) We shall thus be able to proceed with our analysis in the following way.

Our hypothesis is that every process taking place within the population and involving the fundamental relations between the genetic pool and the environment (variation and selection) may

16. Of course, I am not maintaining that any "impure" individual genome, by which I mean any cross between the paternal and maternal ancestry, is to be seen, on that account, as a complete endomorphism of the population, having a bi-univocal correspondence between whole and part. But if this individual actually does spring from a sufficient mixture, then it is a bi-univocal reflection of one sector of the population, which means that it is closer to the population laws than were the genotypes of so-called pure stock of formal Mendelian genetics. Moreover, as we were saying just now, it would be possible to conceive of a complete bi-univocity with the whole population under consideration, for example, a case of polyploidia in which all alleles were represented with their relative frequencies, which would be a fine endomorphism of the genetic pool but perhaps a surprise on the phenotypic plane.

correspond to a parallel qualitative process involving the relations between the individual genome (as a sector of the pool, more or less endomorphic to the total population pool) and the individual environment (insofar as it intervenes in the development of the phenotype and the soma).

Where variation is concerned, the qualitative parallelism—individual $\times$ population—can be taken for granted, for the genetic recombinations resulting from crosses or internal disequilibria occur within the individual genomes and not at large among the population, and these genomes are produced by population mixing.[17] To be sure, if genotypes are artificially selected until more or less pure lineages are obtained (although they are never altogether pure), then the Mendelian laws will once more be found applicable, with greater or lesser mutations and constant ratios. But we are talking here about uncultivated [*sauvages*] individuals, or individuals in a natural state, direct products of the population, who therefore reflect it, insofar as they are part of a sector, be it great or small, of the genetic pool.

When it comes to selection, it will be the same thing again if one stops looking at it as some kind of sorting process by which individuals are just lumped into two classes: those condemned to death and those with a survival certificate. As soon as selection is regarded as a probabilistic process, which modifies and restructures the proportions of the genome or of the genetic pool, then the problem takes on a quite different shape, and nothing then prevents our conceiving of two processes, each related to the other and both modifying the proportions and restructurings. First of all, we must remember that such proportions are relative to the probabilities of survival and of viable lineage, and that the process itself is therefore essentially a dynamic one. Next, we must remember that genes are sources of activity, either duplicating hereditary transmission or having a morphopoietic effect in embryogenesis, so that to modify their proportions is the same as modifying these various activities. Above all, we must remember that the survival of the individual, as well as the various degrees of survival right down to nonsurvival, is the final result of a continuous process of epigenetic and phenotypic growth,

17. The frequency of these mixings within the individual naturally depends, from the qualitative point of view, on the frequencies proper to the population as a whole, but insofar as they are qualitative processes, they remain within the individual genomes.

so that the proportions of the genome can be modified at any moment during these activities by means of selective interactions with the environment.

If this is so, then it can be said that selection, considered as a modification of the proportions of the genome which provokes within the genome a series of reequilibrations or readjustments through regulatory interactions, must depend on two factors which usually occur in conjunction:

1. Indirect factors (also known as external factors), which make for the elimination of certain individuals under pressure from an environment in which they either cannot develop or are destroyed.

2. Direct factors (sometimes called internal factors) such as longevity, strength, plasticity, and so on, which depend on the organism but which also depend, of course, upon the environment.

It is when we look at the second of these factors that we can best see how superficial the concept of selection as a mere sorting out process was, for if an individual can only die en bloc, his survival is an uninterrupted process which is a function of innumerable factors, internal as well as external.

5. *Environment and the Genetic System*

It follows from what has just been said that there are two kinds of actions possible for the environment to exert on the genetic system, and these are, moreover, related to each other in a continuous fashion. Let us take a genome G in an environment M which has undergone modification as M'. The elements of G can be divided into three groups (structural and regulatory): A, neutral elements, showing phenotypic characteristics a; B, favorable elements showing characteristics b; and C, unfavorable, showing characteristics b; and C, unfavorable, showing characteristics c. This being so, there are two courses of action open to the environment M', as follows:

1. Selection in the indirect sense (see the last part of subsection 4, point 1) eliminates those phenotypes in which the C elements are more numerous than the B elements and favors those of the inverse proportion: that is to say, it eliminates individuals in which c characteristics are well developed while the b ones are poorly developed, and is favorable to those in which the inverse is true.

2. However, the death or survival of phenotypes with variable adaptive values (0 to 1) is only the outcome, at one particular stage, of a continuous growth in each individual, and this growth may al-

ready be giving rise to the same process, but in direct form; the *B* factors or elements may be improved by some functioning which is reinforced by the environment in the production of *b* characteristics, whereas the functioning of the *C* elements may constantly be inhibited in producing *c* characteristics because of obstacles set up by the environment during the growth period. This modification of the "reactions" leads to a reequilibration in the form of a change in proportions, equivalent to that brought about by direct selection (see subsection 4, point 2).

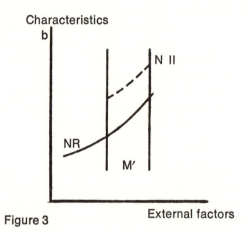

Figure 3

This second process is simply the expression of the formation of phenotypes that have undergone adaptation, but we still have to draw attention to the case in which the equilibrium is only achieved momentarily (in individuals only) and to the case in which it becomes stable by means of "genetic assimilation." And we still have to establish whether this genetic assimilation can be brought about by processes of the second kind or whether it demands selection by elimination (subsection 4, point 1).

The range of phenotypes produced within the environments they occupy, in terms of the variation of one of the factors in an environment, is called the "reaction norm" or adaptive norm of a phenotype or population (see figure 3, curve NR). In the case where a limited environment *M'* is separated from others by modification or isolation, at the extreme end of the reaction norm (see figure 3, the two vertical lines enclosing *M'*), there is a displacement of the reaction norm in the sense that the *b* characteristic is strengthened (see N II, dotted line).[18]

This result (N II) may be brought about by two processes acting independently or conjointly:

1. The first process is selection by elimination (see subsection 4, point 1); those phenotypes with unfavorable *c* characteristics are eliminated, those with *b* characteristics produce a displacement of the norm because they are usually submerged beneath the mass of different variations, which is why there are so few *b* characteristics, whereas in selection by elimination the proportions are changed and the *b* characteristic becomes predominant.

2. The same result can be achieved, however, by the second process. Throughout the animal's growth, the action of the *C* genes is blocked by resistance from the environment, and the action of the *B* genes is encouraged. As the morphogenetic action of the genes constitutes a continuous functional process, within which various stages or degrees $\alpha\beta\gamma\delta$ are beginning to stand out (the action of DNA on RNA in its various forms and from there on the proteins), the resistances or the systematic reinforcements offered by the environment can only have the effect of imposing reequilibrations which become closer and closer in regressive order: reequilibration in δ and reactions upon γ, then reequilibration in γ and reaction upon β. Now there is no reason why, if the genome contains a regulatory system, the reequilibrations produced on the fringes of β should exert no return action in α, seeing that it is the nature of a regulation to record the results obtained by a retroactive process or negative feedback. The genome's "response," as Waddington understands it, will be this final reequilibration, and once it gets beyond a certain threshold there will also be a "genetic assimilation" in the sense of consolidation, running parallel to the responses or "assimilations" that are being set up in the later generations (population).

6. Reorganization of the Genome and New Adaptation

It cannot be denied that the preceding discussion is entirely hypothetical and must therefore be carried farther. In effect, it simply leaves out one factor in such information as we have about genetic populations, and even that is a negative one: namely, the isolation or inaccessibility of the individual genome with regard to its inter-

18. The setting up of this diagram was suggested by E. Binder.

actions with its environment.[19] Still, this is the point over which all biologists have been in the greatest disagreement, and so it is all the more necessary to weigh our evidence carefully.

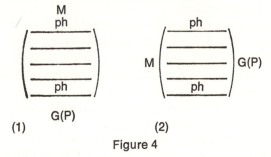

Figure 4

To start with, let us examine the meaning of the difference between processes 1 and 2, as illustrated in figure 4. With process 1, environment M modifies the proportions of genome G or of pool P by means of choices effectuated on phenotype ph (horizontal lines).[20] With the second process, the final proportions and a comparable reequilibration of genome G are deemed to be obtained by means of some inner selection with a bearing on the genes' activities during the development of each successive phenotype as well as the development of one particular phenotype. However, in process 1, selection also had some bearing upon individual development, since selection only applies to phenotypes. These reequilibrations by stages α, β, γ, δ were thus brought about, and in regressive order: actions on δ, then of δ on γ, actions on γ, and from there on β. As to the action of β on α, it was only achieved by selection of individuals which had undergone modification in β, whereas, in hypothesis 2, the action is supposed to be continuous right up to the genome by means of a final reequilibration which is an extension of the preceding ones, the DNA in α being informed by feedback of the modifications imposed on the RNA in β.

Having said this much, we must make clear in what way the supposed process 2 seems to us to differ quite fundamentally from Lamarckian processes and to fit in completely with the logic of con-

19. It is noteworthy that this isolation of the genome is contested by Waddington and that figure 36 of his *Strategy of the Genes* (p. 181) puts forward by way of "speculation" a possible model of the action of the soma, which goes farther than we have done in subsection 5.

20. By genome G we mean, of course, a genome taken as a sector or partial representative of the genetic pool P, or $G(P)$, the final equilibrium depending on the pool as a whole.

temporary genetics. In Lamarckism or empiricism (which I have always criticized on psychological grounds), environment is supposed to introduce new and exogenous characteristics that are, as it were, imprinted on the organism, and thus the morphology of the entire living creature is seen as an amalgam of such imprints. The hypothesis now being put forward shows, on the contrary, the organism to be reacting in an endogenous and active way to the pressures of environment and to be plainly assimilating them into its structures or else differentiating them into reorganizations and reequilibrations by means of the genetic instruments at its disposal. So in this case we are talking not of an imprint but of an active response—and a response qualitatively parallel, in its endogenous recombinations, to that furnished by selection as it effects n generations (process 1).[21]

21. V. Grant, in his book *The Origin of Adaptation* (1963), tells us that among inherited characteristics we must include the genotype's aptitude for responding in appropriate fashion, by means of phenotypic characteristics, to certain environmental conditions. However, what is then transmitted is not the phenotypic characteristic but the genes or constellations of genes which determine what this characteristic will be (p. 132). At once the question arises: By what means is the genetic system able to get information of the necessity for a particular response to the environment? Grant supplies some sort of starting point for resolving this problem in what he says about acquired characteristics. Having first referred to the distinction between the genes of the nucleus and the genes of the ectoplasm, he then reminds us that the latter are more easily influenced by the environment and quotes the well-known example of the euglenes (locomoted Protozoa) with chlorophyll, which, if they lose their chloroplast because of being confined in the dark, will hand on less to their progeniture. He sees a theoretical difficulty in this from his own point of view, but this would be obviated by the fact that in this case it is the same organ (chloroplasts) which responds phenotypically to the environment and which is among the genes in the reproductive cells. In other words, with this example of the phenotype coinciding with the genotype, Grant draws the conclusion that, in pluricellular creatures even of the higher kind, in which the phenomena of growth depend on cytoplasmic genes (and even on the cellular cortex and therefore on the membrane enclosing the cell), it is possible, though not proved, that responses to the actions of environment can be transmitted too.

My own conclusion would be (1) that in certain cases the genotype, insofar as it coincides with the phenotype, gets direct information about the problems presented by the environment and so can "respond" directly by means of a regulation or some appropriate compensation, which it produces from among its own resources, of course, but adjusted to the situation; and (2) that consequently there is nothing in principle to prevent the same being true of genes of the nucleus, when their action (in producing RNA) is reinforced or inhibited by the fact that the RNA itself is, from the somatic fringe first but then working inward, being modified by external causes.

There is one further point about Grant's work, and that is the extent to which the so-called Baldwin effect, which Grant discusses (pp. 137–38) and

The great difficulty here, however, is that in the perspective of present-day geneticists there is no reciprocal relationship between the structure of the genome and its morphogenetic activities. The structure is supposed to be the source of its activities, whereas these activities bring about no reaction in the structure. The question, then, is whether this break between structural and functional (morphogenetic) regulations is a part of the logic of the system or whether it does not, rather, constitute a legacy from the old atomistic genetics, in which genes were seen as "little boxes," enclosing their characteristics once and for all. "Little boxes" are, of course, no longer thought of, but the entire genome becomes a "big box," which opens from time to time in order to manifest activities outside itself, yet receives no information about the results of these activities. Paradoxical as such a break may seem in connection with any anatomical or morphological characteristics, it is even more difficult to maintain such a theory in the area of cognitive adaptations (the instincts, for example). Here, information about the result is necessary and, what is more, cannot be reduced to a mere question of survival of the fittest.

We must therefore try to understand what those affirmations mean which would have us believe (a) that the phenotype is a response by the genome to incitement by the environment, and (b) that selection has a bearing on phenotypes seen as responses. Let us take another look, in this connection, at a phenotypic development in which, when interactions take place between the genome and its modified environment, certain phenotypic characteristics are produced, type a being neutral, type b favorable, and type c unfavorable, these characteristics arising in turn out of the genetic potentialities A, B, and C. Without going back over the whole ques-

---

which J. M. Baldwin himself called "organic selection" (1896), carries the implication of my own second process. Nowadays the term "Baldwin effect" is used to designate genetic reorganization brought about as weak phenotypes finally begin to make the progressive adjustments which render them capable of survival. In this connection, Grant applies the expression "temporary adjustment" of the genotype to the phase preceding the production of the adapted phenotype. Once again, we need to know how the genome gets its information about this and acts upon it so as to make an effective response. How else, except by feedbacks which keep it informed about the success or failure of its structures? Because it is a case here not of selection by death or survival but of "organic selection," which means a change of proportions in terms of the results obtained.

tion of processes 1 and 2, previously discussed, we need only consider, for the moment, the two following kinds of selection:

1. Suppose that during a series of generations the phenotypes with *b* characteristics and (*B* potentialities) find favorable conditions and that those with *c* characteristics (and *C* potentialities) are not favored, so that there is progressive elimination, and by degrees the genetic pool and the genomes are thus being modified as to their proportions, bringing about restructurizations which cause the *B* potentialities and *b* characteristics to develop at the expense of the *C* and the *c*. This kind of development we shall call structural selection (= relative to the composition of the genome).

2. We shall speak of functional selection (= relative to the synthetic activities of the genome) when the interactions with environment during ontogenetic growth have the effect of strengthening *b* and *B*, of inhibiting *c* and *C*, and of leaving *a* and *A* unaffected.

3. Our hypothesis then will be that functional selection (2) plays a part in structural selection (1) and this constitutes "process 2," while "process 1" consists merely of selection, that is, 1 without 2.

4. In both these hypotheses, the phenotype seen as epigenotype constitutes the mold or matrix within which the new genotype is set up by means of genetic recombinations which cause *B* and *b* to survive at the expense of *C* and *c*. The problem, then, is to understand the nature of this connection, which ensures that the new genotype is adequate to the phenotype although the latter is not yet fixed in heredity.

5. Only three solutions can be found to this: (a) that genetic recombinations occur by pure chance, which is to say, without any relation to functional selection (2) or to environment, and that structural selections (1) suffice, on their own, to assure adequation of the new genotype to its mold or phenotypic matrix; (b) that genetic recombinations must have been preformed as part of all the possible combinations and so are not new in any absolute sense; their relative novelty results from a choice made only by structural selection (1) from among the existing potentialities, up to the point where necessary adequation to the phenotypic mold is achieved; (c) that recombination is both new and yet not entirely a matter of chance, which presupposes a process of the second kind and, hence, interactions between the structural selections (1) and the functional ones

(2) brought about by information from feedbacks during development.

6. Solution *a*—chance and mere structural selection—presents two difficulties:

α. From the point of view of the formation of new combinations, the solution implies a probabilistic justification, which would be easy enough with minor variations but quite unacceptable for organs such as the eye, etc.

β. From the point of view of selection, it raises the following objection, which applies equally to minor variations: if the phenotype already presents the characteristics *b* and *B*, which dominate *c* and *C*, there is no need of any genotypic phenocopy to ensure survival, since the phenotypes themselves are assurance enough of this. Where morphogenesis is concerned, we shall be seeing in subsection 8 a clear example of this situation. When it comes to the cognitive field, there is no need for the elementary operations of the intelligence to be hereditary before they can function perfectly, because the phenotypic acquisitions of each generation have always been sufficient.

7. There is always some credibility in the predetermination solution just because any new factor can always be said to have been preformed, but:

α. This is merely a verbal solution so long as there is no calculation possible or any verification by experiment (the notion of the virtual can have no meaning except within the context of deductive conservation).

β. The elimination of all novelty and all constructivism should be quite unacceptable from the cognitive point of view; to say that the eye, the brain, and the intelligence are an integral part of the human being's preformation by virtue of possible recombinations within the genome of bacteria is considered absolutely meaningless today.

8. Supposing genetic recombination to be a new factor and not just a matter of chance, all that remains to be done, in order to explain its adequation to the phenotypic matrix, is to advance some theory that there is feedback information about the successes and failures of the adequation, which is the same process as 2. But:

α. That certainly cannot mean that the phenotypic mold is the cause, that is, that it produces the genetic recombinations of itself.

β. These recombinations are purely endogenous and consist of modifications in the proportions of the pool and the genomes which continue until adequation to the phenotypical matrix is achieved. The matrix alone brings about the causal interactions with the environment.

γ. But we must put forward some theory about information by feedbacks bearing on the results (success or failure) in genetic restructuration, if the latter is a new factor and not altogether a matter of chance.

In fact, if the type 1 processes affecting the population as a whole are not accompanied by parallel processes of the second type produced during the course of individual development, there is no guarantee that the reequilibrations and regroupings brought about by selection under the influence of the environment really will be new and not simply the outcome of something predetermined or of groups that were, to all intents and purposes, preformed. This brings us back to where we started, as mystified as ever with regard to evolution and especially cognition, unless we attribute everything to chance, which, from a probability angle, is absolutely out of the question. Of course, we are told that the phenotype is the result of interactions between the genotype and the environment and that the phenotype is therefore a response to the environment; thus, in making the right responses, selection ends up with a "new" genetic reequilibration. All very well, but if the reequilibrations of the phenotype are not reflected back, step by step, to the individual genome, then the selection of phenotypes is nothing but a sorting out process from among factors that are already present, and the recombination is only a subcombination among all possible combinations (there are still mutations, of course, but, in principle, they are not adaptive; otherwise they themselves could be preformed). On the other hand, the phenotypic response is a response made to some new problem posed by the environment, and this response is the only guarantee that there are "new" interactions, however much these may be a part of previously established structures. Thus, it is in proportion as the genome, in its turn, reacts to the problems presented by the reorganization of the phenotype that one can be certain of the novelty of its reequilibrations.[22]

22. Here one must mention the fact that several current research projects on the interactions of cytoplasm and nucleus would seem to be pointing more and more toward the intervention of form 2 processes, which, although they may not yet be fully demonstrated, are nevertheless becoming more likely all the time. In this connection, one should first refer to the fine work done

But there is a second reason to be added to what has just been said, and it concerns instincts, hereditary cognitive adaptations, and the adaptation of the organic instruments of knowledge, as if the brain, the eye, and the hand had been predetermined from the first in the possible genetic combinations of bacteria and Protozoa,

---

by Jacob and Monod on the *Escherichia coli*, which demonstrates by means of modifications on the environment that there must be interactions between the cytoplasm and the genome that can be followed up in detail as far as the production of the enzymes and then reveal themselves by induction effects on the *opérons* or by repressive action on the regulators. Thanks to Beerman, it has been known for a long time that, in insects, hormones react in a similar fashion upon genetic mechanisms, and now this is being found among vertebrates. But, so far, these various discoveries only apply to the functional activity of certain substances which are capable of modifying one or the other of the four DNA bases.

One field in which the connection between cytoplasm and genome will probably have to be admitted sooner or later—and this actually in the sphere of hereditary structures—is that of extranuclear heredity affecting, among other things, fibers and pigmentation, or the sense of direction in the shell of the gastropode (and, according to Ruth Sager, it is the same with the inheritance of resistance to streptomycin in chlamidomones). Some have attributed this heredity to "plasmagenes," a term which is still rather obscure and puts a name to the problem rather than solving it, but Sonneborg and Preer have demonstrated, in the particular instance of paramecia, that these "plasmagenes" were DNA fragments either having emigrated from, or having been propelled into, the cytoplasm. Moreover, Sonneborg has recently proved, by making a comparison of two distinct types of *Paramecium aurelia*, that it is possible, by transplanting a piece of cellular membrane from one type to the other, to induce the formation of characteristics which then remain hereditary. Whether or not the term "plasmagenes" is used, there must be some cytoplasmic heredity, which is modifiable by the environment (inheritance of sensitivity to toxins, of loss of pigmentation, etc.). It would be very hard to try to maintain that no interactions take place between these "plasmagenes" and the genome or that no mutual adaptation takes place between the two genetic systems.

In short, the central problem still outstanding is to understand just how the genetic code has evolved. For instance, Pauling, Zuckerkandel, et al., have demonstrated that the chain of proteins found in the lower types of fish are to be found all over again in human beings, but more are added to them in the latter case. We cannot avoid asking, in this case, how these new chains are set up, and to say that this is a question of chance will not do at all. The hypotheses formulated in the early days, after the classic work done by Dobzhansky, have been expanded by Goldschmidt, with his proposed "macromutations" or hereditary variations brought about during embryonic development. Today, Waddington's theory on the importance of the genetic system is leading one to wonder whether one ought not substitute the words "in terms of" for "during the." In other words, since epigenetic processes are partly, though only partly, determined by the genetic system in the broad sense, why exclude the possibility of return actions by the former on the latter, now that we are reasoning, no longer by linear causality with its one-way traffic, but by cybernetic circuits?

which, without going any farther, is manifestly absurd. But then, what are we to say about preformation having always existed in the behavior of taenia, before there were any vertebrates? Or about the cuckoo's instincts? Or the termite's? Or the spider's? If those are not "new" combinations, then words have lost their meaning.[23]

23. There is an article by that great biologist Theodosius Dobzhansky, in the 1960 volume *Hundert Jahre Evolutionsforschung*, to the effect that the theory of preformation in evolution—which amounts to denying evolution in favor of a purely endogenous unfolding, predetermined once and for all—is "irrefutable" in principle and that all one can do with it is show where it is useless. But if one attaches any importance at all to the influence of environment, even by means of some purely structural selection, it becomes very hard to view as deducible the sort of evolutionary history which then emerges. It has been demonstrated, by working on Gödel's theorems, that a machine whose inputs, internal workings, and outputs are all thoroughly "determined" and known, still will not allow of calculating, at a given moment, what its condition will be by the time it reaches $t + 1$. What, then, would be the case with a machine whose mechanisms underwent environmental modification for a period of time? Dobzhansky himself declares in the very same article that "evolution is a creative response made by living matter to the opportunities offered it by its environment" (pp. 96–97). He defines the term "creative" as being the appearance of new characteristics. Of course, he makes it clear that environmental influence is exerted by means of selection, although this selection never becomes operational except at some precise moment and "has no foreknowledge of the future" (p. 43). But the genes, according to him, act rather like the members of an orchestra, not like soloists, so that, as he has emphasized elsewhere (*American Naturalist*, November-December 1956), selection operates not upon separate characteristics but upon overall reactions both of the polygenic kind (concurrent action of the genes) and the pleiotropic kind (modification of a single gene with repercussions on two or more characteristics). What decides success or failure is, moreover, not only the final phenotypic state reached, but all the stages along the line. On the other hand, variability is due not simply to mutations but, above all, to genetic recombinations; it will be remembered that Dobzhansky originated the "hypothesis of balance" (1955), according to which the adaptive norm is an arrangement of a number of genotypes, multiple heterozygotes predominating. (For a particularly clear exposition, see Dobzhansky's article "Variation and Evolution" in *Proc. Amer. Phil. Soc.* 159 vol. 103, no. 2.) The vital factor is then seen to be the internal equilibrium of the genetic pool with what Lerner has called the "genetic homeostasis." The important part played by equilibration is stressed as much by Wallun (1957) and others as by Dobzhansky and Spassky in their classic experiment. However, if equilibration of the genetic recombinations in response to external conditions is thus brought in as an alternative explanation to the old idea of direct, or "Lamarckian," action by the environment, the essential question is to find out whether the stages of individual development, on whose importance Dobzhansky insists, are simply the end product available to selection among these recombinations by death or survival (process 1 in subsection 5), or whether, as I myself have suggested (process 2) they are opportunities which allow the processes of internal reequilibration in the genome to get information by feedback—in the course of the growth period

Now, if these are new characteristics from the evolutionary point of view, how is it possible to conceive of their coming into existence without any information about the environment? It is here, in the cognitive aspects of behavior, that the parallel between modes 1 and 2 of obtaining information (end of subsections 4 and 5) seems to me to be indispensable; for any new kind of behavior, however transindividual it may be, can only be acquired and fixated by genetic assimilation during the realization of the corresponding behaviors (although this is not to say there is any overall training period).

The selection process in its ordinary sense (process 1) can, of course, be compared to a series of individual combinations by trial and error, the only difference lying in the kind of sanction involved: the individuals that succeed survive and continue to act, while the individuals that fail become extinct (death of the phenotype). This comparison no doubt holds good in the case of morphological and physiological adaptations on a wide enough scale to omit differentiated adjustments in individual cases to particular situations in an environment. But to try to apply this pattern to the formation of an instinctive behavior is to forget one essential difference: individual behavior of a trial and error kind implies a continuous feedback mechanism aimed at improving later behavior by the lessons learned from previous errors. In other words, behavior is constantly guided by the results it has obtained so far, whether good or bad. Now, in type 1 selection, the survivors learn nothing from those that become extinct, and, if they continue to act, the only feedback they have is at the phenotypic level as far as behavior is concerned, and this would mean that the accumulation of information could not possibly be explained. The type 2 process, on the other hand, generalizes selection with feedbacks right up to the level of the individual genome, and this, let it be repeated, is part of the logic of the system, for if the genome possesses regulatory systems, as everyone now admits that it does, it is by this very fact in possession of all the necessary equipment for obtaining information about the results of its actions during morphogenesis; so it is conceivable that the activities of the phenotype should have repercussions which take it

which is the manifestation of their activity—about the results which are successively being obtained. The effect of this, in fact, is to bring about that regulation whose workings would remain incomprehensible without it.

nearer and nearer to getting responses from the genome (stages $\gamma\beta\alpha$).

To sum up, whatever modes of selection intervene on the plane of behavior, they cannot possibly be restricted to the type 1 processes. A mere enumeration of deaths and survivals will not explain how different species of spiders each make such very distinct webs, or help us to decide whether perception of the third dimension in man and the primates is innate or acquired shortly after birth, because this all comes back to the question of selection. Even in the field of hereditary organs involved in behavior, it is very hard to see how their individual differentiations, which are so well adapted to the particular circumstances of the external environment, could be explained if no system of feedbacks in series of distinctive retroaction levels were linking behavior with the genome both centripetally and centrifugally. The *Drepanididae* of Hawaii, for example, have beak forms that are adapted to every kind of ecological nook or cranny, species for species, whereas on the mainland distinct differentiations are found in different families. This, then, implies a much more rapid kind of evolution, in which case it is hard to see how the beaks that develop special characteristics to cope with all sorts of different situations, according to whether their food is found in the bark of trees, in the ground, or in flowers, could have been formed in such a relatively short time[24] from one single common stock by simple type 1 selection, that is, without the genome's having been informed by feedback of the results of the behavior connected with such beaks.

It is true that in section 17 we admitted the possibility that instinctive inventions might result at the genome level, from coordination of schemata bound up in the construction of some instinct and relatively independent of the individual's behavior. It is also true that in the same connection we emphasized the transindividual character of the instinctive cycles. These spontaneous coordinations of schemata at the genetic or epigenetic level would explain why instinct, in particular, can far out-distance the learning or intelligence capacities of corresponding species. But this does not alter the fact that such coordinations presuppose the existence of elementary schemata that can be coordinated: it is in view of these schemata

24. Short in relation to the differentiation which takes place among families on the mainland.

and their formation that we are here stressing the necessity for a link by successive and regressive feedbacks, which leads from the individuals' behavior to the genome itself.

7. Relationship between the Preceding Model and the Models of Organic Selection, together with the Regulation of Mutations in the L. L. Whyte Sense

The idea—central to our argument—that genetic recombinations succeed, by means of feedbacks or progressive regulations, in molding themselves into the framework or phenotypic model built up by interactions between the genotype and its environment, can be backed up by a whole group of theories known as organic selection.

As long ago as 1881, W. Roux wrote *The Battle between the Different Parts of the Organism*. Fifteen years later, the idea was taken up again by A. Weismann himself and given the name "intraselection," but he did not fully realize the bearing it had on indirect influences of the environment, which it made possible. At about the same time, Baldwin formulated it into a rather general principle, which he called "organic selection" and which R. Hovasse, in the fine volume on biology edited by J. Rostand in *L'encyclopédie de la Pléiade*, defined purely and simply as "the possibility of replacing an *accommodat* by a mutation" (p. 1656). Hovasse points out (pp. 1678–81) how often situations occur in which a phenotype is replaced by a genotype—situations which "mimic, as it were, heredity by acquisition" (p. 1679). In the case of the *Solarnum dulcamara* var. *marina*, whose leaves are thick and pointed when they grow by the seashore, Hovasse singles out three stages: (1) a pure *accommodat*, which is not hereditary; (2) a mixture of *accommodats* and "mutations parallel to the *accommodat*, which thereupon undergo the same kind of selection as did the *accommodat*; and (3) "total replacement of the *accommodat*" by the new genotype (p. 1678). But if this is so, how else but by a miracle or the merest chance can we explain the way in which the phenotypic *accommodat* and the new genotype converge? "We cannot yet be sure about this. However, the fact that an organism may react to some environmental influence by means of somation does imply that there is, within its cytoplasm and quite independent of its genes, a possible effectuating mechanism [*méchanisme réalisateur*], which is a deviation from a genic or even, perhaps, a plasmagenic mechanism. Would it not be possible for this mechanism, once formed, to be set in motion again far more easily by some genic phenomenon? The somation would, as it were, initiate the mutation" (p. 1679). This, then, is his explanation of phenocopies. It would also explain the effect of temperature on size (Bergmann and Allen's laws) an effect which, "although phenotypic in origin, would have become genotypic by the operation of Baldwin's law" (p. 1679).

However, if it is admitted that somation "initiates" mutation, this must mean that, in addition to the centrifugal action of the mutation or genetic recombinations which are all remolded within the "effectuating mechanism" of the phenotypic somation, there must be some return centripetal action by feedback, as we conceded in subsections 5 and 6. When Baldwin talked of "organic selection," it was still only a word and a rather ambiguous word at that, for although external selection may proceed by eliminations and survival of the fittest, any organic or internal selection is much more like a "choice" of a more or less active kind, which means that is is, properly speaking, a regulation.

Such is not the opinion of Lancelot Law Whyte (*Internal Factors in Evolution*). Whyte is a mathematician whose work has been concerned with ordered systems and whose great ambition is to discover the general algebraic conditions which would make it possible to define the precise order of the parts of the cell. In his book (reviewed by E. Wigner in *Physics Today*, by Dalcq in *Embryology* and in *The Science Journal* of January 1966) he starts out from the classic theory that every mutation has first of all to survive the internal conditions imposed by the cell, and that the germinal cell is a very strongly integrated and structured system whose functioning can continue only according to a limited number of modalities. It might, in that case, be possible for a number of simultaneous mutations to cause the system to jump from one mode to another, even if these mutations taken singly would, as sometimes actually happens, eventually render the cell sterile. Whyte therefore suggests that the cell possesses regulatory mutation mechanisms which are capable of "demutating" some of them and rendering them compatible with the rest of the system or even of transforming them into positive ones. Such homeostatic mechanisms built up during the course of evolution would evince themselves, among other things, in the "nonsense suppressors" recently described as occurring in bacteria (*Science*, 149, 3682: 417, 1965) and which might well be found elsewhere.

In this way, to the explanations of organic selection under Baldwin's law and of "genetic assimilation" put forward by Waddington, Whyte adds an explanation in the direction of regulation, that is, a capacity in the component parts for joint functioning. This is what gives real significance to the idea that the mutation is initiated by somation, as was discussed just above. This example demonstrates that the return action of genic regulations—which, as hypothesized in subsections 5 and 6, may occur during morphogenetic functioning— is an idea in the wind (when writing the preceding pages I did not know of Whyte's work) because it is a necessary part of the logic underlying all contemporary thinking about regulations, and because to talk of regulator mechanisms without taking their results into account is absolutely meaningless.

8. An Example of "Genetic Assimilation" in the Kinetogenetic Field

In our search for a tertium quid between the Lamarckian and the neo-Darwinian theories, I did attempt in 1929, and have recently taken up again, the study of some situation which might serve as an example of morphological adaptation allied to behavior in an animal.[25] I took as specimen the pond snail (*Limnaea stagnalis* L.), whose elongated shape is familiar to everyone (figure 5a) but which in the great Swiss and Swedish lakes produces a *lacustris* Stud. variety of a much shorter kind (figure 5b), and in Lakes Neuchâtel and Constance produces a still shorter kind (var. *bodamica* Class.), though both of these in places where the lake bed is flat, stony, and very much exposed to the wind. Now these varieties, which are only found in the situations described (as I have proved by a close study of fauna records, which are copious, having been kept for more than 150 years, and by an examination of all those collections devoted to this species), owe their contracted form to the snail's movements. Throughout its growth period (there being only one or two twists to the shell when it emerges from the egg, whereas there are six or seven in the adult stage) the creature attaches itself as firmly as it can to the pebbles every time there is a wave or other disturbance

25. My preliminary article on the lacustrine races of the *Limnaea stagnalis* L., "Recherches sur les rapports de l'adaptation héréditaire avec le milieu," *Bulletin biologique de la France et de la Belgique*, vol. 63 (1929), pp. 424–59, closed with the following words: "Between integral mutationism and the hypotheses of some continuous heredity of the acquired, there must therefore be a tertium quid."

of the water, and this dilates its aperture and shortens its conical shape by causing the contraction of the columellar muscle. So here we have a typical case of kinetogenesis as Cope explains it.

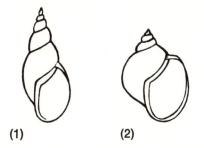

(1)   (2)

Figure 5

The more contracted forms (*lacustris* and *bodamica*) are heredi-tary. We will call them races IV and V, among the five races we have identified, of which the elongated ones, I and II, are found in still water and the intermediate one, III (var. *intermediar* God.), in marshy ground and sheltered coves. Races I and V, for example, can be crossed; the individuals F_2 are the intermediaries, and F_3 gives us an example of Mendelian segregation.[26]

It must further be noted that races IV and V evince specialized behavior. In the first place, they "choose" their environment, as Waddington says; for instance, there is nothing to prevent their bur-rowing five to thirty meters into the sublitoral zone, should some pebbly or exposed position not suit them. It is at this sublitoral level that are found the little elongated variety to which I have given the name var. *Bollingeri* Piag. Now, if crossings are possible between *lacustris* and *Bollingeri*, a frequency curve set up at Lake Neuchâtel based on 750 specimens from one single observation post proved to be distinctly bimodal, and there was no sign at all of any migration by the *lacustris* down into the lower regions. On the other hand, *lacustris-bodamica* do have their own habits; if their aquarium is shaken, they will cling to the glass (just as *Patellae* do, and this in fact is what is meant by the patella reflex), whereas a marsh speci-men will immediately be knocked down by the movement, a thing

26. For all these facts, see J. Piaget, "L'adaptation de la *Limnaea stagnalis* aux milieux lacustres de la Suisse romande," *Revue suisse de zoologie*, vol. 36 (1929), pp. 263–531, plates 3–6.

that would prove fatal if it were in a lake, where the shell would be broken, the liver thus injured, and so on.

Granted this, how were the contracted species IV (*lacustris*) and V (*bodamica*) formed? A hypothesis on mutational lines was at once put forward to me by my colleague Guyénot to the effect that (1) contracted forms may always be found anywhere, by pure chance, and quite independently of the contracted, but not heredi- tary, phenotypes (the latter alone, then, are dependent on our kine- togenesis theory); (2) contracted mutational types which grow in marshy places would become extinct for various reasons—lack of oxygen, etc.; (3) in the parts of large lakes where the water is rough—and in these parts alone—they may, however, be able to survive, thanks to their fortuitous "preadaptation," as Cuénot puts it. With this in mind, in 1928, I took some eggs belonging to race V, selected from the sixth generation of some aquarium-bred types, and placed them in a pool on the Vaudois plateau where there were no *Limnaea stagnalis*. Unfortunately the pool dried up in 1943, but, among 527 samples that we found, there was a contraction index (comparing the height of the aperture to the overall height) of 1.39, whereas the index of the phenotypic *lacustris* is 1.35, and 575 aquarium specimens gave an index of 1.43 (in their natural state, those inhabiting marshland giving indices of from 1.65 to 1.89, the lake dwellers going down to as low as 1.31 on average). Furthermore, among 65,000 samples, the first millesile was at 1.529 in nonlacustrine habitats; the 527 samples from my test pond had lengths varying from 1.20 to 1.68 (in lakes the minimum is 1.14), and 9 out of 10 of them were lower than the millesile of 1.53. It is therefore indisputable that the variety *lacustris* can survive in a stagnant pool and preserve its shape.[27]

In that case, why is it not found in different kinds of places but only in large lakes, where the water is roughest? It is clear that there is some continuity between the phenotypes and this lake strain *bodamica,* which means that we are dealing with a case of Wad- dington's "genetic assimilation," that is, hereditary fixation in a phenotypic variation that was not originally stabilized. So there is some "heredity of acquired characteristics" in this, but it should be looked at as a kind of selection among phenotypes.

27. See J. Piaget, "Note sur des *Limnaea stagnalis* L. var. *lacustris* Stud. élevées dans une mare du Plateau vaudois," *Revue suisse de zoologie,* vol. 72 (1965), pp. 769–89.

What, then, is the method of selection that can explain the genetic assimilation in this particular case? (My purpose in giving the above details was to tackle this very question.) It must be remembered, if we are to get our ideas straight, that what we have here is a situation like that found in figure 3: the reaction norm *NR* would represent the contraction index variations within the species (characteristic *b* seen in decreasing values of the index and therefore in increasing values of the index), and the increasing roughness of the water would be given in abscissa; the segment *N* II in a dotted line would represent the *lacustris* and *bodamica* varieties in rough waters.

The first thing to be noticed is that the contracted varieties do represent a genuine novelty in relation to the usual distribution of the species' shapes; nonlacustrine inhabitants extend, as we have seen, from 1.65 to 1.89 on average in their contraction (divergence of 0.24), whereas lake dwellers exceed this by 1.31 up to 1.65 (divergence of 0.34). It cannot be said, therefore, that this divergence of from 1.31 to 1.65 was included in the normal variability of the species, and so we have to find some explanation for the divergence.

The two processes which might be involved are process 1 (selection by the survival of the fittest) and 2 (modification of the proportions within the genome, as in 1, but by reequilibration in terms of the feedbacks which intervene while the individual specimen is growing). The two processes can naturally be combined, but we are trying to show that, in this particular case, process 2 seems to be the necessary one.

The first reason for this is that the roughness of the water simply does not eliminate the noncontracted types III–V. An elongated individual specimen is, of course, eliminated by the waves, whereas a contracted type can survive anywhere. However, race III and even races IV and V are capable of producing nonhereditary phenotypes in lakes, and this I have proved many times myself with race III, found both in lakes and marshlands; such nonstabilized phenotypes will be just as contracted as races IV and V. It might very well have been the case, therefore, and this is what I was afraid of when I started, that the *lacustris* and *bodamica* strains had nothing hereditary about them, since the phenotypic variation was sufficient in itself. So there is no necessary motive for selection in type 1.

My second point is even stronger. Race IV (*lacustris*) is found in Switzerland in Lakes Constance, Neuchâtel, and Geneva, whereas race V (*bodamica*) is found only in the first two of these lakes, the shores of Lake Geneva being steeper and less exposed. In Lake Neuchâtel one can find specimens of race IV having the same average length as race V (indices 1.34 to 1.37), the phenotypes being indistinguishable, but not the genotypes. How, then, can we explain the evolution of the race *lacustris* into the even more contracted *bodamica* as being due to type 1 selection? There is no possible reason for eliminations, since the phenotypes are identical. On the other hand, in the type 2 process, where environmental influences on growth finally make themselves felt in the genome through feedback action at various levels, it is quite understandable how the cumulative influence of behavior and motion during development should continue to be exerted upon the phenotypes of race IV up to the point where an even more contracted genotype of race V is produced by means of progressive reorganization or gradual change in the proportions of the genome.[28]

9. Conclusions

I judged it necessary to dwell on this example at some length because it is particularly instructive, being typical of countless situations in which the shape of an organ, or even of an entire body, is connected with the behavior of that organ or body. A bird's beak, skin callosities where the foot touches the ground, prehensile or locomotive organs, sensory organs, even bilateral symmetries in creatures that

28. That is, except in the case of some extranuclear heredity. It is known, in fact, that whether the spiral of the shell winds to the right or to the left depends on the plasmagene and not on the genome. (Diver, Boycott, and Garstang [*Journal of Genetics*, vol. 15, p. 113] demonstrated this with the *Limnaea peregra*, which winds to the left.) This could be the explanation of the contraction of the spiral. Indeed, if the turning of the spiral to left or to right does not depend on the creature's motions, as contraction does, it does nevertheless seem to be connected with embryonic development, since Conklin attaches to it the disposition of the "quartletts" during the first segmentations of the egg. As for the connection between the creature's motions and its morphology, we should remember what Naef said about this (A. Naef, "Studien zur generellen Morphologie der Mollusken, *Erg. und Fort. der Zoologie* 3 [1913], pp. 73–164). According to him, the twisting process itself, which is the most general anatomical characteristic of the gastropods, was caused by the crawling motion when the transformation from pelagic ancestors (cf. Veliger's test) to crawling life took place, so that the shell became exogastic instead of endogastic.

search for their food and radial symmetries in those that let it come to them because they are either unable to move or are unable to direct their own course in the water[29]—all these belong to the considerable area of morphology that is functional in essence, that is to say, allied to behavior.

The problem as to how modes or instruments of hereditary knowledge are formed is thus one of the central problems of biology. Contemporary population genetics would seem to be nearing the point at which it might produce a solution for us, but still, on a number of points, it remains strangely in thrall to the mutationist and neo-Darwinian traditions, which overestimated the possibility of explaining things by chance and were satisfied with a simplistic model or selection by a sorting-out process. On the other hand, when we turn to cyberneticians, their way of thinking leads us to realize that there is nothing contradictory in the autoconservation of the genetic system and its undergoing environmental influence, nor is there even anything contradictory in saying that the nature of its recombinations is essentially endogenous. However autonomous a regulatory system may be, that is no reason for depriving it of information about the results of its activity—on the contrary! And if the genome gets information about these results in its morphogenetic actions during its development, there is no reason why we should consider it blind to the endless problems set it by the environment, since phenotypic development is always confronted with the task of conciliating its genetic programming with every new demand made by its environment. It was thus in keeping with the logic of the new biology to risk putting forward the hypotheses developed in subsections 4–7 of section 19.

Section 20. Logico-mathematical Structures and Their Biological Significance

The problem of logico-mathematical knowledge comes midway between that of knowing how knowledge is acquired by heredity (a subject to which one was bound to revert in order to understand the biological nature of knowledge at the higher levels), and how it is acquired by learning—a process which is, of necessity, acquired

29. See E. Binder, *La forme et l'espace*, Musées de Genève, no. 36 (1963).

and not hereditary. Logico-mathematical knowledge belongs to neither of these categories and yet it is a necessary part of the second one.

Such knowledge is not hereditary, since it is acquired and often only with difficulty; thus, it entails a sort of learning period which is often confused with authentic learning. However, logico-mathematical knowledge cannot be reduced to authentic learning in the sense of being drawn from experience of the external world, and it can be distinguished from authentic learning by a whole series of endogenous characteristics. Nevertheless, it is important to examine these problems closely, for logico-mathematical structures occupy a special place, and they seem to hold as great a significance for biology itself as for the epistemology of mathematics.

1. Mathematics and Logic

The first hypothesis, which initially seems unavoidable, is that arithmetic structures or, at any rate, geometric ones, are acquired through experience of objects, hence by empirical learning, whereas logical structures would seem to be hereditary in that they are linked with the functioning of all behavior and consequently with some common, innate stock, which is apparent in varying degrees in all species and particularly dominant in man as a "rational" animal. But before proceeding to any real biological analysis of the problem, we must take note of certain epistemological and psycho-genetic data which, because they are apparent in human thought, are apt to exert a measure of refinement on these somewhat simplistic hypotheses.

1. If we take the development of the human child from two to fifteen years, it is obvious that logic becomes "necessary" in the sense that it is impossible for an adolescent to think without using a certain number of inferential mechanisms and without experiencing, as he draws his conclusions from them, some feeling of deductive "necessity": as, for example, that if A implies B and B implies C, it is impossible or absurd not to admit that A implies C. So there is a relation sui generis, which goes far beyond mere noticing or inductive and experimental regularity and derives from de facto probability or inevitability but not from intrinsic necessity. It is in the light of such personal experience, and of the algebraic or logistic calculations which free that experience from the illusions to which it may be subject, that we are bound to end up by con-

sidering logic as innate and not dependent on any mere learning process. Even if we take any note of what sociologists affirm—that logic is first and foremost an instrument of exchange, imposed by the social group in the normative constraint which it puts on the individual—that will not alter the case, because the social group is essentially a system of interactions, implying the nervous and cerebral coordinations of each of its members just as much as the laws of exchange and of communication. The relations between socialized individuals and the group are thus of the same order as those of the individual phenotype and the population which were studied in section 19, subsection 4; that is to say, every logical connection is simultaneously—and indissociably—individual and social.

However, although logic becomes necessary, it certainly is not so during the years of infancy, and, as was seen in section 1, it is not until the age of seven or eight that a child in human society opens his mind to the transitivity, not of implication (for that we must wait until eleven or twelve years of age), but of equalities or transitive asymmetric relationships ($A = C$ if $A = B$ and $B = C$, or $A < C$ if $A < B$ and $B < C$). One is aware, even, of a very progressive build-up of logical operations and their constants, presenting a very different picture from that of instinctive behavior, which appears quite suddenly at some moment determined by hormonal influence. If logic were present before birth or at birth, or developed by some speeding-up process at a definite age, or if it developed in conjunction with the maturation of the nervous system, it could certainly be placed in the context of hereditary knowledge, but none of the criteria which have been established about that form of knowledge can possibly apply here. As a result, we are confronted with a sort of evolution which is to a great extent endogenous but is not programmed as to the details of its content; it is reminiscent of epigenesis (as we saw in section 2), but from a purely functional point of view that allows of no outright assimilation of logic into some hereditary mental mechanism, while compelling us to look for its origins in those functions which appertain to the living organization.

2. Numerical or arithmetic structures seem, on the other hand, to occasion a definite learning period, and we shall come back to this question in subsection 2 in connection with children and the exciting experiments carried out by Otto Köhler on budgerigars

and jackdaws. However, before embarking on this topic, we should remember that, from the angle of scientific logic (a particular instance of general algebra), number in all its forms is composed exclusively of logical elements, whether it is conceived merely as something reducible to the logic of classes or the logic of relationships, or as something leading to new syntheses altogether. In both cases, however, it is out of the question that any sort of partition should be set up between arithmetic and logic; this might even be regarded as an essential fact which the biologist is compelled to take into account. Thus, to attempt to classify the inferential mechanisms of logic simply as part of innate behavior, and arithmetic structures as the product of learning or experience, would present insuperable difficulties. Both classifications apply at the same time, but since this exacerbates the difficulty, neither must apply, which brings us back to the quest for a third possible biological source of knowledge.

3. Where spatial or geometric structures are concerned, the situation is quite different, and once again we have to bear in mind certain epistemological data before we can launch out upon a biological discussion. A few decades ago, geometry was still considered a kind of mathematics applied to experimental or perceptual data, as against "pure" mathematics or theory of number—algebra and analysis. The advances made in axiomatic method by Hilbert and others, and in physics by Einstein and others, have, in fact, made it possible to overcome this ambiguity by means of a clear dissociation. There is on one side, not a physical geometry, but a geometric physics, which absorbs the spatial properties of an object, as measured experimentally, into the general properties of the object. The theory or relativity thus endows bodies with space, in Riemann's sense of the word (contrary to Poincaré's theory, which was that a physical phenomenon could, or could not, be translated at will into Euclidian space merely by juggling with language), and considers the curves made within this space, which are measurable in ds^2 as they are in Pythagoras' theorem, to be dependent upon the masses themselves. But on the other side there is such a thing as pure geometry, dependent upon nothing but its own axiomatic logic without the need of any intuition (as to truth values). Now this pure geometry resorbs itself, as geometric, into topological structures, which—along with algebraic and order structures—constitute the essential foundations of the architecture of mathematics, as the

Bourbakis put it. Moreover, topology is closely linked to logic, as can be seen, for instance, in the seminal work of Kuratowski, who imperceptibly passes from inclusions of logical classes to topological relations of closure and boundary.

As a result, spatial structures, from the biological point of view, bridge the gap between logico-mathematical structures, the nature of which is still unknown, and those structures which are either hereditary or, as is sometimes the case, acquired by learning.

2. Mathematics and Learning

Let us now look more closely into the reasons why logico-mathematical structures cannot be interpreted by means of the ordinary learning mechanisms. We have, moreover, to distinguish here between the child's construction of number and the kind of learning in birds and mammals effected by Otto Köhler, for these two kinds of behavior are naturally not to be seen as of equal status.

In the case of a child, construction of number is carried out in close collaboration with construction of logical structures of class groupings (inclusions and classifications) and of order relationships (seriation or linking up of asymmetric transitive relationships), and both these types of construction obviously necessitate the handling of objects and, consequently, experiment. For example, it is only after much groping that any subject succeeds in making a connection, item by item, between two collections of objects, and he will take longer still to discover that the numerical sum of each collection remains the same even though the spatial arrangement of its components is altered. We can justly speak of experiment, then, but this type of experiment or learning is not, as we have seen, the same type that the child makes use of in discovering that the weight of bodies is generally—though not constantly—proportional to their size. In this second type of experiment the child certainly performs an operation upon an object, weighing it and so on, but the knowledge thus acquired is drawn from the object itself insofar as its weight and volume were part of it before the action taken upon it. On the other hand, with logico-mathematical experimentation (and such experimentation plays a necessary role long before any active deductive operation is possible, and an auxiliary role, bordering on deduction, when a problem becomes too great for deduction), the information thus obtained is drawn, not from the objects as such, but from the operations performed upon them. It is the operation of putting them all together which gives them an amount in terms of logical or numerical totality; it is the operation of relating them to one another which makes it possible for them to achieve numerical equivalence (although not necessarily an equivalence of shape or color).

Seen from this angle, number appears to be an endogenous construction in that it is produced by highly generalized operations in the subject, who then coordinates them; number is a synthesis of inclusion (the operation of including 1 in 1 + 1, and 1 + 1 in 1 + 1 + 1) and of order (the operation of seriating 1, 1, 1, . . . , which is the only way to distinguish between them), and the relating of 1 to 1 is the expression of this synthesis in comparison between two quite separate groups.

Now from the biological point of view the operations of putting together, including, putting in order, and so on are in no way the products of learning, for the connections of inclusion, order, and correspondence intervene as previously existing conditions, and not merely as results, in all coordinations of behavior, of the nervous system, of the physiological functions, or of the functioning of the living organization in general. There is, of course, some learning involved in the adaptation of these basic connections to each new problem, but it is in the capacity of experiments or of accommodations of previous assimilation schemata. On the other hand, the sources or roots of these connections are to be found within the organism and not in the objects, so that it is impossible to speak of learning or structures or acquired habits in their normal sense.

To take the case of "numeration" in jackdaws or budgerigars that Otto Köhler noted, we know that he succeeded in training the birds to pick out the fourth in a series of bowls he lined up upside down so as to conceal which was empty and which contained food. This training finally led the birds to see the connection between the ordinal number that they had learned and a complex signal consisting of simultaneous visual indices (four objects laid out in a particular way) or successive ones (four flashes of light) or even sounds. But however spectacular these results may be, there are limitations to them, which are also instructive in their way. The figural numbers obtained never go beyond 5 or 6. More important still, the system obtained is not iterative; that is, the bird that has been trained to recognize 5 does not, on that account, know how to distinguish 3 from 4. In a child, number construction will even-

tually enable him to see numbers in series as part of a system
$(1 + 1 = 2; 2 + 1 = 3;$ etc.) and also as a system with a "group"
structure by means of the synthesis of two "groupings" of classes
and of seriation. But all that Köhler's birds can do is master figural
numbers that are comparatively independent of one another but
dependent upon spatiotemporal "Gestalts." It is worth pointing out
here that, in man and in the child, the same level can be observed
in perceptions of "numerosity" together with the illusions it has
been seen to cause: for example, Ponzo's visual illusion, with
twelve little horizontal bars placed one above the other at equal
distances in a vertical column, which appear less "numerous" than
the same bars placed in an oblique column (effect of length on
number, as in the case of preoperational notions in a very young
child).

Be that as it may, Köhler's experiments are certainly concerned
with number, although they are relevant also to shapes and spatio-
temporal factors, and yet here we surely have a classic example of
learning. However, two things must be pointed out in connection
with what has just been observed in children. On one hand, the
numerical element cannot possibly be a pure one, since perceptual
learning of shapes, etc., is involved. But on the other hand—and far
more important—inasmuch as the numerical or, rather, prenumer-
ical factor that intervenes here cannot be denied, it is certainly not
learned; what is involved is the actual perceiving of correspondence,
which constitutes the preexisting condition and does not result from
any learning. The same shapes and the same experimental device
will succeed in birds that have sufficient intelligence,[30] but they
will get no result at all with a salamander or even a lizard, simply
because there will be no perception of correspondence. It is true
that there is some such perception in the case of jackdaws, but
this is simply the exercise of an operation possible for creatures at
their level and is not the outcome of repetitions passively registered
by means of external constraint, for the very reason that, without
this same perception of correspondence, no amount of repetition
will achieve any numerical effect. In short, what is learned from
these fascinating experiments is the application of a perception

30. We are not attributing any mystical power to intelligence, which is defined simply by the sum total of the coordinations possible at one level and,
by abstraction, on the basis of analogous coordinations intervening in simpler
behaviors.

of correspondence that is possible with spatiotemporal shapes but not with numerical ones unless there is something else to help it. The numerical aspect is not learned but only exercised, and it constitutes an actualization of general coordinations which are accessible to the level of intelligence under consideration, and which would bring about an immediate "insight" at a higher level. So here we clearly have to deal with a dawning of "logico-mathematical experiment" as defined earlier by relation to physical experiment such as is normally made in learning.

As for learning in the spatial field, two sorts of processes can be observed, according to whether physical space and hence learning are involved, or logico-mathematical space and hence another type of experiment and operations originating in an action of the subject. This distinction may seem abstract and artificial, but in reality it is not so at all; it does correspond to some operational criteria which are rather easy to apply; here again, physical learning leads only to sequences, but logico-mathematical experiment leads to connections which the subject himself sees as "necessary." Let us, for example, present some children with a cardboard triangle or square, the angles of which have been marked in different colors, and let us turn it round in 90° stages, asking them to anticipate where the colors will appear. Two behaviors are then possible.

The first is based on physical experiment. The child registers the order in which the colors come and thus succeeds in making mere "legal" sequences, according to which anticipation becomes possible: green will be at the bottom because it comes after blue according to the sequence red, blue, green, etc. The other behavior is comprehension, based on the operation itself: the green mark being in the top left-hand corner (by virtue of operations connected with the rotation subgroup). At first glance, it might be said that the rotation itself is learned as an action before becoming an operation; so much is obvious, but insofar as it is an action made by the subject, it is allied to logico-mathematical structures of cyclic order, or position permutations, and so on, such as can be utilized on the plane of action, of concrete operations, or of pure abstraction. Next, it will be said that if these operations do, in fact, lead to the making of necessary connections, the mere fact of physical sequence implies some "order." We grant that point too, and we shall, in section 21, be drawing from such facts the conclusion that no sort of learning or physical knowledge is possible without logico-mathematical frameworks. Nevertheless, it is one thing to register, from the outside, a sequence that is written into the object and recognized by the mere process of being noticed, and quite another actively to engender the sequence by some operation on the part of the subject, which can indeed imitate the object but which confers upon the given sequence an endogenous character of necessity and intelligibility that it did not, of itself, possess.

The distinction just made has such general application that, mutatis mutandis, it will be seen to be the same as the one we employed in section 19, subsections 5 and 6, in order to confront the Lamarckian concept of a direct action exerted by environment on the genome (which is like learning or physical knowledge) with the notion of a reequilibration within the genome, which has the resources to make its own response to environmental influence and finally achieves, by means of a sort of phenocopy, the setting up of a similar, though endogenous, construction.

3. Logico-mathematical Structures and Heredity

This brings us to the second possible hypothesis as to the nature of logico-mathematical knowledge: if this knowledge is not brought about by empirical learning but simply constitutes the necessary condition for the organization and recording of the experience, will it then not have to be considered ipso facto as being hereditary by nature?

Yes and no. Yes, if this only means that logico-mathematical knowledge draws its substance from the living organization, which perpetuating or extending itself from one generation to the next, might be said to be hereditary (but in a sense which has to be further defined and is not to be confused with the transmission of personal characteristics). No, if it means that logic and mathematics correspond to clearly defined characteristics which are present in the genome and give information to the individual in the same way that its specific heredity imposes on it a certain morphology or a well-defined number of instinctive behaviors.

Yet this hypothesis has found its adherents. We do not need to go back to Descartes with his "innate ideas," or to Leibnitz's pre-established harmony, for once again (see section 5, subsection 1, and section 8, subsection 5) we must remember that Konrad Lorenz thinks there is a connection between Kant's a priori (which embrace the whole of logic and mathematics) and the hereditary or innate mechanisms of morphology and instinct. It is only on two important points that Lorenz differs from Kant, but he does so in such a way as to better justify his hypothesis that our so-called a priori knowledge is connected with the genetic mechanisms of life.

The first point is really not our concern here, but it does have its interest in the light of what has just been said about the connections between the phenomenon, which can be drawn through intuitive experience and its a priori structuration, and the noumenon or "thing in itself," which, according to Kant, is absolutely impossible to know and bears no relation to the phenomenon from the point of view of the instruments by which knowledge is acquired. Lorenz does not accept this radical distinction, and, being a good evolutionist (that is, from a point of view which remained completely foreign to Kantian thought), he sees progression in the development of knowledge from the level of bacteria up to that of man, which leads him to assume that we have come a little closer to the "noumenon" during this evolution. In other words, for Kant's rigid and resolutely static frameworks Lorenz substitutes the idea of gradual approximations, not—and this is the important point—by virtue of an additive accumulation of experiences, but because of a steady improvement in the hereditary cognitive instruments, hence, because of an ascending evolution of the a priori themselves. With this we can only concur.

To put it another way, a priori frameworks evolve and perfect themselves. In fact, Lorenz goes so far as to say (and I am in full sympathy with him here although I cannot believe in structural a priori) that a priori in animals—in other words, their instincts—help us to a better understanding of a priori in human beings and, therefore, of those among our cognitive structures which we have imprinted on us by necessity (and of these the only ones we can be sure of are the logico-mathematical ones). But logical as all this may seem, touched up, as it is, by Kantianism, once he translates it into biological terms, Lorenz comes up against a second point of divergence from Kant, and this time a far graver one: if a priori evolve like some biological characteristic,[31] being prior conditions for every kind of experimental knowledge and fixed in heredity as

31. Let it be noted that a priori do indeed evolve, but this can only take place by means of internal autoregulations and not because of chance encounters with environment or by some simple interplay of mutations and selections.

instincts or innate conceptual frameworks, then they must lose, along with their uniqueness and their universality (since they vary from species and are fixated in man as he is now, in a certain form, although they will later take a different form through some mutation favorable to cognition), the very thing that gave them their chief value, which was their necessity.

In effect, as has already been seen, Lorenz abandons, apparently without any qualms, the necessity for a priori connections, since he reaches the point at which he seems to consider them "innate working hypotheses," retaining only their innate character, this aspect of it being prior to any experience or any contact with the environment. Now there is something very interesting about this abandonment. It has serious consequences from the epistemological point of view, since it compromises the discipline of logic and mathematics. Biologically and psychologically it has much to teach us, for it seems to indicate, if not yet to demonstrate, that the hereditary character and the intrinsic necessity of logico-mathematical structures are incompatible, so that we have to choose one or the other, making an exclusive disjunction.

Thus, Lorenz sacrifices the necessity of logico-mathematical structures in favor of their innateness, and this is the major stumbling block in his theory. The sacrifice has been keenly felt by another distinguished biologist, B. Rensch of Münster, who, like Lorenz, is interested in the phylogenetic and ontogentic formation of human knowledge. What Rensch does is to knock down not only the Kantian theory but also the idea that endogenous factors could offer any explanation. He thus arrives at the point at which he sees logico-mathematical knowledge as the outcome of an adjustment, made by successive selection, to the "extramental" world. In fact, he considers the laws of logic to regulate the physical world as well as thought. On the other hand, he says: "Throughout phylogenesis, the thought processes have had to adapt themselves to the logical laws of the world in the same way as to the causal laws. If they did not do so, they would bring about reactions which would be hostile to the law of being."[32] But to put it like this raises difficulties of two kinds. If the logico-mathematical laws of "being" are discovered from outside, as the laws of physics are, then there is no longer anything "necessary" about them in the deductive and

32. Lecture given at the Center for Genetic Epistemology in Geneva in June 1965 (to be published in Etudes d'épistémologie génétique).

axiomatic sense of the term, and there is nothing to prove that selection has been enough to ensure our complete adaptation in regard to them rather than merely an approximate adaptation as in other domains (perception, etc.). If, on the other hand, the laws of logic were universal, as Rensch seems to think, that is to say, if they could be applied to atoms "that no one can see," as they can be to human thought, and to the genome as well as to behavior, then they would be innate and would manifest themselves in infancy. Now this is just not so. Their necessity is brought about by a gradual construction.

In fact, a study of the development of logico-mathematical structures in a child reveals that the necessity for them is imposed on the subject, not from the beginning, but, as we have already said, very gradually, often until such time as it crystallizes rather suddenly. There are two reasons for this, complementary to each other, and the two of them together are enough to explain the whole thing in a valid and verifiable way. The first has to do with the closure of operational structures. For so long as seriation, let us say, $A < B < C \ldots$, simply causes the child to make a construction by groping of an empirical kind, the structure cannot be said to be closed, and consequently the transitivity applied to the objects ($A < C$ if $A < B$ and $B < C$) appears to the child to be not necessary but simply possible or probable. As soon as seriation is established operationally by the persistent choosing of the smallest element remaining or available, with the resultant realization that any element E is both bigger than the A, B, C, D that precede it and smaller than the F and G that follow it, then the structure becomes whole and closed; that is, relations within it are interdependent and can be composed among themselves without recourse to anything outside the system. In that case, transitivity appears "necessary," and this logical "necessity" is recognized not only by some inner feeling, which cannot be proved, but by the intellectual behavior of the subject, who uses the newly mastered deductive instrument with confidence and discipline.

The second reason for the development of these "necessary" judgments is the very one that accounts for the formation and closure of the structures and which therefore invalidates the hypothesis about their structural heredity as opposed to some simple idea of functional continuity. The fact is, a structure can impose itself as a necessity and can do this by essentially endogenous means, being the product of a progressive equilibration, although that does not mean it inherits the program of its structural content. To take a quite different example having no connection with the equilibrium of cognitive functions: if an organism obeys, in such and such a sector, the second principle of thermodynamics, it does so from motives of entropic equilibrium, which, though they may be internal, do not on that account necessitate the hypothesis of hereditary transmission. To take yet another example, more closely allied to logic: if a subject, confronted with a slightly irregular shape, sees a perfect circle, he does so by virtue of some immediate equilibration, either of the perceptual field or of the effects of perceptual centering and decentering. However regular and dominant this behavior may be, it still cannot be called hereditary, since the general laws of equilibration are enough in themselves to bring it about, despite external obstacles. So there we have a question of a general kind, and it is vitally important to distinguish, in every domain and much more carefully than is usually done, between hereditary transmissions and those internal equilibration processes which are capable of identical repetition of a fruitful kind with each new generation.

The necessary character of logico-mathematical structures, then, does not in the least prove them to be hereditary but emerges from their progressive equilibration by dint of autoregulation. It has already been seen in section 14 how operations represent the final limit of regulations of error, leading to a level of precorrection and avoidance of error which shows that deductive equilibrium and "necessity" have been reached. This characteristic of internal equilibration within such structures is enough to explain their generality and, above all, their endlessly mobile extension, whereas the hereditary character of an instinct precludes both its generality and its necessity, since it is peculiar to one species only and might have been very different from what it is. Furthermore, one might say there is a striking contrast, which has surely been emphasized often enough, between the limitations of instinct, causing instinctive behavior to be always of a particular and specialized kind, and the mobile universality of intelligence, which may, indeed, be a little uncertain where experimental knowledge is concerned but whose conquests in the logico-mathematical domain cannot be challenged. We cannot hope to explain the nature of these structures by putting them on a par with instinctive heredity.

4. Mathematical Construction

In a sense, every instinct constitutes an invention, since its origin is largely endogenous and it might have been different from what it is. The physical learning and experiment on which it leans cause it to make discoveries, in the sense of an encounter with realities that existed before the action of the subject. The fact that logico-mathematical structures can be reduced neither to hereditary groupings, as instinct can, nor to learning, becomes obvious to us, also, because we see that logical and mathematical constructions are made up neither of inventions nor of discoveries in the precise and limited sense of these terms. They might perhaps be called inventions, since they are new combinations brought about by the activity of the subject and did not exist before the activity took place; for example, the "imaginary" number $i = \sqrt{-1}$ is a combination of a purely invented kind, as its name shows, coming between the extraction of the root and the pure negatives. But an invention implies a free choice and so might be different from what it is. Now once an invention is made, in mathematics, it seems to be determined and even predetermined by all that has preceded it, and so it is imposed by necessity (the proof of this is the surprising way in which the imaginary has been integrated into the theory of number and into the calculus of functions and engendered quarternions, etc.). Is this a matter of discovery rather than invention? But one can only discover what already exists, whether it is within or outside one's person, like America before Columbus or the association of ideas before Descartes or Aristotle. Can it be said, likewise, that the imaginary number existed from all eternity or even from the time that there was such a thing as human thought? And, if so, where and how? And, if this were true, the means of calculating this hidden entity which had been in existence all the time still had to be "invented" or discovered. Now this calculation is sufficient in itself, without our needing to hypostatize its result in the form of "beings" or "essences."[33]

We are thus compelled to think of the construction of logico-mathematical structures in the form, not of a development that is integrated unpredictably with external elements, but as a kind of

33. I hope I may be forgiven in so seriously intentioned a work as this, for quoting the best criticism ever made of the predetermination of concepts. It was Anatole France who said: "Before there were any feet and before there were any rears, the kick in the rear existed and had always existed, from the beginning of time, in the Almighty's bosom."

endogenous evolution going forward in stages. These stages are of such a kind that the combinations characteristic of any one of them will be new as combinations, yet based entirely upon the elements already present in the preceding stage. This description, however, does not go far enough, for the combinations are dependent upon some possible combinatorial calculation, so that, using the elements given at any one stage, one ought to be able to calculate in advance what all future combinations will be, and this is just not possible without a subject to work on. In order to understand the nature of the construction process, one must examine first the reasons which may obstruct the construction of new combinations and then the conditions which may enable them to take place. Now there are at least two such conditions, one of them formal or logical, and the other psychological.

From the logical angle, Gödel demonstrated as long ago as 1930, by some theorems which become famous, that a system which is otherwise sufficient for its own purposes (for example, elementary arithmetic) cannot, by its own or by weaker means, succeed in verifying its own noncontradiction. In order to establish noncontradiction, one has to go beyond the limits of the system and integrate it into a "stronger" one (which is what Gentzen did for elementary arithmetic, backing it up by transfinite arithmetic). In other words, the development of a structure cannot be made entirely on its own level, by mere extension of given operations and combination of known elements; the progress made consists of the construction of a wider structure, embracing the former but introducing new elements. But what do these new elements consist of? In this particular case, Cantor succeeded in constructing transfinite arithmetic by the simple means of generalizing the operation of perception of correspondences, which was not used in elementary arithmetic although it occurred throughout the exchange actions. If one equates, by means of bi-univocal and reciprocal correspondences, two series such as 1, 2, 3, 4 . . . and 2, 4, 6, 8 . . . , one does, in fact, obtain a new number belonging to neither of the two series, which is their common measure of "aleph-zero," that is to say, the power of enumeration. To put it another way, transfinite arithmetic is arrived at from elementary arithmetic, not by generalizing or merely extending it, but by abstracting from its results an operation that makes possible the construction of a new structure, which includes the old. This new structure, as Gentzen demonstrated, is, moreover, capable of assuring noncontradiction of the former structure, but it is not capable of assuring its own non-contradiction; to assure this it must set up a new, stronger structure (for which we shall have to await a new Cantor).

From the psychological angle (and psychology has nothing to add to what has just been said but simply tries to describe the process from the point of view of the subject who is thinking and, more important still, acting), the abstraction process is very characteristic of logico-mathematical thought and differs from simple or Aristotelian abstraction. In the latter, given some external object, such as a crystal and its shape, substance, and color, the subject simply separates the different qualities and retains one of them—the shape, maybe—rejecting the rest. In the case of logico-mathematical abstraction, on the other hand, what is given is an agglomeration of actions or operations previously made by the subject himself, with their results. In this case, abstraction consists first of taking cognizance of the existence of one of these actions or operations, that is to say, noting its possible interest, having neglected it so far; for example, the perception of correspondence was known in children, but no mathematical notice had been taken of it before Cantor. Second, the action noted has to be "reflected" (in the physical sense of the term) by being projected onto another plane—for example, the plane of thought as opposed to that of practical action, or the plane of abstract systematization as opposed to that of concrete thought (say, algebra versus arithmetic). Third, it has to be integrated into a new structure, which means that a new structure has to be set up, but this is only possible if two conditions are fulfilled: (a) the new structure must first of all be a reconstruction of the preceding one if it is not to lack coherence and congruity; it will thus be the product of the preceding one on a plane chosen by it; (b) it must also, however, widen the scope of the preceding one, making it general by combining it with the elements proper to the new place of thought; otherwise there will be nothing new about it. These, then, are the characteristics of a "reflection," but now we are taking the term in the psychological sense, to mean a rearrangement, by means of thought, of some matter previously presented to the subject in a rough or immediate form. The name I propose to give this process of reconstruction with new combinations, which allows for any operational structure at any previous stage or level to be integrated into a richer structure at a higher level, is "reflective abstraction [*abstraction réfléchissante*]."

This will explain why logico-mathematical construction is, properly speaking, neither invention nor discovery; proceeding by means of reflective abstractions, it is a construction in the full sense of the word; that is, it is productive of new combinations. But such combinations can only be brought about by a combinatorial attainable by calculation at the levels below and previous to the construction of the new structure, for the latter, by retroactive effect (cf. the relationship of operations and feedbacks, section 14), demands a reflective rearrangement of the preceding elements, and achieves a synthesis which outstrips the original structures and thereby enriches them.

5. The General Forms of Organization

One of the most remarkable characteristics of reflective abstractions, the mechanism of which can be observed and identified throughout the whole course of logic and mathematics, is that they converge completely with the psychogenetic process of the elaboration of operational structures at that stage in the child's development when it advances from action to operations, that is, from the sensorimotor levels to the subsequent levels, which are characterized first by concrete operations and then by propositional or formal ones (section 1). Indeed, as we have seen, the sensorimotor action schemata (displacement groups, permanent object schemata, inclusion structures, and order structures, such as are found in the coordination of assimilation schemata, etc.) cannot be extended into operations, with a time span ranging between 1–2 and 7–8 years, until these practical structures have been reconstructed into thought structures which reflect them by working outward from them.

The essential thing if we are to understand the biological nature of logico-mathematical structures is, therefore, to start from the sui generis process of construction, constituted by reflective abstraction, and to work backward to its origins. Now reflective abstraction is a cognitive process allied to the exercise of thought, and so we might be afraid that it would not take us back as far as the sensorimotor levels. However, if we dissociate it from the mental aspects—taking cognizance, etc.—and only retain its constructive and functional mechanism, then it will partly correspond to a process which has been well known in biology since the work done on neurology by Jackson and Sherrington: the integration of lower structures into the structures of the subsequent stage to form a hierarchy whose levels correspond to the successive phases of growth. All that remains to be pointed out is that, in the case of the structures from which logico-mathematical structures finally emerge, the development process under consideration must be qualified by the condition that the new structures contain no exogenous elements and do nothing except reorganize and recombine elements which were present at the lower stages in a less differentiated form.

The limitation imposed by this condition may seem to be severe and therefore a hindrance. In reality it is this limitation which should put us on the road to finding the solution we seek, and the solution becomes self-evident if we bear in mind what was accepted in subsections 1–3 above. Logico-mathematical structures cannot arise from any learning in the strict sense, for although they are constantly working upon external data, they assimilate what they learn without being modified by it, except in the shape of some consolidatory and generalizing exercise, but this never produced any change in structure. On the other hand, these structures cannot be caused by mere hereditary transmission, for if they were attached to the genes in the same way that the shape of the cranium, the lobe of the brain, or some particular instinct are attached to them, they would be neither necessary nor general, nor would they have the extraordinary constructive plasticity which they do. If, biologically speaking, learning and heredity and its content are excluded, there still remains this fundamental reality, which need not be stressed because it is obvious, but which does, all the same, constitute the necessary preliminary condition for every kind of learning and even for heredity itself: namely, the organizing function with its absolute continuity—a function which is not transmitted but is continuous, conserving itself from transmission to transmission. This is not at all the same thing as hereditary transmission, since it is itself the *necessary condition*[34] for any transmission (and vice versa, though the two things can be dissociated by analysis).

In the past, when the genome was still thought of as a little bundle or aggregate of particles, each of which conserved itself and transmitted to the next generation the isolated little message it contained, our present problem did not arise, so that there was no need to know anything about the laws of modern genetics. But once organization is seen in everything, and the genome is seen as a regulation system

---

34. Necessary from the biologist's causal point of view but not, of course, from the point of view of the conscious subject, who only accedes to logical necessity at a much higher level—the level of the closure of operational structures (as we saw in subsection 3).

with its genes coadapted into one polygenius, using its recombinations as compensations, and once variations are attributed to overall disequilibria and reequilibrations, not simply to chance mutations, then two levels of process must necessarily be distinguished in any hereditary transmission:

a. There is the genetic information, that is to say, the combination (in its content) of that which is transmitted and that which acts on the morphology of the next generation.

b. But there is also autoconservation, which perpetually reconstitutes itself, not only by some internal metabolism but also by autoregulation of its organization and functioning during all its many activities, from the complex events of fertilization onward.

Now this kind of autoconservation presupposes that there must be some function which runs right through all the transmissions but is not actually transmitted in the normal sense of the word, since all it does is simply to endure and continue uninterruptedly. So it is not transmitted as a message is transmitted, but is conserved during each transmission and is, in fact, the necessary condition for this transmission. It is still a sort of transmission, if you like, but more elementary than a real transmission because it is an active continuation.

It may be objected that any transmission linked to particular genes is, in the same way, simply a matter of conservation and continuation. If that is so, substructures are involved, with their various contents. The general functioning we are speaking of here is the overall organization of these substructures, and if the latter are reproduced by dissociation and multiple reduplications, the total functioning goes forward in its simple stage and remains the same, by means of functional continuity, while all these divisions are going on. Looked at in this light, in fact, the functioning does something more than transmit itself; it gets on with its work and conserves its dynamic organization, insofar as it is dynamic, while at the same time conserving the power of self-modification.[35]

---

35. To put it in a nutshell: amoeba, porifera, fish, and mammals transmit all their characteristics by divisions and multiplications, and that is truly hereditary transmission; but they also transmit the more general properties of life, being organizations, and that is not transmission in the same sense but a continuation or conservation in the sense that, at every stage of hereditary transmission, a *living* organization subsists which is the necessary condition for the particular transmissions, since it determines the *activities* which intervene during this transmission.

Then again, it may be objected that the distinction we are making between the total organization and its organized content is a mere abstraction. Of course it is, but it still remains true that the things transmitted by heredity vary from species to species or even from one race to another, whereas the general functioning that is necessary for the purposes of our argument about cognitive structures is common to all living creatures. This being so, what comes to mind is the distinction that has come to be made between "special" heredity, pertaining to species and races, and "general" heredity, by which are transmitted the main characteristics of the organization—those pertaining to classes, branches, or even kingdoms. In the past, I myself had the idea that logico-mathematical structures might be explained by this general heredity in contradistinction to individual hereditary characteristics such as spatial perception in two or three dimensions. But now this solution appears to me to be inadequate for several reasons, and that is why it is useful to distinguish between the organization as such, in its permanent functioning, and the hereditary transmission of characteristics, however general or specialized they may be.

In the first place, general heredity transmits only virtualities or a limited kind or characteristics that have already been established and elaborated, though generalized throughout one class, which is different from some common functional dynamism, open to every construction. For example, it is very hard to concede that the very general mathematical structure of "group transformations" should be transmitted by heredity, as is the case with the dorsal spine in vertebrates, whereas it is easier to accept the idea that the structure might be prepared for by the more generalized forms of the living organization, though in its functional dynamism and in its quality of producing isomorphisms and endomorphisms of varying kinds.

On the other hand, the entire hereditary transmission of potentialities and real or virtual characteristics presupposes a total organization containing regulatory systems and an overall organization. Let T be this total functioning and the organization structure to which it is attached, and let H be the entire collection of individual transmissions (whether the heredity be general or specialized). It goes without saying that H cannot exist or be transmitted without T, just as T cannot function without H; this is as much as to say that there is no hereditary transmission without an overall regulatory system and vice versa; no functioning without a structure and vice versa; no parts without wholes and vice versa; and so on. But, when analyzed, H can be distinguished from T insofar as the content of H is transmitted by heredity, even if it is "general" heredity, and insofar as the overall organization T may be said to follow through continuously rather than be transmitted in the proper sense. In particular, it would be possible to maintain that H is more rapidly modified than T, in the sense that the variation of one part may leave the structure and the functioning of the whole relatively unchanged (nevertheless they do undergo transformation but in the manner that "functional invariables" do, which only change little by little as to their content: assimilation and so on). So much being said, the central problem is to establish whether the source of the most highly generalized coordinations (relative to the organism, the nervous system, behavior, etc.), from which logico-mathematical structures will eventually be deduced by means of constructive or reflective abstractions, lies with H or with T.

To look for it in H entails seeing these structures as hereditary characteristics, even if they are "general," so that they are reduced in the end to static a priori—quasi-instinctive mechanisms of the kind Lorenz tried to prove existed in the sphere of human knowledge, modeling himself on a sort of biological Kantianism. This brings us to a major difficulty because, if Lorenz is right, mathematics loses all its "necessity," since a hereditary characteristic is no more than what it is and differs from those of all the other "classes" or branches. On the other hand, to go back to T for the source of logico-mathematical structures means inclining toward the idea of an organizing rather than an organized organization, and consequently coordination more general and therefore more "necessary" than any particular or specialized "characteristics" which may be transmitted at any particular moment.[36]

36. What has just been said—and is, indeed, central to our general thesis—may cause several objections to be raised. (In this connection, all my thanks are due to Professor Nowinski, whose penetrating criticism has been of enormous value to me.) These objections must be examined carefully, as much to forestall their arising in the reader's mind as to clarify the hypotheses themselves.

(1) First of all, it will be remembered that (in section 10, subsection 11, introduction) when we were trying to see the general organization function as opposed to the various possible structures of an organized kind, the conclusion was drawn that, if particular functions such as breathing can be defined as the action exerted by the functioning of a substructure on that of the total structure, then conversely the organization qua function is the

If there is, then, some such general functioning T intervening in every living organization, all we need to do in order to understand its relation to the logical or logico-mathematical structures that are reconstructed by our minds is to assume that, being generalized, it carries on its construction process wherever there is an organization

---

action of the total functioning on that of the substructures. However, supposing such a definition should seem logically defensible (because there is obviously some reciprocity between the roles played by the parts and by the whole), then the distinction between function and structure, so far as the organization as such is concerned, will remain a rather formal one as long as people remain ignorant of the logico-mathematical theory of the overall structure of the organization. We are certainly very far from being in that position! In fact, the distinction between the functions and the structures of the organization simply served, in section 11, to separate the more general characteristics that are considered to be functional (insofar as they relate to observable functioning, although they still defy analysis from the structural point of view) from those that are seen to be more specialized (although they may be common to all forms of living organization), which are easier to describe in structural terms. In what now follows (as throughout subsection 5 of the present section) we had better, therefore, be cautious and refer only to "general functioning."

(2) This being agreed, our next main difficulty in trying to maintain that a general functioning of this kind is necessary to the constitution and transmission in heredity of substructures and particular characteristics is that, logically speaking, the parts seem necessary to the whole to the exact extent that the whole can be considered necessary to the parts. This may seem to be a merely formal objection, but it is well known that, in fact, this is the principal obstacle to accepting the entire static a priori argument, so that what we have to do is to examine carefully whether the idea of development might raise this obstacle.

To use the word "organization" at all is to admit, of course, that an organized totality necessarily contains differentiated parts, these parts being as necessary to the whole as such, as the whole is necessary to the parts. But if the existence of the parts is necessary, none of them alone is necessary in itself, and so each is capable of certain variations (within limits that are variable too) without involving the existence of the *whole* as such. If they do vary, or if one of them varies, the whole will of course be modified. But how will it be modified? Obviously in its structure, and that is why we are absolutely compelled to distinguish between structure and function, or, to put it more cautiously, between particular structures and general functioning. Thus, the whole is modified in its structure if at least one of its parts already is, but then either it will die out and so cause dislocation of the whole, or else something will survive as a *totality*, and it is in this respect that we speak of general functioning.

To say that this general functioning is necessary does not in any way mean, therefore, that the whole is prior to the parts, or that the function is prior to the structure. It simply means that no characteristic can be formed or transmitted without some lasting activity which is not transmitted in the same way as the particular structures whose transmission it guarantees.

(3) Another difficulty arises: if a "general functioning" like this outstrips particular structures, is that not saying that some sort of "superhis-

or reorganization, but in increasingly elaborated forms. One process that strikes us as being an intermediate point between the hereditary organization and the laws governing thought is cortical functioning, which has the double quality of being a hereditary functioning inso-

torical" factor is intervening, or a nonhistorical one, like some "vital form" that is supposed to mold each organism in turn? But the great difference between what we are saying here and all explanations of that kind is that we do not see this "general functioning" as a "factor" superimposed on anything, and are confining ourselves to observable data, with the sole aim of finding out what knowledge is, not biological mechanisms. In fact, the observable data show us (H) an uninterrupted series of transformations or transmissions made by division and multiplication and (T) the conservation of the auto-regulatory organization. We therefore conclude that H and T are interdependent; that is to say, T is necessary to H, and, inversely, H is necessary to T, but only as an overall development or vection (see section 8, subsection 6) and not with regard to each particular characteristic (caused by interactions with environment). Furthermore, we may draw the conclusion that if the H mechanisms, which are geared to the environment, are necessary to physical or experimental knowledge, the T mechanisms supply a possible basis for logico-mathematical knowledge after an endless succession of reflective abstractions and advances followed by reconstructions (see subsections 4 and 6). However, I do not see the general function T as being at all a separate or "superhistorical" factor, since all that is involved is a functional continuity (that is, until we know more about the general structure of the organization) immanent to the development and inseparable from it. Everything I have written and done on the subject of the psychogenesis of the cognitive functions in children goes to show how inseparable this functional continuity is from the construction of particular structures during a particular child's growth, the mechanism of which is dependent upon an entire system, not on isolated factors.

(4) It is impossible also to use this "general functioning" as a basis for any cognitive a priori in the sense of static structures prior to, or given at, the beginning (as Kant says). It is, if you like, possible to speak of a functional a priori in the sense that every structure is the result of some activity, and, if the converse is true, their "common basis" (as Hegel says when making dialectic oppositions) is a structural activity or—which amounts to the same thing—an active structure that is under control (autoregulation), which does, nevertheless, imply that there is a general and continuous functioning. Even if the latter is necessary, it still is only the starting-off ground and not the preformation of higher forms of necessity (logico-mathematical structures) producing a series of nonpredetermined reconstructions. To put it briefly, the sort of general functioning we mean has nothing of the cognitive a priori or biological about it, since it is *inseparable from a continuous construction* and is the simple expression of the functional constant which is inherent in any transformation system. This constant can only be sought among elements, as in some atomistic composition (in the broad, not the microphysical, sense of the word) or in the totality as such, and the whole tendency of organicism today goes to show that, in biology, it is the second of these possibilities that must be accepted.

(5) Special emphasis must be placed on the fact that the term "general functioning" is only a provisional term, introduced to serve until we know

far as it is a functioning, but of having almost no hereditary programming by way of cognitive structures.[37]

In fact, the functioning of the brain is hereditary, since the progress made in cerebral and cortical development among primates and hominids, including man, rather precisely determines the progress of intelligence; but this is only a functioning and not a programming in any sense of the word, since it engenders neither "innate ideas" nor particular "knowing how" instincts, and even McCulloch's "neuron logic" is in no way reflected in a congenital logic in the child. This situation, so extraordinary by comparison with behavior at lower levels, leads us to suppose that (1) cerebral functioning is an expression or extension of very generalized forms rather than of particular organization forms, and (2) that logico-mathematical structures, although not written into this functioning at the structure stage, are nevertheless made by this functioning as soon as it comes to be used in solving effective problems, and that this functioning gives rise to a double movement of constructions and reflective abstractions at successive stages of equilibration. The forms of equilibrium thus attained are, in this case, both structures rendered neces-

---

more about the actual structure of any kind of organized system. It is only when we acquire an algebraico-topological mathematical theory or even an algebraico-logical one for the biological organization that we shall be able to verify whether the filiations suggested in this section do correspond to some reality in ontogenetic and phylogenetic development or if they have been nothing but fancies. Now it does seem certain that whatever this future theory of organization is, it cannot possibly be limited to a static analysis of what is already "organized" but will have to supply an expression of the "organizing" organization as development, progressive construction, and even vection, as well as autoregulation, either synchronic or actual. It is therefore possible that this "general functioning" we have been talking about could be reduced, wholly or partly, to continuous auto-equilibration processes, which would be biological as processes but would also be the basis of cognitive structures in that mobile equilibrium leads to reversibility, and reversibility—in the form of inversions and reciprocities—is what goes to make up the essential elements of logico-mathematical operations. However, before hazarding a guess at what general functioning might be, we can simply point out that even the hypothesis of its intervention permits of some approximations.

37. Of course, there are a certain number of innate connections, such as those which link the eye or the hand to their projection zones or those which determine the sucking reflexes, etc. But the tiny number of these links when compared to the endless powers of the human mind bears definite witness to the great diminution, in man, of innate knowledge in relation to the two other kinds of knowing.

sary by the laws of the functioning (logico-mathematical structures) and structures which are open to experiment (physical or experimental knowledge).

6. *Convergent Reconstructions with Overtaking* [Dépassement]

It is not enough, however, to think up some endogenous source of structurations, distinct from particular hereditary transmissions, in order to understand how the functional conditions of the living organization can possibly influence logico-mathematical knowledge. It should be borne in mind that nothing is farther from my thoughts than to attribute to the genome, or even to the brain, some kind of combinatorial intelligence, as Cuénot does, and to locate in that intelligence, a fortiori, the whole of mathematics in a preformed state. What must now be done, therefore, is to indicate what intermediate stages there might be between a living functioning that conserves itself and the construction of structures by means of reflective abstraction in the domain of thought.

The following considerations fall under three headings: (1) an investigation of the necessary conditions for general functioning (about which we have put forward a hypothesis) that could have a bearing on the construction of logical structures; (2) a reminder of the partial isomorphisms examined in chapter 4; (3) suggestions about the possible intermediaries that might confer meaning upon these isomorphisms with respect to development.

1. As for the necessary conditions of any organic functioning which might have a bearing on thought, we can and must limit ourselves to a minimum, because the more generalized they are, the greater chance there is that they will be valid. On the other hand, we are dealing here with an analysis made by a psychologist, not a logician, on the subject of intelligence. It would be of great interest, just supposing there were any sense in doing it, to discover exactly what the necessary postulates are, not only for the construction of structures (in which case these postulates would fuse into the axiomatic nature of each one of them), but also for their filiation or formal genealogy (it is on this that the logicians at our Center for Genetic Epistemology are working[38]) by going right back to conditions

---

38. See L. Apostel, J.-B. Grize, S. Papert, and J. Piaget, *La filiation des structures*, vol. 15 of Etudes d'épistémologie génétique (Paris: Presses Universitaires de France).

for the "weakest" and most elementary structures. However, since I am a psychologist, I must restrict myself to characterizing a few functional conditions.

A necessary but perhaps sufficient minimum of conditions might be the following:

a. Conservation of the whole, as a closed cycle (see section 11), whatever the components of this cycle may be. Whether this cycle is successful or not in any absolute fashion (and it is obvious that it will not be, since all forms of living organization evolve, including those within the genome), the important thing will be, not what is conserved (and what belongs, ipso facto, to the field of hereditary transmissions), but the continuous functional process of autoconservation, a process which lasts as long as life itself.

b. A minimum of differentiation into subsystems and of conservation of these (to which the same remarks apply as in *a*).

c. Order relationships, intervening either in the total cycle or within the subsystems, and whose presence seems all the more likely because the system is functioning in time.

d. Connections, isomorphisms, endomorphisms, and so on, suggesting certain analogies or formal homologies, if only between the subsystems and the total system.

These four characteristics, I maintain, which are so general as to be found in every living organization, are enough to provide the necessary starting-off ground for the construction of structures which may serve, in their turn, as a springboard for cognitive structures. If there is conservation of a whole and of parts, there must eventually be inclusion structures, whose general nature may be algebraic or topological. In conjunction with order relationships, these structures can lead to all sorts of "networks," and the interplay of correspondences or morphisms may constitute a multiplicity of "groups." Of course, a functional starting point will yield none of these structures, but by means of transpositions and abstractions their construction is possible right up to that domain of behavior where knowledge begins.

2. Next we must recall the few scattered examples of partial isomorphisms that we tried to identify in sections 11–14: formal connections were established between certain cognitive structures—such as classifications, order relationships, multiplicative structures of correspondence, "strongly structured" classes, etc.—and organic structures, not to mention the important functions of assimilation

and regulation, of which "operations" themselves would seem to be the ultimate limit.

However, the great problem raised by these isomorphisms, if they are to be used now as they should be in order to establish that there is a transition from the general functioning of every organism to the construction of logico-mathematical structures, is that of the transition itself, chiefly because of the immense hiatus in it: the living organization finally achieves systems of extraordinary complexity— a complexity so great, indeed, that biologists are still a long way from having mastered it, and there is still no mathematical theory to express its essential outlines. On the other hand, human knowledge, in forms of reflective thought, begins from zero as it sets out to master physical or mathematical reality. How, then, are we to conceive of some functional continuity capable of linking these extremes, even though, when compared, they reveal the partial isomorphisms which have already been mentioned?

3. It is in order to get this central difficulty for our thesis out of the way that we must call upon the processes of reflective abstraction and similar processes which can be found in the organic field.

Reflective abstraction is one isolated case, connected with logico-mathematical knowledge, of some very general processes that are to be found throughout living creation and which might be called "convergent reconstructions with overtaking."

Where unorganized creatures are concerned, but in those sectors where the phenomena are obeying a regular historical evolution, constructions often repeat themselves down to the last detail. This is what caused my mentor E. Argand to invent (or rather to "discover," to use the definitions laid down in subsection 4 above) "the stages of Alpine embryology": the drawing closer of two continents (Wegener) compresses the sea between them (in the case of the Alps, this was the Thetys or the old Mediterranean) and thus compels the layers of earth which occupy its bed to overflow onto the nearest land mass; this causes the the formation of a mountain chain, which batters against the old insular shelves (in the case of the Alps, these were the Lercynian shelves). Thus, there are three stages in this whole process: (a) the formation of a chain of volcanic islands alongside the land mass; (b) the overflowing of the chain onto the land mass, along with the whole length of its coast; (c) the aftermath of the overflow in the shape of layers of overthrusts, etc.; and finally (d) the battering against the insular shelves

(Pelvoux, Mont Blanc, the Aare mass), stabilization, followed by various kinds of erosion. Now what interests us here is the fact that these stages recur all over the world; the islands of Japan are new Alps in process of formation (stage *a*) and the Cordillera of the Andes a later stage (*b*). However, the difference between these stages and the stages of living processes is that the former are a series of similar constructions brought about by the application of the same law in situations of a comparable kind; there are stages but no organic development (because there is no integration and no homeorhesis), and there is repetition of these stages but no direct or collateral kinship between the series, which are causally and genetically independent. In the case of the repetition of a biological development, on the other hand, there are "reconstructions," not similar constructions, and such reconstructions are "convergent" in the biological sense of the term, that is, implying (1) some analogy between the formative processes and (2) a common source, however distant. Furthermore, this reconstruction will result in some overtaking, sometimes slight, sometimes appreciable, which may prove negative or abortive.

Starting from a definition such as this, we can find as many examples as we like of reconstructions of this kind. By relation to the preceding generation, each new one includes an ontogenetic reconstruction capable of slight adaptive overtakings (or regressions). The law of ontophylogenetic "recapitulation" (or law of patrogony), which is valid by and large, is a generalized expression of these reconstructions. The "convergence" phenomena, properly speaking (as witness the case of the eye in both cephalopods and vertebrates) are striking examples of analogous structural constructions from a common source which in no way foretold their formation. The development of the nervous system in relation to that of the entire organism is evidence of a transfer of functions with comparable reconstruction (cf. the analogies pointed out by Bertalanffy in connection with equipotentiality). In a general way, all organic reequilibrations, especially those containing differentiated regulation systems, show a common tendency to achieve progress in adaptation by means of convergent reconstructions.

If this is so, it goes without saying that the various hierarchical echelons which lead from genetic, to embryogenetic, to physiological or functional organization, and finally to behavior, and from the elementary, hereditary, or acquired to the higher form of knowledge, cannot possibly be distributed in simple linear series but consist, generally speaking, or more or less complex series of "convergent reconstructions with overtakings," and these overtakings vary a great deal.

As a result, when thought or representative intelligence begins to function, it starts from zero in its conceptual content, though not, of course, in its sensorimotor or perceptual data. It is, however, functionally prepared for, not only by sensorimotor and nervous coordinations, but more important still, by all that the nervous functioning—constantly at work in sensorimotor and representational development—has itself inherited from organic functioning in general. It must, indeed, be clearly understood that the generalized organizational conditions that we proposed in point 1 above as a possible basis for logico-mathematical structurations are not, chronologically speaking, initial ones but generalized and at work all the time. This being so, the mechanisms determined by them are perfectly adapted to channeling the sensorimotor coordinations, themselves based on nervous coordinations, and hence to serving as objects for the reflective abstractions which characterize thought.

To sum up, logico-mathematical structures are thus a much closer extension of the general organizing functioning found in every living structure than at first seemed to be the case. There is sufficient evidence of this in the simple fact that this functioning operates in action and in the nervous system just as it does in any other organization, and in the fact that reflective abstraction has no positive beginning but goes back to the "convergent reconstructions with overtakings" that are common to all organized constructions.

Section 21. Acquired Knowledge and Physical Experiment

The third main type of knowledge is that which begins by learning and which achieves its highest expression in what is commonly known as experimental knowledge. In this context we are referring to "physical" experiment as against logico-mathematical experiment (see section 20, subsection 2) simply in order to express the fact that the information, in this case, is obtained from the object and not by action; it is, however, obvious that this object may just as well be the action or consciousness of an external object, insofar as the information is obtained by observation or experiment (physical, biological, or psychological) and not by reflective abstraction; in other words, it is obtained by logical construction or convergent reconstruction of a formal kind (at varying degrees).

1. Experimental Knowledge and Logico-mathematical Knowledge

Experimental knowledge constitutes a considerable part of man's cognitive work, and it is quite as important as logico-mathematical knowledge. Being exogenous in origin (even in the case of psychological introspection,[39] which is unreliable anyway), it is something quite distinct from logico-mathematical knowledge and yet is always inextricably bound up in it, for the following reasons.

The first reason is that logico-mathematical knowledge, although it originates in the general coordinations of action, is always knowledge of an object, because action, in the normal course of events, does not take place in vacuo but is always applied to an object. Even if we go back to the most generalized forms of living organization, there is no functioning without objects, for this organization is open and dynamic, an organization of exchanges between the living entity and its environment. No doubt "pure" mathematics does exist, quite free of any actual application, but it is nonetheless related to objects of some kind and remains essentially an instrument for adaptation to the real world even if it goes beyond it (and because it goes beyond it).

The second reason is vital to the understanding of acquired knowledge and physical experiment. It was seen (section 18) that elementary learning is only possible by reliance on innate behavior, just as conditioning relies on reflexes and so on. At the level of thought, where acquired knowledge is based upon physical experiment of a more elaborate kind, representation no longer unfolds within a hereditary framework, since there are no innate ideas, but it demands—as a necessary and previous condition—a logico-mathematical framework outside which there can be no representation at any observable level, that is, with classifications, perception of relationships or correspondence, measuring, and so on. This is a highly instructive fact, with respect both to the nature of logico-

39. For in introspection, the subject as seen constitutes an external object in relation to the subject as cognitive, whatever "subjective" errors the latter may make.

mathematical structures and to that of physical experiment generally.

To begin with the former, the necessity for a logico-mathematical framework shows that logico-mathematical structures fill the same sort of role at the representational level as do hereditary frameworks at the initial learning stages. And this is no mere chance. Hereditary behavior implies, like every other organization, the use of the general organizing function which we found to be at the root of logical structures, and as we have seen (section 16), instinct itself presupposes the existence of some kind of logic which is isomorphic to that of sensorimotor behavior. It therefore follows automatically that at the levels at which there is no longer any hereditary framework to support the learning process, as is the case with representation and thought, there is then the possibility of— and indeed the necessity for—a logico-mathematical framework, since such a framework was inherent, in a more elementary functional form, in hereditary behavior at the lower levels.

But when we turn to physical experiment at however primitive a level, the necessity for such a framework is extremely significant, since it demonstrates the impossibility of "pure" experiment in the sense of a direct and immediate contact between subject and objects. To put it another way: any kind of knowledge about an object is always an assimilation into schemata, and these schemata contain an organization, however elementary, which may be logical or mathematical.

Even at the level of perception, cognitive contact with the object perceived is not just a recording or a mere "reading" of experience. Psychologists of the Gestalt school must be given credit for uncovering what they themselves call the "organization laws" of perception, which are, in essence, a sort of geometrization or construction of spatio-temporal and kinematic structures. Some of these psychologists, however, have tried to account for this geometrization by laws of field equilibrium, belonging to the physical world, before making any study of the subject's activities, and this has caused them to play down such activities as though the subject were simply being subjected to a determinism external to—and the source of—his own determinism. Nevertheless, if perceptual activities are analyzed in detail, especially the way in which they develop with age (a development which the logic of the Gestalt system was bound either to deny or to play down, since the laws of physical equilibrium are quite independent of the subject and of his age level), then, on the contrary, it becomes evident that perceptual organization and geometrization are formed by means of active and progressive relating of objects one to the other. There are simple relations of visual transfer of one element onto another; complex or multiplicative relations in the "transpositions" underlying the sense of proportion; relations of size and direction such as occur in "referring," which is the operation underlying perceptual coordinates; relations of compensation in constancies, and so on. Now relations are logical instruments, and to relate things to one another is a logical activity; in fact, it quickly becomes a logico-mathematical one (properties and coordinates), so that even at the perceptual level physical knowledge presupposes, as a necessity, the logico-mathematical framework discussed just above.

2. The Necessity of Logico-mathematical Frameworks

In the domain of experiment proper, especially that of controlled experiment, it is obvious, a fortiori, that no established fact can remain in its pure stage, in the way classical empiricism claims that the object makes a simple imprint on, or in, the subject, the imprint thus constituting a "copy." In other words, the problem in experimental knowledge is to choose between these two possible concepts of copy-knowledge or assimilation-knowledge.

Now once physical experiment has ceased to be exclusively perceptual (and even before that, since perception is dependent on perceptual "activities"), it inevitably implies the intervention of actions, since the subject can have no knowledge of objects except by acting on them. To "establish" what a weight is, one has to perform the muscular action of feeling it, and, in so doing, one sets up a balance which supplies the weight by means of a collection of metric relations. Even at the stage of immediate experience, therefore, there is always the unavoidable necessity of actions in order to get at the properties of the object. As for the sort of controlled experiment which is aimed at discovering the laws underlying these properties, even more action by the subject is involved, since such laws are more objective. At the macrophysical level, such actions are indispensable if one wishes to dissociate the separate factors and study their effects in isolation, because to dissociate the factors is to modify the bare phenomenon by an action and to encase its elements in forms whose active artificiality alone ensures objectivity. There is no contradiction in terms here, since experimental action is oriented, as we shall see, in the direction of logico-mathematical decentering, whereas the error or subjective illusion corrected by such experiment is brought about by centering upon immediate appearance. At the microphysical level, the intervention of the analyst is still more vital for the understanding of the phenomenon, but at that stage the intervention exerts an even stronger modifying influence, so that it becomes difficult to separate the "observable" into that which depends on the action and that which depends on the object. This being so, action does not exclude objectivity; on the contrary, it is conducive to it, since it is extended into mathematical operators whose coordinations provide laws independent of the subject as individual ego. At the level of astronomy, where the celestial mechanism in the Newtonian system appeared to owe nothing to the action of the subject except—and this is essential—in the form of measurements, the theory of relativity has shown that objectivity is achieved through a coordination of the measurements supplied by different observers and at different scales of speed. In that case, measurement appears to be a much more complex action than it would be without these coordinations. Measurement is the application of a number to size, but this application entails the dividing up of a continuum into units and the methodical shifting of the chosen unit onto the other parts; in other words, a whole series of actions or operations enriching the immediate datum with new relationships. In the case of relative measurement, meters and clocks must also be coordinated at various spatio-temporal distances, which requires signal control, that is, a system of actions all the more complex by reference to the raw datum (a datum only produced by a single observer), since their coordination in terms of speeds shows that the units of spatial or temporal distance do not remain invariant but are involved in a system of covariations which is determined by the coordination of the actions peculiar to all the various observers.

To sum up, physical knowledge is never a "copy" but must, of necessity, be an assimilation into action schemata of growing complexity. Now this assimilation must, also of necessity, be logico-mathematical in nature, primarily because the actions necessary for discovering the properties of the object and the phenomena are not isolated actions, however differentiated they may become by accommodation to the diversity and details of situations. Such actions are coordinated among themselves, and the general coordination of these actions is, in fact, the origin of logico-mathematical operations. That is why, for example, the actions involved in measurement are extended into measurement operations, and these operations at once become part of a "general measurement system" or of one of the variations on this system, be it Euclid's or Riemann's—in other words, a logico-mathematical structure. And that is why the actions of the nuclear physicist, however disturbing they may be, are extended into operators, the coordinations of which nevertheless make possible, not only the sort of calculation by which the most amazing predictions can be made, but a decentering of the subject, who then no longer intervenes as an individual or distorting subject but as an epistemic subject, the condition and instrument of objectivity.

The indissociable union of mathematics and physics has sometimes been grossly misunderstood. The Vienna Circle, with its logical positivism, tried to reduce physics to a collection of reports of data perceived, and mathematics to the role of a mere language giving exact expression to the matter contained in these reports. Against this, we must again remind ourselves, as we did earlier in this book, that in the first place perception itself is a geometric and logical organization. Next, the physicist is not like a newborn infant, limited to perceiving objects only (although the infant even at that stage is very active), for the physicist constantly acts, and the first thing he does is to transform objects and phenomena in order to get at the laws validating these transformations. Finally, mathematics, far from being a mere language, is the very instrument of structuration, coordinating those actions from the outset and then extending them into deductive and explanatory theories. Thus, the union of mathematics and physics is not one of sign and meaning but one of structuring activity and datum, which, without this activity, would remain chaotic, unintelligible, and, most important of all, full of subjective elements because it would be subject to the distorting and egocentric subjectivity of the ego as opposed to the activity of the epistemic subject.

For a biologist there is something extremely interesting about the fact that acquired or experimental knowledge cannot be obtained except within a logico-mathematical framework of a structuring kind, for it proves that the knowledge of environment and of objects which is so admirably attained by the human mind is only so attained by virtue of an extension of the organization's structures into the universe as a whole. To say that physical knowledge is an assimilation of the real world into logico-mathematical structures amounts, in fact, to affirming—if what was said in section 20 is true—that the organization belonging to a subject or to any living creature is a condition of exchanges with environment and cognitive exchanges, as we have seen, just as much as it is a condition of material and energy exchanges. In this respect, conceptual and operational "forms" appear yet again as the extension of organic "forms."

3. *The Harmony between Mathematics and the Real World*

This interpretation of physical knowledge, like the interpretation of logico-mathematical structures put forward in section 20, raises a problem that has been curiously neglected as to its biological aspect. How, in fact, are we to explain the harmony that exists between mathematics and the real world?

First, we must remember that this harmony is a real fact—and a surprising one at that. It must be emphasized at once that the entire world of reality can be expressed in mathematical terms and, a fortiori, in logical terms. There is no known physical phenomenon which has defied expression in mathematical form, and attempts that have been made to prove the contrary, such as Hegel's *Naturphilosophie*, have come to nothing. Biology still finds itself confronted by a succession of unknown forms, and some have concluded from this that there is a limit to what can be expressed in mathematical terms. However, before any decision is reached, we shall have to examine by what means such mysteries might be cleared up. Can an explanation be found that is intelligible although not mathematical? Philosophers think so, although no one has ever been able to give any epistemological proof that there is a kind of knowledge which can properly be called philosophical as distinct from scientific.[40] Or can there be an explanation which is intelligible just because it is logico-mathematical? Since setting oneself up as a prophet is a tricky business, I shall only say that, up to now, any rational, biological explanation of phenomena such as heredity and regulations has proved to be consistent with logico-mathematical models, and that, insofar as the arguments of the vitalists and finalists have any validity, this has been to the extent of their conformity to cybernetic models of which they themselves knew nothing and whose discovery

40. See J. Piaget, *Sagesse et illusions de la philosophie* (Paris: Presses Universitaires de France, 1965).

owes nothing to them. This only goes to show that the concept of finality as irreducible to mathematicization was, in fact, false. In the realm of psychology we are very far from being able to express things in any satisfactory mathematical form; yet very few psychologists are attracted to vitalism on account of the many ordinal processes and the way in which algebraic logic can be utilized. Generally speaking, mathematics today is taking a decidedly qualitative trend, and its involvement with isomorphisms and morphisms of all kinds has opened up such broad structuralist perspectives that there is apparently no field—human, biological, or physical—that cannot now be reduced to fairly elaborate mathematicization.

In the second place, a considerable and growing number of phenomena do seem to be deducible. For a long time, the main obstacle to this was the part attributed to chance, but ever since the theory of probability enabled us to realize that a collective stochastic phenomenon can be calculated even though certain events within it cannot be predicted, chance itself has become both assimilable and deducible. Thermodynamics and microphysics bear witness to this. On the other hand, there is one important field which resists deducibility, and it may even prove to do so for all time (we must retain the "may" lest we seem to be making prophecies): namely, the field of historical development. An authentic "history," such as that of the evolution of organized beings, does, in fact, contain a mixture of the inevitable and the random, but it does so precisely in the sense of individual events which could not be foreseen. Most important of all is the fact that history cannot repeat itself and cannot go backward. There is thus little likelihood of its providing any basis for deduction. On the other hand, to say history is not to be deduced does not mean that it cannot be reduced to logical terms after the event, and there are grounds for hope that this sui generis character of historical development may translate itself into a kind of logic, a specific one at that, which would be dialectical. It is true, of course, that so far no one has succeeded in formalizing a dialectical logic, so that such a concept is still open to discussion. But that is no reason for abandoning the project, for it would be interesting, for example, to establish what would be the outcome of a calculation of results that were dependent on the path followed in reaching them, and so forth.

On the other hand, if not everything is deducible, it should be noted, in the third place, that within the very wide sector of phenomena that are deducible, deduction sometimes takes place before and not after the experiment, that is, in anticipation. The best known examples of this are the discovery of Neptune by Leverrier, or the way in which the still-empty files in Mendeleev's classification theory were filled up after the revolution in contemporary physics. But even more striking and more common is the construction of purely abstract mathematical structures, which afterward serve as indispensable frameworks for physical phenomena, without having been intended as such beforehand. Well-known examples of this are Riemann's expression of space and Einstein's use of tensorial calculus, as well as the many geometric and algebraic models used in microphysics. The physical applications of the imaginary number are equally amazing.

These meeting points between mathematical deduction and physical reality, some of them anticipatory of, and others subsequent to, experiment, raise a vital problem which is of far-reaching importance both for epistemology and for biology. We say biology, not simply because the whole aim of this book is to emphasize the general parallelism between cognitive questions and solutions and biological questions and solutions, but because in this particular case there is a striking point of contact between the problem of the adaptation of mathematics to the real world and the general biological problem of adaptation and preadaptation.

The empiricist solution which, in biology, is the Lamarckian one, is altogether too facile, simply allowing that mathematics is born of physical experiment or constitutes a language evolved especially for describing it. In fact, this still leaves us with the need to explain why this language is so good that, unlike ordinary language, it can sometimes foretell something that has not yet been perceived. Still to be surmounted, however, are the difficulties of such a thesis, which were examined in section 20, subsection 1.

The old a priori solution, taken up again by D. Hilbert, amounts to a statement that mathematical intuitions are a priori simply because of "preestablished harmony" (Hilbert actually uses "preestablished" in a positive sense, not a critical one) between the existing frameworks and the experimental data which are to be shaped by them. This is the sort of thing that, in biology, is repeated by the vitalists and finalists, either explicitly or implicitly, and it is hardly necessary to point out yet again that it is not an answer. Konrad Lorenz's version of apriorism is more intelligible, since what he does is to interpret the adaptation of mathematics to the real world as the equivalent of an instinctive adaptation or even, as he says, of a morphological adaptation, just like hooves on horses or fins on fish, which develop in the embryo long before they are ever used. That random mutations and Darwinian selection should explain how hooves and fins come to be formed is conceivable, strictly speaking (although I myself do not believe it); but to explain on the basis of this model why Riemann's work on abstraction should have acquired a meaning in physics thanks to Einstein—that is endowing chance with remarkable intelligence and turning selection into an intentional choice capable of influencing, in a rather frightening way, the part that is still behind the scenes.

Let us get back, then, to the hypothesis put forward earlier that logico-mathematical structures owe their origin neither to physical experiment nor to instinctive or hereditary transmission but are derived by reflective abstractions from the general coordinations of action and, farther back still, from nervous coordinations, and so on back to the most widely generalized of the organizing functions in life. Since we have just seen that physical and experimental knowledge cannot possibly be established without some structuration and logico-mathematical framework, the simplest way to explain the harmony between these frameworks and their contents is, of course, to say that the contents act in return upon the frameworks and hence that the adaptation under discussion is carried out by means of progressive gropings, in other words, by an equilibration between the assimilation of the contents into the frameworks and the differentiating accommodations of the frameworks to the contents.

Such a concept, however, is tantamount to saying that logico-mathematical structures are not derived solely from the actions of the subject upon objects but also from the objects themselves, since physical experiment will gradually bring about modifications in them. This is, of course, possible, and, if it were so, my interpretation would need some rather basic revision. It would just be one of those unfortunate things that happen, but that is not the point. Only we must weigh the consequences carefully: to say that logico-mathematical structures undergo modification under the influence of physical experiment would simply mean that there is no difference, except a basic one of degree, between physics and mathematics, in which case both would be assimilated into a general knowledge which might be called logico-experimental.

Therefore, the only proper way to solve this problem is by epistemological analysis, making use especially of the historico-critical method, which is the only one capable of judging the real relationship between physicists and mathematicians (on condition, of course, that the task is entrusted to professionals in the respective disciplines and not to philosophers, who think themselves capable of judging such cases without any technical training, either logico-mathematical or in physics). Now we do have at least two decisive studies on this. The first, by A. Lichnerowicz, is a short chapter that he was kind enough to let me include in my work "Logique et connaissance scientifique"[41] and in which he puts forward his ideas on mathematics and reality as a "mathematician turned physicist," to quote his own words. The second is by S. Bachelard[42] and contains a very remarkable historico-critical study of this same problem, while fortunately remaining entirely independent of the phenomenological intentions to which Bachelard artificially links the problem. There is a complete convergence of views in these two articles, summarized as follows.

Physics deals with experimental problems and solves them as such, with the necessary help of adequate mathematical instruments. Next, experimental physics duplicates itself with a quest for explanation, which utilizes all available mathematical instruments in order to end up with a theory whereby phenomena can be deduced. This theory, however, still has to face the verdict of experiment: such is the part played by "theoretical physics," which is still a branch of physics, being subject to experiment, however mathematical its techniques may be. The problem, then, is to specify the relations between this kind of "theoretical physics" and so-called "mathematical physics," the object of which is to treat the problems of physics in a mathematical way (and in which, in fact, Lichnerowicz is a great expert). Now mathematical physics claims to be mathematical and can no longer be classed as a branch of physics because it no longer bases itself on experiment but reaches its conclusions by strictly deductive methods. In so doing, it often overlaps with physics and has a wider scope than either theoretical or experimental physics, although it never seeks to establish its proofs by reference to physics.

At once the question arises whether the truths of theoretical phys-

41. "Logique et connaissance scientifique," ed. J. Piaget, in *Encyclopédie de la Pléiade*.

42. S. Bachelard, *La conscience de rationnalité* (Paris: Presses Universitaires de France, 1958).

ics do not have some secret influence—dissimulated either on principle or out of theoretical hypocrisy—on mathematical physics. This might explain how mathematical physics comes to cover the same ground as theoretical physics, although it does go farther toward the realization of every possible structure but keeps within the same bounds in those spheres that concern phenomena in the real world. Indubitably, there must be some influence there. But the whole problem is to know whether this influence is psychological, that is, relating to the choice of problems and the interests dictated by these choices, or whether it is epistemological—that is, including a transfer of truth. Now physics certainly sets the mathematician some problems which would not occur to him if it were not for physics and which interest him on that account. But he assimilates these problems into questions of abstract structures and studies the properties and transformations of these structures as being mathematical and abstract. To the extent that the correspondence is successful, the mathematician still achieves nothing by "imitating" the physical data by means of his abstract structures; it is only by means of internal and endogenous recombinations that he can reach those data, borrowing nothing from the external "representations" which he integrates and reconstructs with full autonomy.

Any biologist reading this summary of analyses is bound to think of situations in which phenotypic variation precedes the appearance of a genotype that seems to be an imitation of it, which is sometimes called a phenocopy precisely in order to show that an active and endogenous imitation has taken place, not a mere transmission of external causal influences. Taking the model used in section 19, subsections 5 and 6, the genome is supposed, in the same way, to respond by recombinations or endogenous reequilibration to the problems set it by the environment.

But to get back to the question of the harmony between logico-mathematical structures and experiment, the mathematician's supposed independence of physics, even of theoretical physics, thus seems to preclude a solution simply of progressive accommodation. We must therefore look for something else. Now, if this harmony is not effected from without—that is, by some progressive adjustment of the mathematical framework and the experimental content in the course of the experiment itself, in the form of an exchange between subject and object or between organism and environment—then this must mean that the harmony was set up beforehand, not exactly preestablished, but within the organism at levels anterior or inferior to the general coordination of the actions affected the environment.

In fact, to suppose that the ultimate origin of the coordinations underlying logico-mathematical structures is to be found at the very center of the most highly generalized functioning of the living organization is itself a solution of a kind, insofar as it concerns the harmony between these coordinations or structures and the outer environment. The living organization, as Bertalanffy has never ceased to maintain, is an "open system," and, as we have seen (sections 11 and 12, propositions [1] and [4]), although it does not preclude the necessary presence of a cycle which, being a cycle, is of necessity closed, an open system means that each element within the cycle can only produce or support the element that succeeds it by dint of combining with previous elements. Thus, the living organization is the organization of an exchange system, and the term "organization" simply designates the internal aspect of a system which is in a state of perpetual adaptation. This is not to say that the organization is a mere replica of the environment, even if one admits that those characteristics which are transmitted by heredity are responses to the situations imposed by the environment. But it does mean that there is no organizing function, at whatever level, that does not harmonize with the environment; the harmony between mathematics and experience is just one example of this but a particularly interesting one. So to attribute logic and mathematics to the general coordinations of the subject's actions is not an idealistic overestimation of the part played by the subject; it is a recognition of the fact that, while the fecundity of the subject's thought processes depends on the internal resources of the organism, the efficacy of those processes depends on the fact that the organism is not independent of the environment but can only live, act, or think in interaction with it.

7

Conclusions: The Various Forms of Knowledge Seen as Differentiated Organs of the Regulation of Functional Exchanges with the External World

Having reached the end of our analysis, we shall find it useful here to take another look at our main hypothesis, as set out in section 3. What it amounts to is, on one hand, the supposition that cognitive mechanisms are an extension of the organic regulations from which they are derived, and, on the other, the supposition that these mechanisms constitute specialized and differentiated organs of such regulations in their interactions with the external world. In essence, chapters 3, 4, 5, and 6 of this book are an attempt to prove the first of these suppositions. Where the second one is concerned, all we have been able to do is to bring out certain elements of a possible verification; what remains to be done, therefore, is to coordinate these and develop them so as to reach the answer.

But before we tackle this final argument, certain introductory remarks may be of use, since the reader may have had the impression that we were pushing our analogies too far at certain points, for example, as between the synchronic processes of equilibrium or general structuration, and the diachronic processes of historical construction, or, more especially, between the endogenous factors, which, at certain points, we have emphasized almost exclusively, and the exogenous factors, to which some may think we have occasionally accorded exaggerated importance.

To deal with the first of these basic questions, one might be tempted to draw a distinction between the problems of evolution and development and the problems of synchronic organization, in relation, for example, to the analysis of "open systems" or of what we have called "general functioning" in every organism, which intervenes as a condition from hereditary transmission onward. Now, it is essential to point out very clearly from the beginning that no synchronic biological system, however dependent on existing equilibrium conditions, can be independent of history, because it is itself a product of evolution. Reciprocally, no development, either phyletic or individual, can be independent of a progressive organization or, therefore, of equilibrations. There are certainly other spheres, such as linguistics or economics, in which the opposition between the synchronic and the diachronic is much more clearcut because there one is dealing with "arbitrary" symbols or with values of temporary efficacy, whose significance or sum total depends far more upon present equilibrium than on their past history. But, as has been shown elsewhere in this book, the closer the realities under consideration come to structures, whether normative (as with cognitive structures) or merely dominant and comprising an opposition between the "normal" and the aberrant or even the pathological (as in the case of living things), the slighter the opposition between the diachronic and synchronic factors becomes, just because such structures have a tendency to be conserved in time. To talk about conservation within a reality that is functioning, not static, is, ipso facto, to imply continuous reconstruction and construction of a kind in which even the functional invariants are constantly related to development.

Thus, the fundamental reality about living things is constituted neither by timeless structures, standing outside history or dominating it like equilibrated organization forms with permanent conditions, nor by a historical succession of chances or crises like a series of disequilibria without equilibrations. It consists, rather, of continuous processes of autoregulation implying both disequilibria and a constant equilibration dynamism. All that needs to be said here is that at all levels, whether historical stages or the echelons of some organizational hierarchy, we find the simultaneous intervention of exogenous factors, causing disequilibria but also setting off "responses," and endogenous factors, producing these responses and acting as equilibration agents.

This means that anyone who sees, in the present study, a belief in the systematic primacy of one or the other of these factors will have failed to understand me, my central idea being constantly that of interaction. If, however, one were to take some passage or other in the preceding chapters out of its context, one might have the opposite impression or else an impression of oscillation rather than of a continual quest for synthesis. In this connection, it will be helpful to note, before going any further in this summing up, that the main difficulty about what I have been trying to do is that I am addressing two kinds of reader. Psychologists, with their common-sensical approach, lay all the stress on learning factors and environmental influence, forgetting, when it comes to cognitive functions, the implications of modern biology and failing to see the contradiction between biological mutationism and epistemological Lamarckism (integral empiricism). Thus, when addressing myself to them, I had to emphasize the endogenous factors, especially in connection with progressive equilibration and the logico-mathematical structures which are largely dependent upon it. Biologists, in their turn, have their own kind of common sense, which takes no account of epistemology or thought processes and likes to treat the human brain as the mere product of selection, just like horses' hooves and fishes' fins; with them in mind, I had to remember that the harmony between mathematics and physical reality is not all that easy to conceive, so that perhaps we have to recast our models of interaction between environment and the organization itself. It is to be hoped that biologists and psychologists will collaborate in future, so that together they may uncover the secrets of the organizing organization, once they have discovered those of the already organized organization.

Section 22. The Functions Proper to the Acquisition of Knowledge

During our study of the functional connections and partial structural isomorphisms between cognitive and organic functions, we noted the existence of a remarkable number of points of contact. We also saw, however, that there were a number of differences which demonstrated the fact that knowledge, too, fulfills functions proper to itself. Indeed, to deny this would be unthinkable, for if the organism were self-sufficient without the aid of instinct, learning, or intelligence, this would be an indication of some radical separation between life and knowledge, since cognitive mechanisms undoubtedly exist. It might be possible to recognize this separation from various metaphysical points of view, but it would raise insoluble difficulties for any epistemology which was aimed simply at explaining why science can come to grips with the real world.

1. Behavior, the Extension of Environment, and the Closing up of the "Open System"

If one is to base one's conclusions on the elementary data of ethology, by far the greatest part of the knowledge that can be had from animals is of a "knowing how" type, utilitarian and practical. The instinct is always at the service of the three fundamental needs of food, protection against enemies, and reproduction. If, with migration or various modes of social organization, instinct seems to pursue secondary ends, they are only secondary as being interests grafted onto the three main ones and still dependent upon them, so that in the last resort they are subordinated to the survival of the species and, as far as possible, of the individual.

The elementary forms of perceptual or sensorimotor learning do not emerge from a functional framework of this kind, and the same is true of a great deal of practical or sensorimotor intelligence. However, in the latter field, one would probably have to admit that, in the case of mammals and particularly of anthropoids, there is a slight advance beyond this in the direction of a pleasure in understanding for understanding's sake, although this may be functional too. We do, in fact, know that the young mammal plays, and that this play is not, as K. Groos tried to prove, simply an instinctive exercise but a general one of all the kinds of behavior possible at any given level, without any utilitarian purpose or consummation at the time. Now play is only one pole of the functional exercises which take place during an individual's development, and the other pole is nonplayful exercise in which the young subject "learns how to learn" (Harlow),[1] not only in the context of play but in that of

---

1. Cf. Butler's experiment, suggested by Harlow, in which the only external aid used in training well-fed young monkeys to discriminate between things, was to let them look, when they were successful, through the window of their shuttered cage and thus satisfy their curiosity (with no relation to the discrimination called for).

cognitive adaptation. One of my children, at about one year old, who had succeeded by chance in getting a toy he wanted through the bars of his playpen when the toy was too big to go through horizontally and so had to be turned vertically, was not at all satisfied by this chance success. He put the toy out again and began all over again until he "understood" what was being done. No doubt this kind of disinterested knowing is equally possible in monkeys.

But whether exclusively utilitarian or attaining advances beyond "knowing how" to "understanding," knowledge in animals is evidence of a definite and particular function, like survival or feeding or reproducing in their organic aspects, properly speaking; it is the function of the extension of the environment, discussed in section 14, subsection 1. To seek food, instead of drawing it out of the soil or the air as plants do, is in itself an extension of one's environment. To seek out a female and engage in furthering one's species is giving reproduction a greater spatiotemporal extension than the mere physiological function allows. To explore for exploration's sake, without any immediate need (as the rats did in Blodgett's experiment about "latent learning"), right up to "learning for the sake of learning," as can be foreseen at the level of sensorimotor intelligence—this too is a further extension of the available environment.

It is clear that, at later stages, the mere fact of having elaborated instruments of intelligent knowing, even if this knowing only began with a utilitarian purpose, sets up a new functional situation, since all organs tend to develop and feed themselves for their own ends, which accounts for the basic cognitive needs of understanding and inventing. These needs, however, lead to an ever increasing extension of the environment—this time the sum total of the objects of knowledge.

We can, then, express in biological terms this slow—though, with man, more and more accelerated—extension of the environment accessible first to vital needs and then to truly cognitive needs, by relating it to the basic traits of the living organization. And organism, Bertalanffy tells us, is an "open system," by which he means precisely that the organism only succeeds in preserving its form through a continuous flow of exchanges with the environment. Now, an open system is a system that is perpetually threatened, and so it is not for nothing that the basic aspects of survival, feeding, and reproduction are extended into behavior whose result is the extension of the usable environment. This extension must, then, be translated into a language which expresses its effective functioning; it is essentially a search for the means to close the system simply because it is too "open." From the probabilistic point of view, which is the only valid one in this case, the risk adhering to the open system is the fact that its immediate environment or frontier does not supply the elements necessary for its survival. On the other hand, if the system constitutes a limit which is constantly sought for but never attained, this does not mean that the primary needs of food, protection, and reproduction are limitless; the truth is quite the other way. What it does mean is that, with the invention of the various behaviors used in the quest for means to satisfy these needs, thanks to a slight extension of the original environment, the cognitive regulations of these behaviors sooner or later produce a limitless extension of the system. There are two reasons for this.

The first concerns the probability of encounter with the desired elements (food or sex) or the dreaded ones (protection). So long as the living creature does not possess differentiated sensory organs, external events only become of concern at moments of immediate contact and cease to exist for it as soon as they are at a distance. Thus, its only needs are momentary ones, extinguished as soon as satisfied, recurring only later in the course of a periodic cycle of greater or lesser length. On the other hand, as soon as a perceptual regulation appears and olfactory or visual organs signal the distant approach of food or danger, needs are modified by this very extension; even if the appetite is satisfied for the time being, the absence of food that can be seen or smelt becomes worrying, as being a modification of the probabilities of occurrence. This will create a new need in the shape of a need for seeking food even thought there is no compelling need for an immediate meal. In the same way, to catch sight of enemies, at even a relatively safe distance, arouses a new need for vigilance and alertness. In other words, the appearance of a perceptual control leads to its improvement as a functional consequence, and this improvement leads to an extension of the environment with no possibility of the closure of the "open system" at that elementary level. It should be noted, moreover, that a general extension process of this kind is built up already on the organic plane, before there is any sensory control. This is the case with the dissemination of seeds in vegetative sexual reproduction, a fine example of spontaneous extension without cognitive regulation; what would it be like if some perceptual control made it possible for the plant to get feedback information of the poor success rate of this kind of propagation?

2. Behavior and Cognitive Regulations

The second reason for the extension of environment in order to close the "open system"—which, however, constantly pushes the limits of this closure farther back—is the progress of the cognitive regulations in their internal mechanism itself. This brings us up against an essential point as to the nature and method of development of the processes by which knowledge is acquired.

Let there be a physiological cycle of some kind $(A \times A') \to (B \times B') \to \ldots (Z \times Z') \ldots (A \times A') \to$ (prop. 1), in which $A, B, \ldots Z$ represent the elements of the organism, and $A', B', \ldots Z'$ the elements of the environment with which they inevitably interact. One can then schematize the intervention of a cognitive mechanism at its inception in the form of a regulation which reveals the presence of some external element, informs the corresponding A organs of it, and thus intervenes in the $A \to B$ process by facilitating its unfolding.

Thus, from the outset, cognitive reactivity has a part to play in regulation and serves to facilitate, reinforce, moderate, compensate, or otherwise control the physiological process. It is, however, obvious that this elementary reactivity, which may be evidenced in the form of tropisms or faintly differentiated reflexes, contains, just because it is a regulatory mechanism, possibilities and even exigencies of unlimited development, because the very nature of a regulation enables it to bring about its autocorrection by dint of regulating its regulations. In the case of the elementary pattern given above, the feedback from A' to A, which includes some system of signs to A', and indeed to A (afference and effection), brings in its train two sorts of possible improvement of behavior regulations to the second power, while physiological or internal regulations can improve the $A \to B$ process. First, there can be refinements in the recording of A', such as various conditionings which assimilate new signals or indices into the original perceptual schemata and thus are constantly widening the perceptual scope by means of regulations differentiating the initial overall assimilation. Second, and more important, there are refinements in the reaction schemata intervening in *A,* and this is where new regulations prove possible in an uninterrupted series, a very striking example of which is the sensorimotor development of the human infant.

Here we see a whole succession of increasingly complex acts built up on the initial reflex schemata of sucking, grasping with the hand, and moving the eyes. Of these the two general principles are the accommodation of assimilation schemata, which leads to their differentiation, and, more especially, the reciprocal assimilation of the schemata (vision, prehension, etc.), which leads to their coordination. Now, to look at this from the point of view which concerns us here, the two basic lessons to be learned from this pre-sensorimotor development of the intelligence are (a) that the progress observed is due to regulations of regulations entailing the exercise of cognitive functions for their own sake, quite apart from any utilitarian purpose or originally strictly biological one such as feeding, and (b) that this progress therefore postpones indefinitely the "closure" of the system that is open to the environment.

The fact that progress is made by regulations of regulations is immediately apparent in the case of differentiation by means of accommodation of assimilation schemata. In effect, this accommodation is carried out by gropings, and these are a prime example of feedbacks in which an action is corrected in terms of its results. On the other hand, this groping regulation does not take place as an absolutely new development but from within a previous framework, thus from acquired assimilation schemata or reflexes, and these initial schemata constitute the basic regulation whose differentiation is brought about by an additional regulation.

As for the coordination of schemata by reciprocal assimilation, here again there are regulations regulating previous regulations, and these second-power regulations are of particular importance, since they tend toward operations (see section 14). In fact, a schema coordination is a process at once pro- and retroactive, because it leads to a new synthesis by modifying, in turn, the schemata thus coordinated.

This internal development in the mechanism of cognitive regulations therefore presupposes the exercise of them, that is to say, the formation of a series of new interests which are no longer confined to the initial interests which were aroused simply by the functioning of the system. These interests are the functional expression of the very mechanism of cognitive assimilation, but, as again we have just seen, they are so by direct extension of the original assimilations. The extension of environment brought about in this way, therefore, concerns the environment in the biological sense of the sum of the stimuli which are of interest to the physiological cycle of the organization, as well as the cognitive environment as the sum of the objects challenging knowledge.

Now this new extension of the environment is equally incapable of closing the "open system," since it is always at the mercy of whatever may happen, in other words, of the chances that may arise in the experience of the subject. It is only when it comes to representation or thought, which speeds up the multiplication of spatio-temporal distances characteristic of the subject's field of action and of his comprehension, that some possibility of closure comes in sight. But then closure assumes a collection of interindividual or social exchanges as well as the exchanges with the individual environment, and this problem will have to be faced later on.

3. Organic and Cognitive Equilibrium

If the first essential function of cognitive mechanisms is the progressive closure of the "open system" of the organism by means of an unlimited extension of the environment (certainly an essential function in the light of the processes involved, even if—or especially if—it never actually achieves completion from a static point of view), then this function entails a whole series of others.

The second function to be borne in mind is of supreme importance because it appertains to the equilibration mechanisms of the system. The living organization is essentially an autoregulation. If what we have just observed is true, then the development of the cognitive functions does indeed seem, according to our main hypothesis, to be the setting up of specialized organs of regulation in the control of exchanges with the environment—exchanges that are initially physiological and have to do with matter and energy, and then exchanges of a purely functional kind, that is to say those involved with the functioning of actions or behavior. But if differentiated organs are formed, are their own regulations identical to those of the organism? In other words, are the equilibrium forms attained the same in both cases?

Everything said in this book leads to the answer yes and no. They are the same regulations or the same forms of equilibrium in the sense that the cognitive organization is an extension of the vital organization and so introduces some equilibration into those sectors where the organic equilibrium remains insufficient both in its scope (as has just been seen) and even in what it achieves. However, cognitive regulations and equilibrium differ from vital equilibrium in that they succeed where the latter fails.

To start with the evolution of knowledge itself, at first sight we might think ourselves confronted with a phenomenon of exactly comparable type. Leaving out of account the instincts and the elmentary kinds of learning, in all their diversity, the evolution of human knowledge does not always give us the impression of a coherent development in which each new accommodation caused by experiment is written into some assimilating framework of a permanent kind, with no opposition, and then either widens or merely differentiates that framework. There is, however, an exception, and it is the one which has been most difficult to integrate into the usual biological systems: the major exception of logico-mathematical structures, extremely important in itself, and all the more so because such structures produce the chief assimilatory schemata utilized in experimental knowledge. Logico-mathematical structures do, in fact, present us with an example, to be found nowhere else in creation, of a development which evolves without a break in such a way that no new structuration brings about the elimination of those preceding it; the earlier ones may be said to be unadapted to such and such an unforeseen situation, but only in the sense that they proved insufficient to solve some new problem and not that they are contradicted by the very terms of this problem, as may be the case in physics.

Thus, as has already been emphasized, logico-mathematical structures involve a sui generis equilibrium situation with regard to the relationship between assimilation and accommodation. On one hand, they appear to be a continuous construction of new assimilation schemata: assimilation of a previous structure into a new one, which integrates it, and assimilation of the experimental datum into the structures thus set up. But, on the other hand, logico-mathematical structures give evidence of a permanent accommodation, insofar as they are modified neither by the newly constructed structures (except, of course, by being improved thereby) nor by the experimental data whose assimilation they make possible. It is true that new data from physical experiment may set mathematicians some unforeseen problems and thus lead to the invention of theories aimed at assimilating them; but in such a case the invention is not based on accommodation as a physical concept is, but, as we have seen, it is an integral derivation from previous structures or schemata, though at the same time accommodating itself to the realities of the new situation.

One might, then, put forward an interpretation of a rather daring kind, which does, nonetheless, appear to contain a profound biological truth if it is admitted, in accordance with our conclusions of section 20, that the primary source of the coordinations of actions on which mathematics are based is to be sought within the general laws of the organization. We suggest that the equilibrium between assimilation and accommodation which is brought about by logico-mathematical structures constitutes a state—mobile and dynamic and, at the same time, stable—aspired to unsuccessfully by the succession of forms, at least where behavior forms are concerned, throughout the course of the evolution of organized creatures. Whereas this evolution is characterized by an uninterrupted succession of disequilibria and of reequilibrations, logico-mathematical structures do, in fact, attain permanent equilibrium despite the constantly renewed constructions which characterize their own evolution.

This brings us back to the problem of "vection" or "progress," which was raised at the end of section 8. The chief characteristic of the vection which seems to be evinced by organic evolution is a remarkable alliance between two features that are antipathetic at first sight, although their working together is a necessary factor in the adaptations achieved at the higher levels. The first of these was brought out principally by Schmalhausen: the ever-deepening integration making the development processes more and more autonomous in relation to the environment. The second, stressed by Rensch and Julian Huxley, is the increasing "opening" of possibilities of actions upon the environment and, consequently, insertion into wider and wider environments.

It is obvious, in the first place, that these two interdependent aspects are to be found yet again in the development of knowledge; insofar as human intelligence uses logico-mathematical structures as an instrument of integration that is more and more independent of experiment, it achieves an ever greater conquest of the environment on which it experiments. But in this connection again, cognitive structures overtake organic ones by extending them, and this because of the very nature of the form taken by their equilibration—a common nature but, as has just been seen, carried on in the cognitive domain to forms which organic equilibrium can never achieve. Where vection is concerned, the difference is shown in the following way. Progress in integration, as Schmalhausen emphasized, is only concerned with the sort of integration that is, as it were, existing now, or synchronic, which means that it always has to be reconstituted in every new group without integrating the entire phyletic past as subsystems that are both conserved and overtaken. (To give a concrete example of this, mammals lost a part of their reptile characteristics in becoming mammals.) On the contrary, integration, as found in cognitive evolution, has the unique quality, as we have just seen, not only of existing now but of integrating the whole body of previous structures as subsystems into the integration now taking place. This integration, amazingly both diachronic and synchronic at the same time, is carried out in mathematics without disturbance of any kind, for, in mathematics, "crises" merely mean growth, and the only contradictions in it are temporary. In the field of experimental knowledge, however, a new theory may contradict those that have gone before, but it is noteworthy that a new theory always aims at the maximum integration of the past, so that the best theory is, once again, that which integrates all the preceding ones and simply adds on to this integration such retroactive corrections as may be necessary.

4. Dissociation of Forms and Conservation

This victory, however, is due to another specific characteristic of the cognitive functions as compared to the forms of living organization: the possible dissociation of forms and contents (section 11, subsection 2). An organic form is inseparable from the matter organized within it and is only suited, in any particular case, to a limited and clearly determined body of matter whose eventual modification will entail a change of form. This sort of situation is again found (given the continuity linking the living to the cognitive organization) in the case of elementary forms of knowledge, such as sensorimotor and perceptual schemata, although these may be much more highly generalized than the countless forms of the living organization. But, as the intelligence develops, operational schemata also become very generalized, although at the level of concrete operations they are still attached to their content as a structuration is to structured matter, when the former only acts approximately without sufficient deductive mobility. But with hypothetico-deductive operations, by a system of all possible combinations of propositions, a formal logic can emerge in the form of an organizing structure applicable to any content whatever. This is what makes possible the constitution of "pure" mathematics as a construction of forms of organization, ready to organize everything, but from time to time organizing nothing, insofar as it becomes dissociated from its application! Here again we are confronted with a biological situation which would be unthinkable in the organic domain, where micro-organisms are seen to "transduce" a genetic message from one species to another, but in the form of content or matter, and where genetic "transduction" has yet to be seen affecting the organization alone as a form dissociated from all substance!

Now this purifying of form achieves, in the cognitive domain, successes that are constantly being sought after, so to speak, in the organic domain, but never fully attained. Emphasis was laid in section 11 on the analogies between the conservation of biological forms, which is so evident in the regulating autoconservation of the genome, and the exigencies of conservation found in the various forms of intelligence, starting from the sensorimotor type (for example, the schema of the permanence of objects) and on up to operational conservations. The reader may get the impression, as often in reading this book, that I am making an artificial comparison between quasi-physical systems on one hand and normative or ideal ones on the other. But since the time that a clearer view emerged of the essential nature of the regulation pertaining to elementary cognitive functions (see above, subsection 2) and the way in which the regulations become operations (section 14), my comparison has become more easily acceptable, since organic conservation is, in fact, brought about by regulatory mechanisms. However, these analogies we have been talking about lead to one important difference, and this is precisely what interests us here: organic conservations are never anything more than approximate. This is the case, too, with preoperational cognitive forms (perceptual constancies, etc.), whereas only the operational conservations of the intelligence are binding and "necessary," on account of the dissociation of forms and contents that has just been noted.

Conservation is closely linked to operational reversibility, which is its source and evinces, moreover, the particular form of equilibration attained by logico-mathematical structures. Here we have certainly reached the crux of the differences which, at the heart of their analogies, distinguish the constructive work of intellectual operations from organic transformations. The profound analogy is, we have seen, that both of them have constantly to struggle against the irreversibility of events and the decay of energy and information systems. Again, both of them succeed in their struggle by means of elaborating their organized and equilibrated systems, the principle of which is compensation for deviations and errors. Thus, as soon as there are regulations of any homeostasis, genetic or physiological, there is a fundamental tendency to reversibility, the outcome of which is the approximate conservation of the system. Whatever solutions, as yet undecisive, may eventually be found to the problem of the anti-chance function which is necessary both to organization and to evolution (with the exception of Carnot's principle and the various attempts at conciliating this), it does, in fact, remain true that an autoregulatory system includes actions directed in two opposite ways, and that the progress of this approximate reversibility can be followed during the development of cognitive regulations. But, as was pointed out above—and is generally the outcome of the interplay between reflective abstractions and convergent reconstructions with overtakings, the overtakings that mark the progress of each stage in relation to the preceding one are more dependent on regulations of regulations—which means on a reflexive fining down of the system or of the controls superimposed—than on a simple horizontal extension. It is thus that the "operations" mechanism of thought is something more than a mere extension of regulations at a lower stage and marks a kind of transition up to the point (see section 14) at which strict reversibility is constituted when the retroactive feedback action becomes an "inverse operation" and thus guarantees an exact functional equivalence between the two possible directions of construction.

5. Social Life and the General Coordinations of Action

The most remarkable aspect of the way in which human knowledge is built up, as compared with the evolutionary transformations of the organism and such forms of knowledge as are accessible to animals, is that it has a collective as well as an individual nature. One can, of course, see this characteristic faintly sketched out in a few animal species, notably the chimpanzee. But the novel aspect of it where man is concerned is that external or educative transmission, as opposed to the hereditary or internal transmission of instincts, has culminated in the sort of organization that has been able to engender civilizations.

It was noted in section 6 at the end of point 1, that even though two sorts of development have to be recognized—one organic (belonging to a single organism) and the other genealogical (including filiation trees, either social or genetic)—yet the history of human knowledge unites these two developments in one whole; ideas, theories, schools of thought are engendered in genealogical order, and trees can be constructed which represent their structural filiations. But these structures are integrated into a single intellectual organism to such a point that the succession of seekers is comparable, as Pascal said, to one man continuously learning throughout time.

Human societies have been viewed in turn as the result of individual initiative perpetuated by imitation, like totalities shaping individuals from outside or as complex systems of interaction, whose products are individual action—always part and parcel of some more or less important sector of the group—as well as the whole group constituting the system of these interactions. In the realm of knowledge, it seems obvious that individual operations of the intelligence and operations making for exchanges in cognitive cooperation are one and the same thing, the "general coordination of actions" to which we have continually referred being an interindividual as well as an intraindividual coordination because such "actions" can be collective as well as executed by individuals. Here again, we return to the observations made about "population" in terms of genetics (section 19, subsection 4), and so the question whether logic and mathematics are essentially individual or social attainments loses all meaning; the epistemological subject constructing them is both an individual, though decentered in relation to his private ego, and the sector of the social group decentered in relation to the constraining idols of the tribe. This is because these two kinds of decentering both manifest the same intellectual interactions or general coordinations of action of which knowledge is constituted.

The result of this, then, and it is the last fundamental difference we shall have to point out between biological and cognitive organizations, is that the most generalized forms of thought, those that can be dissociated from their content, are, by that very fact, forms of cognitive exchange or of interindividual regulation, as well as being produced by the common functioning which is a necessary part of every living organization. Of course, from the psychogenetic point of view, these interindividual or social (and nonhereditary) regulations constitute a new fact in relation to the thought processes of the individual—which, without them, would be subject to all the egocentric distortions—and a necessary condition for the formation of a decentered epistemological subject. However, from the logical point of view, such higher regulations are nonetheless dependent upon the conditions of any general coordination of actions and thus become part, once more, of the common biological foundation.

Section 23. Organic Regulations and Cognitive Regulations

This collective overtaking of forms constructed originally on the basis of the living organization presents the right framework for the conclusions that must now be drawn from our discussion. The hypothesis still to be justified is that cognitive functions constitute a specialized organ for regulating exchanges with the external world, although the instruments by which they do so are drawn from the general forms of the living organization.

1. Life and Truth

It may be said that to talk of the necessity of a differentiated organ falls short of the meaning we are trying to convey, since the property of knowledge is the attainment of truth, whereas the property of life is simply the quest for survival. While we may not know exactly what life is, we know still less about the meaning of cognitive "truth." There is a sort of general agreement that it is something more than a faithful copy of the world of reality for the very good reason that such a copy could not possibly be made, since only the copy could supply us with the knowledge of the model being copied, and, moreover, such knowledge is necessary for the copy to be made. Attempts to make this copy theory acceptable have only resulted in simple phenomenalism, in which the subjectivity of the ego is perpetually interfering with the perceptual datum—a theory which itself betrays the inextricable mixture of subject and object.

If the true is not a copy, then it must be an organization of the real world. But an organization due to what subject? If this subject is merely a human one, then we shall be in danger of extending egocentrism into a sort of anthropo- or even socio-centrism, with minimal gain. As a result, all philosophers in search of an absolute have had recourse to some transcendental subject, something on a higher plane than man and much higher than "nature," so that truth, for them, is to be found way beyond any spatiotemporal and physical contingencies, and nature becomes intelligible in an intemporal or eternal perspective. But then the question is whether one can possibly jump over one's own shadow and thus reach the "Subject" in oneself, without its remaining "human, too human," as Nietzsche put it. Indeed, the whole trouble has been, from Plato to Husserl, that this transcendental subject has been changing its appearance all the time but with no improvements other than those due to the progress of science—the progress of the real model rather than the transcendental one.

Thus, what we must try to do here is not to get away from nature, for no one can escape nature, but to penetrate it gradually with the aid of science, because, despite all that philosophers say, nature is still very far from having yielded up all her secrets, and before we locate the absolute up in the clouds, it may well be helpful to take a look inside things. Once we do that, if the true is an organization of the real, then we first need to know how such an organization is organized, which is a biological question. To put it another way, as the epistemological problem is to know how science is possible, then what we must do, before having recourse to a transcendental organization, is to fathom all the resources of the immanent organization.

Just because the true is not egocentric and must not remain anthropocentric, do we have to reduce it to a biocentric organization? Just because truth is greater than man, do we have to look for it back among the Protozoa, the termites, and the chimpanzees? If we defined truth as being that which there is in common between all the different views that all creatures, including man, have held about the world, we would get a rather poor result. But the very nature of life is constantly to overtake itself, and if we seek the explanation of rational organization within the living organization *including its overtakings*, we are attempting to interpret knowledge in terms of its own construction, which is no longer an absurd method since knowledge is *essentially construction*.

2. *The Shortcomings of the Organism*

These overtakings, as essential a part of the organization as its original data are, seem to us, from the cognitive point of view, to be inherent in the living organization. Such an organization is a system of exchanges with the environment; it therefore tries to extend as far as the environment as a whole does, but it does not succeed. This is where knowledge comes in, for knowledge functionally assimilates the whole universe and does not remain within the limits of material physiological assimilations. This living organization is capable of creating forms, and its tendency is to conserve them in a stable state, but it does not succeed, and this is why knowledge is necessary—to extend these material forms of actions or operation so that it becomes possible to conserve them through applying them to the various contents from which they have been dissociated. This living organization is the source of homeostases at every rung of the evolutionary ladder. These proceed by means of regulations, which guarantee the equilibrium of quasi-reversible mechanisms. This equilibrium, however, is tenuous and can resist environmental reversibility only at momentary periods of stability, so that evolution appears to be a series of disequilibria and reequilibrations, which then—without attaining it themselves—give place to a mode of construction with integrations and reversible mobility that only cognitive mechanisms will be able to realize by integrating regulation into construction itself in the form of "operations."

To put it briefly, the necessity for differentiated organs for regulating exchanges with the external world is caused by the living organization's inability to achieve its own program as written into the laws which govern it. On one hand, the organization does contain genetic mechanisms which are not only transmitters but are also formative, but the modes of formation known of at present by recombinations of genes are only one limited sector of construction, confined by the exigencies of a hereditary program which is itself always limited because it cannot reconcile construction and conservation in one coherent dynamic whole, as knowledge can, and because its information about the environment is not sufficiently fluid. On the other hand, phenotypes, which achieve quite a detailed interaction with the environment, are distributed in a "reaction norm," which is itself limited, but, above all, whose every achievement remains both limited and of no influence upon the whole—since phenotypes lack the social or external interactions that man will have in his cognitive exchanges—other than by means of genetic recombinations, the limitations of which have been pointed out.

This dual incapacity of organisms in their material exchanges with the environment is partly compensated for by the way behavior is constituted—invented by the organization as an extension of its internal program. In fact, behavior is simply the organization of life itself, applied or generalized to a wider range of exchanges with the environment. Such exchanges become functional, since material and energy exchanges are guaranteed from the outset by physiological organization. Here "functional" means that actions or action forms or schemata are involved, extending the scope of the organic forms. Nevertheless, these new exchanges, like all the others, consist of accommodations to the environment, taking account of the events in that environment and their consequences; but above all they consist of assimilations which exploit the environment and often even impose forms upon it, using constructions or arrangements of objects in terms of the organism's requirements.

Behavior, as with all kinds of organization, includes regulations, whose function is to control constructive accommodations and assimilations on the basis of the results obtained as the action goes on, or by means of anticipation, which allows it to foresee what events may prove favorable or unfavorable and to make sure the necessary compensations are provided. It is these regulations, differentiated from the internal controls of the organism (since now we are dealing with behavior), that constitute cognitive functions. The problem, then, is to understand how they can surpass organic regulations to the point where they can carry out the internal program of the organization in general without being limited by the shortcomings just referred to.

3. Instinct, Learning, and Logico-mathematical Structures

The fundamental facts to be borne in mind here are, first, that cognitive regulations begin by using the only instruments used by organic adaptation in general, that is to say heredity, with its limited variations, and phenotypic accommodation; hereditary modes of learning, instincts in particular, follow this pattern. But then the same shortcomings as those seen in the original organization, and for which the new echelon of behavior is only a mild corrective, are found in innate knowledge; hence, though only at the higher stages of evolution, the final bursting of the instinct, leading to dissociation between its two component parts—internal organization and the phenotypic accommodation. The result, as we have seen—not because of this dissociation but by means of complementary reconstructions in two opposite directions—is the dual formation of logico-mathematical structures and experimental knowledge, remaining undifferentiated in the practical intelligence of anthropoids (which are geometers as well as technicians) and in the technical intelligence of the beginnings of humanity.

The three basic types of knowledge being innate knowledge, whose prototype is instinct, knowledge of the physical world, by which learning is extended in terms of the environment, and logico-mathematical knowledge, the relationship between the first and the two last appears to be essential if we are to understand how it is that the higher forms do in fact constitute an organ for regulating exchanges. We shall therefore return to this for our conclusion.

Instinct certainly includes cognitive regulations, as witnessed, for example, by the feedback system set up by Grassé's "stigmergia" [*stigmergies*]. But such regulations are only of a limited and inflexible kind, because they take place within the framework of a hereditary program, and a programmed regulation is incapable of inventing anything. Of course, it may happen that an animal succeeds in coping with some unforeseen circumstance by means of readjustments which herald the dawn of intelligence (section 18, subsection 2), and we have seen that the schema coordinations produced on such an occasion are comparable to the innate coordinations of the transindividual instinctive cycle—a valuable indication of the possible similarity of function between instinct and intelligence, despite the difference in epigenetic and phenotypic levels which separates them. However, such phenotypic extensions of the instinct are very limited and their incapacities are thus chronic, which shows that a form of knowledge still subject only to the instruments of organic adaptation, although it may have the beginnings of a cognitive regulation, cannot go very far toward achieving what intelligence can in relation to life (section 32).

The sphere of learning proper, which is beyond the innate, begins even at the protozoic level but develops very slowly up to cerebralization in the higher vertebrates, and however remarkable the exceptions may be in the case of certain insects, there is no sign of any systematic spurt until the primate stage.

4. The Bursting of Instinct

The basic phenomenon of the bursting—in other words, the almost total disappearance, in the case of anthropoids and man—of a cognitive organization which has remained dominant throughout the entire evolution of animal behavior, is thus of the very greatest significance. It is significant, not, as is usually said, because a new mode of acquiring knowledge—namely, intelligence considered as a unit—suddenly replaces a worn-out mode. There is much more to it than this. It has the much deeper significance that a still virtually organic form of knowledge is extended into new forms of regulation, which, though substituted for the preceding form, do not really replace it but inherit it, dividing it and using its component parts in two complementary directions.

What does disappear, with the bursting of instinct, is hereditary programming, and this is in favor of two new kinds of cognitive autoregulations, mutable and constructive. It will be said that this is surely a replacement and a total one at that. But to say so is to ignore two essential factors. Instinct does not consist exclusively of hereditary apparatus; Viaud wisely calls this a limit-concept. On one hand, instinct derives its programming and its "logic" from an organized functioning typical of the most highly generalized forms of the living organization. On the other, it extends this programming into individual or phenotypic actions, which include a considerable margin of accommodation and even of assimilation, partly learned and, in certain cases, quasi-intelligent.

What vanishes with the bursting of instinct is exclusively the central or median part, that is, the programmed regulation, whereas the other two realities persist: the sources of organization and the resultants of individual or phenotypic adqustment. Thus, intelligence does inherit something from instinct although it rejects its method of programmed regulation in favor of constructive autoregulation. The part of instinct that is retained allows the intelligence to embark on two different but complementary courses: interiorization, in the direction of its sources, and exteriorization, in the direction of learned or even experimental adjustments.

The condition which must exist before this dual advance can take place is, of course, the construction of a new method of regulation, and this must be recalled before we go any farther. Such regulations, which now become mobile instead of being set in a program, consist, first of all, of the usual correction processes expressed in terms of the results achieved by actions or anticipations. But being an integral part of assimilation schemata and their coordinations, these regulations develop, as we saw in section 14, into operations, thanks to a combination of proactive and retroactive effects. Such operations are no longer correction but precorrection regulations, and the inverse operation guarantees complete rather than approximate reversibility.

With the aid of this new type of regulation constituting a differentiated organ of deductive verification and of construction, the intelligence now embarks simultaneously in the directions of reflective interiorization and experimental exteriorization just referred to. It will be clearly understood that this dual orientation does not by any means imply a mere dividing up of what is left of the instinct. On the contrary, all that is left of the instinct is the source of its organization and its resultants of individual exploration and research. In order to get back to its source and to extend the resultants, the intelligence must therefore undertake new constructions—some by means of reflective abstractions, by identifying the necessary conditions for the general coordinations of action, others by means of assimilation of the experimental datum into the operational schemata thus constructed. In remains true, nevertheless, that these two directions are extensions of two former components of the instinct.

With the bursting of instinct, a new cognitive evolution thus begins, and it begins all over again from zero, since the inner apparatus of instinct has gone, and, however hereditary the cerebralized nervous system and the learning and inventive powers of the intelligence may be, the work to be done thereafter is phenotypic. It is, moreover, just because intellectual evolution begins all over again from zero that its relations with the living organization are so rarely perceived, still less its relations with the constructions of the instinct, striking as these are. Here we have a fine example of what I called "convergent reconstructions with overtakings" (section 20, subsection 6, point 3). In human knowledge, in fact, the reconstruction is so complete that almost no theorist of logico-mathematical knowledge has thought of explaining that knowledge by going back to the obviously necessary frameworks of the living organization. This was true, at least, until work done in the field of mechano-physiology showed the affiliation between logic, cybernetic models, and the workings of the brain, and until McCulloch began talking about the logic of neurons.

5. *Knowledge and Society*

If such a complete reconstruction is possible, it is because, when abandoning the support of hereditary apparatus and developing constructed and phenotypic regulations, the intelligence gives up the transindividual cycles of the instinct only to adopt interindividual or social interactions. Nor does there seem to be any discontinuity in this, since even chimpanzees work only in groups.

It has already been pointed out (section 22, subsection 1) that the social group—in this connection and in cognition—plays the same role that the "population" does in genetics and consequently in instinct. In this sense, society is the supreme unit, and the individual can only achieve his inventions and intellectual constructions insofar as he is the seat of collective interactions that are naturally dependent, in level and value, on society as a whole. The great man who at any time seems to be launching some new line of thought is simply the point of intersection or synthesis of ideas which have been elaborated by a continuous process of cooperation, and, even if he is opposed to current opinions, he represents a response to underlying needs which arise outside himself. This is why the social environment is able to do so effectively for the intelligence what genetic recombinations of the population did for evolutionary variation or the transindividual cycle of the instincts.

But however externalized and educative its modes of transmission and interaction may be as opposed to hereditary transmissions or groupings, society is nevertheless a product of life. Its "collective representations," as Durkheim calls them, still presuppose the existence of a nervous system in each member of the group. So the important question is not how to assess the respective merits of individual and group (which is a problem just like that of deciding which comes first, the chicken or the egg), but to see the logic in solitary reflection as in cooperation, and to see the errors and follies both in collective opinion and in individual conscience. Whatever Tarde may say, there are not two kinds of logic, one for the group and the other for the individual; there is only one way of coordinating actions A and B according to relationships of inclusion or order, whether such actions be those of different individuals A and B or of the same individual (who did not invent them single-handed, because he is a part of society as a whole). Thus, cognitive regulations or operations are the same in a single brain or in a system of co-operations.

6. Conclusion

On the whole, I think that I have justified the two hypotheses which were linked together in my main thesis in section 3: that cognitive functions are an extension of organic regulations and constitute a differentiated organ for regulating exchanges with the external world. The organ in question is only partially differentiated at the level of innate knowledge, but it becomes increasingly differentiated with logico-mathematical structures and social exchanges or exchanges inherent in any kind of experiment.

There is nothing unusual about these hypotheses, I know, and I am sorry that it should be so. Nevertheless, they are hypotheses which must be constantly and more extensively explored, because, strangely, specialists in epistemology, particularly mathematical epistemology, are too much inclined to leave biology out of account, while biologists, as a rule, completely forget to ask why mathematics is adapted to physical reality.

This book has many shortcomings, the principal one being that it proves nothing and that I put forward nothing except possible interpretations based on facts, although constantly going beyond them. Nevertheless, this essay seemed worth writing, for to provide proofs would necessitate the sort of collaboration between biologists, psychologists, and epistemologists that hardly exists at the present time but is devoutly to be wished. It is only by interdisciplinary effort that a scientific epistemology is possible, and such cooperation is still much too rare to respond to the outstanding problems. It is in the hope of furthering this cooperation that I have attempted to project the ideas contained in this volume.

Index

Aber, A., 198n

Abstraction: Aristotelean, 320; reflective, 15, 28, 182, 267–68, 320–21, 325, 331, 333, 342, 359, 367

Accommodation, 8n, 56, 352–53, 355–56, 364; and adaptation, 172–76; and assimilation, 172–82, 184

Accommodats, 173, 174, 298

Acquired: behavior, 2–3, 10–12, 227, 281; characteristics, 105–7, 110–12, 272–77, 300–304; knowledge, 9, 69, 272–77, 333–45, 348–61

Action schemata, 6–8, 97, 150, 220; and assimilation, 32–33, 181–82, 218, 219, 337; conservation of, 13; coordination of, 18, 28; and instinct, 229; organization of, 9–10, 13; and perception, 250

Activity, 7, 9, 32–33; experimental, 336–37; pole of, 253–56

Adaptation, 61, 122–23, 206–7, 287–88; and assimilation-accommodation, 172–82; and behavior, 177; cognitive, 66, 180–83, 271–77, 350; and genome, 174–75; and heredity, 171–76, 241–44, 271–77; mathematical, 341–42; nature of, 171–74; and nervous system, 217; and operations, 182–85; organic, 182–83; and selection,